VIDEO GAME DESIGN

and Programming Concepts

Text and Software Design Guide

D. Michael Ploor

Learn programming concepts in a fun way by building video games!

Guided Tour

Learning Objectives provide expected outcomes to help you prepare for the lesson.

Reading Material provides the theory behind programming and video game concepts as well as academic information so you can make cross-curricular connections.

Game Build presents you with the opportunity to apply concepts by programming functional video games.

Review Questions cover concepts presented in the lesson so you can assess your comprehension of the reading material and game build programming applications.

Higher-Order Thinking Strategies challenge you to apply what you learned in the lesson to synthesize viable solutions.

Office Technology Integration provides an introduction to basic elements of Microsoft Word, Excel, and PowerPoint to offer exposure to this software.

Capstone—Exhibition of Mastery is a concluding project in which you must apply all of the skills and knowledge gained throughout the textbook to construct and program a complete video game from scratch.

Review Questions

Language Arts

1. List four synonyms for a frame used in game design.

Applied Technology

2. How is the illusion of movement created in a game?

Applied Technology

3. List three sound formats commonly used in game design.

Applied Technology

4. What is the action event in this logic statement?
IF the car collides with the wall, **THEN** destroy the car.

Applied Technology

5. List six common computer languages used in game design.

Higher-Order Thinking Strategies

Applied Technology

6. Create pseudocode for this event: a dart pops a balloon.

10

Office Technology Integration

Setting Object Order, Scale, and Position

1. Launch Microsoft Excel or other spreadsheet software, and open the vocabulary spreadsheet you updated in previous lessons.
2. Applying what you have learned, add a new worksheet, and name it Lesson 19.
3. Add each of the vocabulary words and definitions from the Vocabulary section of this lesson.
4. Save the spreadsheet, and then close it.
5. Open the *LastName*_Art PowerPoint file created in this lesson, and save it as *LastName*_Scene in your working folder.
6. Click the drop-down arrow next to **Home>Slides>New Slide**, and click **Title Slide** in the drop-down menu. A new slide is added after the current slide.
7. In the slide sorter on the left side of the screen, click the mini slide for the new title slide, hold, and drag it to the top.
8. On the title slide, click in the top text box, and enter Cannon Scene.
9. Click in the bottom text box, and enter your name, class, and period.
10. Click the second slide in the slide sorter to make it active.
11. Arrange the objects to create a game scene similar to the one shown. Demonstrate proper alignment, nudge, and ordering to place objects. Copy and paste objects as needed. The scene should depict a cannon firing cannon balls to knock over boxes. Resize objects as needed.

Goodheart-Willcox Publisher

12. Save your work, and submit it for grading.

276

Lesson 28

Capstone—Exhibition of Mastery

Learning Objectives

After completing this lesson, you will be able to:

- demonstrate mastery in the design process from conception to production.
- develop design plans, character sketches, documentation, and storyboards for a proposed video game.
- construct an original video game.
- use a variety of software tools to design and construct a video game.
- provide and receive constructive criticism on a video game build.

Situation

The Awesome Game Company has asked your team to submit a proposal for a new video game design. A client named Jam Bee Yoose has contacted the company about having a game made for it. The client provided little details, but offered a huge bonus because the company is overflowing with cash. The Awesome Game Company needs to do well on this first game as this client could easily afford to buy more games in the future.

Game Build

Jam Bee Yoose shared some information about the company that could be used in a game context. Jam Bee Yoose produces and bottles a line of nutritious and healthy drinks from scratch every morning. It has a complex assembly line that peels fruit, removes seeds or pits, and carries the fruit to a machine that turns the fruit into pulp. Each fruit has its own assembly line. Once the fruit is turned into pulp, another machine creates the various flavors of drinks by mixing the fruit pulp in various proportions and bottles each flavor. The bottles are sent to the final station where they are boxed and prepared for shipment. The drinks are sold at the factory store, shipped to local grocery stores, and sold to local vending machine stockers.

Anything you would like to use from this information would make the customer smile. Use your imagination. There is only one restriction on

375

Tools for Student and Instructor Success

Student Tools

Student Text

Video Game Design and Programming Concepts is a contemporary approach to introducing basic programming concepts. Students will experience hands-on programming by building video games in an object-oriented game engine.

By studying this text, students will learn about the fundamental programming concept of the **IF**...**THEN** statement. This foundation will help prepare students for further study in programming and coding. Additionally, students will apply cross-curricular knowledge in the completion of lessons.

G-W Companion Website

The G-W Learning companion website provides selected files needed to complete the game builds in this text. This website can be accessed from any digital device.

Instructor Tools

LMS Integration

Integrate Goodheart-Willcox content within your Learning Management System for a seamless user experience for both you and your students. LMS-ready content in Common Cartridge format facilitates single sign-on integration and gives you control of student enrollment and data. With a Common Cartridge integration, you can access the LMS features and tools you are accustomed to using and G-W course resources in one convenient location—your LMS.

When you incorporate G-W content into your courses via Common Cartridge, you have the flexibility to customize and structure the content to meet the educational needs of your students. You may also choose to add your own content to the course.

Online Instructor Resources (OIR)

Online Instructor Resources provide all the support needed to make preparation and classroom instruction easier than ever. Available in one accessible location, this resource provides you with time-saving preparation tools, such as answer keys, game build solutions, editable lesson plans, and other teaching aids. The OIR is available as a subscription and can be accessed at school, at home, or on the go.

VIDEO GAME DESIGN

and Programming Concepts

by **D. Michael Ploor**

Publisher
The Goodheart-Willcox Company, Inc.
Tinley Park, Illinois
www.g-w.com

Introduction

Video Game Design and Programming Concepts is a fun and easy text-software design guide combination that uses an activity-based integrated curriculum: theory-based reading with game-building application lessons. It supports cross-curriculum and STEM learning as you will use math and science principles, in addition to language arts, social science, and applied technology knowledge, to program your own games. No knowledge of programming or game design is needed before beginning with this textbook.

Pseudo Code Programming

This text teaches the coding and programming of games through the use of pseudo code. Pseudo code is not a coding or scripting computer language, rather it is the logic needed to properly program and code applications. Interactions are broken down into pseudo code and then you must translate the pseudo code into the game programming. This will help you understand and learn the programming logic needed for further study in computer languages.

Clickteam Fusion 2.5 Game Engine

The lessons in this text are built for the free version of Clickteam Fusion 2.5. Clickteam Fusion 2.5 is an object-oriented game design engine. It is easy to use, making it ideal for beginners. While the activities in this text focus on several arcade-style games, the Clickteam Fusion 2.5 software can be used to create advanced games. The software employs a simple programming interface that does not require any coding or scripting. A drag-and-drop environment is used to place design elements into the scene, while menu-driven selections allow advanced programming without entering code.

Clickteam Fusion 2.5 is regularly patched and updated. Be aware that the instruction presented here may need to be adjusted for the version you are using.

STEM

Science, technology, engineering, and mathematics (STEM) form the foundation on which society in the 21st century builds and maintains economic growth. This curriculum integrates the rigor and relevance of STEM into fun and exciting classroom lessons. Taking rigor from each of the core areas of study and placing it in the context of programming video games allows you to recognize the relevance of study. STEM curriculum provides experience in the skills needed for most of the new jobs projected over the next two decades.

Cross-Curricular Activities

Through application and integration of all academic core content areas of applied technology, language arts, science, mathematics, and social science, you will be engaged in learning through doing. Application and synthesis levels of learning are maintained for a truly unique experience. This meaningful engagement in learning will help you become better at all core subject areas and the foundations of technology as presented in this text.

The review questions and higher-order thinking strategies at the end of lessons are identified with an icon. This icon is keyed to a cross-curricular topic. Refer to the key shown here.

Applied Technology   Language Arts   Mathematics   Science   Social Science

About the Author

D. Michael Ploor is the author of *Video Game Design and Programming Concepts*. Mr. Ploor is also the author of three textbooks on the subject of video game design— *Introduction to Video Game Design, Video Game Design Foundations,* and *Video Game Design Composition*—as well as the Microsoft and Adobe series of certification prep guides published by Goodheart-Willcox. He is a National Board Certified Teacher in Career and Technical Education and holds an MBA degree from the University of South Florida. He maintains professional teaching credentials in Business Education and Education Media Specialist.

Mr. Ploor is at the forefront of innovative teaching and curriculum. He developed STEM curriculum while serving as the lead teacher in the Career Academy of Computer Game Design at Middleton Magnet STEM High School. Mr. Ploor has applied his skills as a STEM Curriculum Integration Specialist in designing innovative curriculum and by collaborating to construct the state standards for video game design in several states. He has also been instrumental in authoring competitive events for Career and Technical Student Organizations such as the Future Business Leaders of America (FBLA) and Phi Beta Lambda (PBL).

In addition to publishing textbooks and lessons, Mr. Ploor provides professional development as a frequent presenter at regional and national conferences to promote CTE education and video game design curriculum.

Reviewers

Goodheart-Willcox Publisher would like to thank the following teachers and administrators who reviewed selected chapters and contributed valuable input to this edition of *Video Game Design and Programming Concepts.*

Dr. Joan Glover
Web Applications and
    Game Development Teacher
Great Oaks High School
Cincinnati, Ohio

Jesse Mignogna
Computer Science Teacher
Bluffton High School
Bluffton, South Carolina

Jennifer Norton
Computer Science Teacher
River Ridge High School
Woodstock, Georgia

Diana Penning
Career and Technology Education Teacher
Spring Hill High School
Chapin, South Carolina

Jon Phillips
AP Computer Science Teacher
Academic Magnet High School
North Charleston, South Carolina

Kacithia Wright
Business Education Teacher
Battery Creek High School
Beaufort, South Carolina

Contents

Lesson 1   Game Design Vocabulary 1

Lesson 2   Software Basics 15

Lesson 3   Click Ball 37

Lesson 4   Quality Assurance 59

Lesson 5   Scene Construction 63

Lesson 6   Iterative Design and the Scientific Method 77

Lesson 7   Digital Art 87

Lesson 8   Parent and Child Objects 101

Lesson 9   Graphing Game Coordinates 113

Lesson 10   Spawning 119

Lesson 11   Software Ratings 141

Lesson 12   Game Critique Exposition 147

Lesson 13   Proof of Concept: Launching 153

Lesson 14   Beta Build: Launching 169

Lesson 15   Quality Assurance 189

Lesson 16   Global Variables 193

Lesson 17   Sensory Detection and Navigation 209

Lesson 18   Challenges Using Variables 229

Lesson 19   Two-Dimensional Game Art 247

Lesson 20   Gravity and Ballistics 277

Lesson 21   Game Mod: Particle Physics 303

Lesson 22   Quality Assurance 323

Lesson 23   Binary Number System 329

Lesson 24   Project Management 343

Lesson 25   Concept Documents 349

Lesson 26   Construction Documents 361

Lesson 27   Completion Documents 369

Lesson 28   Capstone—Exhibition of Mastery 377

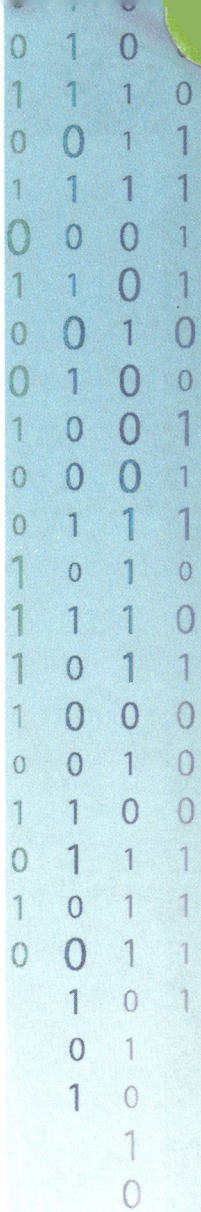

Office Technology Integration

Formatting a Spreadsheet 14

Managing Worksheets 36

Using Word Processing Software 58

Using Spreadsheet Formulas 75

Determining Readability Statistics 85

Using Shapes and Gradients in Presentation Software 99

Drawing and Grouping Vector Images in Presentation Software. 111

Creating PowerPoint Frame Animation. 139

Using Word Processing Software Thesaurus 152

Using SmartArt Graphics. 168

Using a Template to Write a Résumé 188

Using a Job Description Template. 208

Using Mouse-Over Commands 227

Using Animation Presets 245

Setting Object Order, Scale, and Position 276

Using Data in Tables 301

Creating Spreadsheet Charts 322

Creating a Blog Post 327

Using Functions in a Spreadsheet 341

Creating a Spreadsheet Gantt Chart 348

Creating a Word Processor Letter 359

Creating a Slideshow Sales Pitch 364

Spreadsheet Table 375

Lesson 1

Game Design Vocabulary

Learning Objectives

After completing this lesson, you will be able to:

- define common game design vocabulary.
- list computer languages used in game design.
- compare and contrast Fusion 2.5 with other common software applications.

Situation

The Awesome Game Company is looking to hire some interns for the 2D game development division. You have been recommended to intern and build games with the Awesome Game Company professionals. To get this internship, you will need to pass a basic vocabulary test for the game-design software being used. Good luck!

How to Begin

1. Read the passage below.
2. Complete the vocabulary and review questions.
3. Complete the vocabulary puzzle game.
4. Turn in all materials.

Reading Material

A video game is an electronic game that creates an artificial game environment on a video screen. A *game designer* is a person who is involved in the development of a video game. Game designers must have a strong understanding of how to create games. This includes the technology used to create the games. Once you understand this information and terminology, you can begin your journey on becoming a game designer, game programmer, or game artist.

Scene

Games created using Clickteam Fusion 2.5 are built around the concept of frames. The *frame* is where you place game objects to create a scene. In other types of two-dimensional (2D) game-design

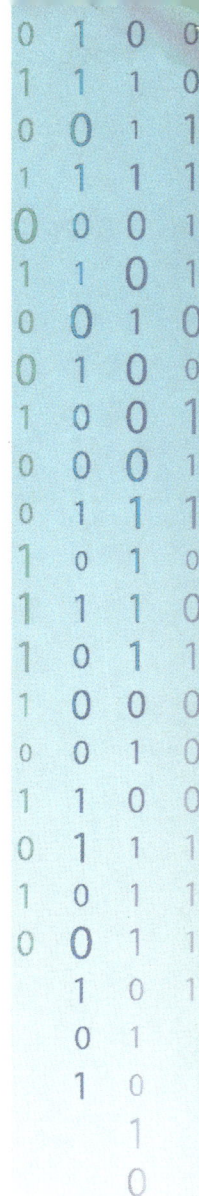

Name: _____

Date: _____

Class: _____

software, the terms *map, room, slide,* or *level* may be used instead of frames. In general, these terms all refer to the same concept.

A frame is like a blank sheet of paper on which you can design your game. You start with a blank screen, then add a background, images, objects, and text to the frame to build a scene. A *scene* is the placement of objects on the frame to convey the story and mood. This process is very similar to creating a PowerPoint presentation slide. After the scene has been constructed on the frame, programming of the animation and interactions can begin.

When a player moves from one frame to another, a transition can be added. A **transition** is a visual effect placed between the frames to gradually move to the next frame. Programs such as PowerPoint also use transitions so the viewer is not faced with an abrupt change in the display.

The background of a frame can be a solid color or an image that you create and import from another program. For example, suppose you have made a cool background using PowerPoint or Paint. You can save the background scene as an image file and then import that image into the frame in Clickteam Fusion 2.5. You could also select an image from the image library files that come with the Clickteam Fusion 2.5 software or from an online resource.

Graphics and Objects

An **artist** is the person who creates images and graphics used in a game. A two-dimensional (2D) scene uses two-dimensional graphics. Two-dimensional graphics have only height and width dimension (or X and Y dimensions). When a 2D image is used in a game, it is called a **sprite.** When a 3D image is used in a game, it is called a *model.* A sprite is simply an image. Sprites themselves cannot be placed in a frame. They must be attached to an object that is placed in the frame.

An **object** is a programmable container that can have an interaction or event. The object can also receive a sprite. The two types of objects used to construct a scene are active objects and background objects.

An **active object** can receive programming. Active objects are things like the player avatar, obstacles, and rewards. A gold coin active object would have programming attached so that when the player collects it, then it will be removed from the scene and added to the coin total. The object would also have a sprite attached to it so it looks like a gold coin.

A **background object** cannot receive programming. The background objects are used mainly to provide artistic design to the scene. A cloud that an airplane can fly through or a distant mountain range backdrop are examples of background objects. These objects develop the scene, but do not affect gameplay.

Each time you place an object on a frame, you are creating an instance of that object in the game. An **instance** is an exact copy that inherits all the properties of the original object. For example, if you are creating a brick wall, you will create several instances of a brick object to construct the wall. Each copy of the original brick will inherit the same properties assigned to the original. Changing the properties of any instance of an object will change *all* of the instances at the same time. So, if you change the color of one instance of the brick object to blue, all instances of the brick object are changed to blue.

An instance differs greatly from a clone. A **clone** is an exact copy of an object, but its properties are *not* linked to the original. The clone is a new object, not an instance of the original. Suppose a brick object is cloned, and then the original brick object is changed to blue. The clone will not be changed because there is no link between the clone and the original.

Animation

An object can have more than one sprite assigned to it. Several sprites can be assigned to an object to form an animation. Unique sprites can also be assigned to the different directions an object can face. If a character turns to the left, the character object should display a left-facing sprite. The same object should display a right-facing sprite when it turns to the right.

The sprite graphics for an object may be contained in an animation set. An ***animation set*** is a series of images, or frames, with slight differences that are played in sequence to create the illusion of movement. To make a character walk, the animation set must include several frames of a single stepping motion, as shown in **Figure 1-1.** In this example, 15 frames are needed to make the character take two strides, one with the right foot and one with the left foot, before returning to the original standing position in frame 1. Additionally, the walking animation set for this object has two directions, left and right. Each direction has a unique set of frames to display movement in that direction.

A ***loop*** is a repeating of an animation or sound when it reaches the end. By looping the animation, a character can take several steps even though only a single step is animated. This is done to simplify the animation.

The animation must be synchronized with the motion of the object. The walking animation should take a step that matches the forward motion of the object the player sees in the game. Movement of an object is referred to as ***translation.*** In **Figure 1-1,** the walking animation set for movement to the right is shown. When the object translates motion to the right, this animation set should be played. This provides the illusion that the character is walking to the right in the game. The process of matching the footsteps to the translation motion of the object is called ***synchronization,*** or *sync* for short. Without proper sync, a character might be running in place or dragging its feet.

Not every object in a game will be animated. In many cases, there is no reason for an object to be animated. Objects that are not animated are ***static objects.***

Sound

A game can be programmed so a sound plays when a collision is detected. Sounds can be added as background music or as part of the action. For example, if a brick will break when the player throws a ball at it, a cracking sound can play to help with the illusion of an actual brick being destroyed. Additionally, you might want to have music playing during the introduction or title frame of the game. A long sound file is typically referred to as ***music.*** This may be as long as a complete song. A short sound file is typically referred to as a ***sample.*** A sample may be less than one second in duration.

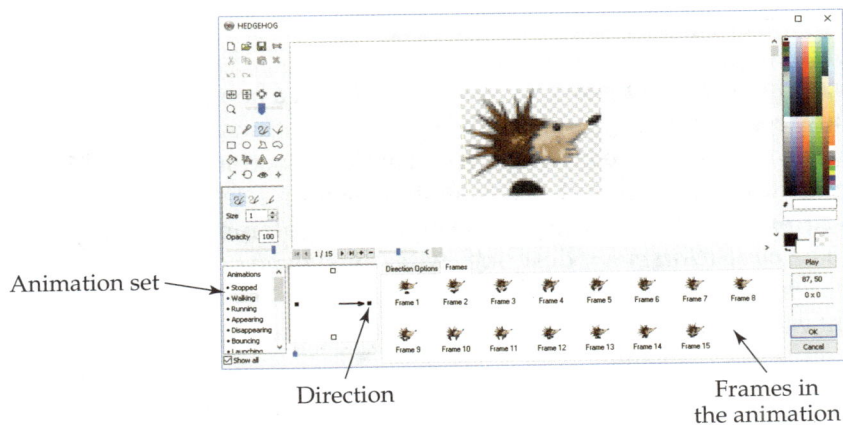

Goodheart-Willcox Publisher

Figure 1-1. An animation set consists of several individual images, or frames. When played in sequence, these frames will appear to give motion to the character.

The small pieces of sound used in a video game are called sound effects, or sound FX. Sound files can be formatted in many ways. The most common types used in games are MP3, WAV, OGG, and MIDI formats.

User Interface

To allow the player to interact with the game, a user interface is needed. A *user interface (UI)* is how the player (user) connects to (interfaces with) the game. As a game programmer, you will need to program a UI.

The games you will build in this course will use a variety of user interfaces. Most of the games compiled for the personal computer will use the keyboard and mouse as the input interfaces. *Input interfaces* allow the user to give information to the computer. When you press the keys on the keyboard, you are inputting letters and numbers into the computer. *Output interfaces* allow the computer to give you information. The computer monitor and speakers are the output interfaces on a personal computer. The monitor displays information for you to see. The speakers create sound for you to hear.

A mobile device, such as an Android device, will likely use input interfaces of a touch screen and tilting for gameplay. A *touch screen* is a video screen that senses pressure or electrical resistance from your finger to activate commands. *Tilting* uses an accelerometer to sense how quickly you move the device and at what angle it is being held. An accelerometer works like a marble in a box. When you change the position of the box, the marble moves. The accelerometer senses the movement of a mass like the marble and can calculate how much the mass has moved.

Event Programming

The objects displayed on the screen are just pixels, not real objects. *Pixels* are the smallest picture elements displayed on a video screen. The word *pixel* is a combination of the words *picture* and *element* as a single pixel is the smallest picture element of a digital image.

In the real world, a ball would not pass through a solid brick. In the virtual world, since objects are just pixels on a screen, they can pass through each other unless an event has been programmed to prevent this. The programming of objects is typically done in a programming or event editor screen, not in the design frame (scene). The programming follows a logical design process that makes it easy to interpret an *IF/THEN logic statement.* Almost all game interactions follow the **IF...THEN** logic of an event.

> **IF** the ball object hits a wall object,
>> **THEN** the ball object bounces.

The above example is written in pseudocode. *Pseudocode* is not actual programming code, rather it is based on English and used to record the programming logic. Pseudocode is a quick way of documenting the action and reaction of an event so it can be coded later in the programming language.

Events describe the *action-reaction relationships* in a computer program. They are the foundation of any computer program. Action-reaction relationships happen all around you in the real world. The easiest way to break down an action-reaction relationship is to put it in the **IF...THEN** format. **Figure 1-2** details how an action-reaction relationship can be described.

An *event editor* breaks down the pseudocode logic statement into condition events and action events. The *condition event* describes what must exist or become true. The *action event* describes what occurs when the condition is met. **IF** the condition event is true, **THEN** the action event will execute. While specific terminology may vary between game-design software, the concept is the same.

In Clickteam Fusion 2.5, the game designer programs event lines. An *event line* is a single action-reaction relationship for the game. Each event line has a place to input the condition

Action-Reaction Relationships			
Operator	**Action**	**Operator**	**Reaction**
IF	Action	THEN	Reaction
IF	Cause	THEN	Effect
IF	Condition is true	THEN	Action is executed
Common Real-Life Action-Reaction Relationships			
Operator	**Action**	**Operator**	**Reaction**
IF	You turn in homework	THEN	You get a good grade
IF	You buy a ticket	THEN	You watch the movie
IF	You miss the bus	THEN	You are late to school
Common Computer Action-Reaction Relationships			
Operator	**Action or Condition Event**	**Operator**	**Reaction or Action Event**
IF	User presses the [R] key	THEN	Letter R appears on the screen
IF	User double-clicks a program icon	THEN	Launch the program
IF	Dart object collides with a balloon object	THEN	Destroy the balloon object

Goodheart-Willcox Publisher

Figure 1-2. Action-reaction relationships are the basis of all computer programs, including video games.

(action) and another place to input the events (reactions), as shown in **Figure 1-3.** The pseudocode for the action-reaction relationship shown in the figure is:

 IF a collision between the ball and the brick,

  THEN destroy the brick.

A collision is a typical condition that occurs in a game. In this case, a ball collides with a brick. The computer has to detect the collision between objects. Without programming the computer to detect when the ball and brick collide, the ball would not have any effect on the brick.

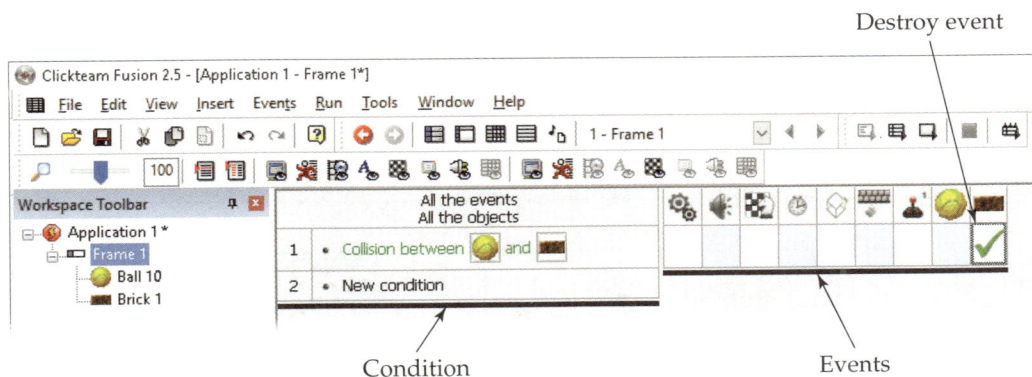

Goodheart-Willcox Publisher

Figure 1-3. An event line in Clickteam Fusion 2.5 describes a single action-reaction relationship for the game.

Programming Languages

Programming, or *coding,* is the process of inputting commands that a machine will execute. Programming is not limited to a computer or even an electronic device. An alarm clock is programmed to ring at a certain time. A game programmer can create a game using game-design software or by programming directly in a computer programming language.

Game-design software, known as a *game engine,* makes the job of computer programming much easier. Clickteam Fusion 2.5 is game-engine software is object-oriented software. *Object-oriented programming (OOP)* assigns programming to objects. An object is a container that has properties and methods (actions). In the example above, the brick object holds the programming for the destroy action. Clickteam Fusion 2.5 and other object-oriented programming allows for a visual programming interface. There, the programmer can see the game objects and use drag-and-drop programming commands for each object.

A more complex way to design a game is to write a set of computer commands using a programming language. A programming language is similar to a verbal language, like English or Spanish, except it is a written language that a computer can understand. Coding is the process a computer programmer uses to input the words and symbols that a computer can understand. The collection of words and symbols themselves are called *code.* Lines of code are assembled to build a script. A *script* is a list of computer commands. There are many computer programming and scripting languages. The most common of these include C, C++, C#, Java, Python, and Ruby.

The process of changing computer codes, scripts, and other programming into a file that can run on a specific type of device is called *compiling.* When a computer compiles, it takes the script the programmer wrote and rewrites it as an executable file. As the name implies, an *executable file* is a program file that a computer can read and run. The executable tells the computer exactly what it is supposed to do in its own language.

Different devices require different formats of executables. For example, an iPhone cannot read most files made for a personal computer. When an executable is changed to make it compatible with a different device, it is called *porting.* Clickteam Fusion 2.5 allows the designer to create an executable for a personal computer and port the same file as an iPhone or Android executable. This is done using an expansion package that can be purchased.

Vocabulary

Write a definition for each of the key terms from this lesson. You will develop a personal glossary of key terms throughout this course.

game designer

_____

_____

frame

_____

_____

transition

_____

_____

Name: _____

artist

_____

_____

sprite

_____

_____

object

_____

_____

active object

_____

_____

background object

_____

_____

instance

_____

_____

clone

_____

_____

animation set

_____

_____

loop

_____

_____

translation

_____

_____

synchronization.

_____

_____

static object

_____

_____

music

_____

_____

sample

_____

_____

user interface (UI)

_____

_____

input interface

_____

_____

output interface

_____

_____

touch screen

_____

_____

tilting

_____

_____

pixel

_____

_____

IF/THEN logic statement

_____

_____

pseudocode

_____

_____

action-reaction relationship

_____

_____

event editor

_____

_____

condition event

_____

_____

action event

_____

_____

event line

_____

_____

programming

_____

_____

game engine

_____

_____

object-oriented programming (OOP)

_____

_____

coding

_____

_____

code

_____

_____

script

_____

_____

compiling

_____

_____

executable file

_____

_____

porting

_____

_____

Review Questions

Language Arts

1. List four synonyms for a frame used in game design.

_____

_____

_____

Applied Technology

2. How is the illusion of movement created in a game?

_____

_____

_____

Applied Technology

3. List three sound formats commonly used in game design.

_____

_____

_____

Applied Technology

4. What is the action event in this logic statement?
   IF the car collides with the wall, **THEN** destroy the car.

_____

_____

_____

_____

Applied Technology

5. List six common computer languages used in game design.

_____

_____

_____

_____

Higher-Order Thinking Strategies

Applied Technology

6. Create pseudocode for this event: a dart pops a balloon.

_____

_____

_____

_____

Name: _____

7. Compare and contrast *active object* and *background object* in the Venn diagram below.

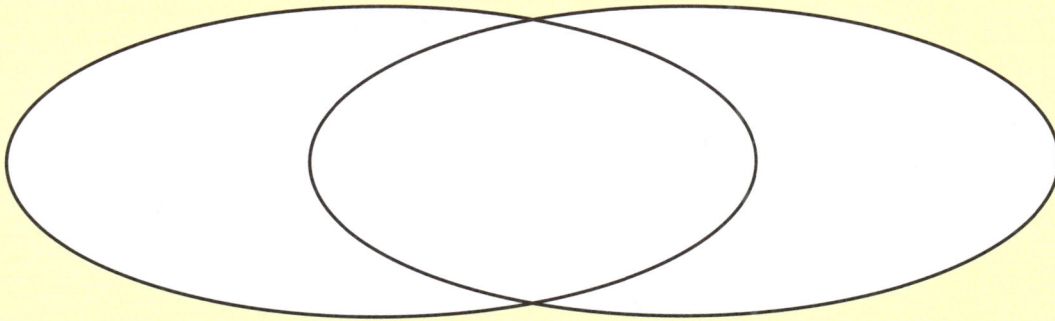

Language Arts

8. Compare and contrast *instance* and *clone* in the Venn diagram below.

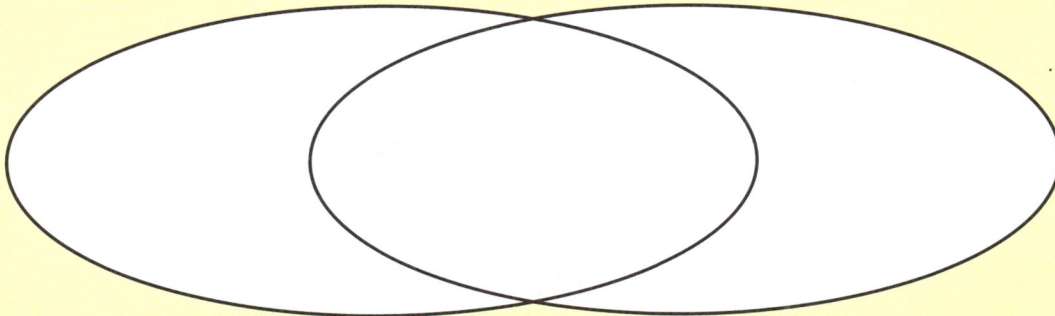

Language Arts

9. Compare and contrast sound *sample* and *music* in the Venn diagram below.

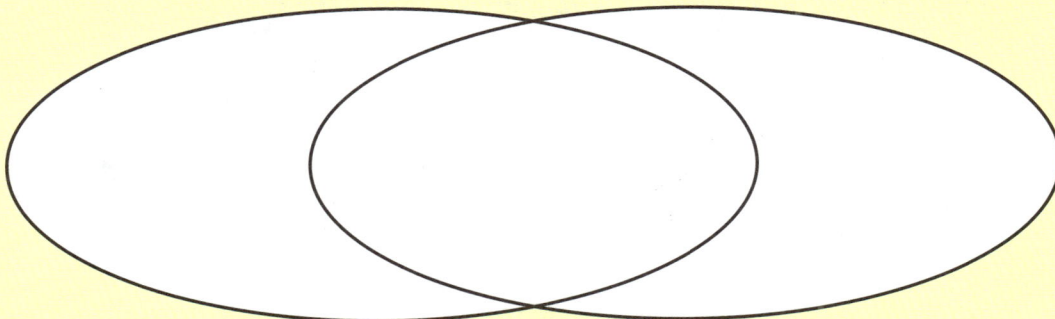

Language Arts

10. Analyze and describe the user interface of your computer.

_____

_____

_____

_____

Applied Technology

Word Hunt

```
J  C  E  S  L  G  A  T  V  U  S  X  E  X  K
I  O  C  Y  P  O  N  I  P  A  E  E  M  Q  L
D  T  N  N  Y  R  O  I  M  I  G  P  A  S  X
D  Q  A  C  F  C  I  P  L  N  R  P  R  E  B
K  L  T  H  Q  Q  L  T  I  I  T  C  F  O  A
Y  E  S  R  B  E  S  T  E  R  P  A  S  B  W
R  A  N  O  E  Z  R  J  A  E  Z  M  X  J  L
O  Z  I  N  Q  O  I  N  Z  X  P  Q  O  E  Y
O  K  O  I  P  E  S  A  R  T  I  S  T  C  T
G  L  E  Z  S  L  E  X  I  P  L  G  T  T  S
C  Y  V  A  A  K  C  M  U  S  I  C  C  C  L
L  P  C  T  G  N  I  M  M  A  R  G  O  R  P
G  T  I  I  P  M  G  S  C  D  F  I  D  D  R
W  O  P  O  S  X  M  F  W  O  I  K  E  Z  H
N  Z  C  N  J  C  D  H  A  P  J  T  W  A  P
```

Find the following terms in the grid above. Circle each term. Terms may appear forward or backward in horizontal, vertical, or diagonal orientation.

frame	music
artist	sample
sprite	pixel
object	programming
instance	code
clone	script
loop	compiling
translation	porting
synchronization	

Name: _____

Crossword Puzzle

Across

2. repeating of an animation or sound
4. does not move
6. writing the symbols a computer can read
7. synonym for a frame
9. a sound format
11. programmable item in a game
12. person who creates games
13. when this occurs, an action will be triggered in the game
14. converting script into computer language
15. matching animation or sound to movement
16. 2D image used in a game
18. connects the player to the game
20. short sound
22. video screen used as an input device
23. commands written in a computer language
24. long sound file
25. a programming language
26. movement of an object

Down

1. list of computer commands
3. English-based recording of programming logic
5. exists as height and width only
8. _____ programming; drag-and-drop method of creating games
10. allows the user to give information to the computer
17. what happens to an object after a condition is met
19. inherits properties from the original object
21. smallest picture element

Office Technology Integration

Formatting a Spreadsheet

In this Office technology activity, you will use spreadsheet software to create a glossary in which to record your vocabulary definitions for all lessons. You will format the spreadsheet in two columns.

1. Launch Microsoft Excel or other spreadsheet software, and begin a new blank workbook.
2. Click in cell A1, and add the text Computer Game Design Vocabulary.
3. Click in cell A3, and add the text Vocabulary Words.
4. Move the cursor to the top of the worksheet, click the line that separates columns A and B, and drag the line to the right to increase the size of column A. Drag until the column is as wide as the text in cell A3.
5. Click in cell B3, and add the text Definition.
6. Click the **File** tab on the ribbon, and click **Print** or **Print Preview**.
7. Close the print preview, and return to the spreadsheet. A vertical dashed line should appear to indicate the right-hand edge of the printed page.
8. Applying what you have learned, resize column B so it extends to the edge of the page (the dashed line).
9. Click the header for column A. This selects the entire column.
10. Locate the **Borders** command, and select the option to include **All Borders**.

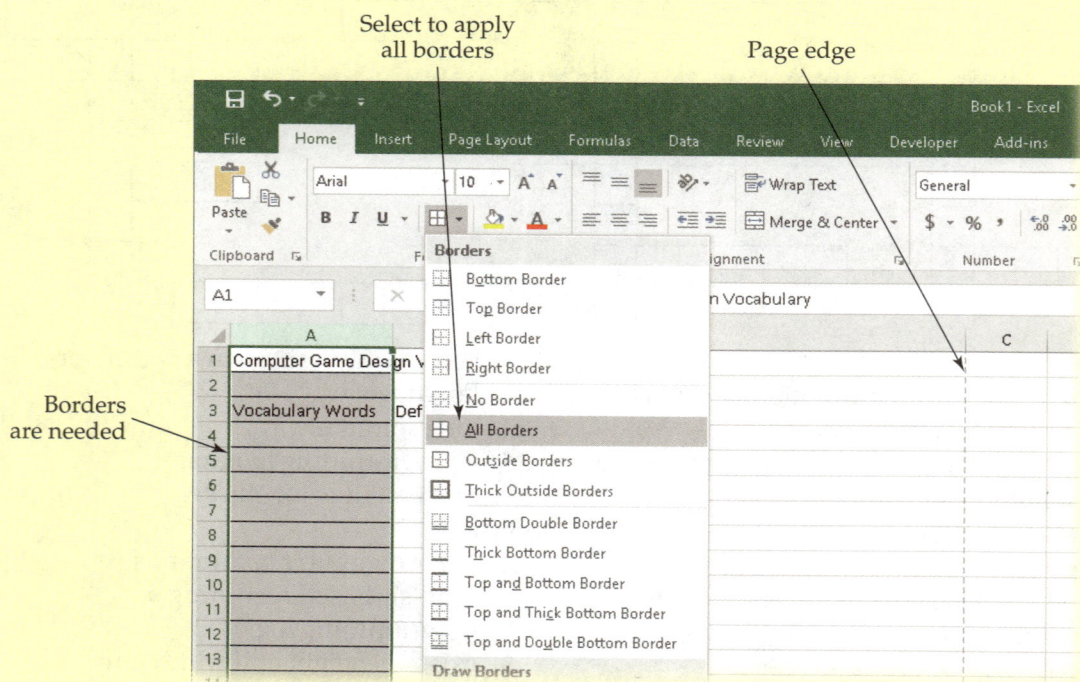

Goodheart-Willcox Publisher

11. Applying what you have learned, format column B with all borders.
12. Click cell A1, hold, and drag to cell B1 to select the range A1:B1.
13. Locate the **Merge and Center** command and use it to combine the two selected cells into one cell.
14. Add each of the vocabulary words and definitions from the Vocabulary section.
15. Save your work as *LastName_*Vocab in your working folder.

0 1 0 0
1 1 1 0
0 0 1 1
1 1 1 1
0 0 0 1
1 1 0 1
0 0 1 0
0 1 0 0
1 0 0 1
0 0 0 1
0 1 1 1
1 0 1 0
1 1 1 0
1 0 1 1
1 0 0 0
0 0 1 0
1 1 0 0
0 1 1 1
1 0 1 1
0 0 1 1
1 0 1
0 1
1 0
1
0

Lesson 2

Software Basics

Learning Objectives

After completing this lesson, you will be able to:

- describe the user interface of the Clickteam Fusion 2.5 software.

- identify command buttons, toolbars, panels, tabs and other user interface structures.

- activate help text to identify command buttons and hot key commands.

Situation

The Awesome Game Company thinks you have the right stuff to become a successful intern in the company. The next step to designing games is to learn how to use the game design software. Complete these learning activities before starting on some skill building designs.

Before beginning this lesson, go to the student companion website (www.g-wlearning.com), and download the asset files for this lesson. Place the downloaded files in your working folder.

How to Begin

1. Launch Clickteam Fusion 2.5 by double-clicking the icon on the desktop or clicking the icon in the start menu.
2. If any pop-up windows appear, close them.
3. Locate the menu bar at the top of the screen, as shown in **Figure 2-1.** The *menu bar* holds pull-down menus, which allows the user to select commands from a list. Click **File** to display the **File** pull-down menu.
4. In the **File** pull-down menu, click **New.** This opens a new Clickteam Fusion 2.5 application.
5. Click **File>Save As...** on the menu bar. The **Save As** dialog box is displayed, as shown in **Figure 2-2.** This is a standard save-type dialog box.
6. Using the drive and folder tree on the left, navigate to your working folder. Note: your instructor may provide you with different instructions on where to save files.
7. Click the **New folder** link. This places a blank new folder in the current location, and the default name can be changed.
8. Name the new folder Video Game Design.
9. Double-click the new folder to navigate to it and make it current.

Clickteam
Fusion 2.5

15

Click to begin a new application

Pull-down menus

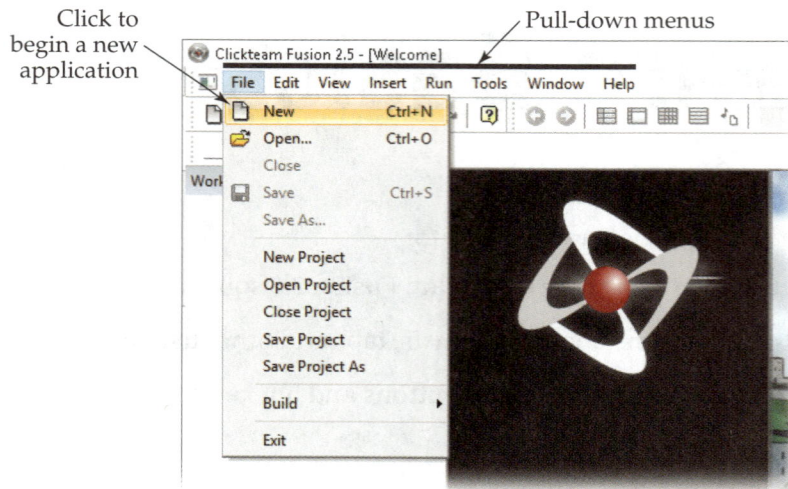

Goodheart-Willcox Publisher

Figure 2-1. Pull-down menus contain commands. Clicking the name of the pull-down menu displays the menu. To activate a command, click the name of the command in the menu.

Click to create a new folder

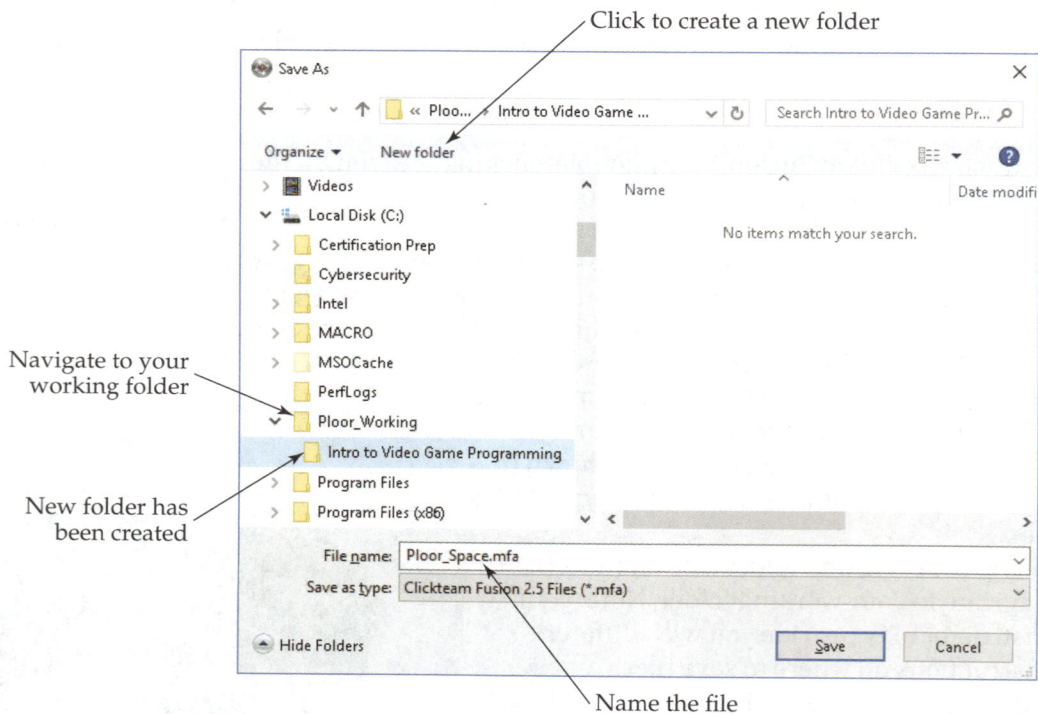

Navigate to your working folder

New folder has been created

Name the file

Goodheart-Willcox Publisher

Figure 2-2. A save-type dialog box is used to name and save a file. A new folder can be created within the selected folder if needed.

10. Click in the **File name:** text box at the bottom of the **Save As** dialog box. Enter *LastName_Space* using your last name.

11. Click the **Save** button to save the file in the folder you just created.

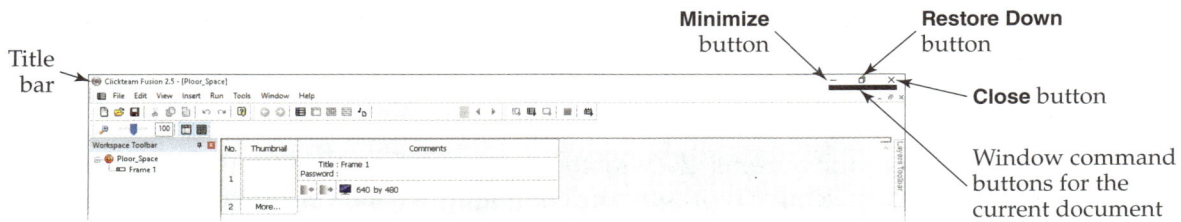

Goodheart-Willcox Publisher

Figure 2-3. The title bar contains the name of the current file as well as command buttons for managing the application window.

User Interface

12. Look to the very top of the screen. This is the title bar, as shown in **Figure 2-3.** The *title bar* displays the name of the software; the name of your file; and the **Minimize**, **Restore Down**, and **Close** buttons. Clicking the **Close** button will exit the program, but do not click it at this time.

13. Click the **Minimize** button. The application is reduced to an icon at the bottom of the screen. Click that icon to again display the application on screen.

14. Click the **Restore Down** button. The application is displayed in a floating window. The button is also replaced with the **Maximize** button. Click the **Maximize** button, and the document is toggled back to full-screen display, and the **Restore Down** button returns. To *toggle* is to switch back and forth.

15. Look to the far-right side of the menu bar. Notice the three window-command buttons below the same buttons on the title bar. These three buttons perform the same actions, but on the current document, not the application.

16. Click **View**>**Toolbars** on the menu bar. A cascading menu is displayed that contains a list of the available toolbars and toolbar panels, as shown in **Figure 2-4.** A check mark means the toolbar is currently displayed. If there is no check mark, the toolbar is currently hidden.

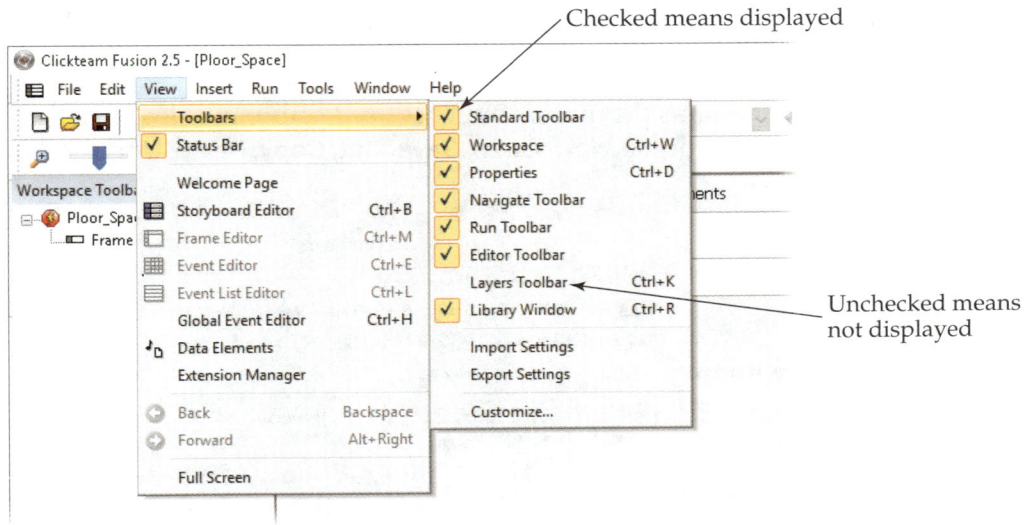

Goodheart-Willcox Publisher

Figure 2-4. Clickteam Fusion 2.5 has several toolbars that can be displayed or hidden. A check mark in the pull-down menu means the toolbar is displayed.

17. Refer to **Figure 2-4,** and make sure a check mark appears next to the toolbars shown in the figure.

Toolbars

Toolbars hold command buttons. Each toolbar contains a group of similar commands. Command buttons have an icon to represent the command. An *icon* is a small image. If you need to understand what a specific button is named, you can hover to display help text. To *hover* means to pause the cursor over the button without moving or clicking. *Help text* is a pop-up text box with a short description or help topic displayed.

18. Hover the cursor over the first button on the **Standard Toolbar,** as shown in **Figure 2-5.** After a second or two, the help text is displayed. The first part of the help text tells you the name of the command is **New.** The information inside the parentheses is the hot key shortcut for the command. A *hot key shortcut* is the key combination that will activate the command. To activate the **New** command, you could press the [Ctrl] key and the [N] key at the same time. At the end of the help text is a brief description of the command.

19. Locate the thick dashed line on the left-hand end of the **Standard Toolbar.** This is the toolbar handle. A *toolbar handle* is used to select and move the toolbar. Click and hold the toolbar handle, and drag the **Standard Toolbar** to the middle of the screen. Then, release the mouse button to undock and float the toolbar. *Floating* means a toolbar is in a window that can be moved around the screen and placed over other elements, such as the editor window. *Docking* is the process of arranging toolbar and panel position next to each other. Docking occurs in a docking area such as the area under the menu bar or the side bar on the left and right of the screen. Note: when floating, the **Standard Toolbar** is labeled as the **Main Toolbar.**

20. Click and hold the title bar on the **Main Toolbar,** and drag the toolbar back up to the top docking area where the **Standard Toolbar** was removed. When in position, release the mouse button to drop the **Main Toolbar** and dock it. Note: toolbars can be docked to the top, bottom, left-hand, and right-hand edges of the screen.

21. Dock the toolbars and panels so that the layout matches what is shown in **Figure 2-6.** Note: to have the **Library Toolbar** displayed, you must click the button in the upper-right corner to "pin" it open, as shown in the figure.

22. Save the file by clicking the **Save** button on the **Standard Toolbar.**

Save

Standard Toolbar

The **Standard Toolbar** contains the most commonly used commands found in the pull-down menus. Basic commands such as **New, Open, Save, Cut, Copy, Paste, Undo, Redo** and

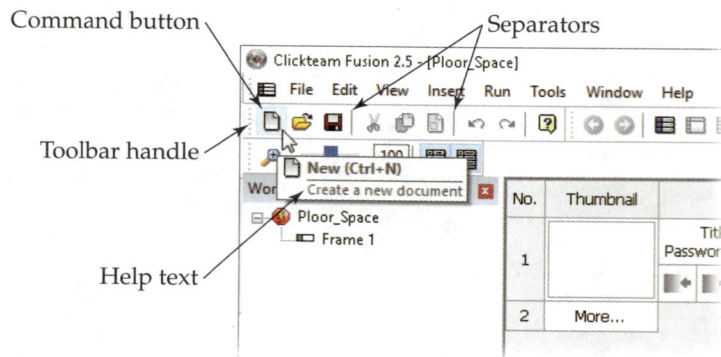

Goodheart-Willcox Publisher

Figure 2-5. Help text can be displayed by hovering the cursor over a command button. The toolbar handle can be used to move the toolbar, including floating or docking the toolbar.

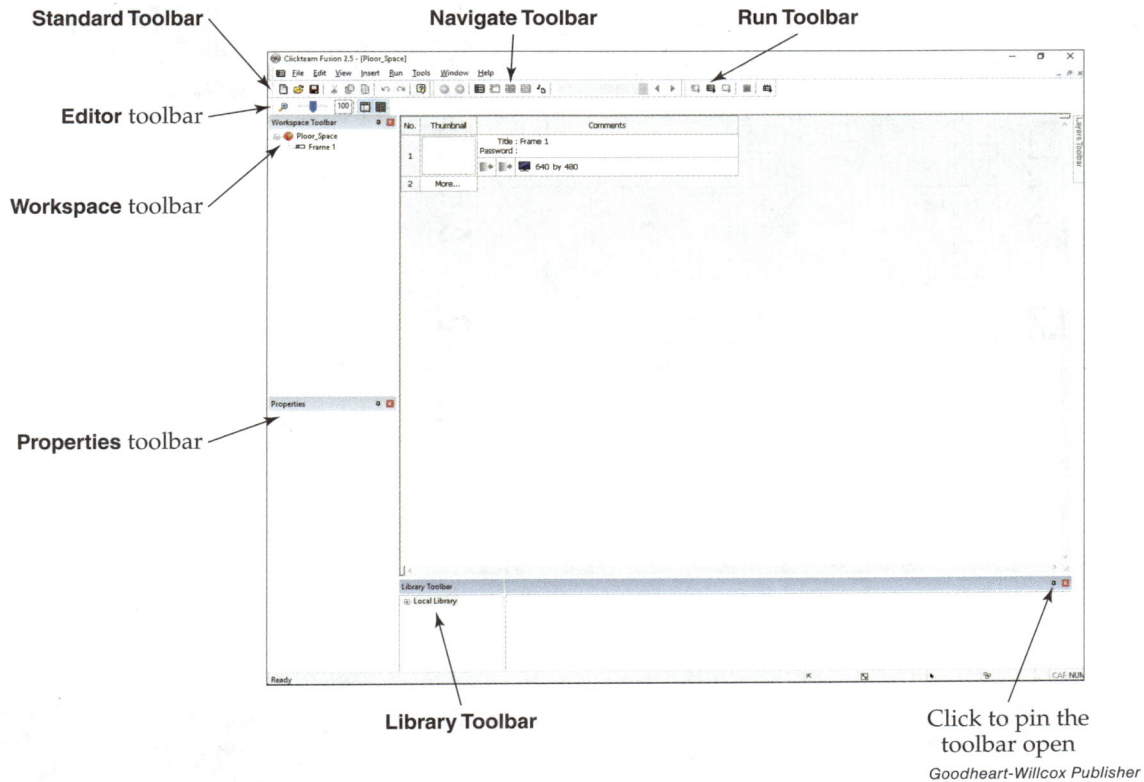

Standard Toolbar   Navigate Toolbar   Run Toolbar

Editor toolbar

Workspace toolbar

Properties toolbar

Library Toolbar   Click to pin the
                                                     toolbar open

Goodheart-Willcox Publisher

Figure 2-6. Display the toolbars shown here. If needed, move them to match.

Contents (help) are located on the **Standard Toolbar**. Since the commands are placed on a toolbar, they are just a mouse click away.

23. Hover the cursor over each button in the **Standard Toolbar** to display the help text.
24. Record the name of each command shown in **Figure 2-7** that is located on the **Standard Toolbar**.

Navigate Toolbar

To move quickly from one area of the game programming to another, use the commands on the **Navigate Toolbar**. Included on this toolbar are commands such as **Back**, **Forward**, **Storyboard Editor**, **Frame Editor**, **Previous Frame**, and **Next Frame**. Also included on this toolbar is the frame identification and selection drop-down list.

25. Hover the cursor over each button in the **Navigate Toolbar** to display the help text.
26. Record the name of each command shown in **Figure 2-8** that is located on the **Navigate Toolbar**.

Run Toolbar

The commands on the **Run Toolbar** are helpful to see how your game is working. These commands allow you to test the game to see if everything is working properly. The **Run Project** command opens the entire project and plays it from the first frame of the first application. A project can be made up of several applications. Each application in a project is saved as a separate file. The **Run Application** command opens the application and plays it from the first frame. The **Run Frame** command opens and plays only the current frame. The **Stop** command ends the game and returns to the editor. The **Build and Run** command builds the game as an executable so it can be tested as a stand-alone program on a computer or mobile device.

27. Hover the cursor over each button in the **Run Toolbar** to display the help text.
28. Record the name of each command shown in **Figure 2-9** that is located on the **Run Toolbar**.

Command Button	Command Name	Command Button	Command Name
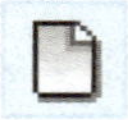 📄		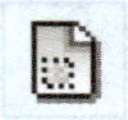 📄	
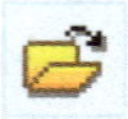 📂		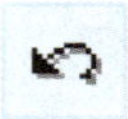 ↩	
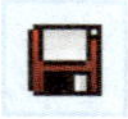 💾		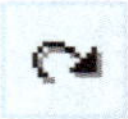 ↪	
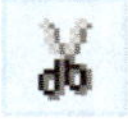 ✂		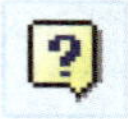 📋?	
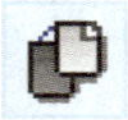 📋			

Figure 2-7. Use help text to discover the name of each command on the **Standard Toolbar**, and record the names here.

Command Button	Command Name	Command Button	Command Name
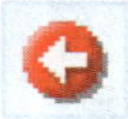 ⬅		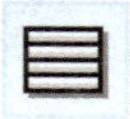 📃	
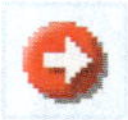 ➡		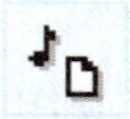 ♪📄	
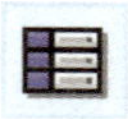 📑		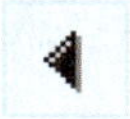 ◀	
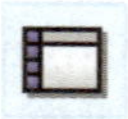 🗔		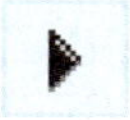 ▶	
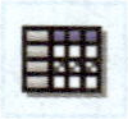 ⊞			

Figure 2-8. Use help text to discover the name of each command on the **Navigate Toolbar**, and record the names here.

Editor Toolbar

The **Editor Toolbar** is only displayed in the frame editor view. The **Editor Toolbar** includes commands for the zoom setting and to control the use of grids. Grids help align objects on the frame and can be modified to any size. If a text object is selected, the commands for formatting and aligning written words are active on the **Editor Toolbar**. These include commands to change the font and the paragraph alignment.

29. You are currently in the storyboard editor. Double-click the number 1 in the editor window to open Frame 1 in the frame editor. The default frame is blank with a white background.

Command Button	Command Name	Command Button	Command Name

Goodheart-Willcox Publisher

Figure 2-9. Use help text to discover the name of each command on the **Run Toolbar**, and record the names here.

30. Hover the cursor over each button in the **Editor Toolbar** to display the help text.
31. Record the name of each command shown in **Figure 2-10** that is located on the **Editor Toolbar.**

Command Button	Command Name	Command Button	Command Name
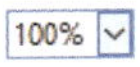 100%		 *I*	
		 U	

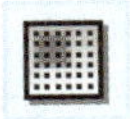			

 B			

Goodheart-Willcox Publisher

Figure 2-10. Use help text to discover the name of each command on the **Editor Toolbar**, and record the names here.

Storyboard Editor

Clickteam Fusion 2.5 has three different views for editing the game. The first editor view shown is the storyboard editor. The storyboard uses thumbnail images, or thumbnails, to show the game frames. **Thumbnails** are small images that represent a full-size image. Double-clicking a thumbnail in the storyboard editor opens the frame in the frame editor. The frame editor is where art is positioned on the frame. The third editor view is the event editor. The event editor is where all the programming is created.

Storyboard Editor

32. Click the **Storyboard Editor** button on the **Navigate Toolbar** to display the storyboard editor.

33. Click the number 2 in the editor window to add a second frame to the application. The new frame is given the title Frame 2. The default frame is titled Frame 1.

34. Click and hold the Frame 2 thumbnail, and drag it upward so it is positioned above Frame 1. Then, drop to reorder the frames, as shown in **Figure 2-11.** Notice that the frame names are not changed.

Show Headers

35. Locate the **Storyboard Editor Toolbar** above the editor window. This is a contextual toolbar that is only displayed in storyboard editor. Click the **Show Headers** and **Show Comments** buttons on this toolbar. These are both on by default, so clicking each will toggle the header and comments to not display.

36. Click both buttons again to display the header and comments.

Show Comments

37. In the Comments column, click the Title: setting that currently is Frame 2. The title now can be edited. Change the title to Inner Planets. Press the [Enter] key to complete the edit.

38. In the Comments column, click the **Add fade in transition** button for the Inner Planets frame. The **Transition set-up** dialog box is displayed, as shown in **Figure 2-12.** A **fade-in** transition displays as the frame enters. A **fade-out** transition displays as the frame exits.

39. Click the **Transition** drop-down arrow, and click **Door** in the list.

40. In the **From/To** area, click the **Background** radio button.

41. Click the **Duration:** slider, and drag until the setting is approximately three seconds.

42. In the **Parameters** area, click the **Horizontal, from left & right to center** radio button to set how the transition will be applied.

43. Click the **OK** button to apply the transition. Notice the button for the Inner Planets frame is now displayed in color to indicate a transition has been applied. Also notice the name of the transition appears above the Inner Planets frame.

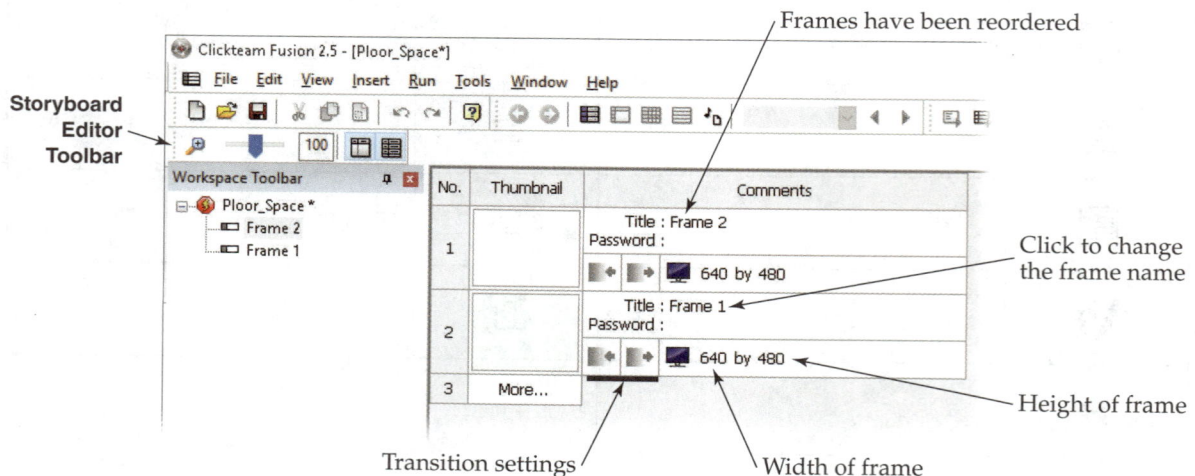

Goodheart-Willcox Publisher

Figure 2-11. Frames can be reordered in the storyboard editor. The name and size of each frame can also be changed, and transitions in and out of the frame can be added.

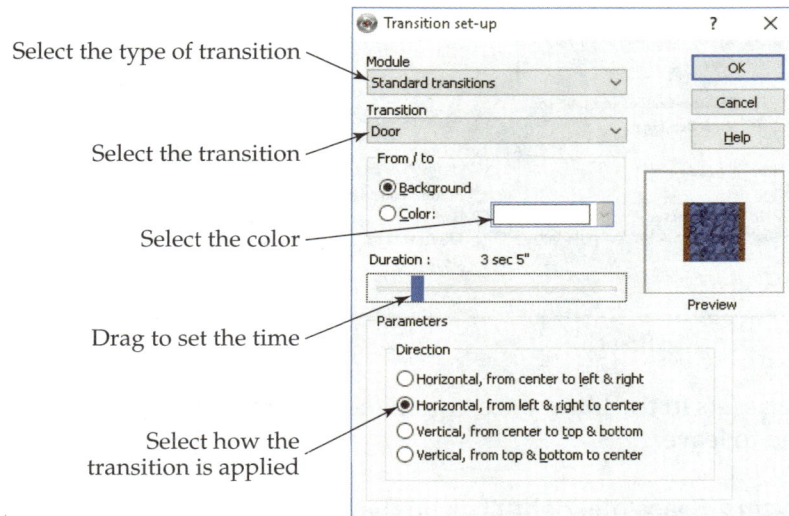

Select the type of transition

Select the transition

Select the color

Drag to set the time

Select how the
transition is applied

Figure 2-12. A transition can be added into or out of a frame. There are many options for creating a transition.

44. Click the width setting for the Inner Planets frame, and change the value to 800. Similarly, change the height to 800.

45. Applying what you have learned, rename Frame 1 to Gas Giants, and resize the frame to 800 by 800.

46. Applying what you have learned, add an exit transition of your choice to the Gas Giants frame. Notice the name of the transition appears below the Gas Giants frame.

47. Applying what you have learned, add a third frame at the bottom, name it Outer Planets, and size it to 800 by 600.

Frame Editor

48. Applying what you have learned, open the Inner Planets frame in the frame editor. Note: the frame editor can also be accessed by selecting the frame in the storyboard editor, and then clicking the **Frame Editor** button on the **Navigate Toolbar**.

Frame Editor

49. In the **Library Toolbar** at the bottom of the screen, click the plus sign next to Local Library. This panel holds art assets that come with the software. The assets are organized in a tree format, as shown in **Figure 2-13.** Similar in structure to a real tree, a *tree organizational format* has branches that expand. The first item in the tree is the *trunk,* which in this case is Local Library. *Branch* folders expand off the trunk and hold more branch folders or other tree structures. A *twig* is a branch that contains no other branch folders. A *leaf* is an end file with no additional branches. You are not limited to using art from the library. In later lessons, you will learn how to add custom art and animations to your games.

50. Launch file explorer, and navigate to the folder where you saved the downloaded files for this lesson. Then, double-click on the SpaceArt.mfa file. The .mfa file extension is for files created in Clickteam Multimedia Fusion 2.5. A new session of Clickteam Fusion 2.5 is launched, and the file is opened.

51. In the SpaceArt.mfa file, right-click on the Frame 1 branch in the **Workspace Toolbar**, and click **Copy** in the shortcut menu. Then, close the session of Clickteam Fusion 2.5 that has the SpaceArt.mfa file open.

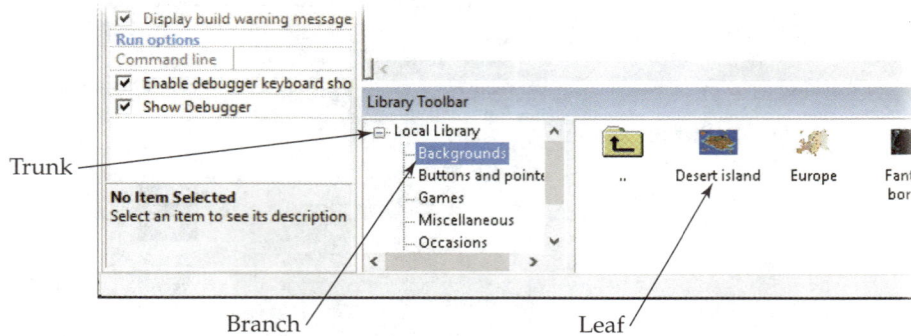

Goodheart-Willcox Publisher

Figure 2-13. The assets in the library are organized in a tree format. From the trunk there are branches that lead to leaves.

52. In the *LastName_*Space file, right-click on the trunk in the **Workspace Toolbar**, which is the name of the file, and click **Paste Frame** in the shortcut menu. The copied Frame 1 is added to the file. This frame contains the art assets you will use in this application. Note: if you receive a message that you have reached the limit of the free version, click the **OK** button. You will correct this later.

53. In the **Workspace Toolbar**, click the plus sign next to the Frame 1 branch to expand it. The art assets contained on the frame are displayed as leaves under Frame 1.

54. Right-click the Inner Planets branch in the **Workspace Toolbar**, and click **Delete** in the shortcut menu. When asked if you want to delete the frame, click the **Yes** button. If you previously received a message about disabled features, you should now receive a message that features have been restored.

55. Right-click on Frame 1 in the **Workspace Toolbar**, and click **Rename** in the shortcut menu. Change the name from Frame 1 to Inner Planets.

56. Click and hold the Inner Planets branch in the **Workspace Toolbar**, drag it up until the Gas Giants branch is highlighted, and drop to reorder the frames. Inner Planets should be the first frame listed. This is another way to reorder frames without using the storyboard editor.

57. Applying what you have learned, display the Inner Planets frame in the frame editor. Note: you can double-click the branch in the **Workspace Toolbar** to quickly move between frames in the frame editor.

58. Click the *LastName_*Space branch in the **Workspace Toolbar** to select the main application. With this selected, global settings can be changed. *Global settings* affect the entire game. A setting such as the score should be global. Otherwise, the score would reset on each frame. *Local settings* affect only a specific frame. These settings are not carried over from one frame to the next.

59. Look at the **Properties** toolbar. Notice the title bar includes the name of what is selected. In this case, the name of the application is displayed.

60. Click the planet Mercury to select it. This can be done in the **Workspace Toolbar** or on the frame. Notice the title bar for the **Properties** toolbar tells you which object's properties are displayed.

61. Applying what you have learned, display the application's properties. Notice that the Properties toolbar has tabs below the title bar. A *tab* is a flap attached to the top of a window, sheet, or toolbar to allow similar items to be grouped. Words or icons are used to help identify the content in the tab.

62. Hover the cursor over each tab in the **Properties** toolbar to display the help text, and record the name in **Figure 2-14.**

Tab	Tab Name	Tab	Tab Name
☑		▦	
🖥		💬	
▶		5	
A·Z			

Figure 2-14. Use help text to discover the name of each command on the **Properties** toolbar, and record the names here.

63. Click the **Window** tab in the **Properties** toolbar.
64. Locate the Size property. The size of the window does not match the size of the frame. Change the Size property to 800 by 800. This is a global setting, so the windows size is changed for all frames. Without changing this setting, part of the frame would not be visible in the window when the game is played.
65. Click the **About** tab in the **Properties** toolbar.
66. Locate the Author property, and enter your name.
67. Locate the Copyright property, and change it to today's date.
68. Click the **Runtime Options** tab in the **Properties** toolbar.
69. Locate the Frame Rate property, and change it to 50. The *frame rate* is how quickly what you see on the screen during gameplay is refreshed. A frame rate of 60 indicates the screen is refreshed 60 times per second. Changing the frame rate will change the global speed of the game. A frame rate of 50 will slow the game down 17 percent from the default rate of 60. Increasing the frame rate will speed up the game.
70. Click the **Values** tab in the **Properties** toolbar. Notice global values and global strings can be edited here. A *value* is a data type such as a number or date. A *string* is text. **Figure 2-15** shows common data types.
71. Select the **Events** tab in the **Properties** toolbar. Notice global events can be edited here. Events that are used on every level like the user interface controls can be programmed here. Note: this feature is disabled in the free version of Clickteam Fusion 2.5, but is not needed for this game build.
72. Applying what you have learned, display the properties for the Inner Planets frame.
73. Click the **Settings** tab in the **Properties** toolbar.
74. Click the color swatch for the Background property, and click the black swatch in the pop-up menu. A *swatch* is a small, square color sample. The default color for the background is white. A *default setting* is the value as it was when the program was installed. When you modify a default setting, you create a custom setting. A *custom setting* is a program feature that has been modified by the user.
75. Click the backdrop object in the editor window to select it. Notice it is outlined in blue and a number is displayed in its upper-left corner. This number is the asset number for the object. The properties for the backdrop are also displayed in the **Properties** toolbar.
76. Using the **About** tab in the **Properties** toolbar, change the name of the object to Backdrop Space. Adding the word *space* helps the name to be more descriptive and, therefore, easier to work with in the future.
77. Click the **Size/Position** tab in the **Properties** toolbar.

🖥 Window

💬 About

▶ Runtime Options

A·Z Values

▦ Events

☑ Settings

Size/Position

Data Type	Content	Range	Description	Example
integer	Whole Number	–2,147,483,648 to 2,147,483,648	Number value up to 4 bytes	X = 4568974
short	Whole Number	–32768 to 32767	Number value up to 2 bytes	X = –12345
long	Whole Number	A very large amount	Number value up to 8 bytes	X = 123456789101112
string	Character	Any size text amount	Holds text only shown in "quotation." Numbers entered into a string variable are text and not numbers, meaning those numbers will not be able to be used to calculate.	X = "Hello World" X = "4" X = "anything"
Boolean	True/False	On or off state only	Use to check if something is true/active/enabled or not	X = true X = false
single	Decimal Number	Short decimal values	Number with decimal value up to 4 bytes. Single precision floating point.	X = 3.14159
double	Decimal Number	Long decimal values	Number with decimal value up to 8 bytes. Double precision floating point.	X = 12345.1234567890

Goodheart-Willcox Publisher

Figure 2-15. These are the common data types in computer programming.

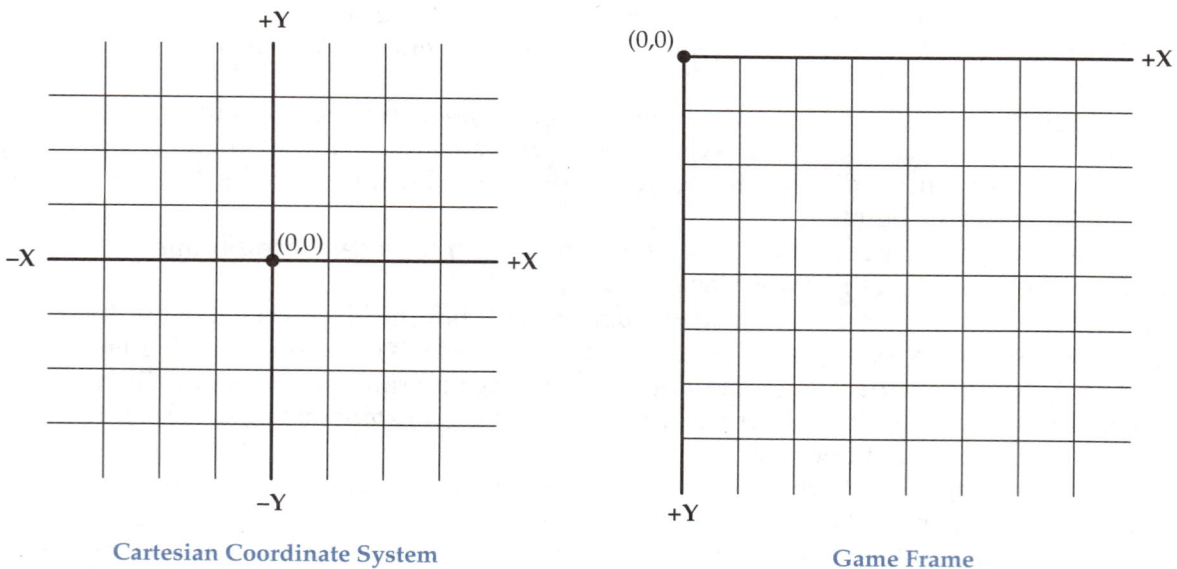

Cartesian Coordinate System

Game Frame

Goodheart-Willcox Publisher

Figure 2-16. The coordinate system for a game frame in Clickteam Fusion 2.5 is similar to the familiar Cartesian coordinate system. However, notice that the Y directions are flip-flopped. The positive Y direction is down on the game frame, not up as in the Cartesian coordinate system.

78. Change the X and Y properties both to 0. This places the object at the origin of the frame. A game frame is set up similar to the Cartesian coordinate system you learned about in your math class, as shown in **Figure 2-16.** The *Cartesian coordinate system* uses values on X and Y axes to locate points. The *X axis* extends to the left and right. In Clickteam Fusion 2.5, the 0 value is the left edge of the frame. X values are positive moving to the right and negative moving to the left. The *Y axis* extends up and down. The values for the Y axis in Clickteam Fusion 2.5 are opposite of the Cartesian coordinate system from your math class. Y values are positive moving *down* and negative moving *up*. The *origin* is where both X and Y values are 0 (0,0). In Clickteam Fusion 2.5, this is the top-left corner of the frame.

79. Change the Width and Height properties to 800. This will fill the frame with the Background Space object.

80. Using the table below, set the size and position of the objects.

Object	X	Y	Width	Height
SUN	−150	250	300	300
MERCURY	275	400	30	30
VENUS	430	400	65	65
EARTH	575	400	70	70
MARS	750	400	35	35
MOON	625	365	25	25

81. Click the JUPITER object in the editor window, and press the [Ctrl][X] key combination to remove (cut) it from the frame and place it on the system clipboard.

82. Applying what you have learned, display the Outer Planets frame.

83. Click in the editor window, and press the [Ctrl][V] key combination. The cursor changes to a large plus sign. Click anywhere on the frame to paste the JUPITER object onto the frame.

84. Applying what you have learned, cut the URANUS, SATURN, NEPTUNE, and PLUTO objects from the Inner Planets frame and paste them onto the Outer Planets frame.

85. Display the Inner Planets frame.

Event Editor

The event editor is where the programming is added to the game. Clickteam Fusion 2.5 does not use a coding language. *Coding* is the use of words and symbols to communicate commands to a computer using a language such as Java or C++. Instead of coding, creating a game in Clickteam Fusion 2.5 requires using a simplified method of programming. *Programming* is inputting instructions for a machine to follow without writing code. Setting an alarm on your phone is programming an alarm. Just by clicking a few buttons, you can program without writing code in a computer programming language.

86. Click the **Event Editor** button on the **Navigate Toolbar** to display the event editor.

87. Locate the icons across the top of the event editor, as shown in **Figure 2-17.** The first seven icons are for standard programming features or functions. The other icons are for the active objects you inserted into the game.

Event Editor

88. Click the words **New condition** in the first line, which is numbered 1. Each event line is numbered. When you click, the **New Condition** dialog box is displayed. This dialog box contains all of the programming icons listed across the top of the event editor.

Click to add a new condition

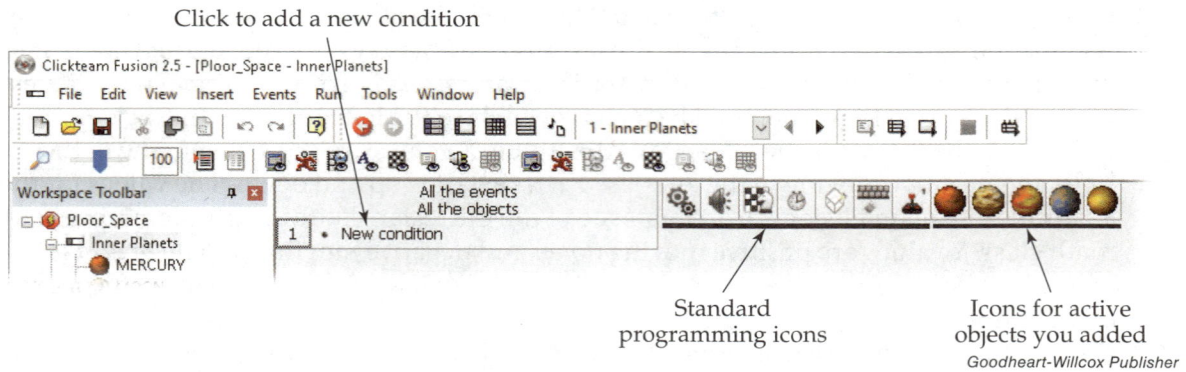

Figure 2-17. The icons across the top of the event editor represent standard programming features and the active objects you have added to the game frame.

89. Hover the cursor over each icon to locate the **The mouse pointer and keyboard** icon, and click that icon. A shortcut menu is displayed.
90. Click **The keyboard>Upon pressing a key** in the shortcut menu. A dialog box is displayed asking you to press a key.
91. On the keyboard, press the [M] key. The message is dismissed, and the new condition is added to event line number 1. Notice that line 1 now reads Upon pressing "M". Also notice line 1 has a rectangle, or cell, below each of the icons along the top. A *cell* is the intersection of a column and a row.
92. Right-click in the cell below icon for the MOON object, and click **Destroy** in the shortcut menu. A check mark is added to the cell in line 1 below the icon for the MOON object.

Pseudocode

Pseudocode is a very simple version of computer coding. In these lessons, you will use pseudocode to develop the programming for your games. Pseudocode is very useful in structuring an event. An *event* is a set of instructions for when a condition occurs and the actions that need to be performed. Clickteam Fusion 2.5 separates the conditions and action sections of programming in each line of programming. The *condition* is what needs to occur to trigger actions. An *action* is what happens when triggered. Pseudocode breaks down conditions as **IF** statements and actions as **THEN** statements. The structure of pseudocode is:

> **IF** condition occurs,
> > **THEN** execute these actions.

To program pseudocode in Clickteam Fusion 2.5, imagine the word **IF** where the line numbers are located and the word **THEN** before the actions icons. Refer to **Figure 2-18.** For the event you just programed, the pseudocode is:

> **IF** upon pressing the [M] key,
> > **THEN** destroy the MOON object.

93. Hover the cursor over the check mark below the icon for the MOON object. Notice the help text displays the action you programmed. This is the **THEN** side of the pseudocode.
94. Click the **Run Frame** button on the **Run Toolbar**. The game is compiled and run in a new window.

Run Frame

95. Inspect the scene to make sure the planets are spinning. These objects have animation sets to create the movement.
96. Press the [M] key on the keyboard. The MOON object should disappear. This is the event you programmed with pseudocode. Note: you do not have to use a capital M.
97. Close the game window.

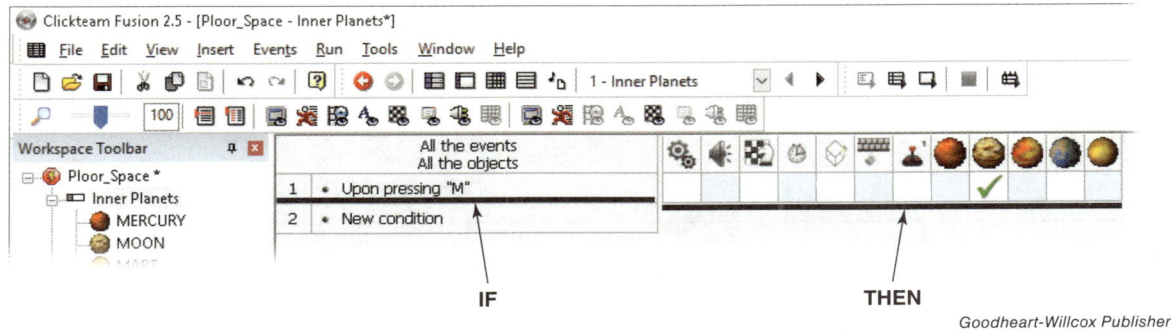

Goodheart-Willcox Publisher

Figure 2-18. In the event editor, the condition is the **IF** side of the **IF...THEN** statement. The action is the **THEN** side.

Programming with Pseudocode

98. Applying what you have learned, program event line 2 using this pseudocode:
    IF upon pressing the [E] key,
        THEN destroy the EARTH object.

99. Applying what you have learned, program event line 3 using this pseudocode:
    IF upon pressing the [V] key,
        THEN destroy the VENUS object.

100. Run the frame. Test the events by pressing the [M], [E], and [V] keys to destroy the objects. Close the game window when done testing.

Programming Using Boolean Operators

The word **AND** in pseudocode can allow more than one condition or action to occur in a single event. This is called a Boolean operator. Boolean operators create a relationship in the statement. The word **OR** is also a Boolean operator.

101. Program event line 4 using this pseudocode:
    IF upon pressing the [X] key,
        THEN destroy the MERCURY object.

102. Drag the check mark from below the icon for the MERCURY object into the cell below the icon for the VENUS object in line 4. This copies the action. The pseudocode on event line 4 is now:
    IF upon pressing the [X] key,
        THEN destroy the MERCURY object
            AND destroy the VENUS object.

103. Program event line 5 using the following pseudocode. Use the drag-and-drop method to copy the actions. Copying existing actions improves programming efficiency. Note: you can drag from one line to another as well.
    IF upon pressing the [Y] key,
        THEN destroy the MARS object
            AND destroy the MOON object
            AND destroy the EARTH object
            AND destroy the VENUS object
            AND destroy the MERCURY object.

104. Run the frame, and test all programmed keys. You will need to run the frame three times to test all possibilities.

105. Save your work, and submit it for grading.

Vocabulary

Write a definition for each of the key terms from this lesson. You will develop a personal glossary of key terms throughout this course.

menu bar

_____

_____

title bar

_____

_____

toggle

_____

_____

toolbar

_____

_____

icon

_____

_____

hover

_____

_____

help text

_____

_____

hot key shortcut

_____

_____

toolbar handle

_____

_____

floating

_____

_____

docking

_____

_____

thumbnail

_____

_____

fade-in

_____

_____

fade-out

_____

_____

tree organizational format

_____

_____

trunk

_____

_____

branch

_____

_____

twig

_____

_____

leaf

_____

_____

global settings

_____

_____

local settings

_____

_____

tab

_____

_____

frame rate

_____

_____

value

_____

_____

string

_____

_____

swatch

_____

_____

default setting

_____

_____

custom setting

_____

_____

Cartesian coordinate system

_____

_____

X axis

_____

_____

Y axis

_____

_____

origin

_____

_____

coding

_____

_____

programming

_____

_____

Name: _____

cell

_____

_____

pseudocode

_____

_____

event

_____

_____

condition

_____

_____

action

_____

_____

Review Questions

1. What is the difference between a fade-in transition and a fade-out transition?

    _____

    _____

    _____

    _____

    _____

    Applied Technology

2. Refer to the game frame coordinate system shown in **Figure 2-16.** What direction would a 2D game object travel when moving from coordinate point (3,5) to (3,0)?

    _____

    _____

    _____

    _____

    _____

    Mathematics

Applied Technology

3. Which is the best data type to store the number 365.2? Use details from the reading to explain why you chose that data type.

_____

_____

_____

_____

Applied Technology

4. Which is the best data type to store the value "awesome"? Use details from the reading to explain why you chose that data type.

_____

_____

_____

_____

Language Arts

5. Which is the best data type to store the number –1? Use details from the reading to explain why you chose that data type.

_____

_____

_____

_____

_____

Higher-Order Thinking Strategies

Applied Technology

6. Summarize how you would move the **Library Toolbar** from the bottom to the right-hand side of the screen.

_____

_____

_____

_____

_____

7. Which of the inner planets is one-half the size of another planet?

_____

_____

_____

_____

_____

Science

8. Use details from the reading, tables, charts, or images to explain why you chose which planet is one-half the size of another.

_____

_____

_____

_____

_____

Language Arts

9. Analyze the structure of the file organization tree. Explain how it is similar to a real tree.

_____

_____

_____

_____

_____

Science

10. Speculate how hot key shortcuts can help a game designer who finds it challenging to use a mouse.

_____

_____

_____

_____

_____

Social Science

Office Technology Integration

Managing Worksheets

1. Launch Microsoft Excel or other spreadsheet software, and open the vocabulary spreadsheet you created in the last lesson.
2. Locate the workbook tabs at the bottom of the screen. These should say Sheet1, Sheet2, and Sheet3. There may be only one tab or there may be multiple tabs.
3. Double-click on the word Sheet1. The name is selected and can be edited.
4. Change the name to Lesson 1, and press the [Enter] to rename the tab.
5. Right-click on the Lesson 1 tab, and click select **Move or Copy...** in the shortcut menu.
6. In the **Move or Copy** dialog box, check the **Create a copy** check box, as shown.

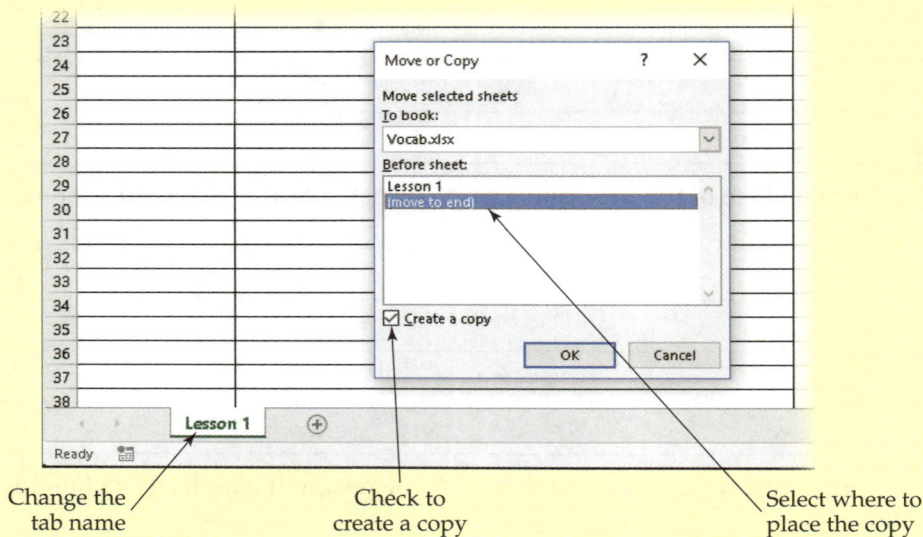

Change the tab name

Check to create a copy

Select where to place the copy

Goodheart-Willcox Publisher

7. Choose to move to the end, or if you have multiple sheets, move before Sheet2.
8. Click the **OK** button to copy the worksheet.
9. Applying what you have learned, rename the copied tab as Lesson 2.
10. Click the Lesson 2 tab to display it.
11. Delete the existing vocabulary on the Lesson 2 sheet.
12. Add each of the vocabulary words and definitions from the Vocabulary section of this lesson.
13. Save your work.

Lesson 3

Click Ball

Learning Objectives

After completing this lesson, you will be able to:

- use game design tools to create a simple game.

- set background and add objects to enhance a scene.

- program objects to react to the game rules.

Situation

The Awesome Game Company wants to create a game for young children to improve a child's control of the mouse and ability to left-click. First, you must learn the definition of a video game and the associated rules and victory condition. The information in this section discusses these aspects.

Before beginning this lesson, go to the student companion website (www.g-wlearning.com), and download the asset files for this lesson. Place the downloaded files in your working folder.

Reading Material

A **video game** is a software-based entertainment product that has a game environment, rules, and a victory condition. The thing that separates a video game from all other games is the game environment.

The **game environment** is a setting or world altered or designed to play a specific game activity. For a game like baseball, the game environment is the baseball field. The outdoor space has been altered to have three bases, home plate, a pitcher's mound, in-bounds areas, and foul areas. None of these things exist in nature. We as humans have changed a piece of land to make this game environment. In a video game, the game environment is a virtual game world. This virtual world is seen through a video screen, thus the *video* in *video game*. The really cool part of a virtual world is that anything can happen. Realistic and unrealistic events can occur. It is up to the designer to create the world he or she wants.

Inside a video game world are the rules that determine the realistic and unrealistic features. A **rule** is a constraint that determines what can or cannot happen in the game. Looking at the baseball example, the rules are clear. Inside the game environment of the baseball field, these rules apply:

- each team fields nine players;
- each team is allotted three outs per inning;
- there are nine innings in a standard game;

Name: _____

Date: _____

Class: _____

- each batter can take up to two strikes to get on base;
- if a batter makes three strikes, an out is recorded; and
- if a ball in play is caught before it hits the ground, an out is recorded.

There are many more rules for the game of baseball. The important point is to understand that these rules make the game environment meaningful. Imagine if the rules did not set out-of-bounds. The batter could hit the ball backward to get a home run. That makes the out-of-bounds rule a very important part of the game environment.

A video game designer has to be very careful when making the rules for video games as well. Making rules that help the player feel the game is fair and winnable is one of the main reasons to construct a rule. Other rules help create the environment, like the out-of-bounds rule in baseball.

Lastly, a video game must have a victory condition. A ***victory condition*** is a point where the player has achieved the objective and is the winner of the game. Levels within the game may also have individual victory conditions. In the game of baseball, the victory condition is the team with the most runs at the end of nine innings. In a video game, the victory may come after defeating a very strong enemy or getting to the end of a quest. A very strong enemy is called a ***boss*** in a video game. It is the imagination of the game designer that determines how the player will win.

Game Build

The Awesome Game Company wants the game to have three levels. Each level will requie better mouse skill and hand-eye coordination than the previous level. The company hopes this approach will improve motor skills for young children in a fun game environment.

How to Begin

New

1. Launch Clickteam Fusion 2.5.
2. Click the **New** button on the **Standard Toolbar** to begin a new application.
3. Click **File**>**Save As...** in the pull-down menu.
4. Save the file as *LastName_*ClickBall in your working folder.
5. Applying what you have learned, use the storyboard editor to change the name of the frame to Level 1.
6. Applying what you have learned, set the size of the Level 1 frame to 640 by 480 if not already that size.

Grids

A ***grid*** is a tool used to help the design place objects on the frame in correct alignment with other objects. The ***snap*** feature moves, or snaps, objects to the closest grid point. The hotspot of each object placed on the frame will snap to the closest grid dot. The ***hotspot*** is the origin of an object. Usually, the hotspot is located in the top-left corner of an object, but can be set by the designer to any point.

Frame Editor

7. Applying what you have learned, display the Level 1 frame in the frame editor.
8. Select Frame 1 in the **Workspace Toolbar** so its properties are displayed in the **Properties** toolbar.

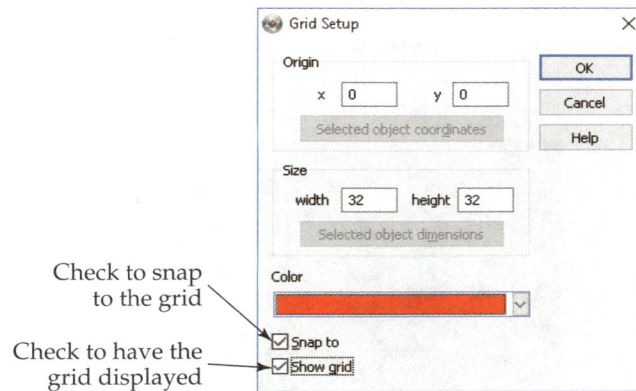

Check to snap
to the grid

Check to have the
grid displayed

Goodheart-Willcox Publisher

Figure 3-1. The grid and snap are useful features to help align objects on the game frame.

9. Applying what you have learned, use the **Properties** toolbar to change the background color of Level 1 to a green color of your choice.
10. Click the **Grid Setup** button on the **Editor Toolbar**. The **Grid Setup** dialog box is displayed, as shown in **Figure 3-1.**
11. In the **Size** area, set the **Width** and **Height** values to 32, if not already.
12. Click the **Color** drop-down list, and click the yellow swatch. You can choose whichever color you feel will contrast with the green background.
13. Check the **Snap to** check box to enable snap.
14. Check the **Show grid** check box to have the grid displayed.
15. Click the **OK** button to close the dialog box and display the grid. The grid is displayed as rows and columns of colored dots.

Grid Setup

Adding and Naming Objects

In naming game assets, you should follow a naming convention. A ***naming convention*** is a standard way of naming items. Following a naming convention makes it easy to identify the proper game asset during game construction. The naming convention used for this game will include the class of object, an underscore, and the name for the object. A ***class*** is a major grouping. This is like stating the noun, an underscore, and an adjective to differentiate the object from all other similar objects. For example, the name Ball_Soccer sets the object apart from all types other balls. The object is in the class of Ball. The type within the class is Soccer.

16. Applying what you have learned, expand the Local Library branch in the **Library Toolbar**. Expand the tree Local Library>Games>Game Objects 2 to show the leaves in the Game Objects 2 branch, as shown in **Figure 3-2.**
17. Click and hold the Ball 10 object, drag it to near the center of the game frame, and drop to add the object to the frame.
18. Applying what you have learned, use the **Properties** toolbar to rename the Ball 10 object as Ball_Tennis.
19. In the **Library Toolbar**, double-click the folder icon to go up one level in the tree. You should see the twigs in the Games branch, including Game Objects 2.

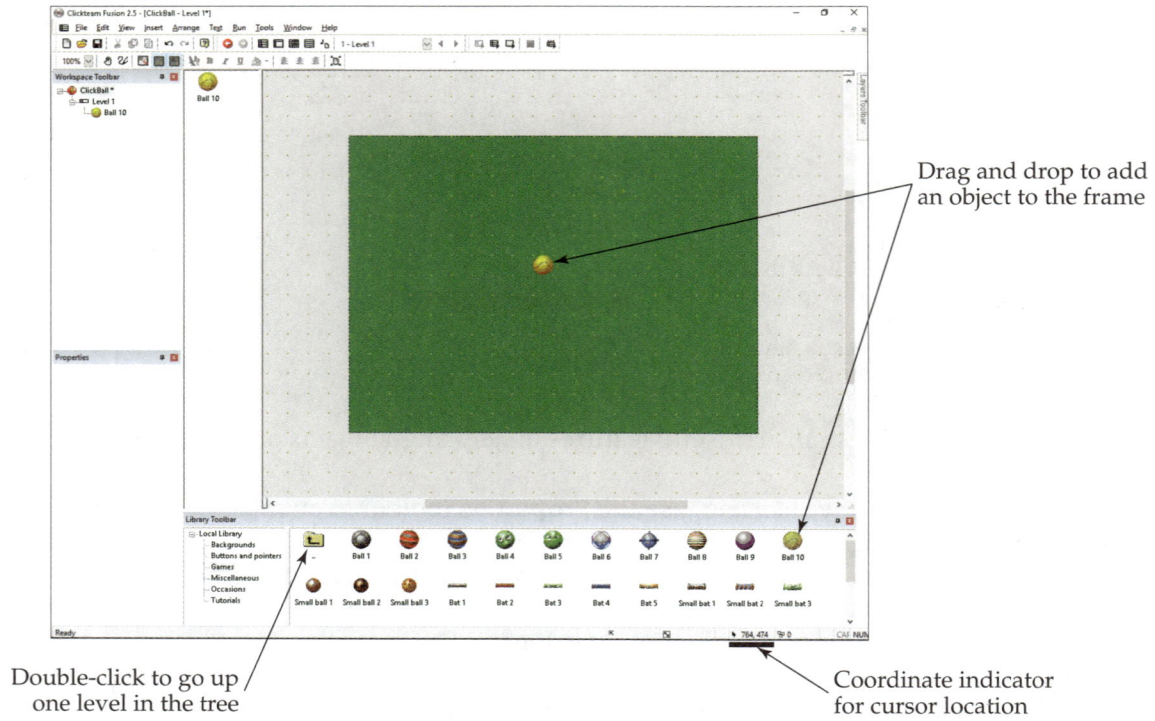

Drag and drop to add
an object to the frame

Double-click to go up
one level in the tree

Coordinate indicator
for cursor location

Figure 3-2. Objects can be dragged from the library and dropped onto the game frame.

20. Double-click the Game Objects 1 twig to open it.
21. Add the following objects to the game frame, and rename them as shown.

Object	Naming Convention
corner wall tile 9	Wall_Corner_Top_Right
corner wall tile 10	Wall_Corner_Bottom_Left
corner wall tile 11	Wall_Corner_Bottom_Right
corner wall tile 12	Wall_Corner_Top_Left
wall tile 6	Wall_Top
wall tile 7	Wall_Right

22. Drag each wall corner object to the correct corner of the game frame. Notice how the grid and snap help you correctly align the objects.
23. Drag the Wall_Top object to the right of the Wall_Corner_Top_Left object.
24. Drag the Wall_Right object below the Wall_Corner_Top_Right object. Notice how the naming convention makes it easy for you to know which objects are being discussed. Using names such as Object 1 or Object 2 would not give you enough information to easily find the object.

Duplicating

25. Right-click on the Wall_Top object in the game frame, and click Duplicate in the shortcut menu. The **Duplicate Object** dialog box is displayed, as shown in **Figure 3-3.** This allows you to specify the placement of the new instances. Remember, an *instance* is an exact copy that inherits all the properties of the original object.
26. Click in the **Rows** text box, and enter 1. This specifies one horizontal row of instances.

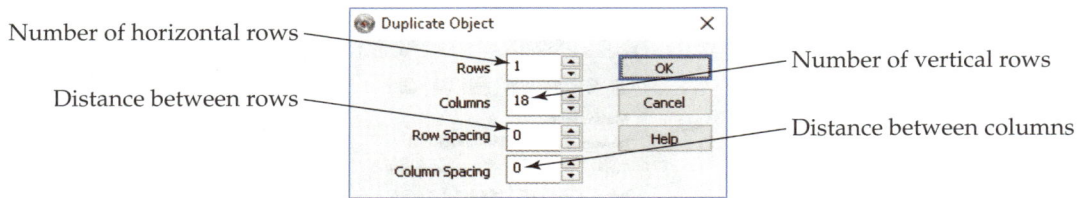

Number of horizontal rows — | Number of vertical rows

Distance between rows — | Distance between columns

Goodheart-Willcox Publisher

Figure 3-3. When creating instances, specify the number of rows and columns as well as the distance between.

27. Click in the **Columns** text box, and enter 18. This specifies 18 vertical columns of instances.
28. Make sure the **Row Spacing** and **Column Spacing** values are 0. This means there will be no space added between the instances.
29. Click the **OK** button to add the instances. Since there is one row and 18 columns, 17 instances of the object are created in the same row as the original for a total of 18 objects. The top wall is now complete. You will add the programming for it later.
30. Applying what you have learned, duplicate the Wall_Right object so there is a total of 13 objects to complete the right-hand wall.

Window Selection

A *marquee* is a window or box dragged around a set of objects to select them. Any object completely contained inside the window will be selected. Any object not *completely* inside the window will not be selected. If even one pixel of the object is outside of the selection, it will be excluded.

31. Move the cursor around the game frame, and look at the coordinate indicator at the bottom-right corner of the screen. Notice how the values show you the exact X and Y location of the cursor.
32. Move the cursor to position (650,30) using the coordinate indicator to properly position it.
33. Click and drag to create a marquee that will completely include all of the Wall_Right objects, but *not* the Wall_Corner objects.
34. With the 13 Wall_Right objects selected, click the **Copy** button on the **Standard Toolbar**.
35. Click the **Paste** button on the **Standard Toolbar**. The cursor changes to a large plus sign to indicate content is ready to be pasted.
36. Move the cursor below the Wall_Corner_Top_Left object, and click to paste the copied objects. The pasted objects remain selected.
37. If needed, drag the pasted objects into place if they were not perfectly aligned when you clicked.
38. Applying what you have learned, copy the Wall_Top objects, and paste them at the bottom edge of the game frame. There should now be a complete wall along the outside of the game frame.

Copy

Paste

Ball Movement

39. Select the Ball_Tennis object, and click the **Movement** tab in the **Properties** toolbar.
40. Click the Type property, and click **Bouncing Ball** in the drop-down menu that is displayed, as shown in **Figure 3-4.**
41. Make sure the Moving at start property is checked. This makes the ball start moving when the frame opens.
42. Change the Speed property to 40, and leave all other values at the defaults. Note: the Randomizer and Security properties are used to keep the ball from getting stuck. These will randomly change the direction of the ball to avoid these issues. Increasing these values will create a more random movement that is harder to predict.

Movement

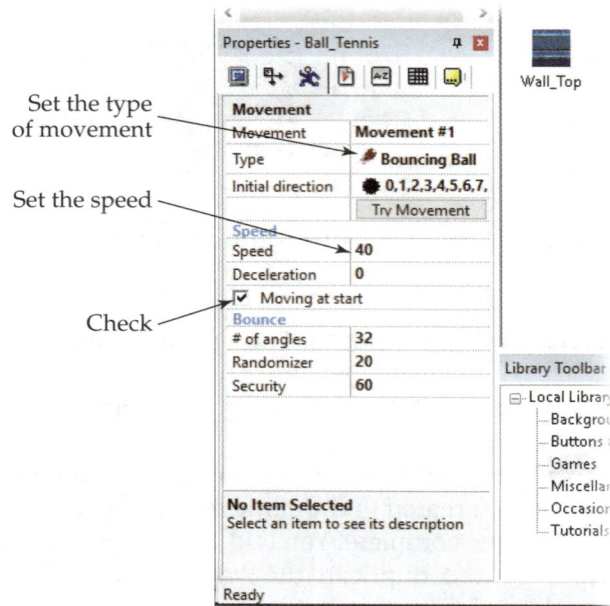

Set the type
of movement

Set the speed

Check

Wall_Top

Goodheart-Willcox Publisher

Figure 3-4. To make the ball object act like a ball, the movement is set to the bouncing ball type.

Run Frame

43. Applying what you have learned, run the frame to see what happens. Close the game window when done.

Collision Detection

As you could see when you tested the frame, the tennis ball moves through the walls and off the screen. This is because collision detection has not been programmed. The walls are not real walls, they are just colored pixels. The wall objects must have programming so the computer will treat them as real walls.

Collision detection is how the computer recognizes when one object has touched another. The designer can specify to have the collision detected by the bounding box for the object or by the object's edge as defined by the pixels of the sprite. Refer to **Figure 3-5.** For rectangular objects like the walls, the bounding box would be used. A *bounding box* is a rectangular region within which the sprite on object fits. For nonrectangular objects like the ball, the object edge would be used.

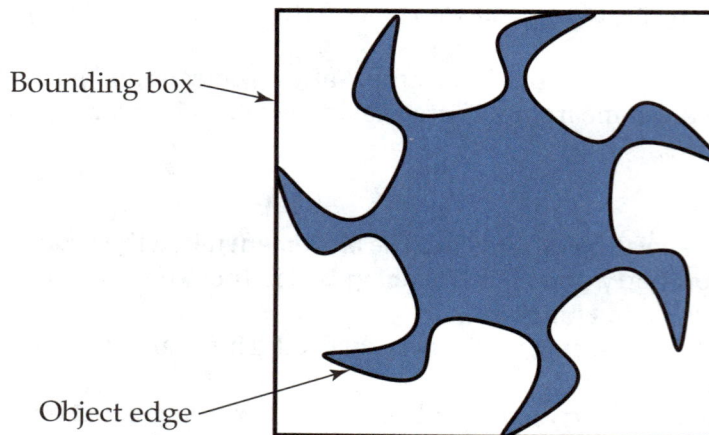

Bounding box

Object edge

Goodheart-Willcox Publisher

Figure 3-5. Collision detection can be based on an object's bounding box or the edge of the object.

44. Select the Wall_Corner_Top_Left object.
45. Click the **RunTime Options** tab in the **Properties** toolbar.
46. Change the Obstacle Type to Obstacle. An object can be set as a basic barrier, such as a platform, ladder, or obstacle. Most background objects are simply set to None as they are decorative and not functional. Game objects can pass over or through these objects.

RunTime Options

47. Check the Collision with box property. This specifies the bounding box will be used for collision detection.
48. Applying what you have learned, set all the wall class objects to be obstacles with collision detection set to the bounding box. Note: you only need to change the properties of one object to change all instances of the object.

Programming Events

Remember, Clickteam Fusion 2.5 uses conditions and actions to create the interactions needed in a game. Your game does not yet have any programming, only scene design. The first programming event will be to make the ball bounce off any obstacle it encounters. The pseudocode for this is:

IF the Ball_Tennis object collides with an obstacle,
THEN bounce the Ball_Tennis object away from the obstacle.

49. Display the event editor.
50. Applying what you have learned, add a new condition. In the **New Condition** dialog box, right-click on the icon for the Ball_Tennis object, and click **Collisions>Backdrop** in the shortcut menu. This creates the condition **IF** the Ball_Tennis object collides with an obstacle. Notice how this is displayed on the event line in the event editor. Note: only background objects set as obstacles will be detected.

Event Editor

51. Right-click in the cell under the icon for the Ball_Tennis object, and click **Movement>Bounce** in the shortcut menu. This creates the action **THEN** bounce the Ball_Tennis object away from the obstacle. If you hover the cursor over the check mark, the help text will indicate Bounce, as shown in **Figure 3-6**.
52. Run the frame to make sure the Ball_Tennis object is bouncing off the walls. Close the game frame when done testing.
53. Debug any errors by setting any wall object as an obstacle if needed.

Run Frame

Victory Condition

Recall from the reading that to be a video game requires a game environment, user interface, and victory condition. Do you think all three requirements have been met? Only one requirement has been met by setting up the scene or game environment. This game will use a score to establish a victory condition.

54. Display the frame editor.

Frame Editor

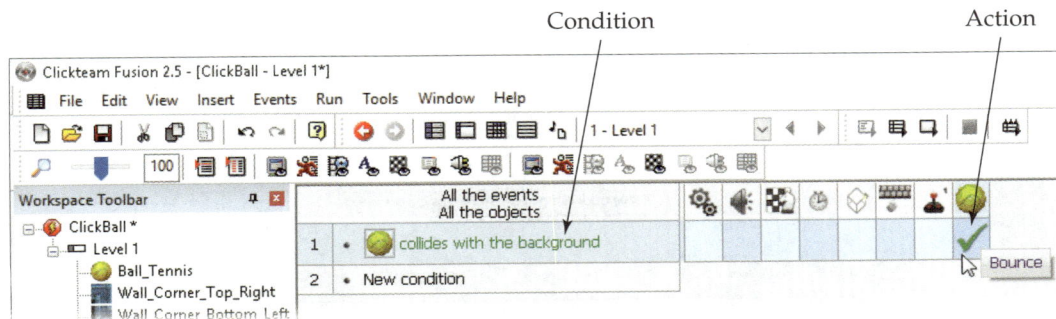

Goodheart-Willcox Publisher

Figure 3-6. Actions are represented by check marks in the event editor. The help text will show what the action is.

55. Click **Insert>New Object** in the pull-down menu.

56. In the **Create New Object** dialog box, click **Games** on the left, and then click **Score** on the right, as shown in **Figure 3-7.** Click the **OK** button. The cursor changes to a large plus sign.

57. Click near the center of the frame to place the Score object on the frame.

58. The Score object should be selected. If so, click it once to display the sizing handles. If the object is not currently selected, slowly click twice on the object to display the handles. Clicking once on an unselected object selects the object. Slowly clicking twice on an unselected object displays the sizing handles.

59. Move the cursor over one of the corner sizing handles so a resizing cursor is displayed. Then, click and drag to make the object larger and easier to see.

60. Double-click the Score object to display the **Image Editor** dialog box. This is the image editor. The tools in the image editor are similar to most painting software, such as Microsoft Paint.

61. Click a yellow color swatch in the color palette. You may choose any color you feel will contrast with the wall objects.

Fill tool

62. Click the **Fill tool** button, and then click in the black area of the number 0 that is currently displayed in the editing area. The black is replaced with the yellow you selected.

63. Select the next frame (the number 1) in the area at the bottom of the dialog box, and recolor the number with the fill color.

64. Recolor the number on all of the frames. Then, click the **OK** button to update the object.

65. Applying what you have learned, use the **Properties** toolbar to change the position of the Score object to (615,20), the width to 8, and the height to 15. This should place the score object in the wall section at the top. If not, reposition the score object so it is visible on top of the wall.

66. Display the event editor. You will now program the victory condition.

Event Editor

67. Applying what you have learned, add a new condition. In the **New Condition** dialog box, right-click on the icon for **Player 1**, and click **Compare to player's score** in the shortcut menu. A new dialog box is displayed, as shown in **Figure 3-8.** This is the expression editor.

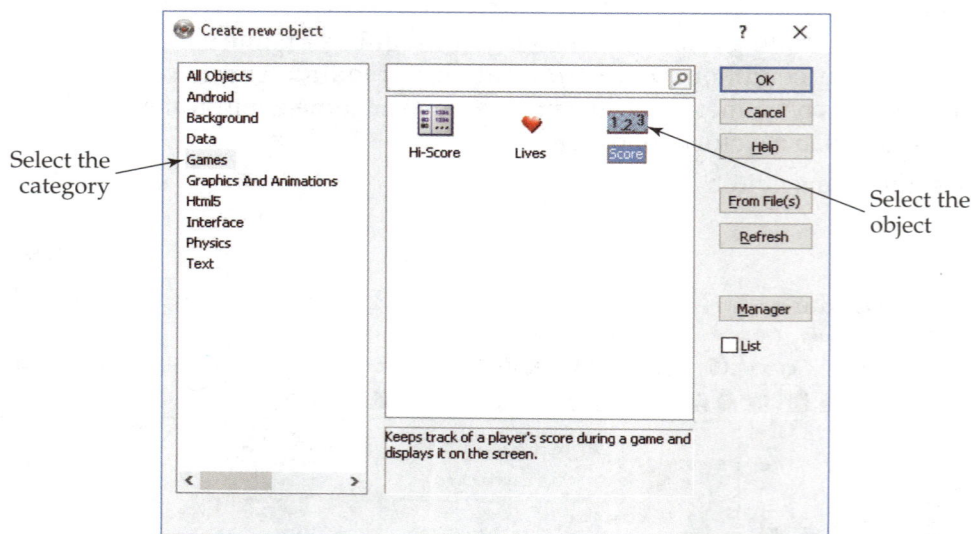

Goodheart-Willcox Publisher

Figure 3-7. The **Create New Object** dialog box contains several categories on the left. Selecting a category displays the objects within it on the right.

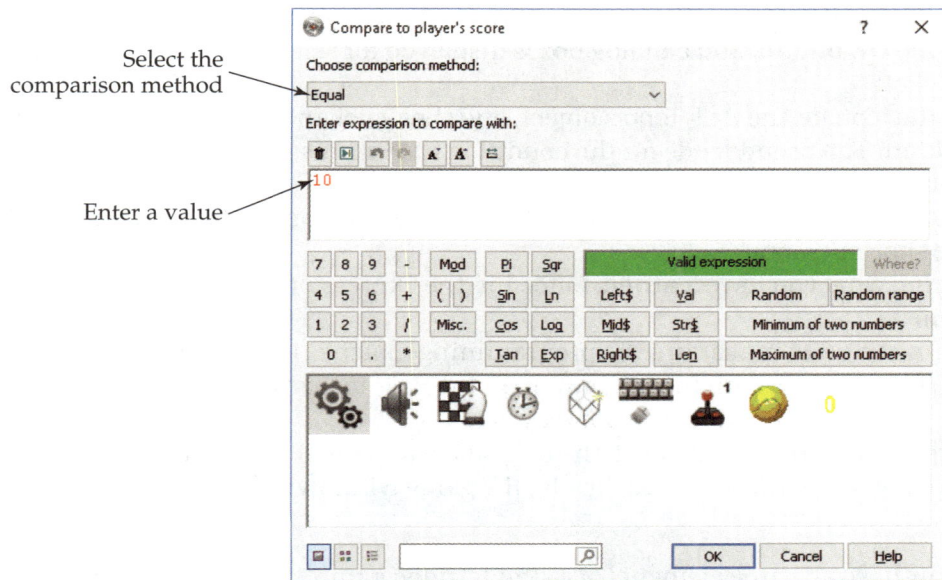

Select the
comparison method

Enter a value

Goodheart-Willcox Publisher

Figure 3-8. The expression editor is used to set up equations and formulas.

68. Click the **Choose comparison method:** drop-down arrow, and click **Equal** in the drop-down list.
69. Click in the **Enter expression to compare with:** text box, and enter 10.
70. Click the **OK** button to complete the condition statement.
71. Right-click in the cell on line 2 below the **Storyboard Controls** icon, and click **Next frame** in the shortcut menu. Line 2 is now programmed for this pseudocode:
    IF the score for player 1 equals 10,
        THEN go to the next frame.

User Interface

The user interface is how the player will interact with this game. For this game, the player will need to click the ball to add one point to the score. This will create the user interface, and you will have all three elements of a video game.

72. Add a new condition. In the **New Condition** dialog box, right-click on the icon for **The mouse pointer and keyboard**, and click **The mouse>User clicks on an object** in the shortcut menu. The **User clicks on an object** dialog box is displayed, as shown in **Figure 3-9.**
73. Click the **Left button** radio button to set which mouse button the user must click.

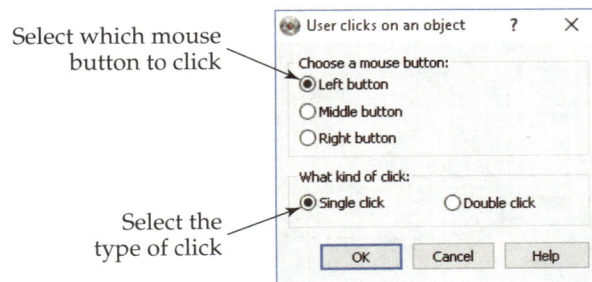

Select which mouse
button to click

Select the
type of click

Goodheart-Willcox Publisher

Figure 3-9. When testing the condition of the user clicking an object, you must select which button is pressed and whether it is a single-click or double-click.

74. Click the **Single click** radio button to set how the user must click.

75. Click the **OK** button, and a dialog box is displayed for selecting which object the user must click.

76. Click the icon for the Ball_Tennis object, and then click the **OK** button to complete the condition. The pseudocode for the condition is: **IF** the user clicks with the left mouse button on the Ball_Tennis object.

77. Right-click in the cell where line 3 under the **Player 1** icon, and click **Score>Add to Score** in the shortcut menu.

78. Applying what you have learned, enter 1 in the expression editor, and click the **OK** button.

79. Examine line 3 to make sure the programming matches this pseudocode:
    IF the user click with the left button on the Ball_Tennis object,
      THEN add 1 to the score for player 1.

80. Run the frame. To test, left-click the ball object and see if the score increases by 1 each time. Note: when the score reaches 10, the game window will close.

Run Frame

Sound

You now have all three elements of a simple video game, but the game needs a little tuning. *Tuning* is improving the game. Start tuning by adding some sound to let the player know when the ball has been clicked and a point awarded. Sounds can be obtained from almost any source or even recorded on your own. You must, however, be mindful of copyrights. When using sounds that you did not create yourself, you must make sure that these sounds are free to use and are not protected by copyright. Clickteam Fusion 2.5 comes with some sound files you can use.

81. Display the event editor.

82. Right-click in the cell on line 3 below the **Sound** icon, and click **Samples>Play Sample** from the shortcut menu. The **Play Sample** dialog box is displayed, as shown in **Figure 3-10.**

83. Make sure the **Uninterruptable** check box is *not* checked. Then, click the **Browse** button to the right of the **From a file** label. A standard open-type dialog box is displayed.

84. Navigate to the folder where the sound files installed with Clickteam Fusion 2.5 are located. This is typically C:\Program Files (x86)\Clickteam Fusion 2.5 Free Edition\Samples.

85. Select the BALL6.WAV file in the folder, and click the **Open** button to finish adding the action.

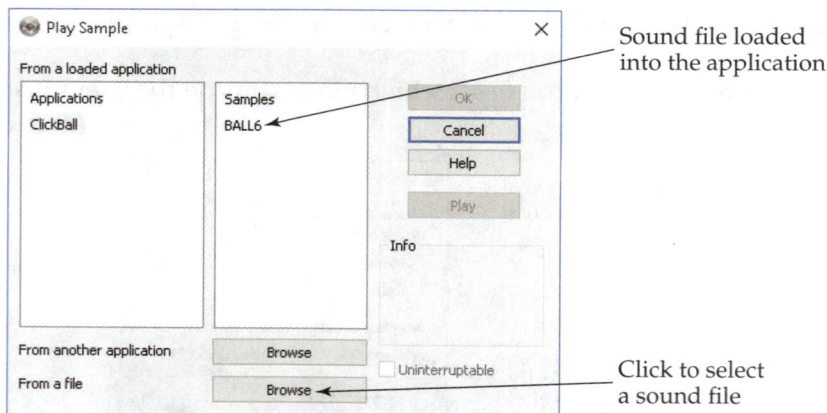

Goodheart-Willcox Publisher

Figure 3-10. Sound files can be loaded into the application to be played in the game.

86. Examine line 3 to make sure the programming matches this pseudocode:
    IF the user clicks with the left button on the Ball_Tennis object,
       THEN play the sound sample BALL6
          AND add 1 point to the score for player 1.

87. Run the frame. Test that the sound plays when the ball is clicked. Note: the first time you click the ball, the game may pause for a few seconds while the sound loads. Close the game window when done testing.

Run Frame

Sound Engineering

A **sound engineer** is someone who locates sounds and configures them for proper use. In a video game design studio, sound engineers are responsible for all of the sounds needed in a game. You get to be the sound engineer for this game.

88. Launch a web browser, and navigate to a search engine. Search for a sound file of a ball hitting a wall. Be sure to locate a copyright-free sound file in WAV format.

89. Download the sound file to your working folder.

90. Rename the sound file as Ball_Wall_Hit using the same file extension.

91. Applying what you have learned, modify the first event line to program the sound to play with this pseudocode:
    IF the Ball_Tennis object collides with an obstacle,
       THEN play the Ball_Wall_Hit sample
          AND bounce the ball.

92. Test the game. Check that the sounds play correctly. Close the game frame when done testing, and replace the sounds if needed.

Run Frame

Room for Expansion

You have reached a milestone of design. A **milestone of design** is a key point in the process of creating a game that represents a significant event. This milestone is the first playable level. The **first playable level** is the prototype version of the game that actually allows someone to play and test all of the interactions in the game. The Click Ball game has reached the first playable level milestone. It is a solid game, but it could still use a little improvement.

The reason why first playable level is so important is that the majority of the programming is in place. To add another level to the game is very easy. You can copy the first level and edit it to require more skill to win. To show the player that a different level is being played, the background color will be changed.

93. Display the storyboard editor.

94. Right-click the thumbnail for Level 1, and click **Copy** in the shortcut menu.

95. Right-click on the thumbnail again, and click **Paste** in the shortcut menu. An exact copy of the Level 1 frame is created.

Storyboard Editor

96. Applying what you have learned, rename the second frame as Level 2.

97. Double-click the Level 2 thumbnail to open that frame in the frame editor view.

98. Applying what you have learned, change the background color to any other color of your choice. Note: avoid yellow as it will not provide enough contrast with the ball.

99. Using the skills you have learned, increase the difficulty for the Level 2 frame. For example, you could increase the speed of the ball, reduce the size of the ball, or add additional wall blocks to the frame. This would give the ball more obstacles to bounce off and change direction more often, as shown in **Figure 3-11**. Additionally, increasing the speed property of the ball makes it harder to track the ball and click on it. Be creative in applying what you have learned.

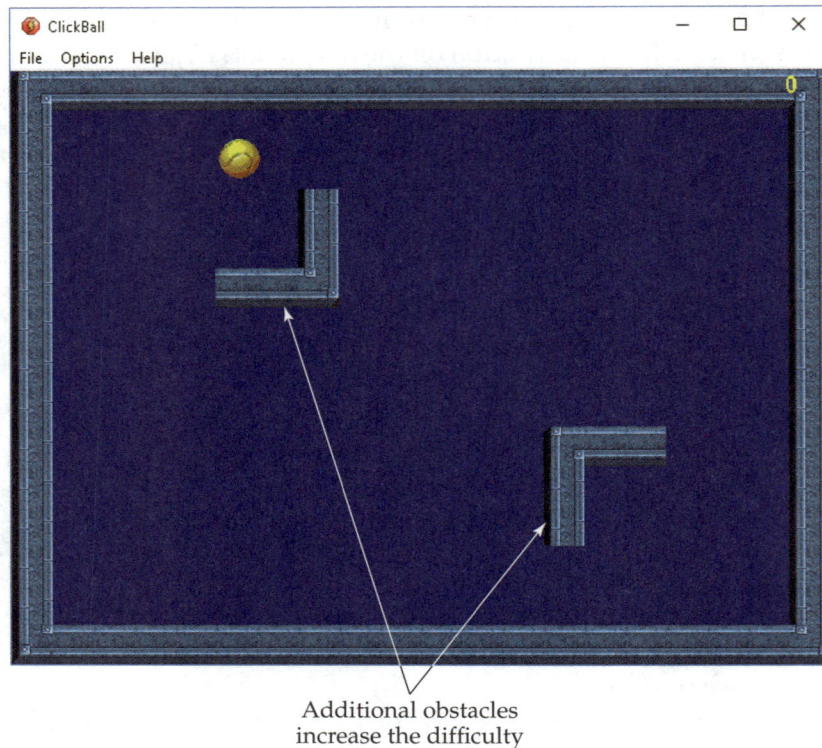

Additional obstacles
increase the difficulty

Goodheart-Willcox Publisher

Figure 3-11. Adding more obstacles is one way to increase the difficulty of a game level.

Cheat Code

A *cheat code* is a shortcut built into a game to help the quality assurance team and programmers test the game. This allows them to jump past certain points without having to complete the task or level. To help you pass each level while testing your game, you will program a cheat code. The pseudocode is:

IF the player presses the [space bar] on the keyboard,

> **THEN** stop the ball movement.

100. Display the event editor. Be sure Level 2 is current, as indicated by the drop-down list on the **Navigate Toolbar.**

Event Editor

101. Add a new condition. In the **New Condition** dialog box, right-click on the icon for **The mouse pointer and keyboard**, and click **The keyboard>Upon pressing a key** in the shortcut menu.

102. When prompted for a key, press the [space bar].

103. Right-click in the cell on line 4 below the icon for the Ball_Tennis object, and click **Movement>Stop** in the shortcut menu.

104. Run the frame, and test the cheat code. Close the game window when done testing.

Run Frame

Debugging

Currently, you can only play one level at a time. You should be able to achieve the victory condition on Level 1 and continue on to Level 2, but this does not happen. This is a bug. A *bug* is an error in programming. In this case, the same programming from Level 1 to move to the next frame when the score is 10 is the bug. Level 1 moves to the next frame, but since the score is already 10, Level 2 instantly moves to the next level. As a result, you never see Level 2.

105. Open Level 2 in the event editor, as shown in **Figure 3-12.**

Event Editor

106. Examine the condition in line 2: **IF** the player 1 score equals 10. Double-click the condition to open the expression editor.

Double-click to
edit the expression

Level 2 is current

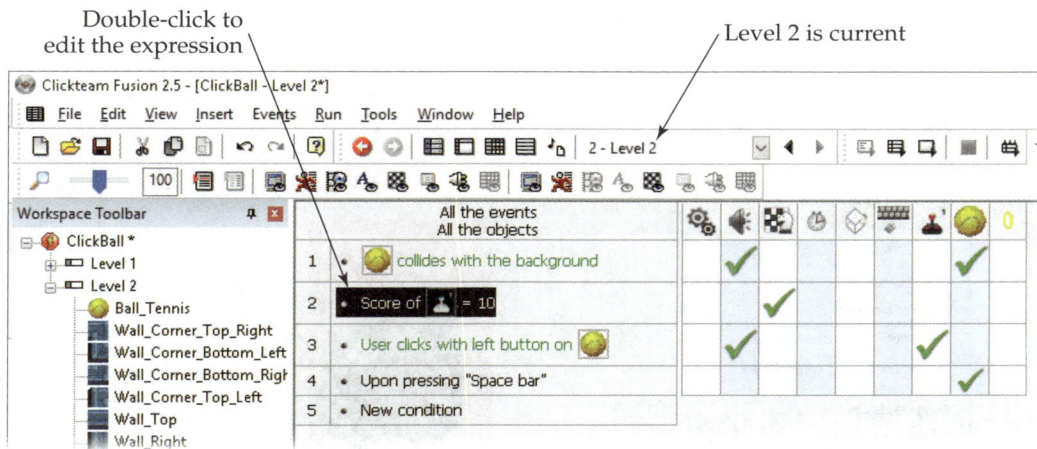

Goodheart-Willcox Publisher

Figure 3-12. To edit an existing condition, double-click it. In this example, double-clicking will display the expression editor.

107. Applying what you have learned, change the expression so the value is 20.
108. Click the **Run Application** button on the **Run Toolbar.** Play Level 1 to achieve the victory condition, and see if the bug is fixed. Close the game window when done testing.

Run Application

Transition Tuning

Adding a transition from one level to the next allows the player a quick break between levels. A transition allows for the next room to move into place smoothly. This is similar to the transition used in a PowerPoint slide show. Without a transition, the next room would begin abruptly when the first one closes.

109. Display the storyboard editor, and click the **Click to add fade in transition** button for Level 2.
110. Applying what you have learned, apply a zoom transition. Notice after you have applied the transition that the word zoom appears between Level 1 and Level 2 in the storyboard editor.

Storyboard Editor

111. Run the application. Play Level 1 to achieve the victory condition to see the transition. Close the game window when done testing.

Run Application

Enemies

To enhance gameplay, some enemy objects can add to the challenge. The idea here is that if the player clicks on an enemy, the game would end or a life would be lost.

112. Open Level 2 in the frame editor.
113. Click **Insert>New Object** in the pull-down menu.
114. In the **Create New Object** dialog box, click **Graphics and Animations** on the left, then click **Active** on the right. Click the **OK** button.

Frame Editor

115. Click anywhere on the frame to add the active object. The default sprite for an active object is a blue diamond. You will change the sprite on this object.
116. Double-click the active object to open the image editor.
117. Click the **Clear** button to erase the default image from the canvas.

Clear

118. Click the **Import** button, and navigate to your working folder.
119. Select the Bomb.gif image file, and click the **Open** button. The **Import Options** dialog box is displayed, as shown in **Figure 3-13.** Notice the image file has a pink background. This needs to be removed.

Import

Click and select the
background color

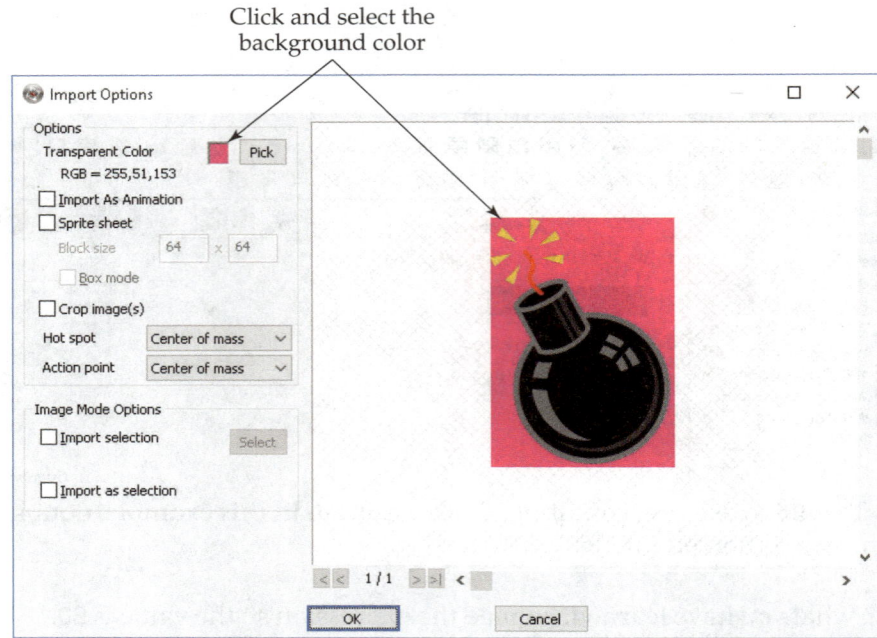

Figure 3-13. When importing an image file, you can select which color will be transparent (not shown) in the sprite.

120. Click the **Pick** button, and then click anywhere on the pink background color. The color swatch next to the button changes to indicate which color will be knocked out to make areas transparent. Note: black is the default transparent color, so if this was left unchanged, the black of the bomb would be invisible in the game, but the pink background would be visible.
121. Click the **OK** button to close the **Import Options** dialog box.
122. Click the **OK** button to close the image editor.
123. Applying what you have learned, rename the active object as Enemy_Bomb.
124. Change the size of the Enemy_Bomb object to 32 pixels wide and 44 pixels high.
125. Change the movement to bouncing ball with a speed of 60.
126. Copy and paste the Enemy_Bomb object so there are a total of eight enemies.
127. Randomly place the bombs around the scene.

Copy and Edit Programming

As you have seen, actions can be copied and pasted to speed up programming. Event lines can also be copied and pasted. Once pasted, an event can be easily edited. This increases efficiency by not having to program the entire event from scratch.

128. Open Level 2 in the event editor.
129. Right-click on the 1 for the first event line, and click **Copy** in the shortcut menu.

Event Editor

130. Right-click on the number for new condition line, and click **Paste** in the shortcut menu. An exact copy of the first event line is added.
131. In the condition for line 5, double-click the icon for the Ball_Tennis object.
132. In the dialog box that is displayed, click the Enemy_Bomb object, and click the **OK** button. The condition now tests for a collision with the Enemy_Bomb object instead of the Ball_Tennis object.
133. Drag the check mark in line 5 from the Ball_Tennis column to the Enemy_Bomb column.
134. Right-click the check mark in the Ball_Tennis column on line 5, and click **Delete** in the shortcut menu.

135. Applying what you have learned, replace the sound for event line 5 with an appropriate sound or delete the existing sound.

136. Try programming a new event line on your own for the Level 2 frame to match this pseudocode:

> **IF** the user clicks on the Enemy_Bomb object with the left mouse button,
> **THEN** go to the next frame.

Level 3: The End

At the end of the game, the player should see some sort of conclusion. In games like Click Ball, this is typically a high score page. This shows the player's score in relation to previous scores.

137. Display the storyboard editor, and click the number 3 on the third line to add a new frame.

Storyboard Editor

138. Applying what you have learned, rename the new frame Winner.

139. Applying what you have learned, open the Winner frame in the frame editor.

140. Applying what you have learned, expand the tree in the **Library Toolbar**: Local Library>Backgrounds>Games—General Playareas.

Frame Editor

141. Applying what you have learned, add the Playtime border object to the frame, and position it to fill the entire frame.

142. Click **Insert>New Object** in the pull-down menu. In the **Create New Object** dialog box, click **Text** on the left, **String** on the right, and then click the **OK** button.

143. Place the object anywhere on the frame. This object is similar to a text box like you might use in PowerPoint or Word. The text can be formatted.

144. Double-click the String object. This makes the text editable.

145. Enter this text: Congratulations! You are a WINNER!

146. Select all of the text, and click the **Font** button on the **Frame Editor Toolbar**. The **Font** dialog box is displayed, as shown in **Figure 3-14.** This dialog box contains text-formatting options similar to what you would find in PowerPoint or Word.

Font

147. Use the **Font:** list to select a typeface you like. Keep in mind the style of the background image. The typeface should fit with the style of the image.

148. Select **Bold** in the **Font style:** list.

149. Click **28** in the **Size:** list to set how big the text will be. Depending on the typeface you selected, the size may need to be larger or smaller.

150. Click the **OK** button to apply the formatting changes. Notice that the text box is no longer large enough to display all the text.

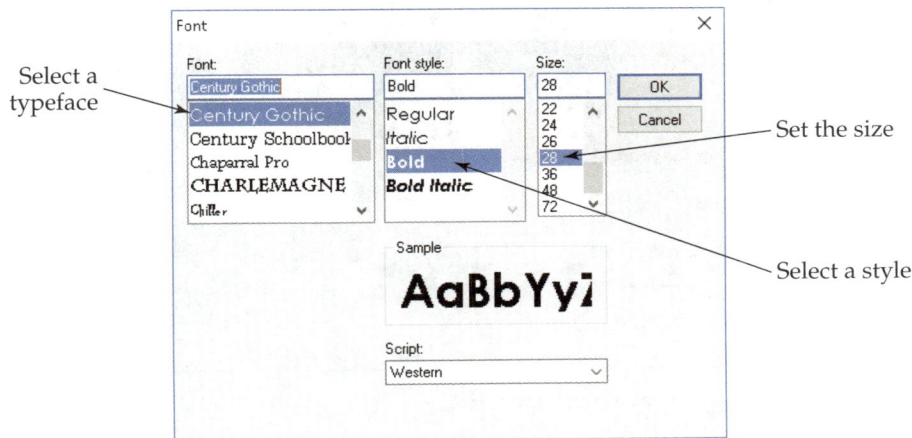

Goodheart-Willcox Publisher

Figure 3-14. The text-formatting tools in Clickteam Fusion 2.5 are similar to those found in PowerPoint or Word.

151. The text box should be selected with the sizing handles displayed. If not, click the text box to select it.

152. Drag the sizing handles to increase the size of the text box until the word Congratulations! fits across the top and You are a WINNER! fits on the second line, as shown in **Figure 3-15.** Always leave room at the bottom. If the bottom is too close to the text, a scroll bar will appear in the text box when the game is played.

153. With the text box selected, click the **Center** button on the **Frame Editor Toolbar.** This sets the text to be center aligned.

Center

154. With the text box selected, click drop-down arrow next to the **Color** button on the **Frame Editor Toolbar,** and click the yellow color swatch. This changes the color of the text.

Color

155. Applying what you have learned, insert a new Hi-Score object. This object is located in the **Games** category in the **Create New Object** dialog box.

156. Move the Hi-Score object to the empty space below the text box. The Hi-Score object is also a text box just like the String object.

157. Applying what you have learned, resize the Hi-Score object to match the string you created earlier. Also, format the text to match the string at the top of the frame, but with a smaller text size.

Adding Buttons

The final frame should include buttons to allow the player to replay or quit the game. A **Quit** button will be added to end the application. A **Replay** button will be added to allow the player to restart the game.

Show Grid

158. Click the **Show Grid** and **Snap to Grid** buttons on the **Frame Editor Toolbar** to turn off the grid and snap.

Snap to Grid

159. Click **Insert>New Object** in the pull-down menu. In the **Create New Object** dialog box, click **Interface** on the left, **Button** on the right, and then click the **OK** button.

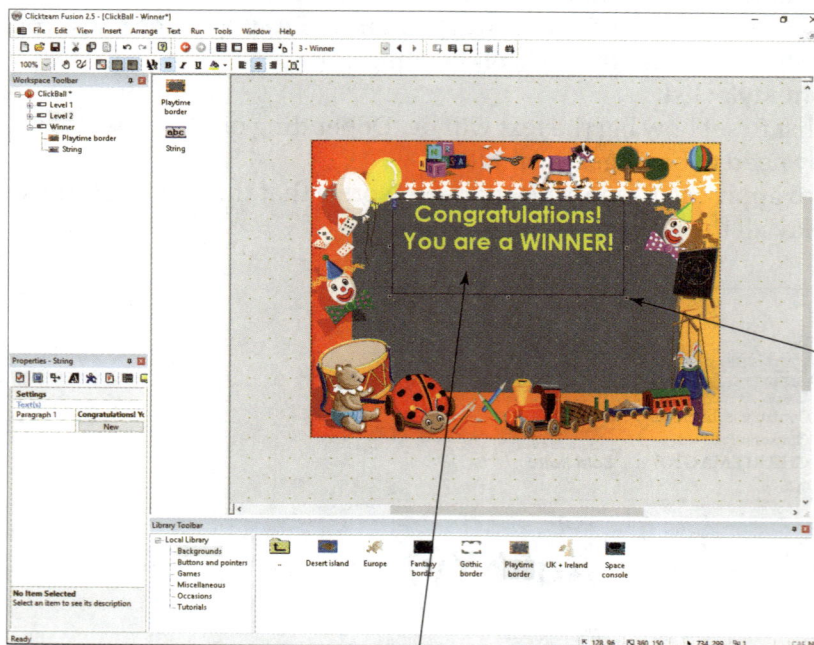

Use the handles to resize the text box

Leave some space below the text

Figure 3-15. The sizing handles can be used to adjust the size of the text box so all of the text is visible.

160. Place the Button object below the Hi-Score object. It can be placed in the border of the background image.

161. Applying what you have learned, rename the Button object as Button_Quit.

162. Double-click the Button_Quit object on the frame. A dialog box is displayed for editing the text. Change the text to Quit, and click the **OK** button to update the object.

163. Applying what you have learned, insert another Button object, place it to the right of the Button_Quit object, rename the new object Button_Replay, and change the display text to Replay.

164. Move the two button objects so they are centered on the frame with some space between them. Users expect these types of buttons to be at the bottom-center of the interface.

165. Applying what you have learned, display the event editor for the Winner frame.

166. Applying what you have learned, add a new condition, and program the following pseudocode. Refer to **Figure 3-16.**
> **IF** the Button_Quit object is clicked,
> > **THEN** end the application.

167. Applying what you have learned, add a new condition, and program this pseudocode:
> **IF** the Button_Replay object is clicked,
> > **THEN** restart the application.

168. Test play the application. Make sure you test the enemies on Level 2 frame and the high score and the buttons on the Winner frame.

169. Debug any errors as needed.

Run Application

Compile to a Distributable Format

So far, you have test played the game at various points during the game build. It is important to make all final changes to the game before it is compiled into a file that can be distributed to players. This distributable file cannot be modified. Clickteam Fusion 2.5 can compile games into a few types of distributable files, but the free version can only compile HTML 5 format. This format can be placed on web pages.

170. Click the **Build and Run** button on the **Run Toolbar**. The **Save HTML 5 Project** dialog box is displayed, as shown in **Figure 3-17.**

171. Click in the **Project name:** text box, and enter Click Ball.

Build and Run

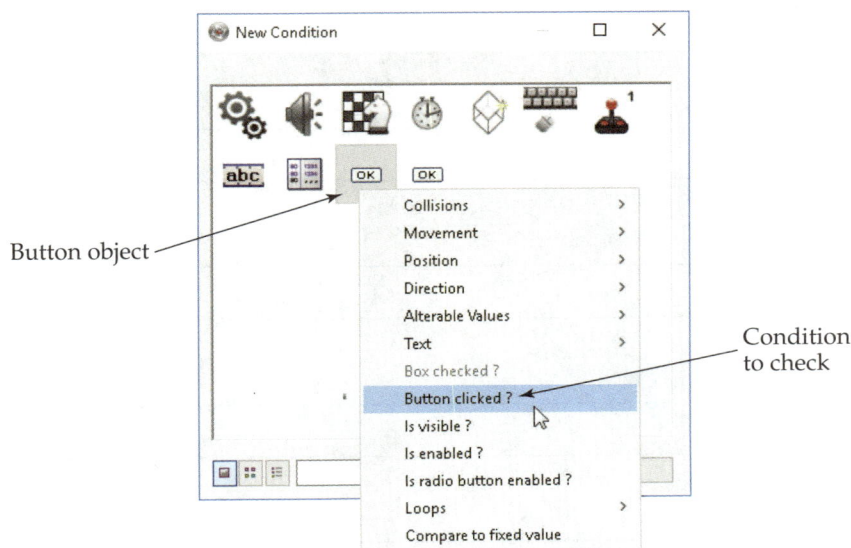

Goodheart-Willcox Publisher

Figure 3-16. To program a button, click the button object in the **New Condition** dialog box, and select the condition **Button clicked?** in the shortcut menu.

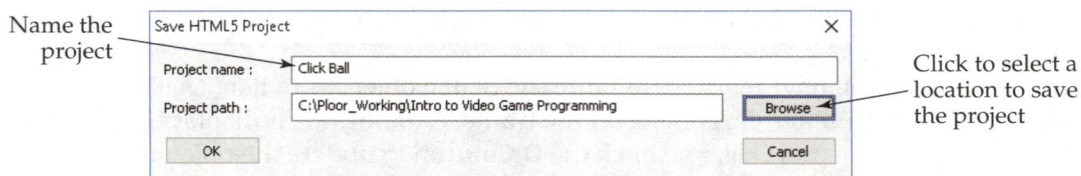

Name the project →

Click to select a location to save the project

Goodheart-Willcox Publisher

Figure 3-17. When compiling a game into distributable format, name the project and specify a location to save the file or files.

172. Click the **Browse** button next to the **Project path:** text box, navigate to your working folder, and select it. The HTML 5 files will be added to a subfolder in this folder.
173. Click the **OK** button to compile your game.
174. Submit all work for grading.

Going Beyond

Going beyond activities are suggestions to challenge your game-building skills. Complete these steps as directed by your instructor.

175. Add a second ball to the game, different from the first ball (like a basketball).
176. Enhance the sounds to have better effects for the game interactions.
177. Program the ball objects to bounce when colliding with enemy objects.
178. Post your game to your school's website, your blog, or your social media outlets so your friends can download and play your creation.

Vocabulary

Write a definition for each of the key terms from this lesson. You will develop a personal glossary of key terms throughout this course.

video game

_____

_____

game environment

_____

_____

rule

_____

_____

victory condition

_____

_____

boss

_____

_____

Name: _____

grid

_____

_____

snap

_____

_____

hotspot

_____

_____

naming convention

_____

_____

class

_____

_____

marquee

_____

_____

collision detection

_____

_____

bounding box

_____

_____

tuning

_____

_____

sound engineer

_____

_____

milestones of design

_____

_____

first playable level

_____

_____

cheat code

_____

_____

bug

_____

_____

Review Questions

Applied Technology

1. Explain how the grid and snap help to speed up scene design.

_____

_____

_____

_____

Mathematics

2. What is the percentage change for an object's speed if it was moving at a speed of 40 and is now moving at a speed of 80?

_____

_____

_____

_____

Language Arts

3. Summarize why a naming convention is important for game elements.

_____

_____

_____

_____

Mathematics

4. If an object moves 30 pixels in 10 seconds, what is the pixels per second for the movement? Reduce your answer to a whole number.

_____

_____

_____

_____

Applied Technology

5. Create pseudocode for this game interaction:
The player clicks on an enemy and the game ends.

_____

_____

_____

_____

Name: _____

Higher-Order Thinking Strategies

6. Explain how the bouncing ball in the game is different from a bouncing ball in the real world.

_____

_____

_____

_____

Science

7. How does increasing the speed of the ball increase difficulty?

_____

_____

_____

_____

Science

8. Summarize how the first playable level can be used as a template for new levels.

_____

_____

_____

_____

Language Arts

9. What changes would you make to this game if you designed it to play on a phone or tablet?

_____

_____

_____

_____

Applied Technology

10. Speculate how you would modify this game and title page if it were exported to other countries where English is not spoken?

_____

_____

_____

_____

Social Science

Office Technology Integration

Using Word Processing Software

1. Launch Microsoft Excel or other spreadsheet software, and open the vocabulary spreadsheet you updated in the last lesson.
2. Applying what you have learned, add a new worksheet and name it Lesson 3.
3. Add each of the vocabulary words and definitions from the Vocabulary section of this lesson.
4. Save the spreadsheet.
5. Launch Microsoft Word or other word-processing program, and start a new blank document.
6. Save the document as *LastName*_Formatting in your working folder.
7. Locate the **Page Setup** group of commands on the **Layout** tab on the ribbon (**Layout**>**Page Setup**).
8. Click the **Margins** button, and select the option with margins set at 1 inch on the top, bottom, left, and right.

Margins

9. Click **Insert**>**Header & Footer**>**Header** on the ribbon, and choose the **Blank (Three Columns)** option. The header area is activated, and three text fields are available for entering text, as shown.

Text field

Header area

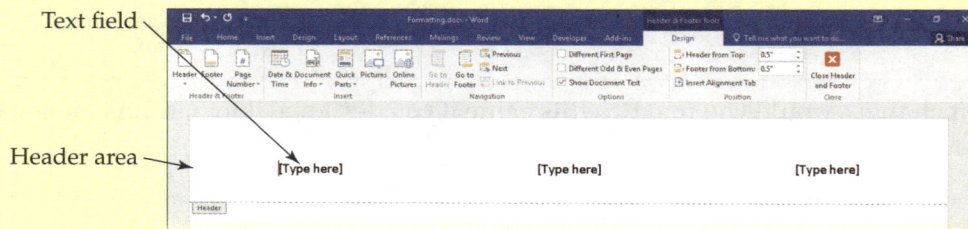

Goodheart-Willcox Publisher

10. Click the left-hand text field, and enter your first and last name.
11. Click the center text field, and enter the name of this class.
12. In the right-hand text field, enter the period or hour this class meets.
13. Double-click below the header area to close the header.
14. Enter the text Writing Prompt #1 on the first line of the document.
15. Press the [Enter] key two times to add space below the text.
16. Select the text and the blank lines.
17. Click **Home**>**Styles**>**No Spacing** in the style gallery on the ribbon.
18. Click anywhere in the line that contains the text.
19. Applying what you have learned, assign the Heading 1 style.
20. Use the down arrow key to move down to the last line. There should be a blank line between the cursor and the text.
21. Add the text Claim:, and press the [Enter] key.
22. Select the text Claim:, and locate the **Home**>**Font** group on the ribbon.
23. Use the formatting commands to change the font to Times New Roman, the size to 12, and apply bold and underline formatting.
24. Save your work, and close Word.

Lesson 4

Quality Assurance

Learning Objectives

After completing this lesson, you will be able to:

- evaluate the quality of your own work and the work of others.
- assess positive aspects of the playability and functionality of a game.
- provide constructive criticism to peers by suggesting possible solutions to problems.

Situation

The client has asked for an evaluation report on the playability and functionality of the Click Ball game created in Lesson 3. Each member of the design team needs to evaluate the product and suggest reasons why each item achieves or does not achieve the objective. An assigned quality assurance (QA) evaluator will also review the game. Be accurate and complete in your evaluations. The personal and peer evaluation are for the same game by the same designer. That means you must give your personal evaluation to a classmate for him or her to complete the peer evaluation for your game.

Quality Assurance Team

Personal Evaluator Name:

_____

_____

Total Score from Personal Evaluation Rubric:

_____

_____

Peer Evaluator Name:

_____

_____

Total Score from Peer Evaluation Rubric:

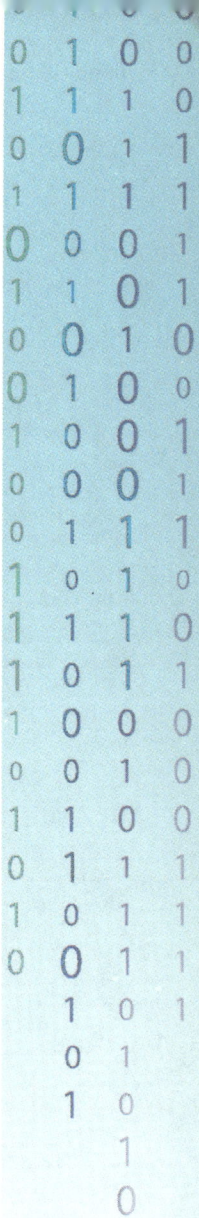

_____

_____

Name: _____

Date: _____

Class: _____

Design Reasoning: Personal Evaluation

1. Reflect on your work, and evaluate your game for each of the five key areas of design identified in the rubric.
2. Rank each key area using a scale from 0 to 5. Record the value in the Score column.
3. Complete the Personal Evaluation rubric in the Commentary and Constructive Criticism section. Explain why you gave the score you did for each area of design.
4. Suggest improvements needed for your game in the Personal Evaluation rubric in the Commentary and Constructive Criticism section.

Key Area	0	1	2	3	4	5	Score
Concept Is the idea well developed?	No main idea or theme.					Clear theme or main idea maintained on all levels.	
Aesthetics Does the look, color, contrast, and placement of objects fit the game?	Poor quality graphics, color, and contrast.					Awesome graphics and animations. Items contrasted well.	
Sound Effects Do the sounds play? Are the music and sounds appropriate?	No sound. Sound is too loud, too soft, or not related to the game.					Sounds enhance gameplay and play clearly.	
Functionality Does everything work as expected?	Unfinished. Could not play. Major errors.					Plays perfectly. No bugs, glitches, or errors.	
Replay How likely are you to play this game again?	Game solved. Too easy. Not interesting or impossible to win.					Cannot wait to play it again! Skill was challenging, but enjoyable.	
Add the values in the Score column to get a total.						**Total Score**	

Name: _____

Design Reasoning: Peer Evaluation

1. Play the game designed by the peer as assigned by your instructor.
2. Reflect on the peer's work, and evaluate the game for each of the five key areas of design identified in the rubric.
3. Rank each key area using a scale from 0 to 5. Record the value in the Score column.
4. Complete the Peer Evaluation rubric in the Commentary and Constructive Criticism section. Explain why you gave the score you did for each area of design.
5. Suggest improvements needed for the peer's game in the Peer Evaluation rubric in the Commentary and Constructive Criticism section.

Key Area	0	1	2	3	4	5	Score
Concept Is the idea well developed?	No main idea or theme.					Clear theme or main idea maintained on all levels.	
Aesthetics Does the look, color, contrast, and placement of objects fit the game?	Poor quality graphics, color, and contrast.					Awesome graphics and animations. Items contrasted well.	
Sound Effects Do the sounds play? Are the music and sounds appropriate?	No sound. Sound is too loud, too soft, or not related to the game.					Sounds enhance gameplay and play clearly.	
Functionality Does everything work as expected?	Unfinished. Could not play. Major errors.					Plays perfectly. No bugs, glitches, or errors.	
Replay How likely are you to play this game again?	Game solved. Too easy. Not interesting or impossible to win.					Cannot wait to play it again! Skill was challenging, but enjoyable.	
Add up the values in the Score column to get a total.						**Total Score**	

Commentary and Constructive Criticism

Explain why you assigned the score for each key item assessed. Provide details on what you liked in that area and what needed improvement. Cite specific examples from the game. Provide suggestions on how to improve the game.

Personal Evaluation

Key Area	Detailed Assessment
Concept	
Aesthetics	
Sound Effects	
Functionality	
Replay	
Suggested Improvements	

Peer Evaluation

Key Area	Detailed Assessment
Concept	
Aesthetics	
Sound Effects	
Functionality	
Replay	
Suggested Improvements	

Lesson 5

Scene Construction

Learning Objectives

After completing this lesson, you will be able to:

- insert active and background objects to a game frame.
- program object movement to simulate natural movement.
- debug errors.
- refine interactions.

Situation

The Awesome Game Company wants you to continue to develop skills as a game designer. Your first task is to develop a simulation for the movement of the inner planets of our solar system. The placement and movement must be accurate to determine the number of days each planet takes to orbit the Sun.

Reading Material

Significant digits are those numbers that are meaningful. *Floating points* is how a computer calculates numbers with a decimal. The computer first determines the number of significant digits and discards any numbers that are not significant. The computer moves the decimal point by the number of places stored in the float. The *float* refers to scientific notation for a base-10 exponent. The resulting number is the *mantissa* or *significand.* The float is also the exponent in scientific notation. Computer science typically uses the term significand instead of the term mantissa. The significand is not the entire number. It is only the base-10 exponent to move the decimal place. The following table shows how the significant digits and floating point determine the significand or mantissa from the original number.

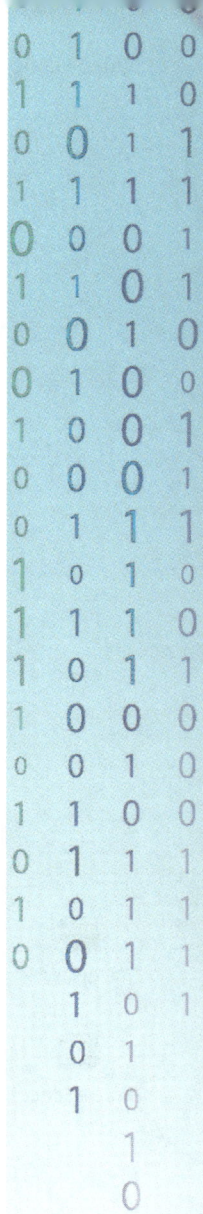

Name: _____

Date: _____

Class: _____

Number	Significant Digits	Whole Number Value	Float	Scientific Notation	Significand (Mantissa)
35.28946	0	35	0	35×10^0	35
352.8946	1	3529	1	3529×10^{-1}	352.9
3528.946	2	352895	2	352895×10^{-2}	3528.95
3.528946	1	35	1	35×10^{-1}	3.5
0.3528946	2	35	2	35×10^{-2}	0.35

Game Build

The Awesome Game Company wants you to create a simulation of the solar system based on the work you did in Lesson 2. It wants the simulation to show the planets orbiting the Sun. It also wants the simulation to report how many Earth days it takes for the planets to orbit.

How to Begin

Open

1. Launch Clickteam Fusion 2.5.
2. Click **File>Open…** in the pull-down menu or click the **Open** button on the **Standard Toolbar**.
3. Navigate to your working folder, and open the *LastName*_Space file created in Lesson 2.
4. Applying what you have learned, display the Inner Planets frame in the frame editor. Note: make sure the objects are in the locations specified in Lesson 2 and have not accidentally been moved.

Frame Editor

Setting Object Motion

Standard movement can be applied to objects in the frame editor. For the planets, the movement will be around the Sun along a circular path.

Movement

5. Select the MERCURY object, and display open the **Movement** tab in the **Properties** toolbar.
6. Change the Type property to Circular. This is a standard movement type. Once it is selected, additional properties appear that can be modified.
7. Change the Angular Velocity property to 60. *Angular velocity* is the speed of rotation about the center point. This setting is measured in degrees per second. If the angular velocity is set to 60, it will take six seconds for the object to complete a full circle. There are 360 degrees in a circle, so 360 degrees ÷ 60 degrees per second = 6 seconds.
8. Change the Radius property to 275. The *radius* of the circle is the distance from the center point to the edge. The Sun will be the center. The visual center of the Sun sprite is at X = 0. Therefore, the radius for the circle Mercury will follow is the current X value for the MERCURY object.
9. Move the cursor to the visual center of the SUN object. This is the white circle. Look at the coordinate indicator at the bottom-right corner of the screen. The coordinates of the visual center point are (0,400), as shown in **Figure 5-1**.
10. Set the Center X property to 0 and the Center Y property to 400. These properties determine the coordinates of the point about which the object will rotate. The planet will rotate around the center of the Sun with these values.

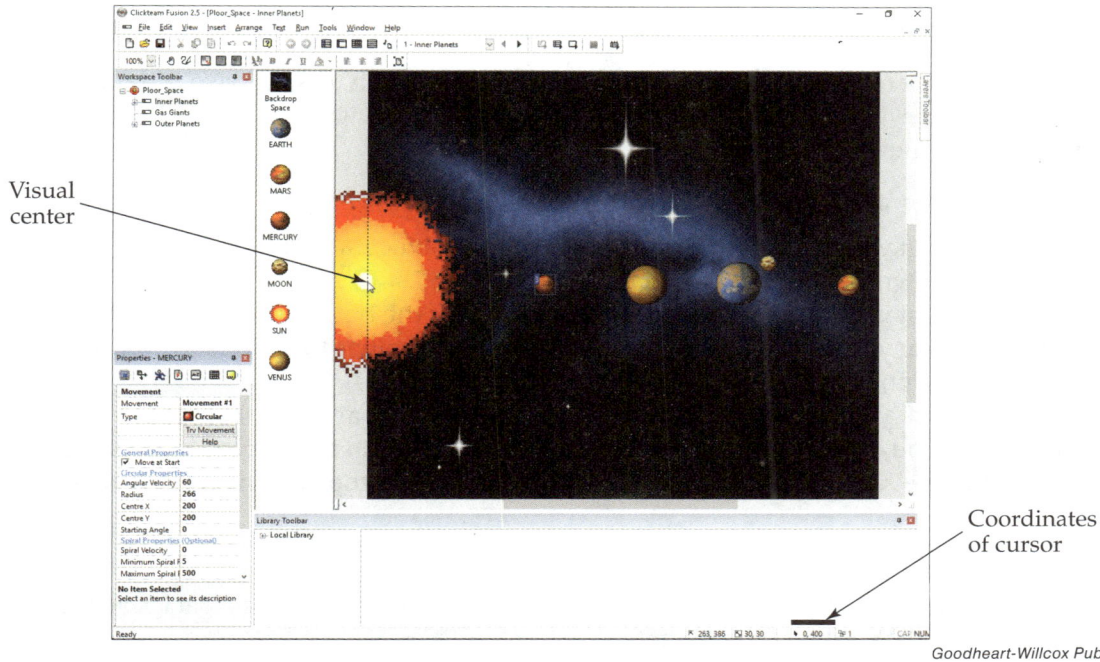

Goodheart-Willcox Publisher

Figure 5-1. Move the cursor to the visual center of the Sun sprite. The coordinate indicator will display the location of the cursor.

11. Applying what you have learned, run the frame to see the rotation of Mercury around the Sun. See if it takes six seconds to complete a single revolution. Also check to see that the planet rotates about the center of the Sun.

12. Close the game window.

13. Using the table below, set the movement Type and Angular Velocity of each planet. Also, calculate the time it takes for one revolution.

Object	Movement Type	Angular Velocity	Radius	Center of Rotation (X,Y)	Time for One Revolution (seconds)
MERCURY	Circular	60	275	(0,400)	6
VENUS	Circular	–24	430	(0,400)	
EARTH	Circular	15	575	(0,400)	
MARS	Circular	8	750	(0,400)	

14. Run the frame to see how it works. What happened to Earth and Mars? Close the game window.

15. Close the game window.

Debugging Errors

You should have noticed that Earth and Mars did not make a full revolution. This is a bug caused by a default setting to destroy an object if it gets too far from the edge of the frame. Destroying objects if they are too far from the frame is usually a good thing. This prevents the computer from wasting resources tracking objects that are far outside the game frame. Unfortunately, the large circular orbits of the planets need to be tracked even when you cannot see them so they will return to complete the orbit.

16. Select the EARTH object, and click the **RunTime Options** tab in the **Properties** toolbar.

Run Frame

Run Frame

RunTime Options

17. Uncheck the Destroy object if too far from frame property.

18. Repeat this for the MARS object.

Run Frame

19. Run the frame to see the planetary rotation. Wait for Earth to make two full revolutions so you can see if Mars shows up properly. Note: the Moon will not move.

20. Close the game window.

Adding Interface Objects

21. Applying what you have learned, add a new Button object near the top-center of the frame, as shown in **Figure 5-2.**

22. Applying what you have learned, change the text for the button to Reset.

23. Applying what you have learned, use the **Properties** toolbar to change the name of the button to Button_Reset.

24. Applying what you have learned, use the **Properties** toolbar to set the button's position to (368,10). The default width of the button is 64 pixels, and the frame width is 800 pixels. So, setting the X coordinate for the button to 368 centers the button on the frame (400 – 32 = 368).

Adding a Counter Object

Planets orbit the Sun in a set pattern. A counter object can be used to track the number of simulated days for the orbit of the planets.

25. Applying what you have learned, open the **Create New Object** dialog box.

26. Click **All Objects** on the left of the dialog box to show all of the preset objects. This is helpful when looking for a specific item by name since the objects are listed in alphabetical order and you do not need to know in which category the object resides.

27. Select **Counter** on the right-hand side, and click the **OK** button to close the dialog box.

28. Click anywhere on the frame to place the Counter object. Note: since the default color of the numbers is black and the background image is dark, it will be helpful to place the Counter object on the gray area outside the frame. It will be moved into a final position later.

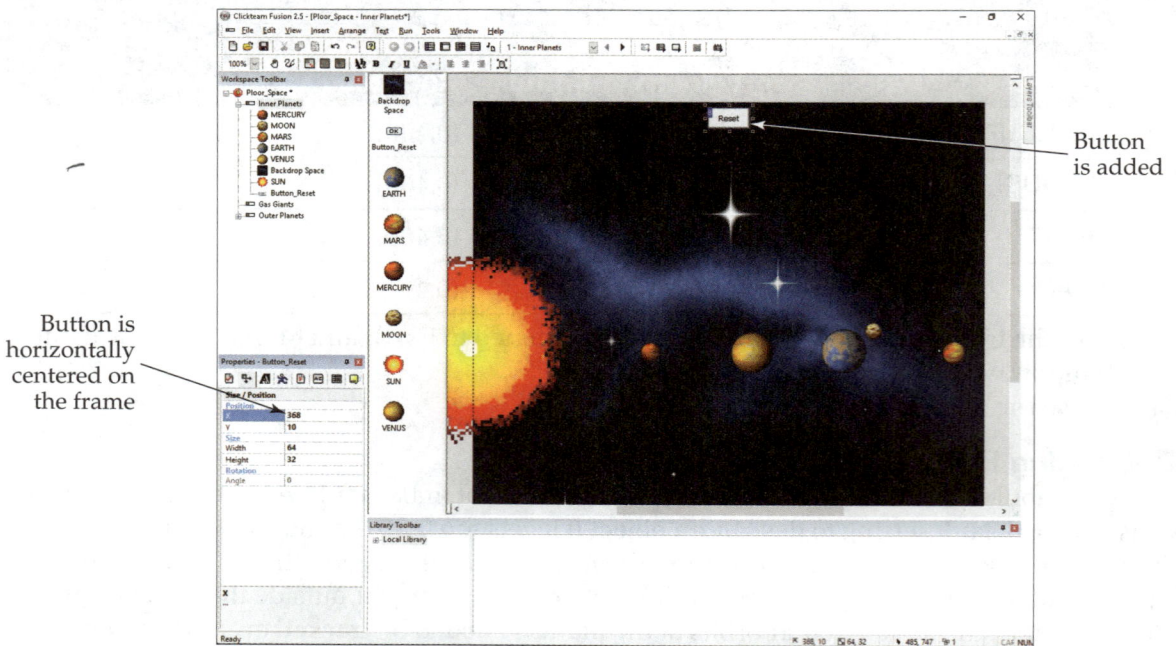

Button is added

Button is horizontally centered on the frame

Goodheart-Willcox Publisher

Figure 5-2. A button is added to the game frame that will be programmed to allow the user to reset the planets.

29. Applying what you have learned, rename the object as Days Counter.

30. Applying what you have learned, change the size of the counter to a width of 40 and a height of 60.

Sprite Image Editor

Right now, there is little contrast between the background and the text color of the counter. *Contrast* is a difference in color. The background is dark and the text is black. If the counter is placed over the background, it would be very hard to see the numbers. This can be fixed by changing the colors of the sprites.

31. Double-click the Days Counter object to open the image editor, as shown in **Figure 5-3.**

32. Click in the **Tolerance** text box, and enter 3. *Tolerance* is acceptable variance. Increasing this value from 0 allows more shades to replace with one click.

33. Applying what you have learned, select a red color, and fill the number on each frame.

34. Click the **OK** button to update the sprites on the object. The Days Counter object should now display a red 0. Red has good contrast with the dark background image.

35. Applying what you have learned, use the **Properties** toolbar to place the Days Counter object at (800,70).

Cloning an Object

Recall, a clone is a copy of the original as a new object that does not inherit properties from the original. Cloning the Days Counter object will allow a new object to be created that has all color changes and sizing, but allow different programming to be applied to the new object. This is different from an instance, which always inherits properties from the original.

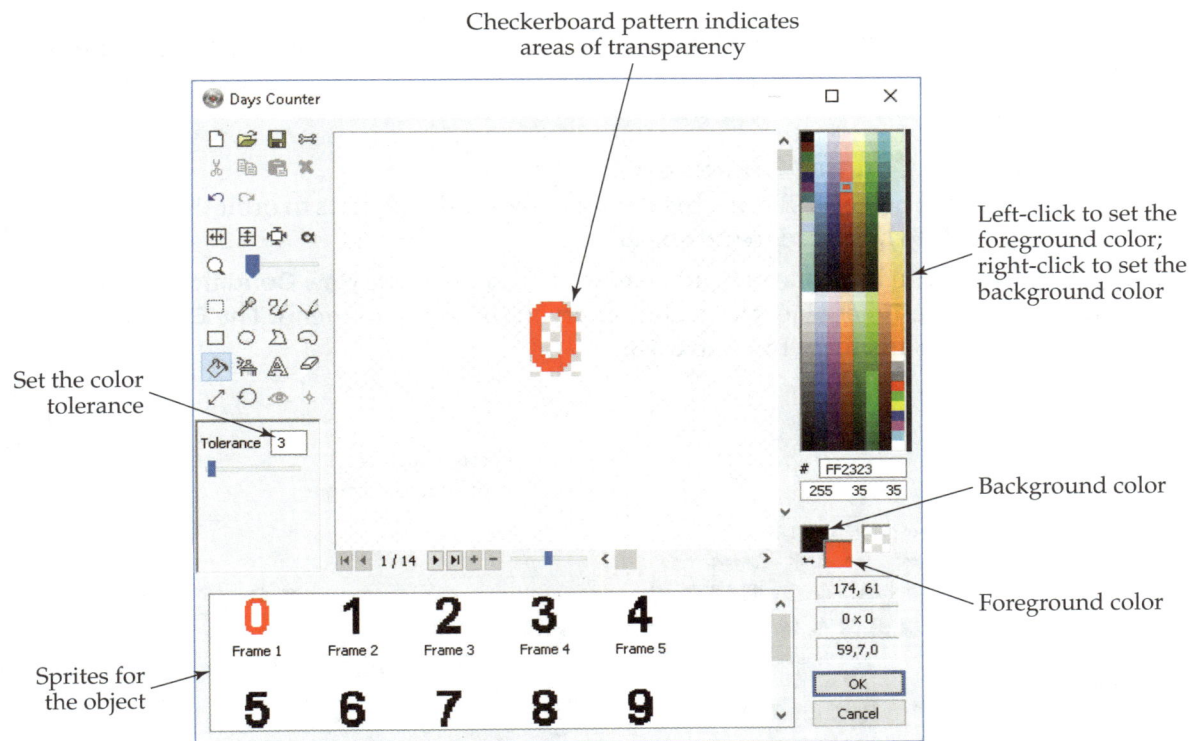

Goodheart-Willcox Publisher

Figure 5-3. To provide contrast with the dark background, the color of the numbers in the sprites for the Days Counter object needs to be changed. Be sure to change each number's color.

36. Right-click on the Days Counter object, and click **Clone Object** in the shortcut menu. The **Clone Objects** dialog box is displayed. Creating a clone is very similar to creating an instance as you learned about in Lesson 3.

37. Applying what you have learned, create two rows and one column with spacing of five between the rows. The clone is placed below the original with five pixels between the two objects.

38. Applying what you have learned, rename the cloned object as Stopwatch.

39. Applying what you have learned, create one clone of the Button_Reset object so it is five pixels below the original.

40. Rename the clone as Button_Time.

41. Change the text on Button_Time object to Stop Time.

Programming the Reset Button

At this point, the button objects cannot do anything. The buttons now need to be programmed to act as buttons. Examine the pseudocode shown below.

> **IF** the Button_Reset object is clicked,
>> **THEN** restart the current frame.

42. Display the event editor for the Inner Planets frame. Currently, the frame contains programming for deleting the planet objects by pressing certain keys.

43. Right-click on the number 1 for the first event line, and click **Delete** in the shortcut menu. The event programming is completely erased. Note: it is important to right-click the number, not the condition.

44. Applying what you have learned, delete all of the events. You should be left with one event line that states New condition.

45. Applying what you have learned, add a new event. In the **New Condition** dialog box, right-click on the Button_Reset object, and click **Button clicked?** in the shortcut menu. The condition **IF** the Button_Reset object is clicked is added.

46. Right-click in the cell under the **Storyboard Controls** icon, and click **Restart the Current Frame** in the shortcut menu. The action **THEN** restart the current frame is added, as shown in **Figure 5-4.**

Programming the Counter Operation

The Days Counter object will track the days it takes for the planets to orbit the Sun. This programming needs to be added to the object.

47. Applying what you have learned, add a new condition. In the **New Condition** dialog box, right-click on the Timer object, and click **Every** in the shortcut menu. The **Every** dialog box is displayed, as shown in **Figure 5-5.**

IF the Button_Reset object is clicked

THEN restart the current frame

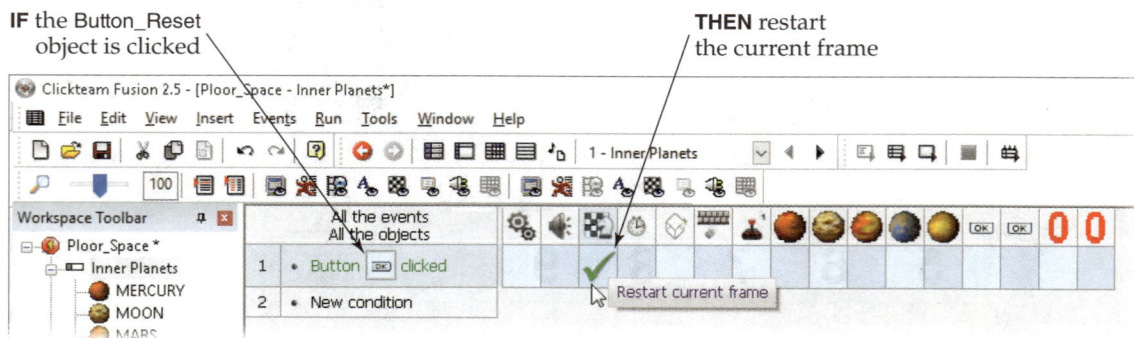

Figure 5-4. The **Reset** button is programmed to reset the planets by restarting the frame.

Entering 10 means
every 1/10 of a second

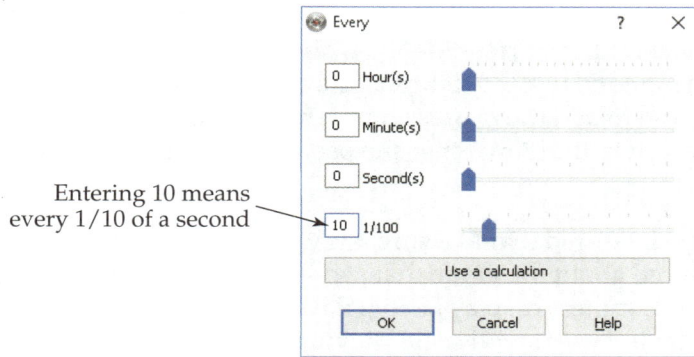

Goodheart-Willcox Publisher

Figure 5-5. Setting how often the object is updated.

48. Make sure the values in the **Hours**, **Minutes**, and **Seconds** text boxes are all 0, and then enter 10 in the **1/100** text box.

49. Click the **OK** button to close the dialog box. The condition **IF** every 10/100 seconds is created. This is the same as **IF** every 1/10 of a second.

50. In event line 2, right-click in the cell under the icon for Days Counter object, and click **Add to Counter** from the menu. The expression editor is displayed.

51. Applying what you have learned, enter 1.52 for the expression, and then click the **OK** button to create the action.

52. Hover the cursor over the check mark in event line 2. Make sure the programming on event line 2 matches this pseudocode:
    IF every 10/100 of a second,
      THEN add 1.52 to the Days Counter object.

53. Display the frame editor for the Inner Planets frame.

54. Select the Inner Planets frame in the **Workspace Toolbar**.

55. Click the **Runtime Options** tab in the **Properties** toolbar.

56. Change the Movement timer property to 50. This matches the frame rate set in Lesson 2.

57. Run the frame to see how the counter tracks the number of days the simulation is running. Check that the **Reset** button functions properly. Try to determine the number of days it takes Mercury to orbit once around the Sun. See if one orbit for Mercury is about 85–95 days. A planet has completed one orbit when it has returned to its starting point. Close the game window when done testing.

Frame Editor

Runtime Options

Run Frame

Programming the Time Button

The Days Counter object is creating data. Specifically, it is creating the number of days the simulation is running. The counter displays numbers too quickly to accurately read the number of days. The Stopwatch object will be programmed to capture the value of the Days Counter object whenever the user presses the **Stop Time** button. The Stopwatch object will show the instantaneous time each time the user clicks the **Stop Time** button. *Instantaneous* means occurring immediately. This is the pseudocode for programming the Stopwatch object:
  IF the user clicks the Time_Button object,
    THEN set the value of the Stopwatch object equal to the value of the Days Counter object.

58. Display the event editor for the Inner Planets frame.

59. Applying what you have learned, create a new condition. In the **New Condition** dialog box, right-click on the icon for the Time_Button object, and click **Button clicked?** in the shortcut menu.

60. In line 3, right-click in the cell below the icon for the Stopwatch object, and click **Set Counter** in the shortcut menu to display the expression editor.

Event Editor

61. At the bottom of the expression editor, click the icon for the Days Counter object, and click **Current value** in the shortcut menu, as shown in **Figure 5-6.** The expression value ("Days Counter") is added to the text box at the top of the expression editor.

62. Click the **OK** button to add the expression as the action.

63. Check that the event in line 3 matches the pseudocode shown on the previous page.

Testing and Tuning

Each game should be tested to make sure it is working properly. During testing, there may be things uncovered about the game that should be tuned to make the game better. For example, currently the counters display partial days as a decimal value. This value is too precise. The simulation is a very small scale. Having the computer track partial days is not a good use of resources. Tuning will correct this.

Run Frame

64. Run the frame, and click the **Stop Time** button. Make sure the Stopwatch counter is working properly.

65. Click the **Reset** button to restart the planets orbiting around the Sun.

66. Click the **Stop Time** button when Mercury completes one orbit. In the real world, the orbit of Mercury is approximately 88 days. The current orbit takes too long and must be adjusted to work properly.

67. Close the game window.

68. Applying what you have learned, change the value of the Angular Velocity property for the MERCURY object to 64. This will increase the speed of the object, which will correct the error in the number of days reported for one orbit.

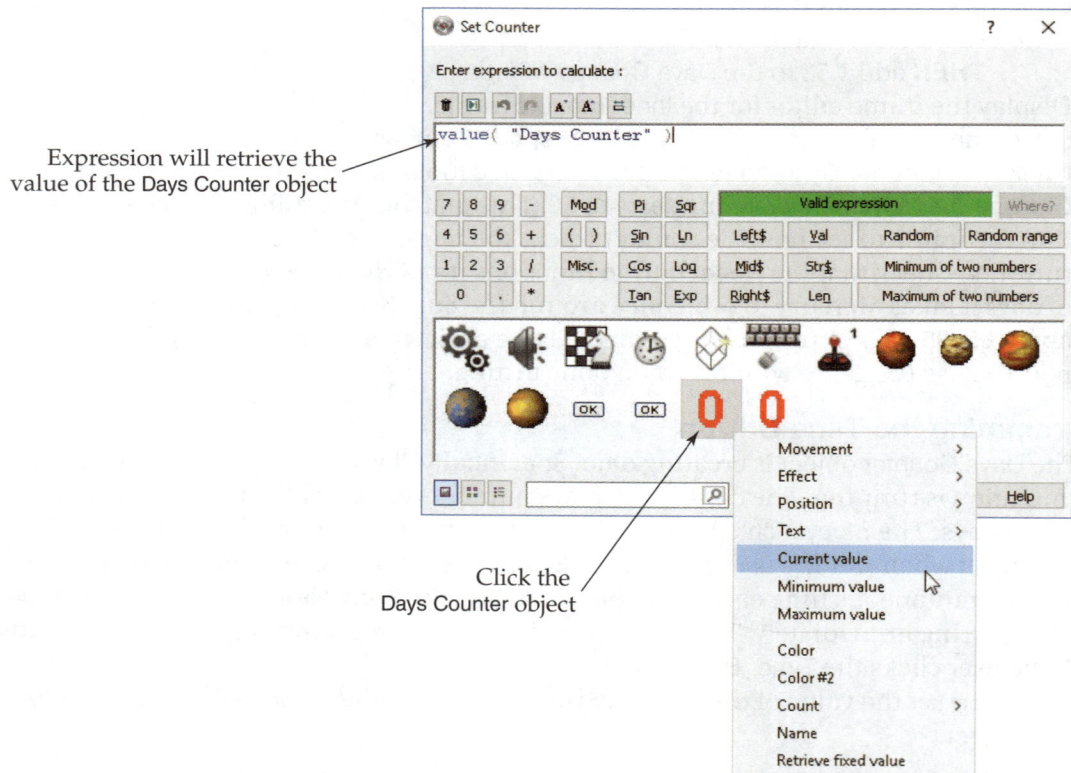

Expression will retrieve the value of the Days Counter object

Click the Days Counter object

Goodheart-Willcox Publisher

Figure 5-6. An expression can be created to retrieve the value of another object. Here, the value of the Days Counter will be retrieved.

69. Run the frame, and test if the adjustment makes the orbit of Mercury close to 88 days. Note: test several times to make sure you are clicking the button at the right point in the orbit.

70. Close the game window.

71. Display the frame editor for the Inner Planets frame.

72. Select the Days Counter object.

73. Click the **Settings** tab in the **Properties** toolbar.

74. Check the Number of significant digits property, as shown in **Figure 5-7.**

75. Click in the text box for the Number of significant digits property, and enter 2.

76. Check the Number of digits after decimal point property.

77. Click in the text box for the Number of digits after decimal point property, and enter 0. This will make the counter display only whole numbers.

78. Applying what you have learned, make the same changes to the Stopwatch object.

79. Run the frame. Check that both counters display only whole numbers. Close the game window when done testing.

80. Save your work, and submit it for grading.

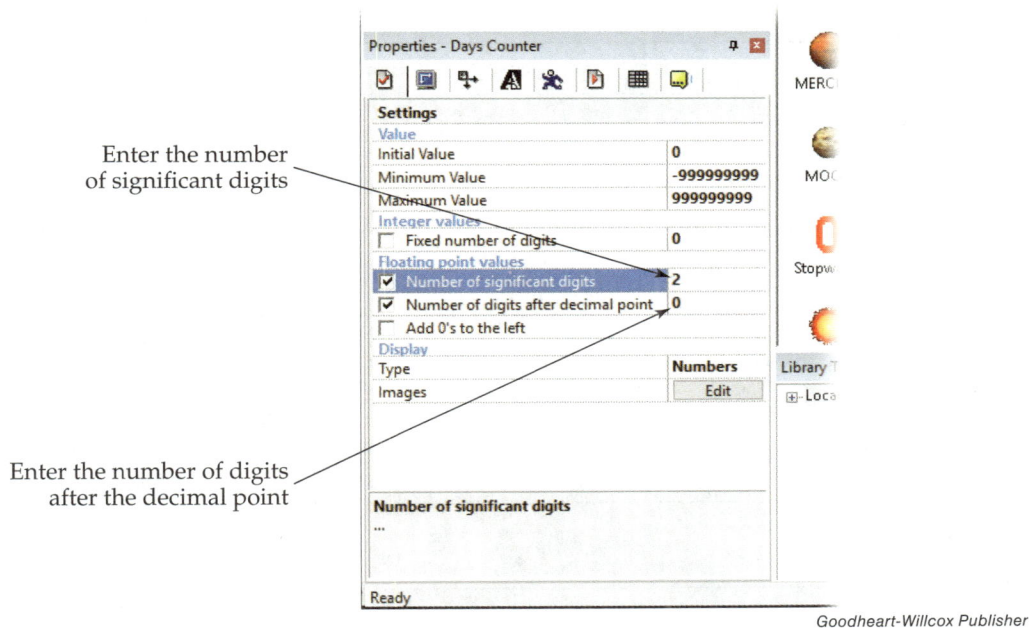

Frame Editor

Settings

Run Frame

Goodheart-Willcox Publisher

Figure 5-7. Setting the number of significant digits and the number of places to the right of the decimal point will limit the counter display to only whole numbers.

Vocabulary

Write a definition for each of the key terms from this lesson. You will develop a personal glossary of key terms throughout this course.

significant digits

_____

_____

floating points

_____

_____

float

_____

_____

mantissa

_____

_____

significand

_____

_____

angular velocity

_____

_____

radius

_____

_____

contrast

_____

_____

tolerance

_____

_____

instantaneous

_____

_____

Name: _____

Review Questions

1. How do you determine the position of the cursor on the frame in the frame editor?

_____

_____

_____

_____

_____

Applied Technology

2. Why was the center of rotation for the circular movement of the planets set to (0,400)?

_____

_____

_____

_____

_____

Mathematics

3. Describe how floating points work with significant digits in a computer application.

_____

_____

_____

_____

_____

Language Arts

4. The value 10/100 was used to set how often the Days Counter object is updated. What does this fraction reduce to in fraction form? What is equivalent decimal fraction?

_____

_____

_____

_____

_____

Mathematics

5. How would you test the Inner Planets frame without having to test the Gas Giants frame and the Outer Planets frames?

_____

_____

_____

_____

_____

Applied Technology

Higher-Order Thinking Strategies

Science

6. The angular velocity for Venus was entered as a negative number. Why was a negative number used?

_____

_____

_____

_____

_____

_____

_____

Language Arts

7. Summarize the cause of the bug that did not allow Earth and Mars to orbit.

_____

_____

_____

_____

_____

Applied Technology

8. Describe how to fix the problem of a red ball in a video game being hard to see on an orange background.

_____

_____

_____

_____

_____

Language Arts

9. Explain the benefits of using the Stopwatch counter to determine the orbit of each planet.

_____

_____

_____

_____

_____

Applied Technology

10. Write pseudocode for this game interaction: The game ends when the user clicks the **Quit** button.

_____

_____

_____

_____

_____

_____

Office Technology Integration

Using Spreadsheet Formulas

1. Launch Microsoft Excel or other spreadsheet software, and open the vocabulary spreadsheet you updated in the last lesson.
2. Applying what you have learned, add a new worksheet, and name it Lesson 5.
3. Add each of the vocabulary words and definitions from the Vocabulary section of this lesson.
4. Save the spreadsheet, and then close it.
5. Begin a new blank workbook.
6. Save the file as *LastName_*Formulas in your working folder.
7. Applying what you have learned, rename the Sheet1 tab as Time.
8. Copy the information in this table into the worksheet. "Object" should be in cell A1. A formula will be used to calculate the time for each revolution.

Object	Angular Velocity	Time for One Revolution (seconds)
MERCURY	60	
VENUS	–24	
EARTH	15	
MARS	8	

9. Double-click the vertical line between the B header and the C header. This will expand the width of column B to match the widest value in the column.
10. Expand column C to fit the content.
11. Select the range from cell A1 to cell C5 (A1:C5).
12. Click the drop-down arrow next to **Home**>**Font**>**Bottom Border**, and click **All Borders** in the drop-down list. Note: the **Bottom Border** button may be different, depending on which border formatting was applied last.
13. Click in cell C2, and add an equal sign (=). All formulas must start with the equal sign. It is like writing a math problem backward, such as = 2 + 2. Once a formula is entered, the cell displays the answer, not the formula.
14. After the equal sign, add 360. There are 360 degrees in a circle.
15. After 360, add a forward slash (/). The forward slash is used as a division symbol in computer applications. It creates a fraction out of the numbers to the left of the symbol over the numbers to the right of the symbol.
16. Make sure the insertion point (vertical bar) is after the forward slash, and then click cell B2. The cell is outlined, and a reference is added to cell C2. This creates a relative reference to cell B2. The value of cell B2 will be used in the formula.

Bottom Border

17. Press the [Enter] key to apply the formula. Cell C2 should display the result of the calculation, which in this case is 6. If you click cell C2, the formula is displayed in the formula bar above the workbook, as shown.

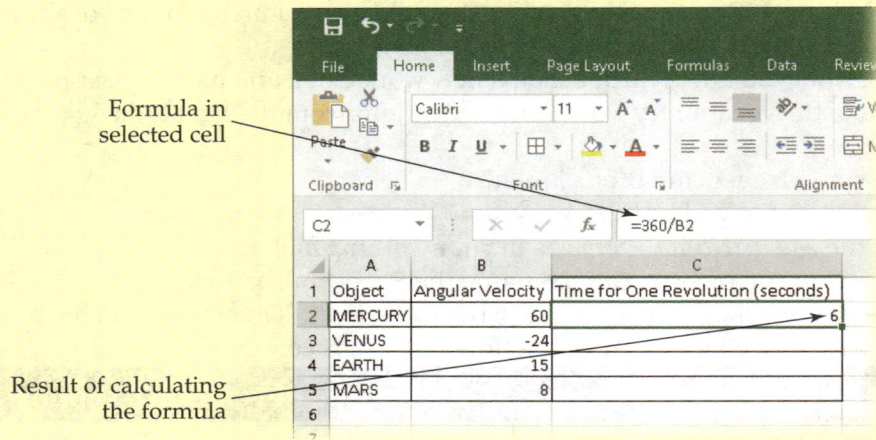

Formula in selected cell

Result of calculating the formula

18. Click cell C2, and copy by clicking **Home**>**Clipboard**>**Copy** on the ribbon or using the [Ctrl][C] keyboard shortcut.

Copy

19. Select the range C3:C5, and click **Home**>**Clipboard**>**Paste** on the ribbon or using the [Ctrl][V] keyboard shortcut. This will fill in a relative formula in the selected cells.

Paste

20. Click cell C3, and look at the formula bar. Notice that the reference to cell B2 has been changed to B3. This is relative copying, and the spreadsheet changes the formula to match to location or the original cells.

21. Change the value in cell B2 to 64. Remember, you changed that value to correct the orbit of Mercury. Notice that the value displayed in cell C3 changes. This is because you used the relative cell reference and not the actual number 60 in the formula.

22. Select cell C3. Notice the calculated value is negative, but elapsed time should be positive. The formula needs to be adjusted to compensate for the negative angular velocity value.

23. Click at the end of the formula in the formula bar, and add *–1. The asterisk is used in computer applications to indicate multiplication.

24. Press the [Enter] key to update the formula. The calculated result is now positive because multiplying a negative number by –1 changes the value from negative to positive.

25. Save your work.

Lesson 6

Iterative Design and the Scientific Method

Learning Objectives

After completing this lesson, you will be able to:

- perform authentic research on a selected topic.
- test a game or simulation to meet performance requirements.
- predict outcomes and evaluate deviations from expected results.
- perform research and evaluate source information.
- analyze data using the scientific method.

Situation

The Awesome Game Company wants to make sure your Inner Planets simulation is an accurate representation of the real solar system. You have been asked to conduct research and test the movement of the planets in the simulation to assure quality. You will use an iterative design process and the scientific method to complete this work.

How to Begin

1. Read the passage below.
2. Complete the required research.
3. Evaluate the validity of the sources for your research.
4. Use the scientific method to predict the outcome of a simulation.
5. Test the Inner Planets simulation to determine errors and record trial data.
6. Make conclusions and suggest improvements.
7. Turn in all materials.

Reading Materials

Video game design follows the iterative design process. In the ***iterative design process,*** the final design is achieved through a series of versions, each one being an improvement over the previous one. A designer will create a working game, test it,

and make changes. Each time a new version of the game is created. Each new version is an *iteration* of the same game.

The design cycle allows for the information from one experiment to be used to refine and retest another attempt. The iterative design process follows the scientific method to go through each cycle of improvement. The *scientific method* is a set of principles and systematic procedures for obtaining knowledge. **Figure 6-1** shows the basic steps in the scientific method. These steps involve the following.

- purpose (problem being solved)
- research
- hypothesis
- experiment
- analysis
- conclusion

Figure 6-2 shows a comparison between the scientific method and the iterative design process.

Purpose

The scientific method starts when you identify a problem to which you would like to know the answer. Identifying a problem will help you ask a question about something that you observe: how, what, when, who, which, why, or where?

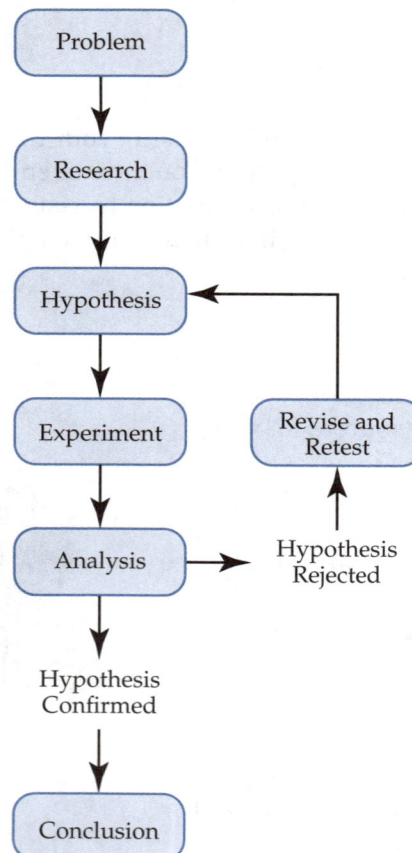

Goodheart-Willcox Publisher

Figure 6-1. These are the basic steps in the scientific method.

Scientific Method	Iterative Design Process
Purpose	Identify the problem
Research problem	Research errors or problems
Hypothesize	Predict game reaction to changes
Build an experiment	Build or refine a game or simulation
Analyze the data	Analyze the results of the game or simulation
Form conclusion	Confirm or deny hypothesis was a success
Recommend changes for retest	Suggest refinements and retest

Goodheart-Willcox Publisher

Figure 6-2. This table shows how the scientific method compares with the iterative design process.

Research

You usually do not have to start from scratch. Other people often have asked the same or similar questions and have recorded the results of their observations. Using the library and Internet for research will help you find out more information about the items you are observing. Be sure to use credible sources of information.

Hypothesis

A *hypothesis* is an educated guess to answer a question. It is a prediction to answer the question stated in the purpose. A hypothesis can often be written as an **IF...THEN** statement similar to pseudocode.

IF this condition occurs, **THEN** this action will happen.

The hypothesis guides the rest of the scientific method. It must be measurable.

Experiment

Test the hypothesis by doing an experiment. The experiment will collect data to see if the hypothesis is supported. Test one factor at a time, keeping all other conditions the same. The experiment should also be repeated several times to make sure the results are consistent and accurate. Averaging data from multiple observations also helps minimize errors.

Analysis

After you collect your measurements, analyze the data to see if the hypothesis is supported or not. Compare the data from the experiment to what would be expected if the hypothesis is true. Often, the hypothesis is not supported by the data. In these cases, the process must begin again or you can decide the hypothesis is incorrect and conclude the process. If continuing with the process, construct a new hypothesis based on the information learned in the experiment.

Conclusion

Make a conclusion as to whether or not the hypothesis was supported. Determine any errors that were made and how to overcome errors in the future. Reflect on the experiment and data to determine the next course of action needed to improve the experiment if necessary. Recommend any changes or refinements that can be made to the experiment. Properly record and publish your results.

Iterative Design for the Inner Planets Simulation

Purpose (Problem)

1. The movement of the planets in the Inner Planets simulation created in Lesson 5 should be as accurate as possible. Write a question to match this purpose.

_____

_____

_____

_____

_____

_____

Research

2. Find two sources from the library or credible Internet sources to determine the amount of time each of the Inner Planets takes to make a single revolution around the Sun. Note: for this activity, Wikipedia is *not* a credible Internet source.

Source Info	Source #1	Source #2
Author		
Title		
Publisher or Web Address		
Publication Date		
Date Accessed		

3. Record the result of your research in the table below.

Source	Mercury	Venus	Earth	Mars
1				
2				

Hypothesis

4. Write a hypothesis to predict the results of Inner Planets simulation.

_____

_____

_____

_____

_____

_____

_____

Experiment

5. Test the Inner Planets simulation created in Lesson 5. Use the **Stop Time** button to determine the time it takes for each planet to complete one revolution of the Sun.
6. Record the total number of days for each planet to complete one orbit in the table.

7. Repeat to fill in all the data values for five trials.

Trial	Mercury	Venus	Earth	Mars
1				
2				
3				
4				
5				

Analysis

8. Using the data collected in the experiment, calculate the averages. Record the results in the table.
9. Compare the calculated averages to the data you found during your research. Record the difference in the table. If the research value is higher than your calculated average, record the value as a negative number.

10. Calculate the percentage change by dividing the difference value by the average value and multiplying by 100 to convert to a percentage.

Calculations	Mercury	Venus	Earth	Mars
Total				
Average				
Difference				
% Change				

Conclusion

11. Write a conclusion with supporting data analysis to back up your claim. A conclusion should state if the data collected support or do not support the hypothesis. Additionally, you should use the data analysis as evidence to support your claim.

_____

_____

_____

_____

_____

_____

_____

_____

_____

_____

_____

_____

_____

_____

12. Write your recommendations to make the experiment better. Note any problems and suggest improvements for the next experiment. If there are any variations between what you expected as a result and what actually happened, these need to be explained.

_____

_____

_____

_____

_____

_____

_____

_____

_____

_____

_____

_____

_____

_____

_____

_____

_____

_____

Vocabulary

Write a definition for each of the key terms from this lesson. You will develop a personal glossary of key terms throughout this course.

iterative design process

_____

_____

iteration

_____

_____

scientific method

_____

_____

hypothesis

_____

_____

Name: _____

Office Technology Integration

Determining Readability Statistics

1. Launch Microsoft Excel or other spreadsheet software, and open the vocabulary spreadsheet you updated in the last lesson.
2. Applying what you have learned, add a new worksheet, and name it Lesson 6.
3. Add each of the vocabulary words and definitions from the Vocabulary section of this lesson.
4. Save the spreadsheet, and then close it.
5. Launch Microsoft Word or other word-processing software, and open the *LastName_* Formatting document created in Lesson 3.
6. Evaluate the Inner Planet simulation. Develop a claim as whether or not the program is a game. Add this statement in the space below the Claim heading.
7. Skip two lines and create a heading similar to the one for Claim that states Single Paragraph.
8. In the space below the Single Paragraph heading, write a single paragraph. Begin with a topic sentence that states your position. Provide evidence to support your position. Include commentary indicating how the evidence applies to your claim. End with a closing statement.
9. Click in front of the first word of the paragraph, and press the [Tab] key. This will indent the first line of the paragraph.
10. Click **File**>**Options** on the ribbon to display the **Word Options** dialog box, and click **Proofing** on the left side.
11. Locate the spelling and grammar section, and check the **Show readability statistics** check box, as shown.

Check to display readability statistics →

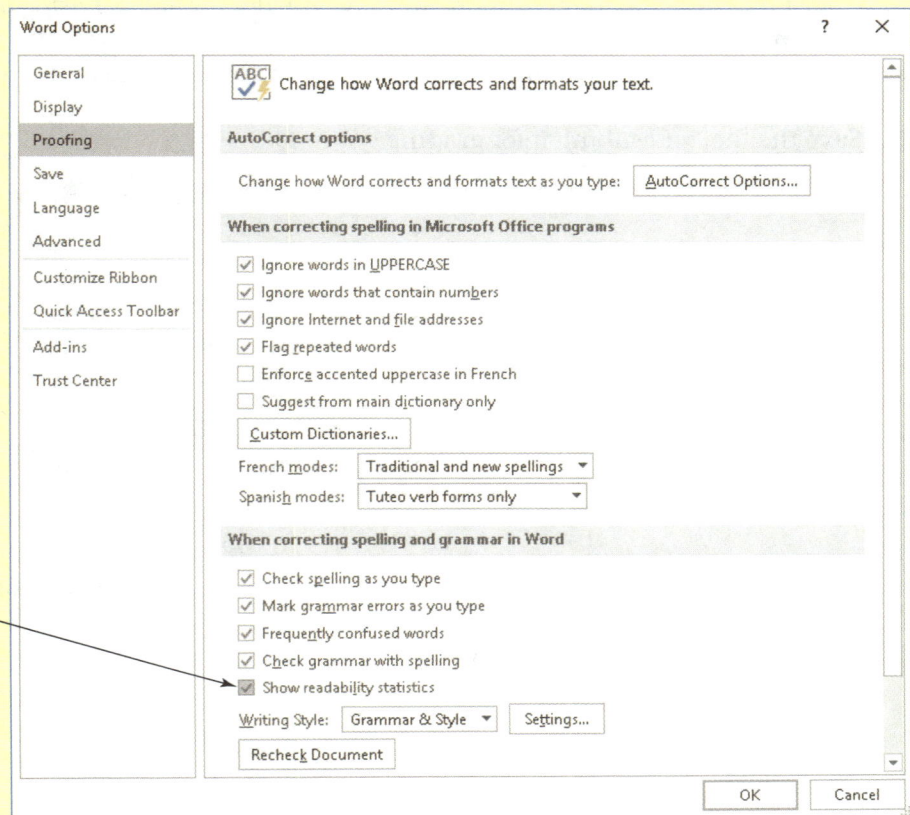

Goodheart-Willcox Publisher

12. Click the **OK** button to close the **Word Options** dialog box.

13. Select the entire paragraph. All words in the paragraph should be highlighted.

Spelling & Grammar

14. Click **Review**>**Proofing**>**Spelling & Grammar** on the ribbon or press the [F7] key to perform a spell-check.

15. Fix any spelling or grammar errors. If the program detects an error that is not really an error, use the **Ignore** button to leave the word as is. When the last error suggestion has been addressed, a message appears asking if you want to check the rest of the document for errors.

16. Click the **No** button. This will limit the check to only the selected paragraph. The statistics are then displayed, as shown.

Readability Statistics	? ✕
Counts	
Words	72
Characters	351
Paragraphs	1
Sentences	4
Averages	
Sentences per Paragraph	4.0
Words per Sentence	18.0
Characters per Word	4.8
Readability	
Passive Sentences	25%
Flesch Reading Ease	48.7
Flesch-Kincaid Grade Level	10.9

Grade level

17. Locate the value for the Flesch-Kincaid Grade Level. This number should be your grade level or higher.

18. Click **File**>**Save As** on the ribbon, and save the document as *LastName*_Prompt-1 in your working folder.

19. Make any corrections or improvements to your document to improve your readability statistics.

20. Save the file, and submit it for grading.

Lesson 7

Digital Art

Learning Objectives

After completing this lesson, you will be able to:

- create custom pixel art graphics for icons and logos.

- differentiate between raster and vector images.

- apply hexadecimal and RGB color models to graphic design.

- calculate pixel dimensions.

Situation

Your team has been assigned the task of creating custom icons and logo images for games that will be offered at the app store. You must first acquire a basic understanding of color theory. This will allow your team to use different color models in digital designs. Next, you will need to understand how raster and vector images are created to required specifications.

Reading Material

Images are created using shapes and colors. Combining shapes results in a composite image. Digital images are images created or displayed on a computer screen. What you see is based on the properties of visible light and the color model used to create the image. There are two basic types of computer-generated images: raster and vector. All images created using a computer fall into one of these categories. Each image type has specific characteristics that give it advantages and disadvantages over the other image type.

Visible Light

Visible light is the portion of light that humans can see. This spectrum, or gamut, of light is displayed by the colors of the rainbow. The basic colors of the visible light spectrum are red, orange, yellow, green, blue, indigo, and violet. Colors are actually different wavelengths of energy, as shown in **Figure 7-1.** Red is the longest wavelength of light humans can see. Energy wavelengths longer than red are called *infrared.* Heat energy emits wavelengths in the infrared spectrum. The shortest wavelength of light humans can see is violet. Energy wavelengths shorter than violet are called *ultraviolet.*

The properties of a wave of energy are measured in length, amplitude, and frequency,

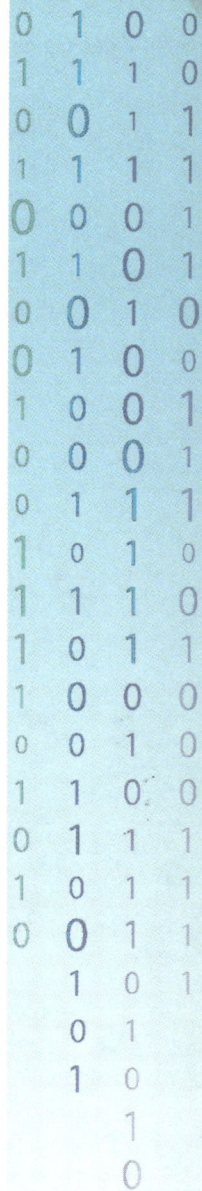

Name: _____

Date: _____

Class: _____

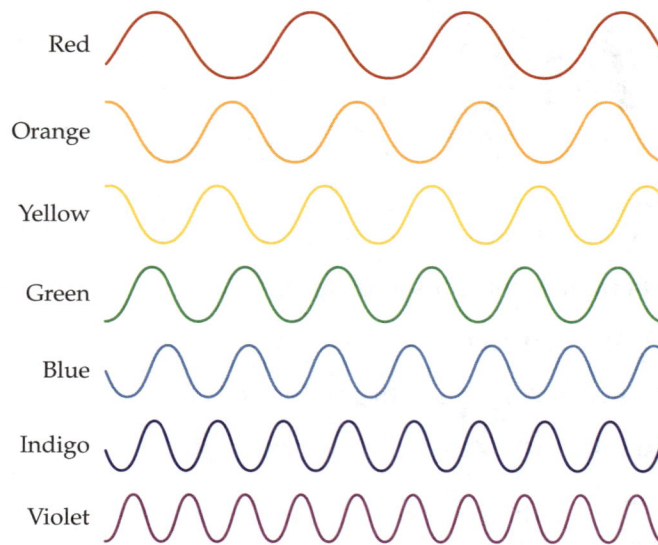

Figure 7-1. The color you see is based on the wavelength of the light reaching your eyes.

as shown in **Figure 7-2.** Length or *wavelength* is the distance from one wave peak (top) or trough (bottom) to the next. *Amplitude* is the height of the wave. *Frequency* is the number of complete waves per a time period, often one second. The wavelength determines the color of light. The amplitude determines the brightness of light.

Color Models

Colors for images are defined using a color model. A *color model* is the way of mixing base colors to create a spectrum of colors. The RGB, HSL, and hexadecimal color models are the most common digital color models.

The *RGB color model* is based on the three base colors red, green, and blue. All of the colors you see on a computer screen are made by mixing these three base colors. The value for each color can range from 0 to 255.

The *HSL color model* creates color by adjusting the values of hue, saturation, and luminescence. Hue is the pigment color. Saturation is the amount of color. Luminescence or brightness is how much light is shining on the color. This model is popular in creating

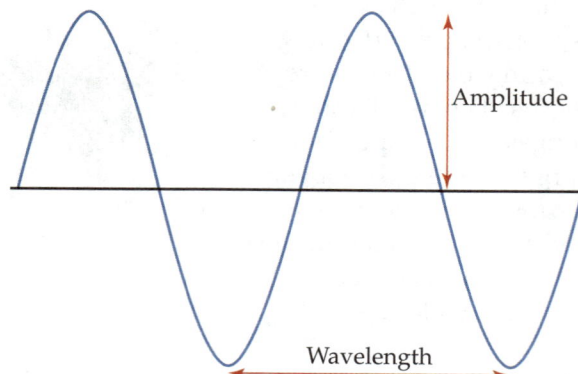

Figure 7-2. An energy wave can be defined by its wavelength, amplitude, and frequency.

textures and surfaces for computer-generated 3D models since these models require the use of light and shadow to define position relative to the light source. Using this color model allows the computer to leave the hue and saturation unchanged while only adjusting the luminescence setting to be brighter or darker. Lighter luminescence would be facing the light source, while darker luminescence would be in shadow. The HSL color model is also known as the hue, saturation, and brightness (HSB) color model.

The **hexadecimal color model** is an RGB color model in which colors are represented by a series of six letters or numbers, such as #FF2500. The first pair is the setting for red (FF). The second pair is the setting for green (25). The third pair is the setting for blue (00). This color model is used in web page design. Many imaging software programs allow the user to limit colors to 16 web safe colors or the 216 colors universally compatible with web browsers.

Raster Images

A **raster image** is made of dots or pixels, as shown in **Figure 7-3.** Each pixel in the image has a specific color and location to construct the final image. A raster image is called a **bitmap** because the location and color of each pixel is mapped. The computer reads a bitmap image by creating a coordinate grid with the origin at the top-left corner. The coordinates change by increasing the X value moving right and the Y value moving down. In each space of the coordinate grid is a single pixel. A pixel can only be one color. To determine the color of a pixel at a particular coordinate location, the color value of a pixel is read by the computer and displayed.

Depending on the file format, a bitmap can also support alpha channels. An **alpha channel** varies the opacity of a color. The alpha channel can support full transparency all the way to full opacity. Alpha channels can also allow for a masking color. A **masking color** is a single shade of a color that can be set to be transparent. If you have ever seen a weather report on TV, you have likely seen them using a masking color. Using a green or blue screen, called a chroma screen, allows the background of the weather map to digitally replace the blank screen. The meteorologist is filmed in front of the chroma screen. This image is placed over the top of the weather map. The masking color of the chroma screen is set to transparent, so the meteorologist appears to be "on" the weather map. In image creation, masking colors are typically chosen so they will not interfere with natural colors. Using a masking color such as white would be a very bad choice. If white were made to be transparent, then the whites in a person's eyes, teeth, and other white items would be transparent.

Goodheart-Willcox Publisher

Figure 7-3. A raster image is composed of dots of color. Lines, circles, curves, and other shapes are just dots.

Vector Images

A *vector image* is composed of lines and fills determined by mathematical definitions, not pixel-by-pixel data. The image is not created by storing the color value and location of each pixel. In other words, in a raster image, a line is composed of dots, while in a vector image, a line is defined by a mathematical equation. For a vector image to be displayed, the software must rasterize the image before it is sent to the display device.

A vector image file can be very small in size. This is because the image is drawn by the computer using a mathematical formula. Since the formula defines the image, the image can be resized infinitely smaller or larger without loss of clarity, as shown in **Figure 7-4.** This is one of the biggest advantages of a vector image.

However, vector images do have a disadvantage that raster images do not. A vector image requires the central processing unit (CPU) of a computer to work hard to draw the image. The CPU is the brain of the computer and performs the calculations needed to create the images, sounds, and other output a computer creates. In the world of handheld devices with small CPUs and low memory, displaying a vector image may take up a large amount of the CPU's ability. Bitmaps do not require a large amount of the CPU's ability, but they have larger files. The designer will need to understand the limits and capabilities of each device on which the

Goodheart-Willcox Publisher

Figure 7-4. A vector image (right) is created by the mathematical definitions of lines, circles, curves, and other shapes. This allows them to be scaled up without loss of image quality, unlike a raster image (left).

image will be rendered to correctly match the file size and CPU usage. This will prevent lag and crashing of the device.

Image Sizing and Resampling

When a bitmap is enlarged, the pixels spread out. This **dithers** the image, which creates holes in the image where the pixels are no longer touching each other. Software uses a process called interpolation to dither an image. **Interpolation** is the refining of the space between pixels. During interpolation the software averages the color of all pixels touching the empty space. The average color of the surrounding pixels is then assigned to the new pixel.

A designer must know the size of the final image to properly create art that will look and work correctly. For example, an app for the Android should have an icon that is 96 pixels × 96 pixels. That is the specification given to the designer so the icon will properly display on the device and in the app store. On the other hand, most images for print publication should be sized to specific dimensions with a resolution of 300 dots per inch (dpi).

Resolution is the measure of the sharpness or clarity of an image. The resolution of an image is measured in dots per inch (dpi) or pixels per inch (ppi). This measurement is the number of dots or pixels along the horizontal and vertical axes of the image. An image that is one inch square with 200 pixels on each axis has a resolution of 200 dpi. If an image with a resolution of 200 dpi is five inches wide, the horizontal dimension contains 1000 pixels (5 inches × 200 dpi = 1000 pixels). The vertical dimension also contains 1000 pixels. The image as a whole contains a total of one million pixels (1000 × 1000 = 1,000,000).

Sometimes, resolution may be expressed as the width by the height. For example, a computer monitor my have a resolution of 1280 × 1024. This display has 1280 pixels along the horizontal axis and 1024 pixels along the vertical axis.

If an image that is one inch square at 200 dpi is stretched to two inches square without resampling, the resolution becomes 100 dpi. This results in a loss of image clarity. When an image is resized, it must be resampled to create a new image without reducing the image resolution. **Resampling** uses interpolation to add or remove pixels as needed to keep the resolution the same.

Game Build

The Awesome Game Company needs to create the logo for some games using Clickteam Fusion 2.5. Now that you and your team have an understanding of digital art and color models, you have been tasked with creating the logo. The first game for which you will create a logo is the Click Ball game created in Lesson 3.

How to Begin

1. Launch Clickteam Fusion 2.5, and open the *LastName*_ClickBall game.
2. Make sure *LastName*_ClickBall is selected in the **Workspace Toolbar**. This is the application branch.
3. Click the **About** tab in the **Properties** toolbar, and locate the Icon property. The current game icon is displayed as a thumbnail in the property. The default icon is a red circle with a yellow lightning bolt in it. The icon is the image that will be displayed as the desktop program shortcut or app to represent the game.

About

4. Click the thumbnail for the current icon. The **Edit** button is displayed to the right of the thumbnail, as show in **Figure 7-5.**
5. Click the **Edit** button. The **Edit Icon** dialog box is displayed.

Pixel Art

Pixel art is digital art in which each pixel is modified to create an image. Program icons are often created as pixel art. The default icon has been created in 11 different sizes

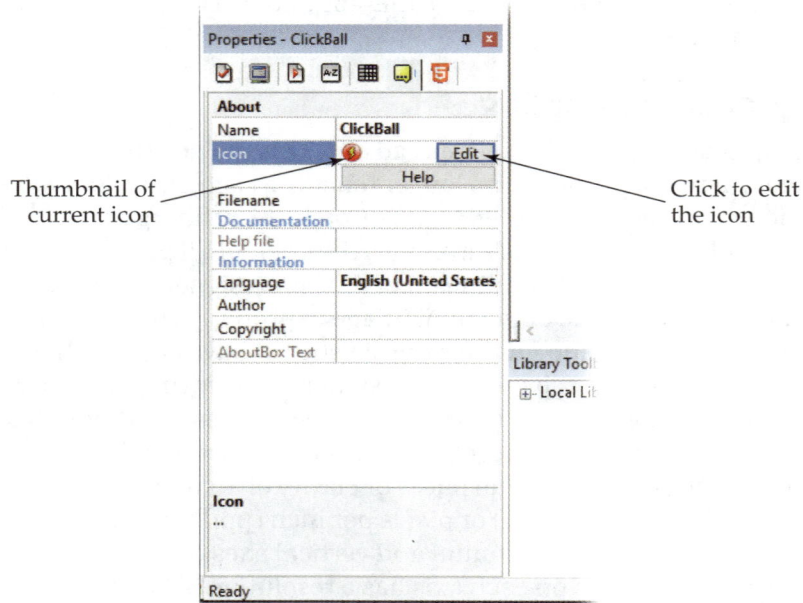

Goodheart-Willcox Publisher

Figure 7-5. The icon for a game can be edited or replaced.

and quality standards. This is done to match the different requirements for several different devices. Each icon appears at the bottom of the **Edit Icon** dialog box similar to frames.

6. In the frames section at the bottom of the **Edit Icon** dialog box, select the 16 × 16 – 16c icon. The icon is displayed in the editing area. This icon fits in a space 16 pixels wide by 16 pixels high and is created with only 16 colors. This is a very small graphic with few colors for low-power devices.

7. Use the window-control buttons to maximize the **Edit Icon** dialog box so it fills the screen.

8. Use the **Zoom** slider to increase the magnification so the image is as large as possible. This will provide the most detail for each pixel of the drawing. Notice how this image looks more like an octagon than a circle.

9. Click the **Color Picker** button. The color picker is used to choose a color in the image and set it as the current drawing color.

10. Left-click the dark red along the outside of the image to choose that color. Notice the foreground color swatch on the right side is now that dark red color. The color is also selected in the color palette near the top right. The settings for RGB and hexadecimal color models are shown below the color palette. Notice the RGB values for this color are 128, 0, 0. The hexadecimal number is 800000.

11. Click the **Line Tool** button. This tool is used to draw straight lines in the foreground color.

12. Click at the top of the image and draw a one-pixel wide, two-pixel long line in the checkerboard area above the center of the circle, as shown in **Figure 7-6.** If you make a mistake, press the [Ctrl][Z] key combination to undo the action, and then try again.

13. Add similar lines on the left, right, and bottom to help make the object a bit more round.

14. Applying what you have learned, change the foreground color to the light red found in the image.

15. Draw a light-red line just below the dark-red lines you drew earlier. This will reduce the thickness of the dark-red line to only one pixel.

16. Click the **Brush Tool** button. This tool can be used to paint single pixels of color.

17. Change the single dark-red pixel in the middle of each of the diagonal lines around the outside to light red.

Zoom

Color Picker

Line Tool

Color Picker

Brush Tool

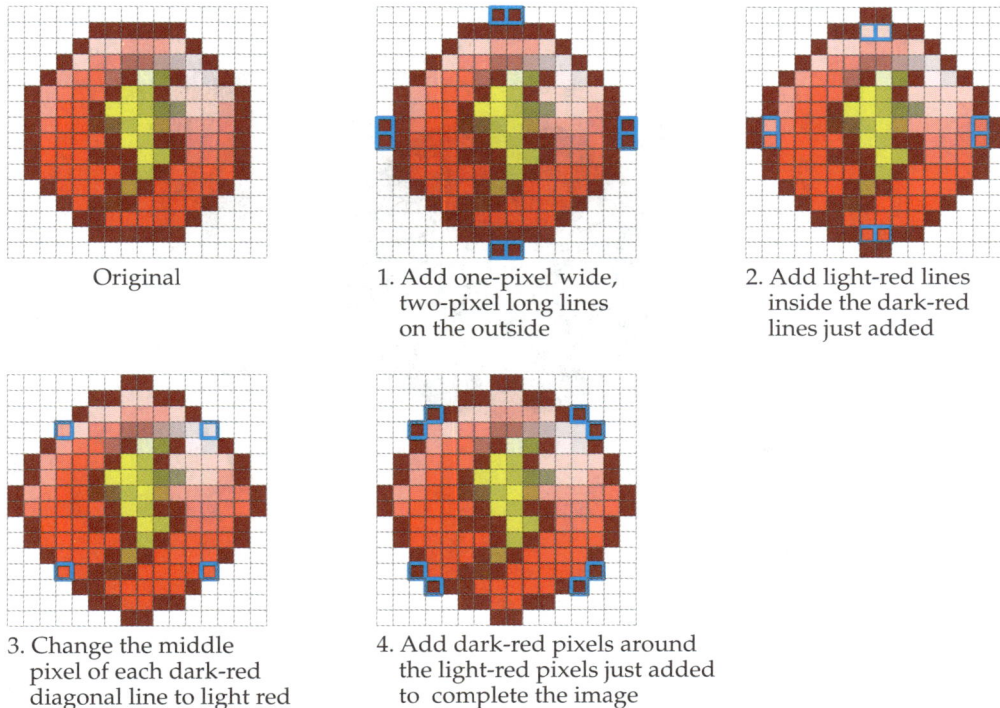

Original

1. Add one-pixel wide, two-pixel long lines on the outside

2. Add light-red lines inside the dark-red lines just added

3. Change the middle pixel of each dark-red diagonal line to light red

4. Add dark-red pixels around the light-red pixels just added to complete the image

Goodheart-Willcox Publisher

Figure 7-6. The small-size default icon looks more like an octagon than a circle. Editing the icon improves the shape of the image.

18. Applying what you have learned, add dark-red lines to create a border next to the light-red pixel you added on each diagonal. This will provide a balanced look to the border with two-pixel lines around the entire image. Notice how these modifications make the image more circular.

19. Click the **OK** button to close the dialog box and save the changes to the icon.

Custom Icon

The default icon can be used for your game. However, it will not really give the user an idea of the game's theme or content. A custom icon can be created to match the gameplay.

20. Applying what you have learned, open the **Edit Icon** dialog box.

21. Select the 256 × 256 icon, and adjust the **Zoom** slider so the entire image fits in the editor window.

22. Click the **Clear** button. The current image is deleted, leaving a blank canvas with transparent background.

23. Click the foreground color swatch, and enter FFFF00 as the hexadecimal color number. This is a yellow color.

24. Click the background color swatch, and enter 0, 0, 0 as the RGB color. This is black.

25. Click the **Ellipse Tool** button. This tool creates a circular line based on the foreground color and fills the inside with the background color.

26. Locate the options for the tool below the tool palette, and click the **Outlined Filled** button, as shown in **Figure 7-7.**

27. Click in the **Size** text box, and enter 4. This will make the outline four pixels thick.

28. Click in the top-left corner of the canvas, drag to the bottom-right corner of the canvas, and release the mouse button to draw a circle that fills the canvas. The *canvas* is the drawing area.

Clear

Ellipse Tool

Outlined Filled

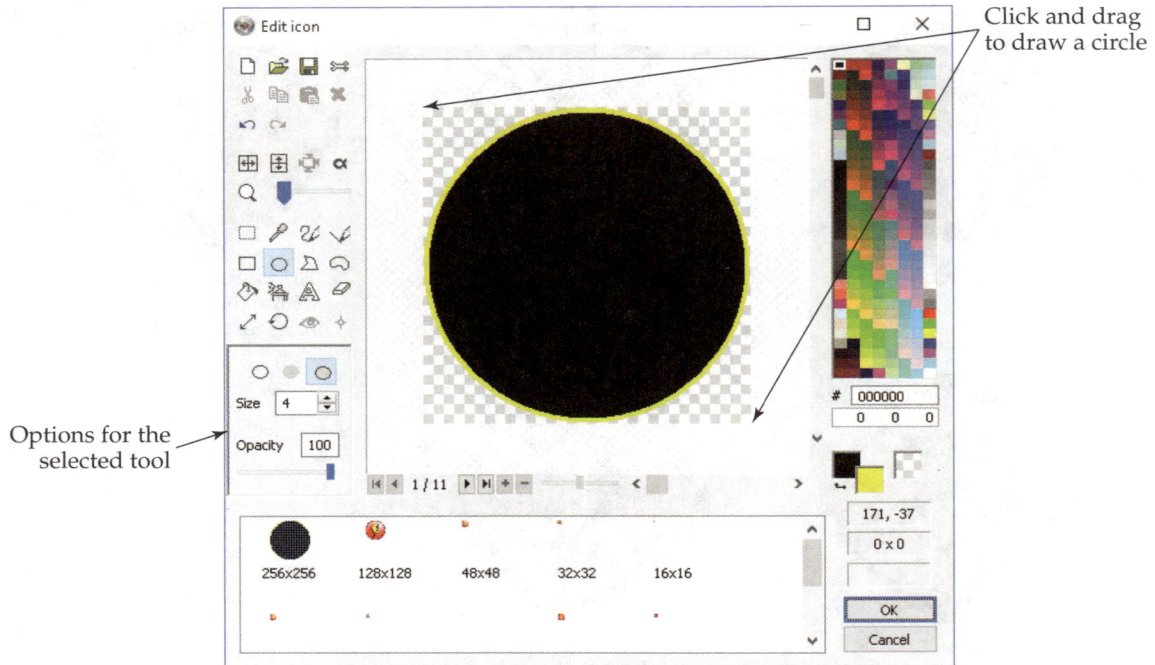

Click and drag to draw a circle

Options for the selected tool

Goodheart-Willcox Publisher

Figure 7-7. Many tools in the image editor have options that can be set to refine the function of the tool.

29. Click the **Text Tool** button, and click the **Font** button in the options area.
30. In the **Font** dialog box, click **Arial** in the **Font:** list, click **Bold** in the **Font Style:** list, and enter 20 in the **Size:** text box. Then, click the **OK** button to update the settings for the tool.
31. Click near the top of the circle. The **Text** dialog box is displayed.
32. Add the text Click, and press the [Enter] key.
33. On the second line, add the text Ball.
34. Click in front of the word *ball,* and press the space bar to move the word over by one space. Important: leave the **Text** dialog box open for the next few steps! Do not close it until told to do so.
35. Move the cursor over the words in the editing area, click, and drag the words so they are centered in the circle. Move the **Text** dialog box out of the way if needed, but do *not* close it.
36. Click the **Font** button in the options area.
37. In the **Font** dialog box, change the **Size:** value to 48. Click the **OK** button to close the **Font** dialog box.
38. Applying what you have learned, move the words as needed so they are centered in the circle, as shown in **Figure 7-8.**
39. Click the **Close** button (X) on the **Text** dialog box to set the text. After the **Text** dialog box is closed, the text cannot be edited as text. The text becomes part of the image.
40. Applying what you have learned, create matching custom icons for the following sizes.

Icon Size	Outline Size	Text Size
128 × 128	3	28
48 × 48	2	10
32 × 32	1	7
16 × 16	1	2 (Note: the text will not be legible at this size)

41. When finished, close the **Edit Icon** dialog box to save the icon changes.
42. Save your work, and submit it for grading.

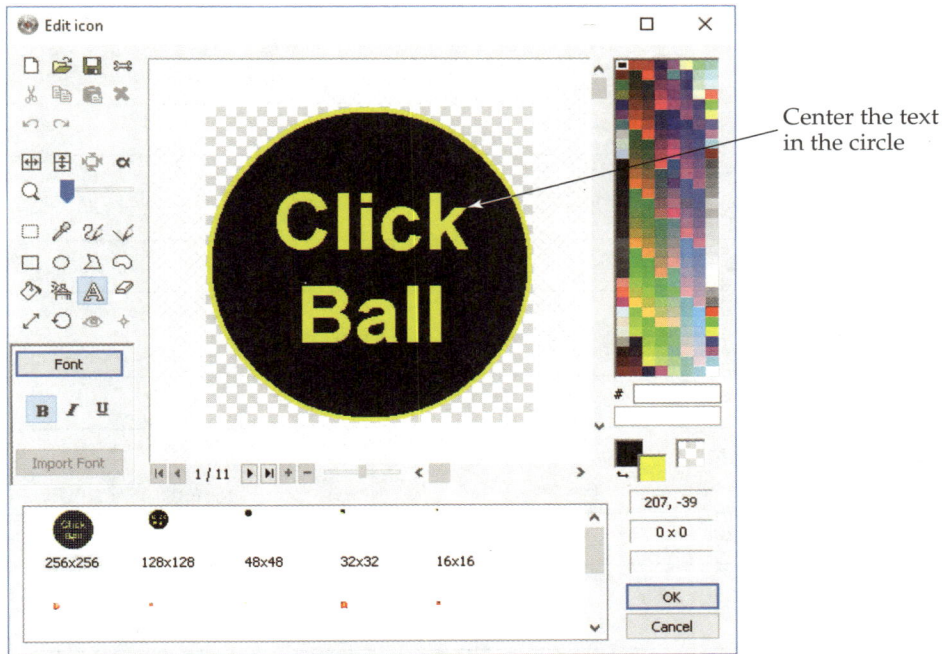

Center the text in the circle

Goodheart-Willcox Publisher

Figure 7-8. Make any adjustments to the text before closing the **Text** dialog box because once it is closed the text is no longer text, it is an image.

Vocabulary

Write a definition for each of the key terms from this lesson. You will develop a personal glossary of key terms throughout this course.

visible light

_____

_____

infrared

_____

_____

ultraviolet

_____

_____

wavelength

_____

_____

amplitude

_____

_____

frequency

_____

_____

color model

_____

_____

RGB color model

_____

_____

HSL color model

_____

_____

hexadecimal color model

_____

_____

raster image

_____

_____

bitmap

_____

_____

alpha channel

_____

_____

masking color

_____

_____

vector image

_____

_____

dithers

_____

_____

interpolation

_____

_____

resolution

_____

_____

resampling

_____

_____

pixel art

_____

_____

canvas

_____

_____

Review Questions

1. Compare and contrast the pros and cons of vector images with raster images. Give one example for each type of where it is the best format to use.

   _____

   _____

   _____

   _____

   Language Arts

2. Complete the table with how many total pixels are possible in each rectangular icon.

Number of Pixels High	Number of Pixels Wide	Total Pixels
16	16	256
48	128	
100		10,000
256		65,536

   Mathematics

3. What three color models are commonly used for digital art?

   _____

   _____

   _____

   _____

   Applied Technology

4. Summarize how a chroma screen and masking color work together.

   _____

   _____

   _____

   _____

   Language Arts

Mathematics

5. If the resolution of an image is 100 dpi and the image is three inches tall and five inches wide, how many pixels wide is image? Show your work.

_____

_____

_____

_____

Higher-Order Thinking Strategies

Applied Technology

6. Speculate for what type of program the $16 \times 16 - 16c$ icon would be used.

_____

_____

_____

_____

Science

7. What is the relationship between the wavelength of visible light and what color you see?

_____

_____

_____

_____

Language Arts

8. Describe why you think it is important to test the program icons on various computers and devices before releasing the game.

_____

_____

_____

_____

Applied Technology

9. If a color's RGB values are 128, 128, 128, speculate what the color is.

_____

_____

_____

_____

Science

10. If a client is color-blind and cannot see long wavelengths of light, what two colors would you choose for a custom icon? Why?

_____

_____

_____

_____

Name: _____

Office Technology Integration

Using Shapes and Gradients in Presentation Software

1. Launch Microsoft Excel or other spreadsheet software, and open the vocabulary spreadsheet you updated in the last lesson.
2. Applying what you have learned, add a new worksheet, and name it Lesson 7.
3. Add each of the vocabulary words and definitions from the Vocabulary section of this lesson.
4. Save the spreadsheet, and then close it.
5. Launch Microsoft PowerPoint or other presentation software, and start a new blank presentation.
6. Click **Home**>**Slides**>**Layout** on the ribbon, and click **Blank** in the drop-down menu. This removes any text boxes or objects that are on the slide.
7. Click **Insert**>**Illustrations**>**Shapes**>**Oval** on the ribbon.
8. Click anywhere on the slide, drag, and release the mouse button to draw a small ellipse (oval). This shape is a vector image.
9. Click the **Format** tab on the ribbon and locate the **Size** group. The text boxes in this group control the height and width of the shape.
10. Change the size of the shape to 7 inches high and 7 inches wide.
11. Click the arrow next to **Format**>**Shape Styles**>**Shape Fill** on the ribbon. In the drop-down color palette that is displayed, click the yellow color swatch. The shape is filled with yellow.
12. Click the arrow next to **Format**>**Shape Styles**>**Shape Outline** on the ribbon. In the drop-down color palette that is displayed, click the black color swatch. The shape is outlined with black.
13. Click the arrow next to the **Shape Fill** button, and click **Gradient**>**More Gradients...** in the drop-down menu. The **Format Shape** pane is displayed along the right-hand side of the screen, as shown.

Layout

Oval

Shape Fill

Shape Outline

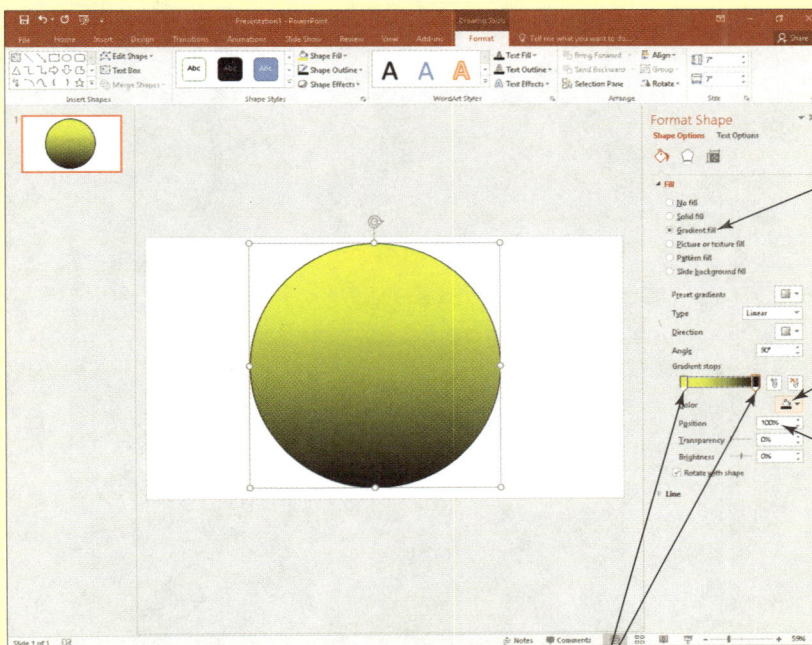

Select to create a gradient

Color of selected stop

Position of selected stop

Gradient stops

Goodheart-Willcox Publisher

14. Click **Gradient fill** radio button.
15. Locate the **Gradient Stops** section, and click one of the triangular gradient stops to select it. Then, press the [Delete] key to remove the stop. Repeat this until only two stops remain.
16. Select one of the remaining two gradient stops.
17. Click the **Color** button in the **Gradient Stops** section, and click the yellow color swatch in the drop-down palette.
18. Click in the **Position** text box, and enter 0%. This places the stop on the left-hand end of the preview stripe.
19. Applying what you have learned, change the other gradient stop to black and position it on the right-hand end of the preview stripe.
20. Close the **Format Shape** pane.
21. **Insert>Text>Text Box** on the ribbon.
22. Click in the center of the circle to add a text box to the circle. When added in this way, the text box automatically becomes part of the circle.
23. Add the text Click Ball, and then select the text.
24. Click the **Home** tab on the ribbon, and locate the **Font** group. Use the tools in this group to change the typeface to Arial, the size to 140, the color to black, and make the type bold. This should fit inside the circle. Adjust the size if needed to fit the text within the circle.
25. Right-click on the circle, and click **Save As Picture...** in the shortcut menu. A standard save-type dialog box is displayed that allows you to save the selected object as an image file.
26. Click the **Save as Type:** drop-down arrow, and click **PNG Portable Network Graphics Format** in the list. The PNG file type is a raster image format.
27. Name the file Click Ball, navigate to your working folder, and click the **Save** button. This graphic image can now be used in other programs such as Clickteam Fusion 2.5 as an icon or on the title frame inside the game.
28. Save the presentation as *LastName_*Vector in your working folder, and submit it for grading.

0 1 0 0
0 1 0 0
1 1 1 0
0 0 1 1
1 1 1 1
0 0 0 1
1 1 0 1
0 0 1 0
0 1 0 0
1 0 0 1
0 0 0 1
0 1 1 1
1 0 1 0
1 1 1 0
1 0 1 1
1 0 0 0
0 0 1 0
1 1 0 0
0 1 1 1
1 0 1 1
0 0 1 1
1 0 1
0 1
1 0
1
0

Lesson 8

Parent and Child Objects

Learning Objectives

After completing this lesson, you will be able to:

- differentiate relative and absolute referencing for plotting points on a game frame.
- position game objects in specified locations within a coordinate system.
- create a parent-child object relationship.
- use ordered pair notation.

Situation

The Awesome Game Company needs to create some games using Clickteam Fusion 2.5 software. It wants all the designers to understand how the program uses a two-dimensional frame to plot the location of game assets. Your team must also understand the parent-child relationship that can exist between game objects.

Reading Material

In game creation, a coordinate system is used to find the location of each object in the frame. As you learned in Lesson 2, this is very similar to the Cartesian coordinate system with a horizontal X axis and a vertical Y axis. However, in a game frame, the positive Y direction is *down,* not up as in the Cartesian coordinate system. The origin (0,0) is located at the top-left corner of the game frame just as it is on computer monitors, televisions, and smartphone screens.

When showing coordinates, we use the ordered pair system. An ***ordered pair*** identifies a single point in the coordinate system. It is written as (X,Y). X is the coordinate value along the X axis. Y is the coordinate value along the Y axis.

Game designers often have to place objects in a specific position within the scene. The true and exact location of an object in relation to the origin is the ***absolute position.*** When placing an object at the absolute position of (25,400), it is placed where X = 25 and Y = 400.

Other times, an object will need to be placed at a relative position. ***Relative position*** is the location

Name: _____

Date: _____

Class: _____

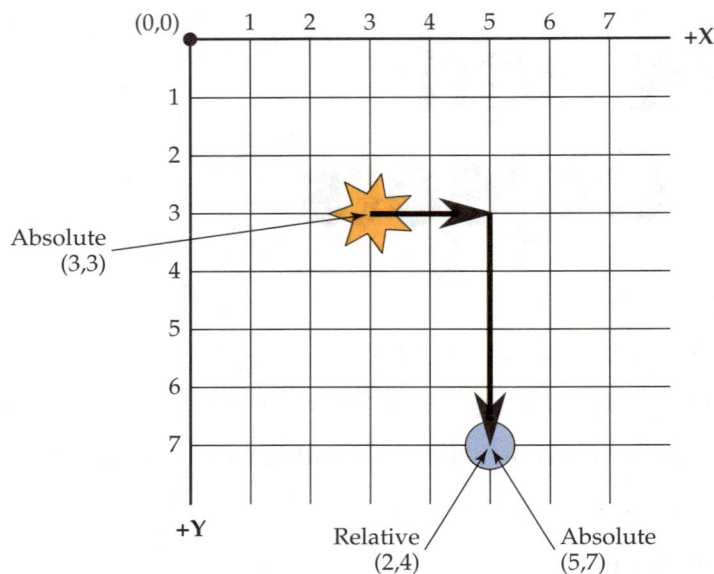

Figure 8-1. Absolute positioning or coordinates are based from the origin. Relative positioning or coordinates are based from another object or a point that is not the origin.

of an object in relation to another object or a point that is not the origin. **Figure 8-1** compares absolute and relative positioning.

One application of relative positioning is when two objects are linked. One object is the parent object. A ***parent object*** is the object to which other objects are linked. Its position is used to calculate the location of the linked objects. In Clickteam Fusion 2.5, the hotspot of the parent object is considered the (0,0) point of the calculation. The ***hotspot*** is the point on the object on which an object's location is based as well as movement and other transformations are calculated. A ***child object*** is an object linked to a parent. The location of the child is based on the coordinates of the parent's position.

Think of the parent-child relationship as a child holding the hand of the parent. If the parent moves, the child will also move. Consider the knight character shown in **Figure 8-2.** The knight character is carrying a sword and a shield. In a game, these objects may be separate from the knight object so they can be picked up or dropped as needed. However, to make them move with the knight, they could be linked. That would make the knight the parent object and the sword and shield child objects. The position of the child object is inherited from the parent object. ***Inherited*** means passed down from a parent.

Relative position can also apply when creating a new object in the scene. When programming a game to have an object that is launched or thrown, the object should always appear relative to the player. Consider making a Snowball Fight game. You program the computer to throw a snowball from the absolute position of the player. However, what happens when the player moves and throws a second snowball? If the snowball is created at the player's original absolute position, it will be far away from the player. This would be a bug in gameplay. To fix this bug, you need to tell the computer to create the snowball relative to the player's hand. That way, wherever the player goes, the snowball will always appear next to the character.

pzUH/Shutterstock.com

Figure 8-2. The sword and shield can be linked to the knight so they move when the knight moves. This would make them child objects of the knight object.

Game Build

Your team has been assigned the task of creating a plotted image using the ordered pairs of X and Y axis points for a two-dimensional game frame. You will create several objects to form a face. In order to have all objects move together, you will need to create parent-child relationships.

How to Begin

1. Launch Clickteam Fusion 2.5.
2. Applying what you have learned, start a new application, and save it as *LastName_* Positions in your working folder.
3. Open Frame 1 in the frame editor.
4. Applying what you have learned, insert a new active object, and place it anywhere on the frame.
5. Rename the object as Parent_Face.
6. Change the size to 300 by 300.
7. Change the position to (320, 240). This is an absolute position.
8. Change the Movement Type property to Eight Directions. With this movement type, the arrow keys on the keyboard are used to move the object.

Image Editing

9. Double-click the Parent_Face object to open the image editor.
10. Applying what you have learned, clear the default image.
11. Using the color palette, set the foreground color to a skin tone.

Clear

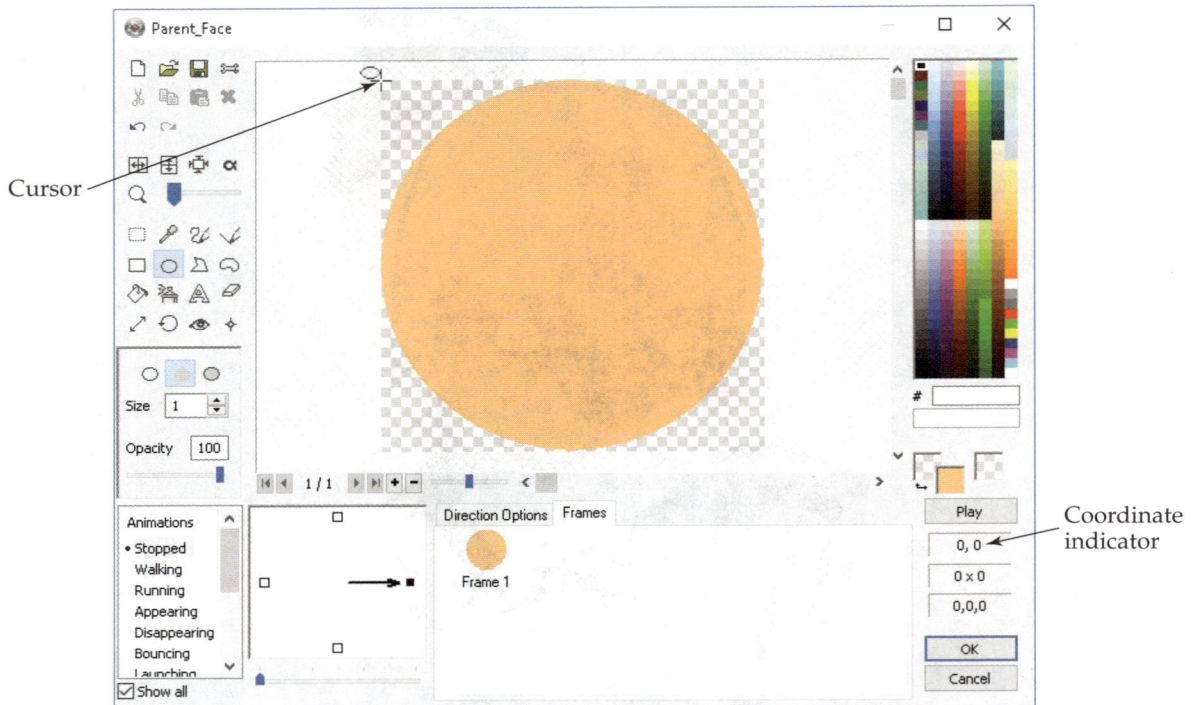

Goodheart-Willcox Publisher

Figure 8-3. Use the coordinate indicator in the image editor to locate the cursor when drawing shapes.

12. Click the **Ellipse Tool** button, and then click the **Filled** button in the options area.
13. Move the cursor to the top-left corner of the drawing canvas, and look at the coordinate indicator. It will display 0,0 display when the cursor is at the exact top-left corner of the canvas, as shown in **Figure 8-3.**
14. Applying what you have learned, draw an ellipse from 0,0 to 300,300.
15. Click the **View Hot Spot** button.
16. In the tool options area, click the center **Quick Move** button, as shown in **Figure 8-4.** This moves the hotspot to the center of the object.
17. Click the **OK** button to close the image editor and update the object.
18. Applying what you have learned, create the following objects, and modify the sprite images using the **Ellipse Tool**. Note that the sclera is the white part of the eye.

Object Type	Size	Position	Name	Movement	Fill Color	Hotspot
Active	32 by 32	(350, 165)	Child_Sclera_R	Static	White	Top-left
Active	32 by 32	(256, 165)	Child_Sclera_L	Static	White	Top-left
Active	16 by 16	(360, 181)	Child_Pupil_R	Static	Black	Top-left
Active	16 by 16	(263, 178)	Child_Pupil_L	Static	Black	Top-left

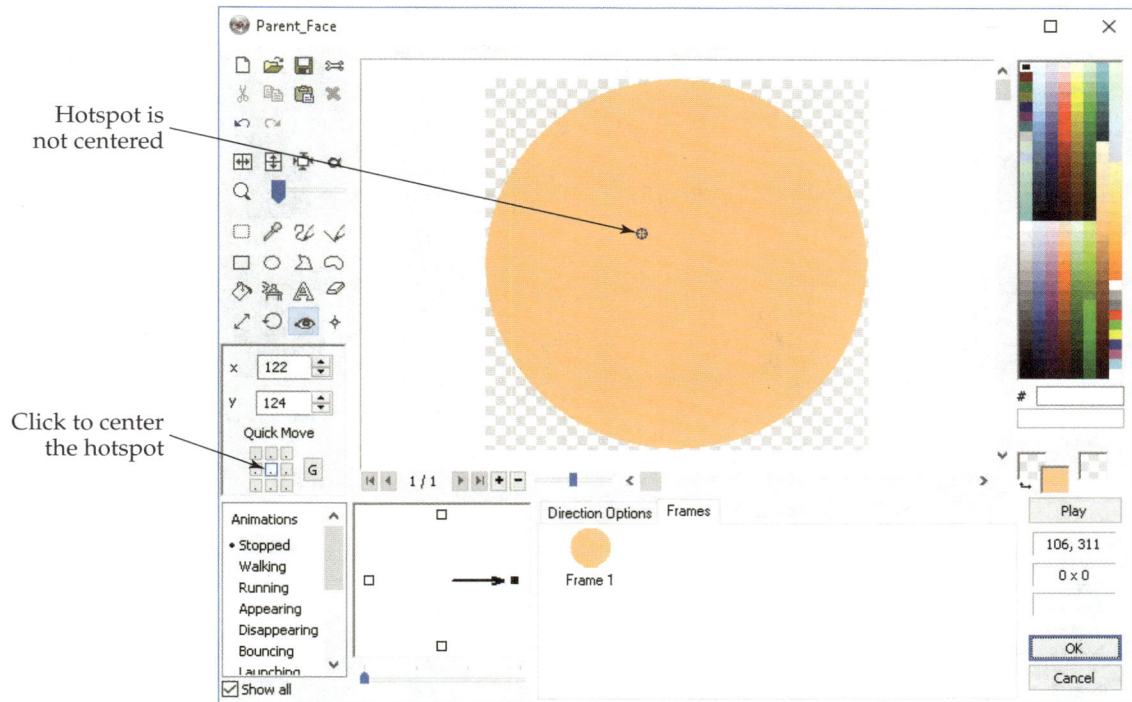

Hotspot is
not centered

Click to center
the hotspot

Goodheart-Willcox Publisher

Figure 8-4. The buttons in the **Quick Move** area of the tool options can be used to move the hotspot to a specific location on the sprite.

19. If the pupil objects are behind the sclera objects, right-click on the sclera object, and click **Order>Backward One** in the shortcut menu. Repeat this as needed until the pupil object is no longer behind the sclera object.

Nose and Mouth

20. Insert a new active object anywhere on the frame, and name it Child_Nose.
21. Set the size to 55 by 55 and the position to (295, 230).
22. Open the object in the image editor, and clear the canvas.
23. Set the foreground color to a color similar to the skin tone, but slightly darker so it will contrast well with the skin.
24. Use the **Zoom** slider if needed so you can see the entire canvas.
25. Click the **Brush Tool** button.
26. Click the **Continuous Brush** button in the tool options area. This will create a solid line.
27. Set the size to 3 pixels and the opacity to 100%.
28. Click and drag in a nose profile similar to the one shown in **Figure 8-5.** If you are not happy with the shape, press the [Ctrl][Z] key combination, and try again.
29. Click the **OK** button to close the image editor and update the object.
30. Insert a new active object anywhere on the frame, and name it Child_Mouth.
31. Set the size to 140 by 40 and the position to (300, 300).
32. Open the object in the image editor, and clear the canvas.
33. Use the **Zoom** slider if needed so you can see the entire canvas.
34. Set the foreground color to a color appropriate for lips for the skin tone you have been using.
35. Click the **Shape Tool** button.
36. Click the **Filled** button in the tool options area.

Continuous Brush

Shape Tool

Draw a nose profile

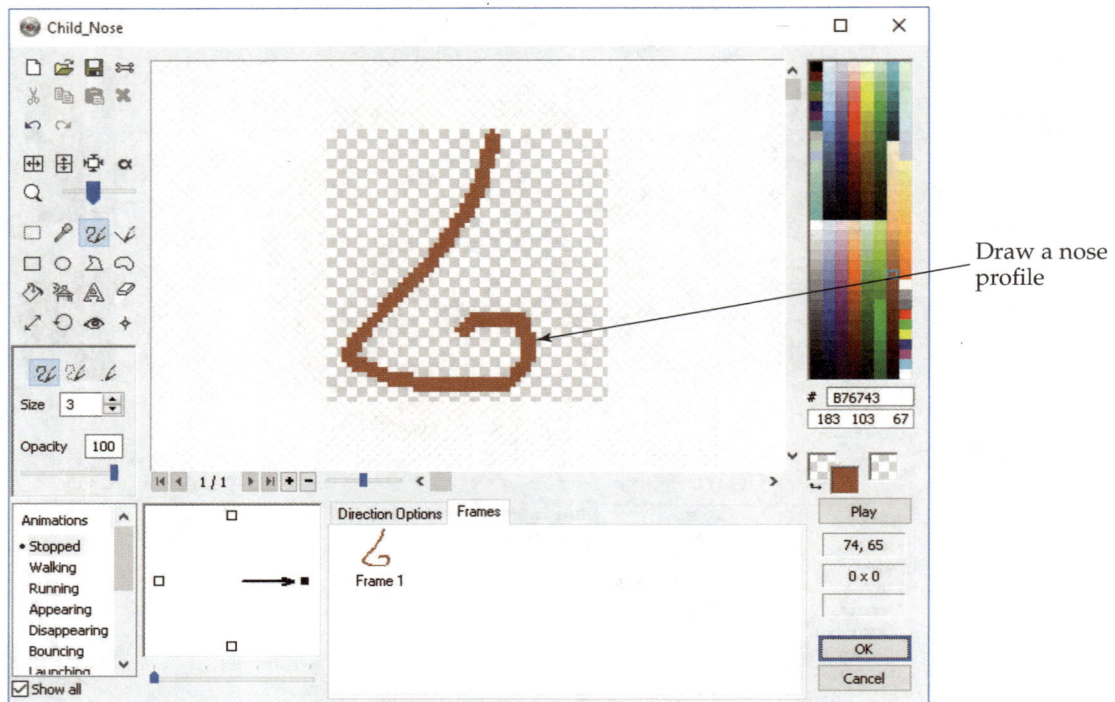

Figure 8-5. The nose profile is drawn freehand using the **Brush Tool**.

37. Click and drag to draw a mouth shape. The tool automatically connects the starting and ending points to create a closed shape. A *closed shape* has no breaks or holes in the outline.

38. Click the **OK** button to close the image editor and update the object.

Relative Positioning for Child Objects

The objects you have created are not connected to each other in any way. The facial features can be set as child objects relative to the face. This will allow the entire face to be moved as a single unit.

39. Run the frame, and use the arrow keys to move the face. The large circle will move, but the individual facial features will not. Close the game window when done testing.

Run Frame

40. Applying what you have learned, display the event editor for Frame 1.

41. Applying what you have learned, add a new condition. In the **New Condition** dialog box, right-click on the **Special** icon, and click **Always** in the shortcut menu. This condition will always be true, so whatever actions are programmed for it will always occur.

Event Editor

42. Right-click in the cell under the Child_Sclera_L object, and click **Position>Select Position…** in the shortcut menu. The **Select Position** dialog box is displayed in the frame editor, as shown in **Figure 8-6.**

43. Click the **Relative to:** radio button. A dialog box is displayed for selecting which object will be the parent.

44. In the dialog box, click the Parent_Face object, and then click the **OK** button. A dashed line appears on the frame surrounding the Parent_Face object and there is a boxed X in the center of the object. This X is the target representing the hotspot of the object.

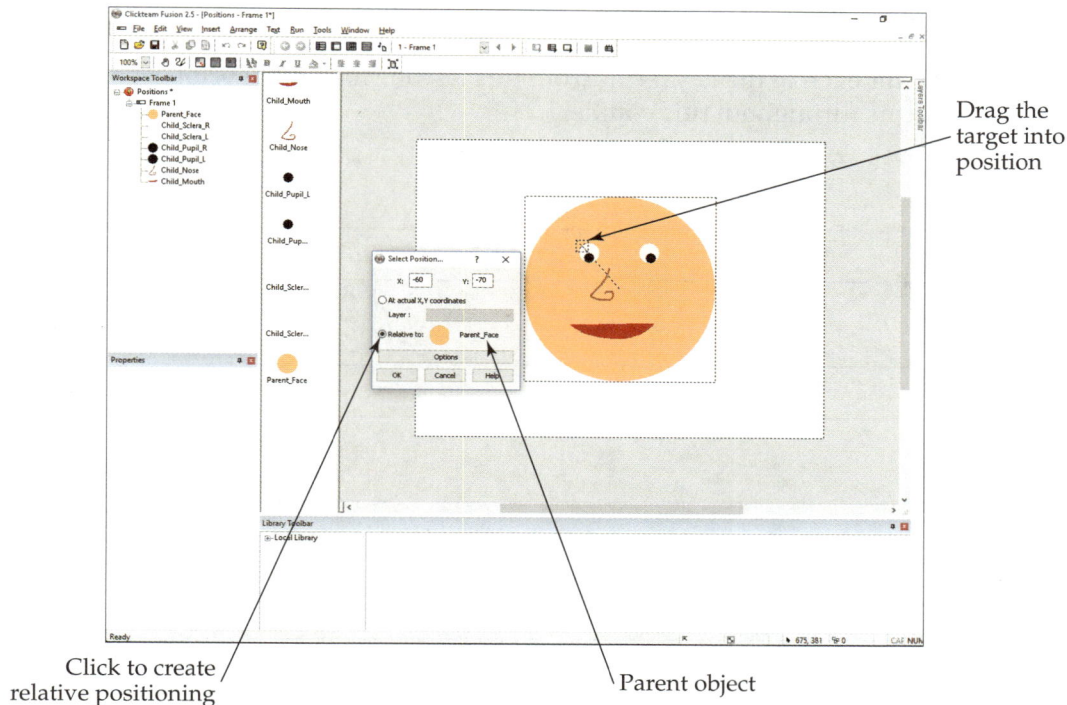

Drag the target into position

Click to create relative positioning

Parent object

Figure 8-6. A child object is linked to a parent object by specifying relative positioning based on the parent object.

45. Click and drag the target to the top-left corner of the Child_Sclera_L object. Release the mouse button when in the correct position. Notice that a dashed line connects the target to the hotspot of the parent object.

46. Click the **OK** button to close the **Select Position** dialog box and return to the event editor.

47. Hover the cursor over the check mark in event line 1. Make sure the programming matches the pseudocode below. It means the child object will always be 60 pixels to the left (–X value is left) and 70 pixels up (–Y value is up) from the hotspot of the parent object. Note: your coordinate values may be different, depending on the position of your objects, which is okay.

> **IF** always,
>> **THEN** set position of the Child_Sclera_L object to (–60,–70) relative to the Parent_Face object.

48. Applying what you have learned, create additional actions on event line 1 to correctly position the remaining child objects relative to the Parent_Face object.

49. Run the frame, and move the face around to check if all the child objects follow properly. Close the game window when done testing.

50. Debug any errors as needed.

51. Save your work, and submit it for grading.

Run Frame

Vocabulary

Write a definition for each of the key terms from this lesson. You will develop a personal glossary of key terms throughout this course.

ordered pair

_____

_____

absolute position

_____

_____

relative position

_____

_____

parent object

_____

_____

hotspot

_____

_____

child object

_____

_____

inherited

_____

_____

closed shape

_____

_____

Review Questions

Mathematics

1. Create an ordered pair for the relative location of the child object located 45 pixels to the right and 70 pixels below the origin of the parent object.

_____

_____

_____

_____

_____

Name: _____

2. Where is the location of the origin on a television, computer monitor, or smartphone screen?

_____

_____

_____

_____

_____

Applied Technology

3. Describe what a hotspot is.

_____

_____

_____

_____

_____

Language Arts

4. What needs to be created or established for a tennis racket object to always follow a character's hand?

_____

_____

_____

_____

_____

Applied Technology

5. Which type of positioning should be used for a child object and why?

_____

_____

_____

_____

_____

Applied Technology

Higher-Order Thinking Strategies

6. Compare and contrast relative and absolute positioning.

_____

_____

_____

_____

_____

Language Arts

Applied Technology

7. Explain how the properties of a parent object are applied to a child object.

_____
_____
_____
_____
_____

Science

8. Using contextual clues from this lesson, speculate a meaning for the word _sclera_.

_____
_____
_____
_____
_____
_____

Language Arts

9. Describe the process needed to draw a closed shape.

_____
_____
_____
_____
_____

Social Science

10. This game build included a stylized human character. Speculate how the facial features and skin tone selected by the designer can affect players who come from diverse backgrounds.

_____
_____
_____
_____
_____
_____

Office Technology Integration

Drawing and Grouping Vector Images in Presentation Software

1. Launch Microsoft Excel or other spreadsheet software, and open the vocabulary spreadsheet you updated in the last lesson.
2. Applying what you have learned, add a new worksheet, and name it Lesson 8.
3. Add each of the vocabulary words and definitions from the Vocabulary section of this lesson.
4. Save the spreadsheet, and then close it.
5. Launch Microsoft PowerPoint or other presentation software, and start a new blank presentation.
6. Applying what you have learned, remove any text boxes or objects that are on the slide.
7. Click **Insert>Illustrations>Shapes>Oval** on the ribbon, and draw an ellipse of any size on the slide.
8. Applying what you have learned, change the size of the ellipse to 1 inch high and 1 inch wide to make a circle.
9. Applying what you have learned, change the shape fill color to black.
10. Click the arrow next to **Format>Shape Styles>Shape Outline** on the ribbon. In the drop-down color palette that is displayed, click **No Outline**. The line around the outside of the shape is removed.
11. Draw a large circle that covers the existing small black circle. Note: if you hold down the [Shift] key as you draw, the shape will be constrained to a circle.
12. Right-click on the large circle, and click **Send to Back>Send to Back** in the shortcut menu, as shown. Objects can be reordered with a bring forward, send backward, Bring to Front or Send to Back command. The object drawn last will be placed on top of the object stack.

Layout

Oval

Shape Fill

Shape Outline

Large circle is behind the small circle

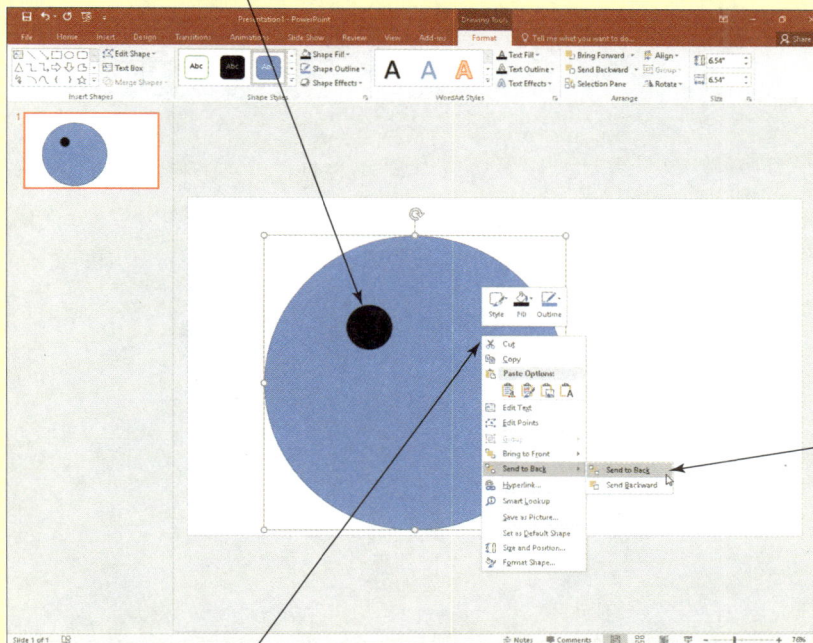

Click to send the object to the back of the stack

Right-click

Goodheart-Willcox Publisher

13. Applying what you have learned, create and modify additional shapes to create a basic face composed of two eyes, a round nose, and an elliptical mouth.

14. Hold down the [Shift] key, click each object to select it. Holding down the [Shift] key allows more than one object to be selected.

15. Right-click on any of the selected objects, and click **Group**>**Group** in the shortcut menu. A single bounding box is displayed around all of the objects.

16. Click and hold on any of the objects, and drag to move it. All objects in the face should act as one object instead of several separate objects.

17. Click and drag one of the resizing handles for the group. All objects in the group are resized at the same time and in the same proportion.

18. Save the presentation as *LastName_*Group in your working folder, and submit it for grading.

Lesson 9

Graphing Game Coordinates

Learning Objectives

After completing this lesson, you will be able to:

- plot two-dimensional points within an X and Y axis system.
- explain path movement and nodes.
- use ordered pair notation.
- apply algebraic thinking skills to solve for relative locations.
- create a path.

Situation

The Awesome Game Company has noticed that some of its designers are not proficient using absolute and relative coordinates. Being able to determine absolute and relative coordinate locations is an important fundamental skill to develop for video game design. Training has been developed to provide practice using these skills, and you have been asked to complete this training.

How to Begin

1. Before beginning this lesson, download the 2D game coordinate system grid from the student companion website (www.g-wlearning.com). You could also choose to complete this activity on a sheet of graph paper.
2. On the coordinate grid, label the X and Y axes.

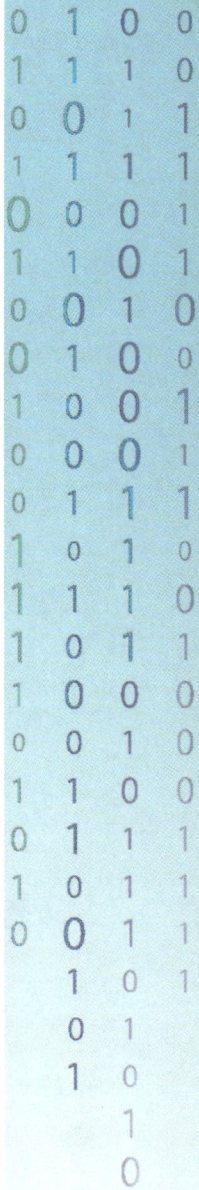

Name: _____

Date: _____

Class: _____

3. Use the absolute location of the ordered pairs listed below to plot the points on the coordinate grid. Plot the points sequentially according to the point order. Each stopping point on a path is called a *node*. Draw a line from one node to the next as you plot them to create the shape outline.

Point Order	Absolute Coordinate	Point Order	Absolute Coordinate	Point Order	Absolute Coordinate	Point Order	Absolute Coordinate
1	(27, 11)	12	(20, 6)	23	(6, 7)	34	(11, 30)
2	(28, 10)	13	(20, 4)	24	(3, 8)	35	(18, 30)
3	(28, 8)	14	(18, 2)	25	(2, 10)	36	(20, 29)
4	(27, 8)	15	(15, 2)	26	(3, 13)	37	(23, 27)
5	(26, 9)	16	(13, 4)	27	(5, 14)	38	(25, 25)
6	(26, 10)	17	(12, 6)	28	(3, 16)	39	(28, 20)
7	(27, 11)	18	(12, 7)	29	(2, 19)	40	(28, 16)
8	(26, 12)	19	(13, 9)	30	(2, 22)	41	(27, 15)
9	(23, 10)	20	(11, 9)	31	(3, 25)	42	(26, 12)
10	(21, 9)	21	(9, 11)	32	(6, 27)		
11	(18, 9)	22	(8, 9)	33	(9, 29)		

4. Using the relative coordinates given below, find the rest of the points for the next shape. All points are relative to location (21, 9), *not* the previous point. Use algebraic thinking to solve for the absolute location of each point by adding or subtracting the relative values from the values of the starting point. Draw a line between nodes as you plot them to create the shape outline.

Point Order	Relative Location	Absolute Location	Point Order	Relative Location	Absolute Location
1	(0, 0)	(21, 9)	6	(6, –3)	
2	(1, –9)		7	(7, –6)	
3	(3, –7)		8	(10, –7)	
4	(4, –4)		9	(11, –7)	
5	(5, –7)		10	(7, –1)	

5. Using the relative coordinates given below, find the rest of the points for the next shape. All points are relative to the location (11, 23), *not* the previous point. Draw a line between nodes as you plot them to create the shape outline.

Point Order	Relative Location	Absolute Location	Point Order	Relative Location	Absolute Location
1	(0, 0)	(11, 23)	11	(–2, –5)	
2	(–2, 1)		12	(–2, –3)	
3	(–3, 1)		13	(0, 0)	
4	(–6, 0)		14	(2, 3)	
5	(–8, –2)		15	(5, 4)	
6	(–8, –3)		16	(8, 3)	
7	(–7, –5)		17	(10, –1)	
8	(–4, –7)		18	(7, 1)	
9	(–3, –7)		19	(3, 1)	
10	(–1, –6)		20	(0, 0)	

6. Using the relative coordinates given below, find the rest of the points for the next shape. All points are relative to the location (10, 17), *not* the previous point. Draw a line between nodes as you plot them to create the shape outline.

Point Order	Relative Location	Absolute Location	Point Order	Relative Location	Absolute Location
1	(0, 0)	(10, 17)	10	(13, 3)	
2	(2, –3)		11	(14, 4)	
3	(5, –4)		12	(16, 3)	
4	(8, –4)		13	(17, 2)	
5	(11, –2)		14	(17, 1)	
6	(11, –1)		15	(14, –5)	
7	(13, 1)		16	(11, –4)	
8	(13, 3)		17	(11, –2)	
9	(11, 5)				

7. For the next shape, create a path where each point is relative to the previous point. Shown below is the starting point and the change in X and Y to move from one point to the next. Draw a line between nodes as you plot them to create the shape outline.

Point Order	Absolute Coordinates	Change in X to Next Node	Change in Y to Next Node
1	(6, 19)	–1	1
2		0	1
3		1	1
4		1	–1
5		0	–1
6		–1	–1
7	(6, 19)		

8. As you did for the last shape, draw the next shape by creating a path where each point is relative to the previous point. Shown below is the starting point and the change in X and Y to move from one point to the next. For point 7, you will need to calculate the change in X and Y as well as the absolute coordinates. Draw a line between nodes as you plot them to create the shape outline.

Point Order	Absolute Coordinates	Change in X	Change in Y
1	(24, 17)	1	–1
2		0	–1
3		–2	–1
4		–1	1
5		0	1
6		1	1
7			
8	(24, 17)		

9. For the next shape, you will use the slope of a line to calculate coordinates. The *slope* of a line is a ratio of the change in X over the change in Y (change X ÷ change Y). The formula $Y = m \times X + B$ can be used to plot a segment on the line with a given slope. The slope is *m*. B is the Y intercept, or the Y coordinate in the ordered pair for the given X coordinate. To solve for Y, multiply the slope (m) times the X value from the ordered pair and add the Y intercept (B).

Node	Point	Y	m	X	B
1	(12, 18)	18	1	12	6
2	(14, 17)	17	1	14	3
3			1	15	4
4			2	15	−9
5			1/2	14	15
6			−1/2	13	28.5
7			1/4	12	17
8			1/4	12	15

10. Create the next shape by calculating the Y intercept given the X coordinate of the ordered pair and the slope of the line.

Node	Point	Y	m	X	B
1	(18, 17)	17	1	18	−1
2	(17, 19)	19	0	17	19
3			2	17	−14
4			1/9	18	19
5			−1/4	20	26
6			−1/7	21	22
7			4/40	20	15
8			2/3	18	5

11. Complete the table by solving for the missing information. Plot the points and connect them with lines to draw the shape.

Node	Point	Y	m	X	B
1			1	4	6
2		9	2		−1
3			2/3	6	5
4		10	2	7	
5		12	12/4		−9
6			2/12	6	13
7		12		4	0
8	(4, 10)	10	3/2		

12. Complete the table by solving for the missing information. Plot the points and connect them with lines to draw the shape.

Node	Point	Y	m	X	B
1			2/3	15	−1
2		6	1/2	14	
3			7/5	15	−17
4	(17, 4)				21
5		6		18	0
6	(17, 9)		0	17	
7		9	3/5		0

13. Locate the following points, but do *not* connect the nodes with lines. Shade the area in which each point is located using the color indicated to make the shapes look more like a character.

Point	Absolute Coordinate	Color
1	(25, 7)	Yellow
2	(27, 9)	Red
3	(12, 12)	Green
4	(16, 26)	Red
5	(6, 20)	Black
6	(23, 15)	Black
7	(16, 16)	Dark green
8	(6, 12)	Dark green
9	(16, 6)	Dark green

14. Submit your work for grading.

Spawning

Learning Objectives

After completing this lesson, you will be able to:

- explain how object movement synchronization is achieved in a game.

- describe animated sprites and moving targets.

- create custom sprite art and animation direction nodes.

- program object spawning.

Situation

The Awesome Game Company has decided to hire you as an intern for its 2D game development division. In order to be assigned higher-level tasks, you must first learn how object movement is created for a game. After learning about motion, you will be assigned a custom game build to put this knowledge into practice.

Reading Materials

Object movement in a game is created in one of three different ways: transportation, animation, and spawning. If you think of the video games you have played, movement within each game falls into one of these categories.

Transportation

In the Click Ball game created in Lesson 3, you made a ball move and bounce on the screen. This form of movement is transportation. In the simplest definition, *transportation* is moving an object from one location to another. An attribution set is associated with the transportation process. An ***attribute set*** is a collection of characteristics or features. The designer can manipulate characteristics such as direction, speed, acceleration, and deceleration. **Figure 10-1** shows how direction of an object can be manipulated in Clickteam Fusion 2.5.

Transportation attributes are easy to understand as they can be seen applied every day in the real world. Suppose you are standing on the sidewalk and a car is traveling down a road. The car's direction attribute is controlling how the car is transported from one position to the next. This may be from your left to your right. The direction attribute in this case is "move right." In this way,

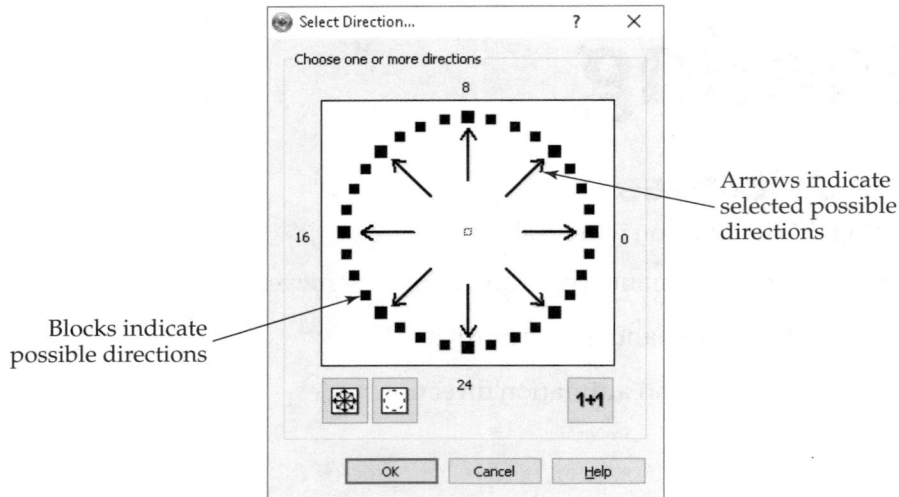

Figure 10-1. In this example, there are 32 possible directions the object can take. Of the possible directions, eight have been selected as possible solutions for the object.

direction determines the path the object will travel. Some game design software may use the term *vector* to describe the direction.

This same car also has a speed attribute. *Speed* is how fast something is moving. In engineering and physics, speed is referred to as *velocity.* Both words have the same meaning, and speed is used more frequently in game programming. If the car is obeying the speed limit of 50 miles per hour (mph), it would have a speed attribute of 50 mph. To calculate speed, use the formula:

$$velocity = distance \div time$$

In the example of the car, the car travels a distance of 50 miles in one hour. The formula works out such that 50 miles ÷ 1 hour = 50 miles/hour, or 50 miles per hour (mph).

Speed can change as the car is moving. The *instantaneous speed* is the exact speed the car is moving at the moment or instant you observe. If you drive down the street and a slow-moving bus gets in front of you, you will need to slow down. Your instantaneous speed might drop to 40 miles per hour until you can pass the bus. You may even speed up a bit to 60 miles per hour as you pass the bus. During your trip, your instantaneous speed may change as you drive through traffic and around corners. In the end, you may still have traveled 50 miles in one hour, but your instantaneous speed will have varied along the 50 mile journey.

To change the instantaneous speed of the car, the driver must press the accelerator pedal to speed up or the brake pedal to slow down. This applies additional force to the car, as shown in **Figure 10-2.** To speed up, the car must accelerate. To slow down, the car must decelerate.

Imagine that the car is stopped. A stopped car has no speed, or an instantaneous speed of 0. If the driver presses the accelerator pedal, the car begins to move. When observed two seconds later, it may be traveling at an instantaneous speed of 20 mph. Applying gas allowed the car to accelerate from 0 mph to 20 mph in two seconds.

Speeding up or changing the instantaneous speed in the positive direction is *acceleration.* In other words, the object is moving faster. Acceleration is calculated using the formula:

$$acceleration = distance \div time^2$$

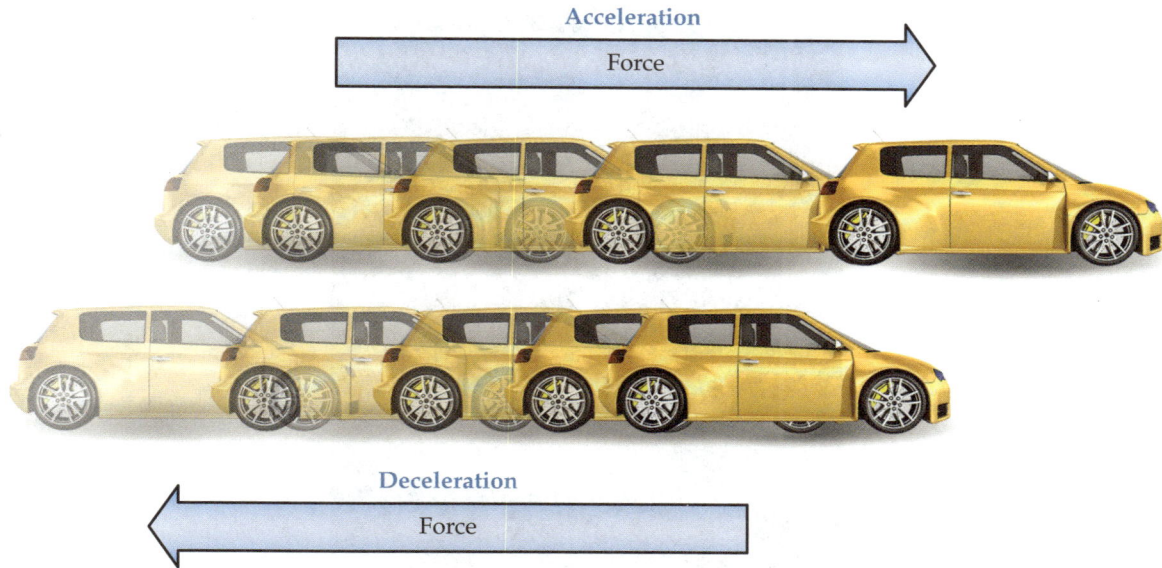

Goodheart-Willcox Publisher; rzymuR/Shutterstock.com

Figure 10-2. Force applied to an object creates acceleration and deceleration.

If the car accelerates from 0 mph to 20 mph, or .006 miles per second, in two seconds, the acceleration is .0015 miles per second^2 (.006 $\div$ 2^2 = .0015).

If the driver applies the brakes, the car will slow down. Slowing down or changing the instantaneous speed in the negative direction is ***deceleration.*** If a dog runs out into the path of the car, the driver slams on the brakes. The speed of the car might change from 30 mph to 0 mph in two seconds.

In game design, it is typical to apply the formulas of direction, speed, and acceleration using the virtual distances in the game. The game frame can be broken down into a grid, like you did in the first lesson. The regular spacing of the grid acts like real-life measurements. In the real world, a meter is 100 centimeters. In the virtual world, one grid section might be 10 pixels by 10 pixels. Just as the virtual world reduces the size of the real-world room, it must also reduce the time intervals to accurately match the scale. In most games, the time intervals are milliseconds, or 0.001 seconds.

Speed in a video game is calculated by how many pixels an object moves in each fraction of a second. If the software speed is calibrated so a speed setting of 1 moves five pixels per second, then it would take 20 seconds to move 100 pixels (100 pixels $\div$ 5 pixels/sec = 20 sec).

Animation

Animation is the creation of a series of images that quickly change to give the illusion of movement. This is similar to a flipbook animation where you draw a series of pictures in the corner of a notepad and then flip the pages to see the object animated. Game design software has some built-in animation features or you can create custom animations on your own and import them.

To animate a sprite is to make it appear to move. To accomplish this, the designer needs to create several animation frames. As you learned in Lesson 1, these images or frames form an animation set. On each frame, the sprite changes a small amount. If you need a sprite to walk, you need to create animation frames for each pose as the characters' arms and legs articulate. ***Articulation*** is the bending and positioning of movable parts. A human character may have articulated legs, arms, fingers, head, lips, eyelids, and many other parts, as shown in **Figure 10-3.**

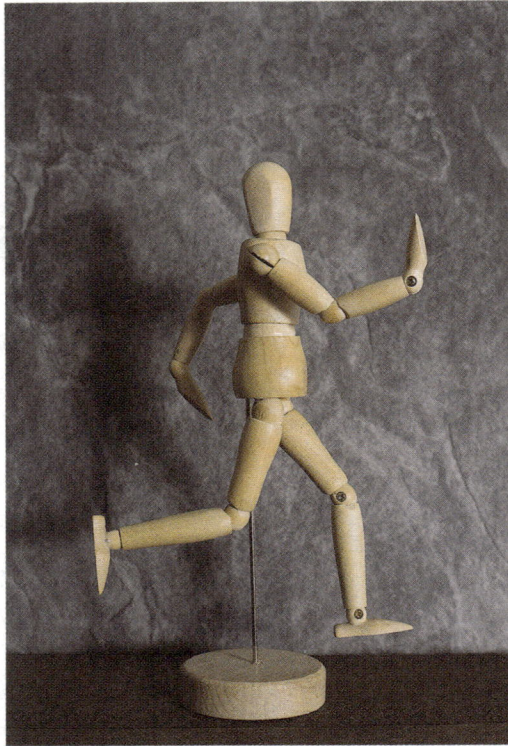

stalk/Shutterstock.com

Figure 10-3. Articulation of this artist figure at joints changes the shape of the character to different poses.

If an object is transported and animated, it is considered an ***active animation.*** An example of an active animation is a character walking where the limbs are articulated synchronized to the transportation to look realistic. ***Synchronizing*** is linking the timing of two events. In this case, the footstep animation distance must link with the transportation distance the object is moved. If the walking animation does not move the character the same distance as the footstep animation, the result will look odd and unnatural.

Spawning

The final object movement option is spawning. ***Spawning*** is the creation of an object within the game. When spawned, an object may be created in a random or set location or teleported to a new location. An obstacle, like a flying meteor, might be randomly spawned for the player to avoid. With a ***teleported*** object, the object is moved from one point within the game to another point. This might occur between levels or could just be an added feature to jump from one spot in the game to another. Teleporting is like using a magic doorway that takes the player to another place within the game. In the classic game of *Pac-Man,* when the player character leaves the right side of the room, it is teleported to the left side. This specific teleporting feature where an object moves from one side of the screen to the other side is called ***wrap.*** An object can teleport in many other ways in addition to wrap. The most common application of teleporting is when the player character is destroyed and is respawned or recreated at a checkpoint.

A ***checkpoint*** is an advancement point within a game that allows the player to teleport back to that point if damaged or destroyed. Without a checkpoint, the player would have to restart from the beginning of the game each time the player character is damaged. The checkpoint allows the player to stay interested in the game and avoid frustration of having to redo sections of the game already mastered.

Game Build

The Awesome Game Company wants to create a mini game that has a gravity element. This game will also need to have a very small file size as it will be exported for play on an Android device. A minimal number of objects must be used so the game will load quickly. The focus will be on gameplay, not on intense graphics.

Before beginning this lesson, go to the student companion website (www.g-wlearning.com), and download the asset files for this lesson. Place the downloaded files in your working folder.

How to Begin

1. Launch Clickteam Fusion 2.5 software, and begin a new application.
2. Save the file as *LastName*_Gravity_PC in your working folder.
3. Display the storyboard editor, and rename Frame 1 as Game Frame.
4. Applying what you have learned, create a new frame, and name it Winner Frame.
5. Create a third frame, and name it Title Frame.
6. Click the thumbnail for the Title Frame, drag it to above the thumbnail for the Game Frame, and drop it to reorder the frames. You could also drag and drop the branches in the **Workspace Toolbar** to rearrange frames. Place the frames in this order from top to bottom: Title Frame, Game Frame, Winner Frame.
7. Applying what you have learned, set the size for each frame to 640 by 480.
8. Display the Game Frame in the frame editor.
9. Applying what you have learned, open the file Spiko art.mfa downloaded from the student companion website, copy the Bonus 1 and HEDGEHOG objects from Frame 1, and paste them onto the Game Frame in your Gravity_PC application. Then, close the Spiko art.mfa file.
10. Move the objects to the side just outside the game frame.
11. Applying what you have learned, insert a new active object anywhere on the frame.
12. Rename the new object as Platform 1.
13. Set the position of Platform 1 to (0, 210), as shown in **Figure 10-4.**
14. Set the size of Platform 1 to 640 wide by 32 high.

Storyboard Editor

Frame Editor

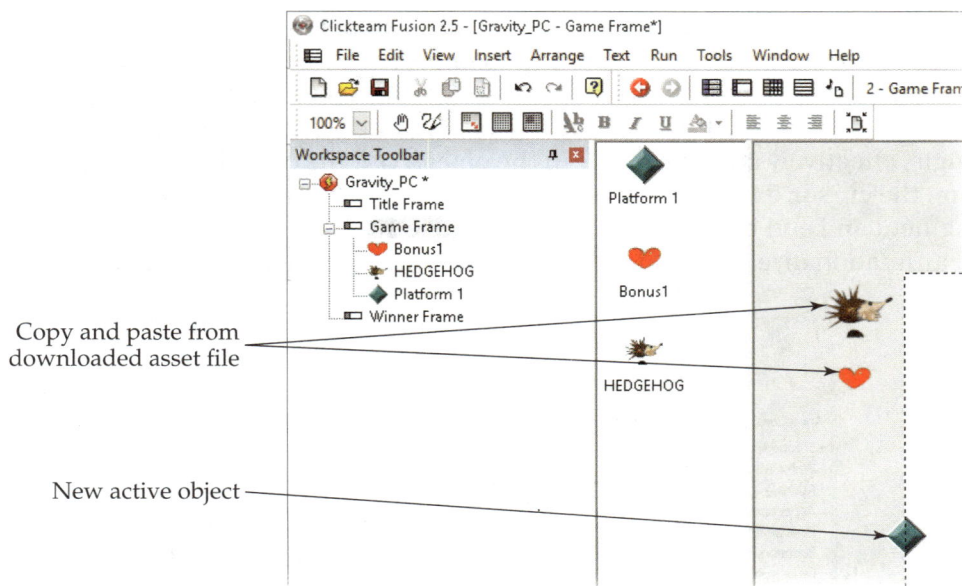

Copy and paste from downloaded asset file

New active object

Figure 10-4. Assets are copied and pasted from another file, and a new active object is placed on the frame.

Clear

View Hot Spot

Fill Tool

Animation Directions

15. Double-click the Platform 1 object to open it in the image editor.
16. Click the **Clear** button to start with a blank canvas.
17. Applying what you have learned, change the hotspot to the top-left corner.
18. Select a shade of green in the color palette that is close to the color of grass, and then use the **Fill Tool** to flood the entire canvas in that color. The sprite should look like a green square.
19. Click the **Frames** tab at the bottom of the image editor, right-click on Frame 1, and click **Copy** in the shortcut menu.
20. Locate the slider below the animation direction nodes. The slider controls the number of directions available for the animation set. Drag the slider to the far right to increase the number of direction nodes to 32, as shown in **Figure 10-5**.
21. Hover the cursor over each of the animation direction nodes to display the direction number for each node. Nodes are numbered starting with 0, which is the right-facing node. Numbers increase as you move from node to node in counterclockwise fashion.
22. Applying what you have learned, show only four animation direction nodes.
23. Click node 8 to select it. The arrow points to that node, and there are currently no sprites in the animation set. Notice that the node numbers are based on position, not how many nodes are displayed.
24. Right-click in the empty space in the **Frames** tab, and click **Paste** in the shortcut menu. A copy of the sprite from node 0 is added to the animation set for this direction.
25. Applying what you have learned, paste a copy of the sprite in the animation sets for nodes 16 and 24. Notice that all four nodes are now black. A black-filled node indicates there is content in that direction's animation set.

Editing Animation Frames

The game will use the Platform 1 object as platforms on which the player character will walk. A hole needs to be created in each of the platforms for the player to fall through to reach the platform below. The four animation directions will be used to achieve this with a single object.

26. Select animation direction node 0.
27. Click the **Rectangle Tool** button, and select the **Filled** option.

Rectangle Tool

28. Click the transparency swatch below the color palette (the checkerboard) to set the foreground to transparent. This will allow the tool to act as an eraser.
29. Move the cursor to (120, 0), click, drag to (255, 32), and release. This draws a transparent rectangle, effectively creating a hole in the object. Use the coordinate indicator to position the cursor. The Y coordinate does not need to be exact so long as you start above the segment and end below it, as shown in **Figure 10-6**.
30. Select animation direction node 8, and remove the segment from (0, 0) to (155, 32).

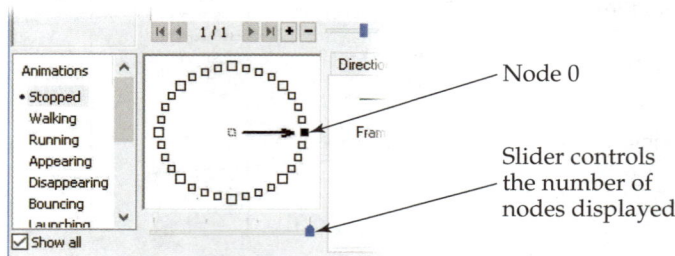

Node 0

Slider controls the number of nodes displayed

Goodheart-Willcox Publisher

Figure 10-5. The number of available direction nodes can be changed. Node 0 is to the right, and nodes are numbered in counterclockwise fashion.

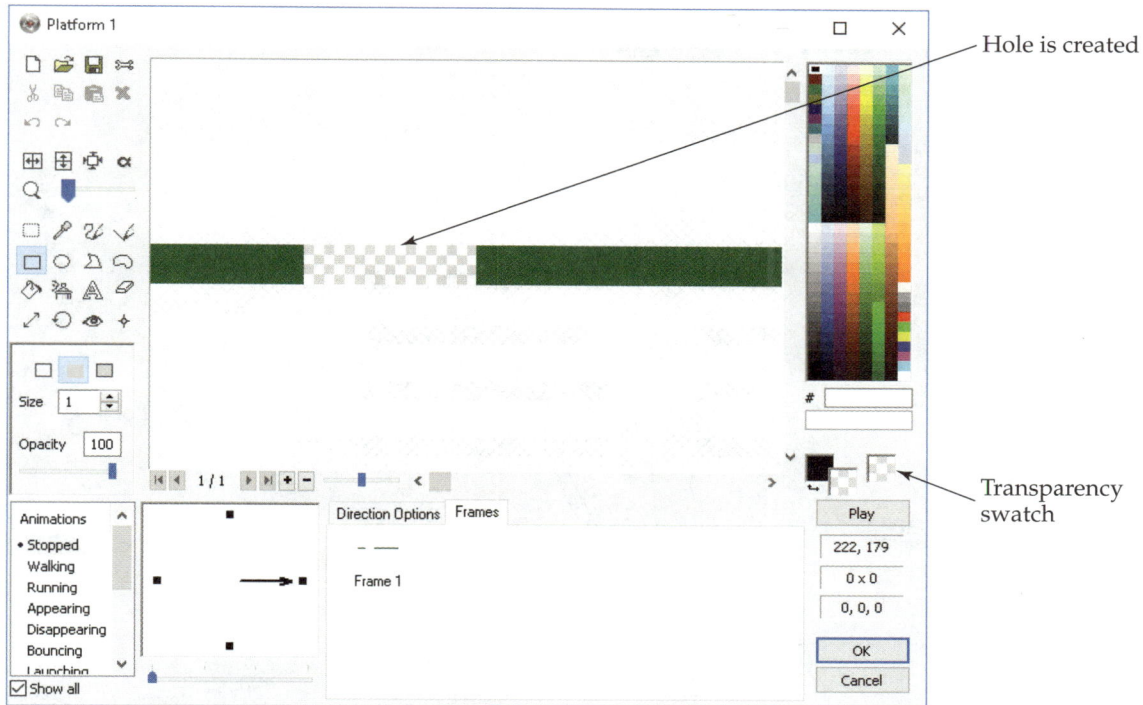

Hole is created

Transparency swatch

Goodheart-Willcox Publisher

Figure 10-6. A hole is created in the platform by setting a portion of it to transparent.

31. Select animation direction node 16, and remove the segment from (465, 0) to (640, 32).
32. Select animation direction node 24, and remove the segment from (400, 0) to (525, 32).
33. Click the **OK** button to close the image editor. The Platform 1 object now has four options to display a platform with a hole. Programming will be used to control which version is displayed.
34. If needed, reset the position of the Platform 1 object to (0, 210).

Avatar Movement

Spiko is the player avatar for this game. An ***avatar*** is a game object used to represent the player in the game. It is the player character. In this game, Spiko will need to move to lower platforms as the platforms move upward. If Spiko leaves the game frame, he will be destroyed.

35. Rename the HEDGEHOG object as Spiko, and set its position at (435, 208). This places Spiko two pixels above the platform.
36. Rename the Bonus 1 object as Heart, and set its position at (280, 195).
37. Applying what you have learned, clone the Platform 1 object. Create a single clone.
38. Rename the clone as Platform 2 if it is not already named that, and set its position at (0, 300). This places Platform 2 below Platform 1 with some space between them.
39. Applying what you have learned, copy the Platform 1 object, and paste one copy at (0, 390) and a second copy at (0, 480).
40. Copy the Heart object, and paste copies at (93, 286), (399, 374), and (191, 462), as shown in **Figure 10-7.**
41. Applying what you have learned, insert a Counter object, and name it Counter_Random.
42. Drag the Counter_Random object anywhere outside of the frame. This prevents the counter from being seen during gameplay.
43. Insert a Score object, and change its size to 32 wide and 50 high.
44. Set the position of the Score object at (640, 50).
45. Applying what you have learned, change the color of the number in each frame of the Score object to light blue.

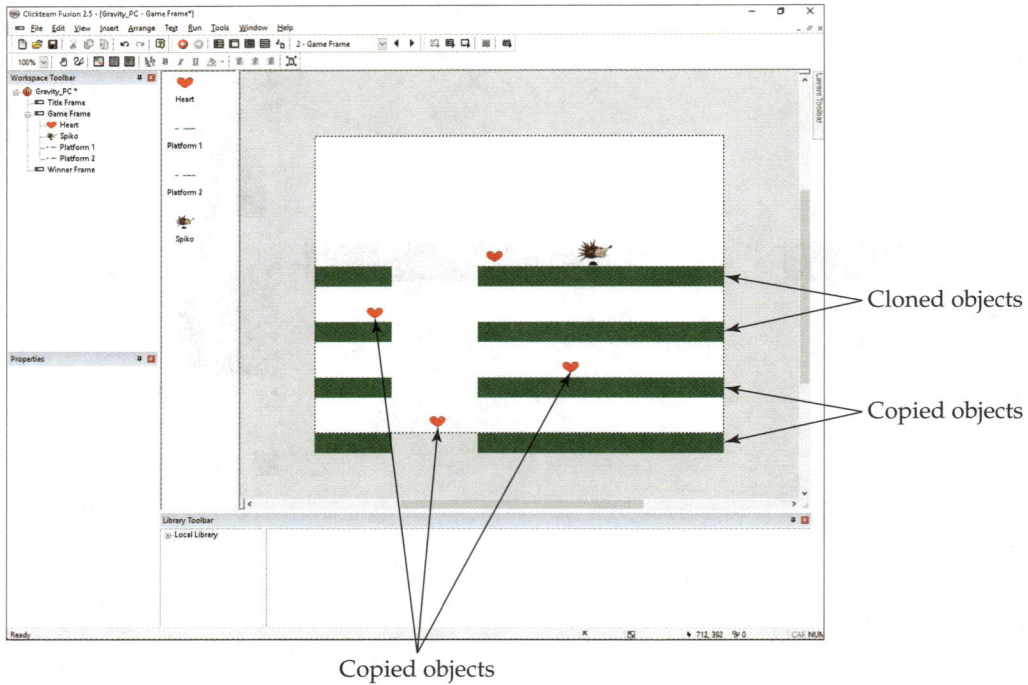

Goodheart-Willcox Publisher

Figure 10-7. A series of platforms and hearts are added to the frame by copying and pasting.

Movement

46. Select Spiko, and click the **Movement** tab in the **Properties** toolbar.
47. Change the Movement Type property to Platform.
48. Change the Initial direction property to direction 16, as shown in **Figure 10-8.**
49. Change the Speed property to 20.
50. Set Acceleration, Deceleration, Gravity, and Strength properties each to 50. By setting the Gravity and Strength properties to the same value, the character will not be able to jump. Spiko will not be able to jump in this game.

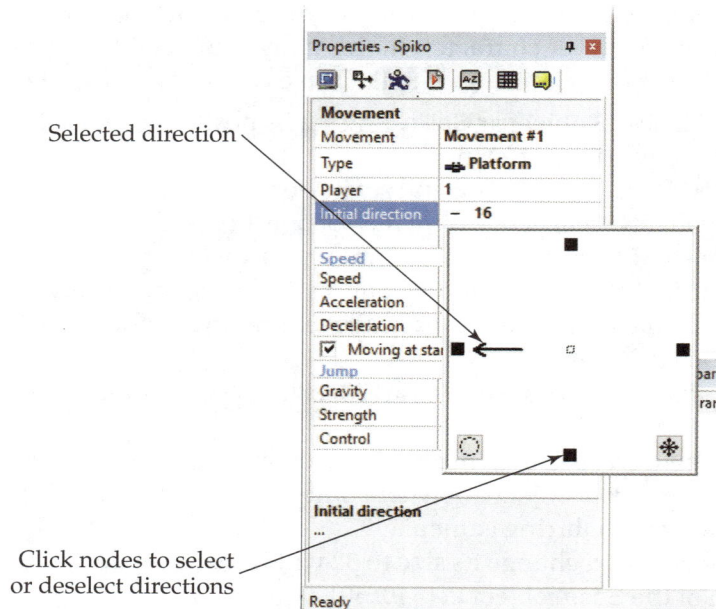

Goodheart-Willcox Publisher

Figure 10-8. The initial direction is set to left (direction 16).

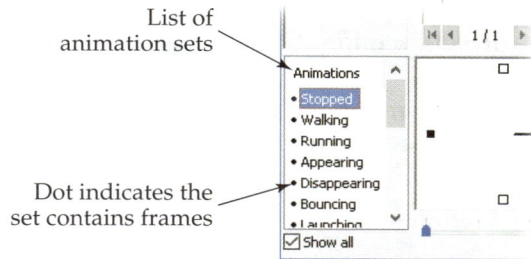

List of animation sets

Dot indicates the set contains frames

Goodheart-Willcox Publisher

Figure 10-9. A list of animation sets appears in the image editor. A dot to the left of the name means the animation set contains frames.

Custom Animation

The art department provided more animation sets than will be used for this game. The animation sets that will not be used need to be removed. This will help to avoid having a large file size or a lag in loading the game. Reducing the file size is a best practice to avoid loading more content than will be used in the game.

51. Open Spiko in the image editor, and locate the list of animation sets, as shown in **Figure 10-9.** Animation sets with a black dot to the left of the name contain frames. The only animation sets needed will be Stop and Walking.
52. Right-click on the Crouch down animation set, and click **Delete** in the shortcut menu. The frames in the animation set are completely removed, but the name remains.
53. Applying what you have learned, delete all animation sets *except* Stopped and Walking.
54. Select the Walking animation set.
55. Select animation direction node 0. This is the animation that should be displayed when the character is walking to the right.
56. Click the **Direction Options** tab to display the playback settings for the animation set, as shown in **Figure 10-10.**
57. Set the **Lower Speed** to 32, **Higher Speed** to 32, **Repeat** to 0, **Back to** to 4, and check the **Loop** check box. These settings will allow Spiko only one walking speed. If the **Lower Speed** and **Higher Speed** were different, Spiko would be able to accelerate. The **Back to** setting tells the computer where to begin looping the animation. In this case, the loop will start at the fourth frame in the animation.
58. Click the **Frames** tab, and examine the frames for this animation. Notice how a walking loop is achieved with only Frame 4 through Frame 15. Frame 1, Frame 2, and Frame 3 get Spiko started moving from a standing position that he does not return to when walking.

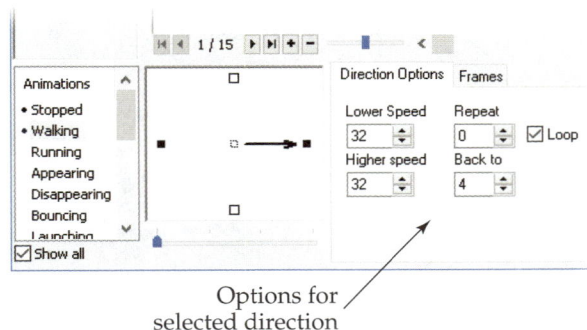

Options for selected direction

Goodheart-Willcox Publisher

Figure 10-10. The **Direction Options** tab in the image editor contains settings for the selected direction.

Run Frame

59. Applying what you have learned, set the **Lower Speed**, **Higher Speed**, **Repeat**, **Back to**, and **Loop** values for the direction node 16 (walking left) to the same as those used for the walking right animation

60. Click the **OK** button to close the image editor.

61. Run the frame to see how Spiko reacts to the game environment. Close the game window when done testing.

Bug Repair

Spiko fell right through the platforms! Remember, just because an object *looks* like a platform does not mean it will *act* like a platform. These objects need to be programmed to tell the computer they are solid objects and Spiko should not fall through them.

Event Editor

62. Open the Game Frame in event editor.

63. Program event line 1 to match this pseudocode:
    IF Spiko collides with the Platform 1 object,
        THEN Spiko's movement will stop.

64. Program event line 2 to match this pseudocode:
    IF Spiko collides with the Platform 2 object,
        THEN Spiko's movement will stop.

Run Frame

65. Run the frame to see if Spiko can walk on the platform without falling through it. Spiko should also fall through the hole in the platform. Close the game window when done testing.

Platform Movement

This game will have unlimited gameplay. That means that the game map will never end. To accomplish this, the platforms will have to move and respawn. The Heart objects should also move along with the platforms. By matching the upward motion settings of the platforms, the Heart objects will appear to be in the same position relative to the platforms.

Event Editor

66. Display the event editor for the Game Frame.

67. Applying what you have learned, program this pseudocode to move the platform up one pixel each time the game runs through the programming loop:
    IF always,
        THEN set the position of Platform 1 to (0, –1) relative to itself.

68. Program the Platform 2 object to match the movement of the Platform 1 object. Note: a new event line does not need to be added, as shown in **Figure 10-11.**

Run Frame

69. Run the frame. Notice how Spiko moves up with the platforms, but the hearts do not. Close the game window when done testing.

70. Applying what you have learned, program the movement of the hearts to match that of the platforms.

71. Test the frame, and debug if needed.

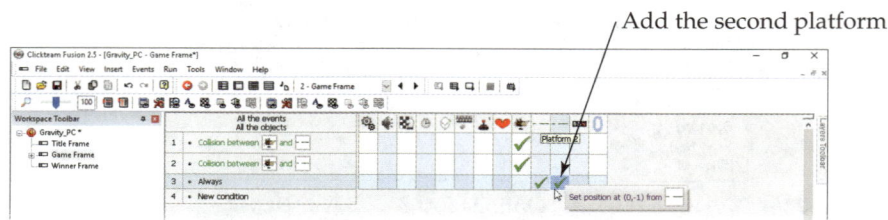

Add the second platform

Goodheart-Willcox Publisher

Figure 10-11. The programming to move the Platform 2 object can be combined with the programming for the Platform 1 object.

Random Number Generator

Random numbers are used throughout video games, from spawning enemies to changing environmental effects, determining which cards are drawn, rolling dice, varying the likelihood of hitting an enemy, and many more applications. The platforms are designed to be different with the hole in different locations. A random number generator will select a number that will be used to vary the random animation direction. This will make different platforms appear in the game. The gameplay will be new each time the game is played. The function random is a computer programming method that randomly selects a number from the set defined by the number specified in the parentheses. The first number available is always 0. In this case, there are four animation directions, so the computer needs to randomly choose from 0, 1, 2, and 3.

72. Open the Game Frame in the event editor.
73. In event line for the Always condition, right-click in the cell below the Counter_Random icon, and click **Set Counter** in the shortcut menu. The expression editor is displayed.
74. Enter random(4) in the expression editor, as shown in **Figure 10-12.**
75. Click the **OK** button to set the expression. Note: if an error message appears, check that you spelled *random* correctly, and try again.
76. Verify the programming matches this pseudocode:
    IF always,
        THEN set Counter_Random to a value from 0 to 3.

Spawning

Spawning is the creation of a new object. This game will spawn new platforms and hearts to keep the gameplay going.

77. Applying what you have learned, add a new condition. In the **New Condition** dialog box, right-click on the **Timer** icon, and click **Every** in the shortcut menu. The **Every** dialog box is displayed.
78. Change the time setting to 1.70 seconds. You will have to use both the **Second(s)** and the **1/100** text boxes to make that setting.
79. Click the **OK** button to apply the setting.
80. On the event line for every 1.70 seconds, right-click in the cell below the **Create new objects** icon, and click **Create Object** in the shortcut menu.

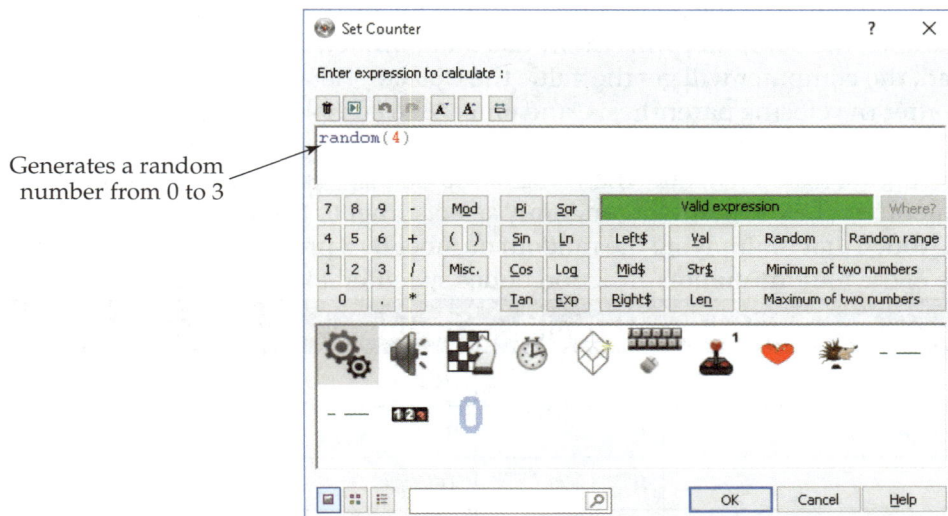

Generates a random number from 0 to 3

Goodheart-Willcox Publisher

Figure 10-12. The expression editor can be used to create code that generates a random number.

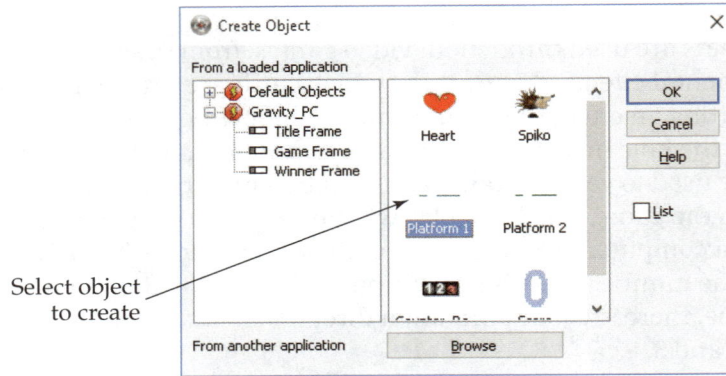

Goodheart-Willcox Publisher

Figure 10-13. When programming spawning, select which object will be created (spawned).

81. In the **Create Object** dialog box, select the Platform 1 object, as shown in **Figure 10-13.** Then, click the **OK** button. The frame editor is displayed for you to select where the object is to be created.
82. Applying what you have learned, set the absolute position at (0, 480).
83. Test the frame to see if the platforms spawn and move up. Note: the Platform 2 object will move off the screen, but it will not spawn. The only platform that needs to spawn is the Platform 1 object. Close the game window when done testing.

Run Frame

Setting a Random Platform

The Counter_Random object has been set to generate a random number. This number will be used in a formula to select the animation direction for the Platform 1 object. In effect, this randomizes where the hole will be in each platform.

84. On the event line for every 1.70 seconds, right-click in the cell below the icon for the Platform 1 object, and click **Animation>Change>Direction of animation…** in the shortcut menu.
85. In the **Direction of Animation** dialog box, click the **Calculate Direction** button (1+1) to display the expression editor.
86. Right-click on the icon for the Counter_Random object at the bottom of the expression editor, and click **Current value** in the shortcut menu. The code value ("Counter_Random") is added to the expression. This code means use the **value** method, which tells the computer to start looking for a value. The item inside the parentheses is the value. If this is a number, the computer will simply use that number, but by adding "Counter_Random" instead, the computer will get the value the Counter_Random object is currently holding.
87. Click after the closing parenthesis, and enter *8 to complete the expression, as shown in **Figure 10-14.** The asterisk (*) is a multiplication symbol (×) in computer applications. The complete expression will take the value of the Counter_Random object and multiply it by 8. Remember, the counter will randomly select either 0, 1, 2, or 3. Examine the following table. Notice that multiplying the random number by 8 produces a number corresponding to one of the four animation direction nodes specified for the Platform 1 object.

Counter_Random **Value**	**Multiplier**	**Resulting Value**	**Animation Direction**
0	8	0	Right
1	8	8	Up
2	8	16	Left
3	8	24	Down

88. Click the **OK** button to add the expression.

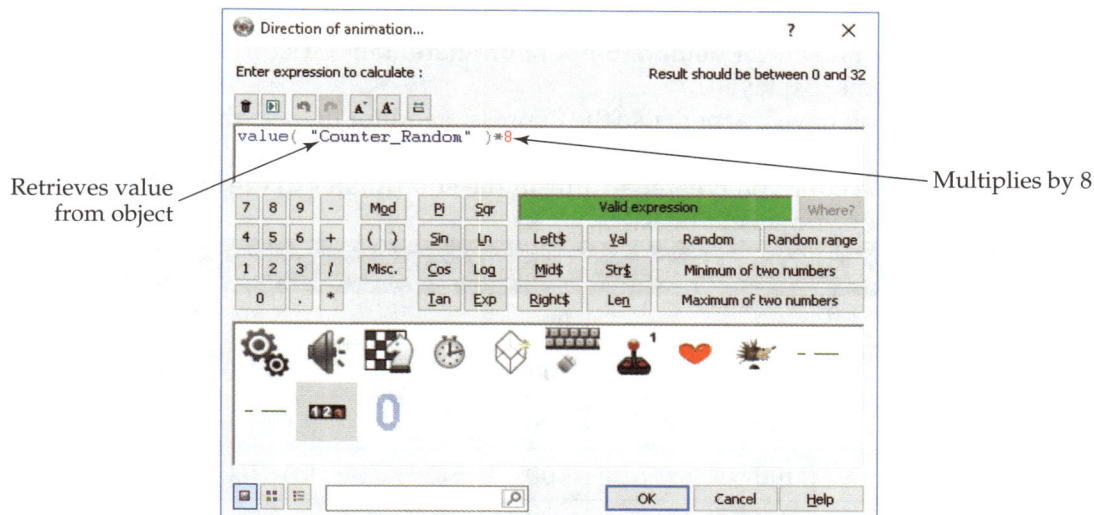

Retrieves value
from object

Multiplies by 8

Figure 10-14. The value retrieved from the Counter_Random object will be multiplied by 8 and the result used in the programming.

89. Test to see if the platforms now have holes in random locations. Note: it may take a few spawns to see all four possible platform configurations. Close the game window when done testing.

90. Debug if needed.

Rewarding the Player

The heart objects will be randomly generated to float above each new platform. Rewards encourage the player to do well and take risks. Right now the player gets to the heart, but nothing happens. You need to get the hearts to award points to reward the player for taking the risk to get the heart.

91. Display the Game Frame in the event editor, and program a new event to match this pseudocode:

>   **IF** Spiko collides with the Heart object,
>
>>   **THEN** destroy the Heart object
>>
>>>   **AND** add 1 point to the player 1 score.

92. Test the frame. Check that the heart is removed and the score is adding up. Debug if needed. If the score is not adding up, be sure the code is *adding* to the score, not *setting* the score.

93. Applying what you have learned, modify an existing event to match this pseudocode:

>   **IF** every 1.70 seconds,
>
>>   **THEN** create a new Heart object at (0, 540).

94. Test the frame. See if hearts are spawned. Note: the hearts will all appear on the left side, but should not overlap a platform. Close the game window when done testing.

95. Debug as needed.

Setting a Random Horizontal Position

The hearts are being spawned, but in a terrible position. The hearts should spawn in random locations to make the game fun and exciting. This requires the X coordinate for each heart to be a random value. However, the Y coordinate must remain the same so the hearts will always float above the platform.

96. Display the Game Frame in the event editor.

97. On the event line for every 1.70 seconds, right-click in the cell below the icon for the Heart object, and click **Position>Set X coordinate...** in the shortcut menu. The expression editor is displayed.

98. Applying what you have learned, use the expression editor to have the computer choose a random number between 0 and 5 and multiply that value by 100, as shown in **Figure 10-15.** The code you created results in the coordinates in the table below. Notice that only the X coordinate changes.

Random Value	Multiplier	Resulting Value	Generated Position
0	100	0	(0, 540)
1	100	100	(100, 540)
2	100	200	(200, 540)
3	100	300	(300, 540)
4	100	400	(400, 540)
5	100	500	(500, 540)
6	100	600	(600, 540)

99. Test the frame. See if the hearts now are randomly spread out when spawned. Close the game window when done testing.

Run Frame

100. Debug as needed.

Creating Risk

Now that the game has rewards, it needs to have some risk. Without risk, the player would have little interest to keep playing.

101. Display the Game Frame in the event editor.

102. Applying what you have learned, add a new event. In the **New Condition** dialog box, right-click on Spiko, and click **Position>Test position of "Spiko"** in the shortcut menu. The **Test Position** dialog box is displayed, as shown in **Figure 10-16.**

103. Hover the cursor over the arrow buttons to show the help text. Note the name of each button.

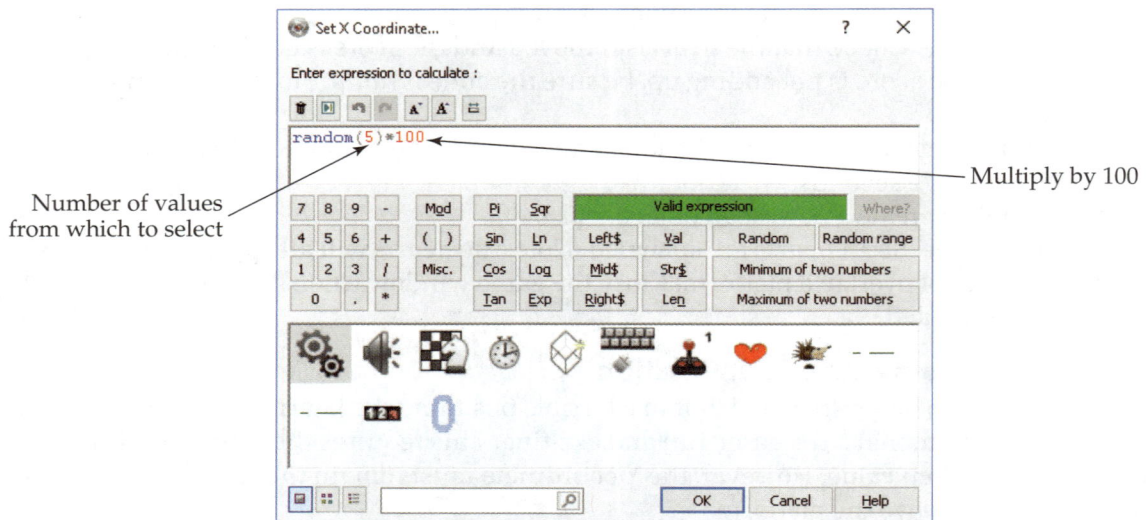

Number of values from which to select

Multiply by 100

Figure 10-15. Specifying a value instead of an object with the random function defines the range of numbers from which the computer will select starting with 0.

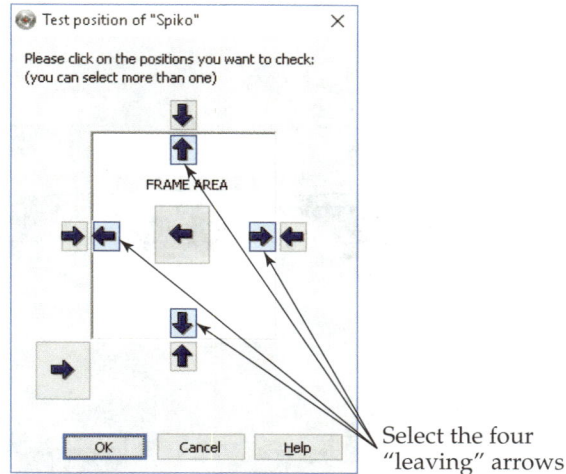

Goodheart-Willcox Publisher

Figure 10-16. Selecting which areas to test for the object's position as it enters or leaves the frame.

104. Select only the **Leaves in the bottom?**, **Leaves in the top?**, **Leaves in the left?**, and **Leaves in the right?** arrows. The button for a selected arrow will be blue.

105. Click the **OK** button to create the condition **IF** Spiko leaves the play area.

106. For the condition just added, program the actions needed to match this pseudocode:
     THEN destroy Spiko
       AND go to the next frame.

107. Test the frame. Check that the frame ends if Spiko exits the play area on any side.

108. Debug as needed.

Run Frame

Title and Winner Screens

A game should always start with some direction on how to play the game. For this game, you will create a title screen to tell the player the name of the game and to give basic directions for how to play. The game also needs a winner screen to display high scores and to cleanly end the game.

109. Display the Title Frame in the frame editor.

110. Applying what you have learned, add a **Play** button that will advance to the next frame and a **Quit** button that will end the application.

111. Design a decorative layout for the frame. Use a background from the library, or experiment with the Backdrop object to use your own image.

112. Add text boxes to explain how to play the game.

113. With the Title Frame displayed in the frame editor, expand the tree for the Game Frame in the **Workspace Toolbar.**

114. Click the Heart object in the tree in the **Workspace Toolbar**, drag it to the Title Frame in the editor window, and drop, as shown in **Figure 10-17.** This copies the object to the Title Frame. Placing game objects on the title screen is a good way to let the player see what will be present during gameplay. The movement of an object can be changed on each level (frame) without affecting the same object on a different level. Movement settings are local to the frame.

115. Complete the design of the title screen using your imagination.

116. Display the Winner Frame in the frame editor.

117. Set the background color of the frame to black or other dark color of your choice.

118. Applying what you have learned, drag the Score leaf from the Game Frame tree, and drop it onto the Winner Frame in the upper-right corner.

Drag and drop the
object onto the frame

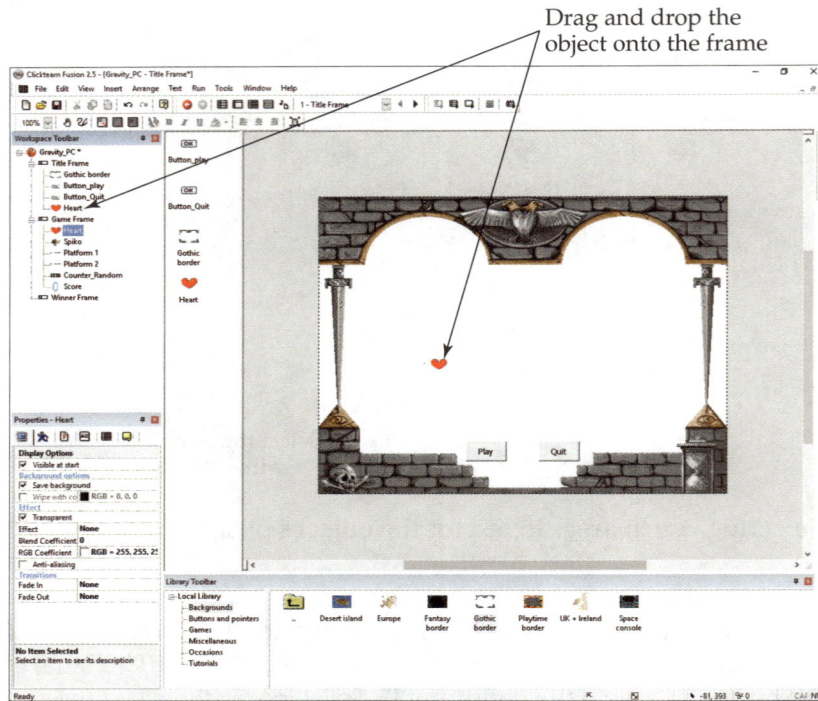

Figure 10-17. Objects can be dragged and dropped between frames using the tree in the
Workspace Toolbar.

119. Add a String object that reads: Number of Hearts Collected. Position, size, and format the
object on the frame as appropriate to be a label for the score.
120. Applying what you have learned, add a Hi-Score object. Format the text as appropriate.
121. Add a **Quit** button that will end the application.
122. Add a **Replay** button that will restart the application.
123. Display the storyboard editor.
124. Applying what you have learned, set entry and exit transitions of your choice for all
frames.
125. Run the application. Fully test all frames.
126. Debug as needed.

**Storyboard
Editor**

**Run
Application**

Tuning

The computer will track the movement and position of objects even if they are outside
the viewable area. To reduce the amount of processor load, or work the computer processor
is doing, the objects outside the viewable area should be destroyed. This will help the game
run without lag on a mobile device. The game should also be debugged for visual clarity.
This means inspecting the game to see that objects can all be seen properly, text is readable,
and objects are in the correct stacking order and fixing any issues. For example, on the Game
Frame, the Score object gets covered by platforms during gameplay and cannot be seen. This
needs to be fixed.

127. Display the Game Frame in the event editor.
128. Add a new event, and program this pseudocode:
 IF the Platform 1 object leaves the play area from the top,
 THEN destroy the Platform 1 object.
129. Similarly, program the Platform 2 and Heart objects to be destroyed when no longer
needed.

130. Test the frame. Notice that the platforms and hearts now disappear when they touch the top of the screen. This may not be easy to see.

131. Display the Game Frame in the frame editor.

Run Frame

132. Right-click on the Score object in the editor window, and click **Order>To Front** in the shortcut menu. This moves the object to the top level. It will appear in front of all other objects.

133. Applying what you have learned, add appropriate sounds to the game interactions. Use sounds supplied in the Clickteam Fusion 2.5 Samples folder or locate your own free-use sound files.

134. Run the application, and fully test the game.

135. Debug other issues of visual clarity or any other issues you find.

Run Application

136. Build the game as HTML 5.

137. Save your work.

138. Collect all files, and submit all materials for grading.

Vocabulary

Write a definition for each of the key terms from this lesson. You will develop a personal glossary of key terms throughout this course.

transportation

_____

_____

attribute set

_____

_____

direction

_____

_____

vector

_____

_____

speed

_____

_____

velocity

_____

_____

instantaneous speed

_____

_____

acceleration

_____

_____

deceleration

_____

_____

animation

_____

_____

articulation

_____

_____

active animation

_____

_____

synchronizing

_____

_____

spawning

_____

_____

teleported

_____

_____

wrap

_____

_____

checkpoint

_____

_____

avatar

_____

_____

Name: _____

Review Questions

1. What is the velocity of a car that traveled 345 miles in five hours and 45 minutes? Show your work.

_____

_____

_____

_____

_____

Mathematics

2. If you drove a car and maintained an instantaneous speed of 40 mph for 20 minutes, 50 mph for 30 minutes, and 60 mph for 10 minutes, how far would you have traveled in one hour? Show your work.

_____

_____

_____

_____

_____

Mathematics

3. Setting which two parameters to the same amount in Clickteam Fusion 2.5 will make it impossible for a character with the platform movement to jump?

_____

_____

_____

_____

_____

Applied Technology

4. How does a checkpoint help eliminate player frustration?

_____

_____

_____

_____

Social Science

5. Is a wrap movement realistic or unrealistic? Why or why not?

_____

_____

_____

_____

_____

Science

Higher-Order Thinking Strategies

Science

6. Describe how virtual world physics such as speed and acceleration are simulated in a virtual world like a video game.

_____

_____

_____

_____

_____

Applied Technology

7. A character moves left at a speed of 60. It seems to move its feet much faster than it is traveling across the screen. What would you do to solve this?

_____

_____

_____

_____

Language Arts

8. For the game build in this lesson, summarize why the Spiko walking animation loops back to frame 4 instead of frame 1.

_____

_____

_____

_____

_____

Social Science

9. Research a world map, and determine the best vector to travel by airplane from Perth, Australia to Colombo, Sri Lanka. Assume that east is direction 0 and use 360 degrees to create the vector. Which directional vector would you use?

_____

_____

_____

_____

Mathematics

10. Complete the table below. Find the multiplier needed to convert the random values into resulting values. Use the expression random(3) to create the counter random values. The multiplier is the same for all values.

Counter Random Value	Multiplier	Resulting Value
		0
		22

Office Technology Integration

Creating PowerPoint Frame Animation

1. Launch Microsoft Excel or other spreadsheet software, and open the vocabulary spreadsheet you updated in the last lesson.
2. Applying what you have learned, add a new worksheet, and name it Lesson 10.
3. Add each of the vocabulary words and definitions from the Vocabulary section of this lesson.
4. Save the spreadsheet, and then close it.
5. Launch Microsoft PowerPoint, start a new blank presentation, and save the file as *LastName*_FrameAnimation in your working folder.
6. Change the layout so the slide is blank with no text boxes.
7. Insert an oval shape, and set its size to 1.0 inch by 1.0 inch.
8. Move the circle so that its center is at the top-left corner of the slide. The object will be partially off of the slide.
9. Draw a rectangle at the bottom of the slide. Make it as wide as the slide and .7 inches tall. Change the fill color to brown and remove the outline.
10. Click the **View** tab in the ribbon. In the **Show** group, check the **Gridlines** check box to display the grid.
11. Copy the circle and place the copy to fit in the grid square that is over one and down two from the top-left corner.
12. Create eight additional copies and place them as shown. Three of the circles should be just touching the rectangle.

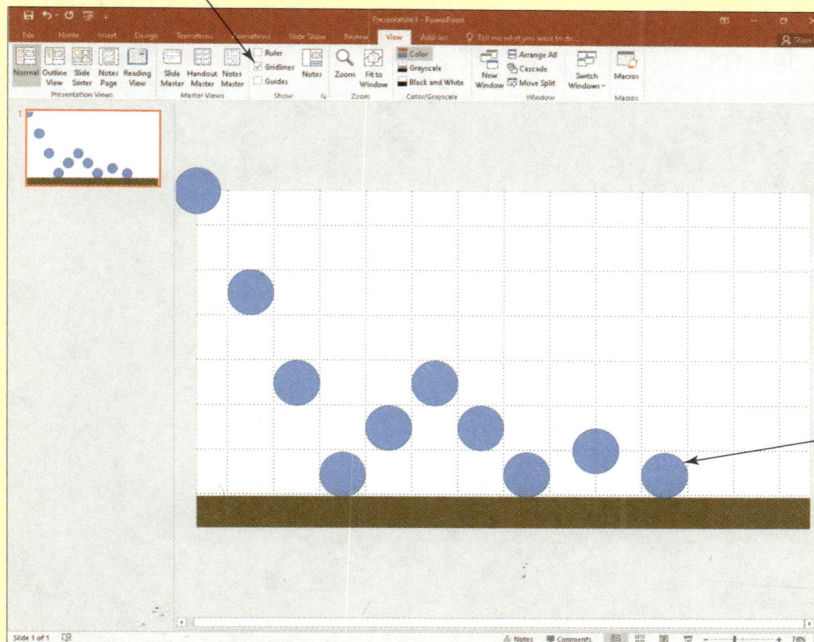

Goodheart-Willcox Publisher

13. Right-click on the mini slide in slide sorter on the left, and click **Copy** in the shortcut menu. Right-click again, and click the **Use Destination Theme** button in the **Paste Options** section of the shortcut menu. Paste nine copies so there is a total of ten slides. Each slide will be one frame in the animation.

14. On slide 1, change the fill color of the top-left circle into red with no outline, and delete all other circles from the slide to leave only the red circle.

15. On slide 2, change the color of the second circle to red, and delete all other circles.

16. Continue the process of recoloring the next circle in sequence on the next slide and deleting all the other circles through slide 10.

17. Click the **Transitions** tab on the ribbon. In the **Timing** group, click in the **Duration:** text box, and enter 00.25. Click in the **After:** text box under **Advance Slide**, and enter 00:00.50. Make sure the corresponding check box is checked. Click the **Apply to All** button to make all ten slides have the same transitions.

From Beginning

18. Click **Slide Show**>**Start Slide Show**>**From Beginning** on the ribbon to see the frame-by-frame animation. The current settings advance one slide every half (.5) second. As such, this creates a frame rate of 2, or 2 frames per second (fps).

19. Applying what you have learned, change the frame rate to 5. Not five seconds, five frames per second. Be sure to apply the change in settings to all slides. Play the slide show to see how that changes the animation.

20. Change the frame rate to 20, and play the slide show. How does changing the frame rate affect the animation?

21. Submit your work for grading.

Lesson 11

Software Ratings

Learning Objectives

After completing this lesson, you will be able to:

- evaluate the quality of your own work and the work of others.
- assess positive aspects of the playability and functionality of a game.
- provide constructive criticism to peers by suggesting possible solutions to problems.

Situation

The Awesome Game Company would like you and a colleague to review the game built in Lesson 10. The results of the review will be used to create a game critique that will be posted to the company website and blog space on the Internet. Complete an evaluation report on the playability and functionality of the game. Each member of the design team needs to evaluate the product and suggest reasons why each item achieves or does not achieve the objective. Be accurate and complete in your evaluations. The personal and peer evaluation are for the same game by the same designer. That means you must give your personal evaluation to a classmate for them to complete the peer evaluation for your game on the same page as your personal evaluation.

Reading Material

The ***Entertainment Software Rating Board (ESRB)*** is the nonprofit, self-regulatory body that assigns age and content ratings for computer and video games, enforces industry-adopted advertising guidelines, and helps ensure responsible online privacy practices for the interactive entertainment software industry. The ESRB ratings provide concise and impartial information about the content and age-appropriateness of computer and video games so consumers, especially parents, can make an informed purchase decision.

ESRB ratings have two equal parts:
- ***Rating symbols*** are found on the front of virtually every game package available for sale in the US and Canada and suggest age appropriateness for the game.
- ***Content descriptors*** are displayed on the back of the game package to indicate elements in a game that may have triggered a particular rating and/or may be of interest or concern.

These ratings are similar to the MPAA ratings assigned to movies in that both systems provide parents with guidance as to whether content is

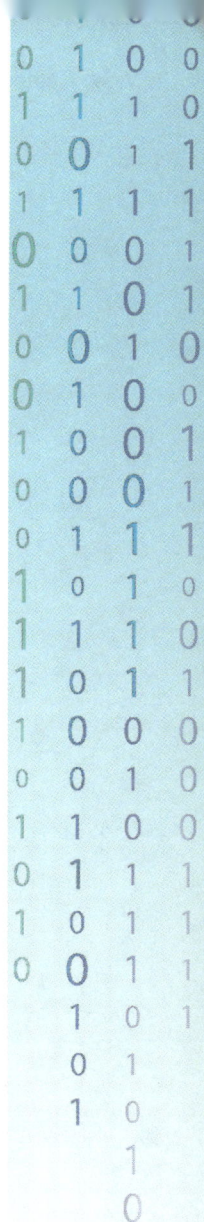

Name: _____

Date: _____

Class: _____

appropriate for various ages. Just like movie ratings, the ESRB ratings are not legally binding, and having a game rated is voluntary.

In addition to the ESRB ratings, parents and players can get information about a game from professional critics and game reviews. A **critic** is someone who evaluates a game and writes a review for others to read. A **game review** is the written opinion and evaluation about the good and bad qualities of a game. Some game websites and magazines hire critics to write game reviews and articles about new games. This gives a reader the chance to learn more about the game and helps decide if it is a game they would like to buy and play.

When writing a game review, the critic will evaluate a game based on several key features to determine how well the game was made. In many cases, critics use a five-star rating system. The **five-star rating system** is a scale of one star to five stars, one star meaning poor and five stars meaning excellent. This is very similar to the letter grades you receive in school. A letter grade of A would be the same as five stars and a letter grade of F would be the same as one star. The five-star rating system helps the critic quickly convey the overall quality of a game on the key features.

In addition to professional critics are nonprofessional critics. The nonprofessionals are not paid or hired by a company to write a review. In most cases, these are user reviews. A **user review** is a game review written by a game player (user). When players like a game, they can post user reviews on a website to tell others how awesome the game is. These reviews do not usually follow the five-star rating system, nor do they focus on evaluating key features. In many cases, user reviews are simply comments related to what the players liked or did not like about the game.

A game beta tester will write a user review that also includes possible improvements to the game. These testers can provide not only evaluation, but also ideas on how to solve problems or improve the game. Since the game has not yet been released, the improvements can often be incorporated into the final game build.

Quality Assurance Team

Personal Evaluator Name:

_____

_____

Total Score from Personal Evaluation Rubric:

_____

_____

Peer Evaluator Name:

_____

_____

Total Score from Peer Evaluation Rubric:

_____

_____

Design Reasoning: Personal Evaluation

1. Reflect on your work, and evaluate your game for each of the five key areas of design identified in the rubric.
2. Rank each key area using a scale from 0 to 5. Record the value in the Score column.
3. Complete the Personal Evaluation rubric in the Commentary and Constructive Criticism section. Explain why you gave the score you did for each area of design.
4. Suggest improvements needed for your game in the Personal Evaluation rubric in the Commentary and Constructive Criticism section.

Key Area	0	1	2	3	4	5	Score
Concept Is the idea well developed?	No main idea or theme.					Clear theme or main idea maintained on all levels.	
Aesthetics Does the look, color, contrast, and placement of objects fit the game?	Poor quality graphics, color, and contrast.					Awesome graphics and animations. Items contrasted well.	
Sound Effects Do the sounds play? Are the music and sounds appropriate?	No sound. Sound is too loud, too soft, or not related to the game.					Sounds enhance gameplay and play clearly.	
Functionality Does everything work as expected?	Unfinished. Could not play. Major errors.					Plays perfectly. No bugs, glitches, or errors.	
Replay How likely are you to play this game again?	Game solved. Too easy. Not interesting or impossible to win.					Cannot wait to play it again! Skill was challenging, but enjoyable.	
Add the values in the Score column to get a total.						**Total Score**	

Design Reasoning: Peer Evaluation

1. Play the game designed by the peer as assigned by your instructor.
2. Reflect on the peer's work, and evaluate the game for each of the five key areas of design identified in the rubric.
3. Rank each key area using a scale from 0 to 5. Record the value in the Score column.
4. Complete the Peer Evaluation rubric in the Commentary and Constructive Criticism section. Explain why you gave the score you did for each area of design.
5. Suggest improvements needed for the peer's game in the Peer Evaluation rubric in the Commentary and Constructive Criticism section.

Key Area	0	1	2	3	4	5	Score
Concept Is the idea well developed?	No main idea or theme.					Clear theme or main idea maintained on all levels.	
Aesthetics Does the look, color, contrast, and placement of objects fit the game?	Poor quality graphics, color, and contrast.					Awesome graphics and animations. Items contrasted well.	
Sound Effects Do the sounds play? Are the music and sounds appropriate?	No sound. Sound is too loud, too soft, or not related to the game.					Sounds enhance gameplay and play clearly.	
Functionality Does everything work as expected?	Unfinished. Could not play. Major errors.					Plays perfectly. No bugs, glitches, or errors.	
Replay How likely are you to play this game again?	Game solved. Too easy. Not interesting or impossible to win.					Cannot wait to play it again! Skill was challenging, but enjoyable.	
Add up the values in the Score column to get a total.						**Total Score**	

Commentary and Constructive Criticism

Explain why you assigned the score for each key item assessed. Provide details on what you liked in that area and what needed improvement. Cite specific examples from the game. Provide suggestions on how to improve the game.

Personal Evaluation

Key Area	Detailed Assessment
Concept	
Aesthetics	
Sound Effects	
Functionality	
Replay	
Suggested Improvements	

Commentary and Constructive Criticism

Explain why you assigned the score for each key item assessed. Provide details on what you liked in that area and what needed improvement. Cite specific examples from the game. Provide suggestions on how to improve the game.

Peer Evaluation

Key Area	Detailed Assessment
Concept	
Aesthetics	
Sound Effects	
Functionality	
Replay	
Suggested Improvements	

Game Critique Exposition

Learning Objectives

After completing this lesson, you will be able to:

- evaluate a project to introduce a precise claim.
- cite specific examples to support a claim and refute a counterclaim.
- integrate vocabulary into formal writing.
- construct claim, evidence, and commentary in a single paragraph format.

Situation

The Awesome Game Company wants to post a written review or critique of the game on the company's website and blog. Your job is to analyze the information from the Quality Assurance documents and summarize your findings in paragraph form.

Reading Material

A *claim* is a position on a topic. For example, you could take a position (claim) as to whether or not toolbars should be used as a means of command access in software. *Pros* are the benefits of a topic. *Cons* are the disadvantages of a topic. Pros and cons are *evidence* used to debate the claim. *Commentary* is an explanation of the evidence. Use the commentary to explain in your own words why the evidence is relevant and applies to the issue (claim).

Planning Guide

A planning guide, such as the one shown in **Figure 12-1**, can be used as a prewriting organizer to develop claim, evidence, and commentary needed to support your position. Make sure to identify cons so you can refute the claims others make in opposition to your claim. A graphic organizer, such as the one shown in **Figure 12-2**, can also be used as a planning guide. This also provides for identifying evidence and commentary, just in a different format.

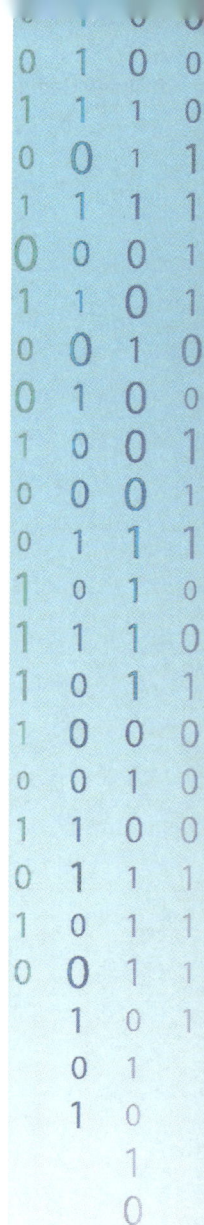

Name: ______________________

Date: ______________________

Class: ______________________

Pros and Cons for My Position

Claim (statement of your position):

____

Pros What arguments support your claim?	**Evidence** What evidence supports your arguments? Use facts, statistics, quotes from experts, personal examples, and so on.
Cons What arguments can be made against your claim?	**Counterarguments** What can you say to refute these counterclaims?

Goodheart-Willcox Publisher

Figure 12-1. A planning guide can be used to develop claim, evidence, and commentary to support a position.

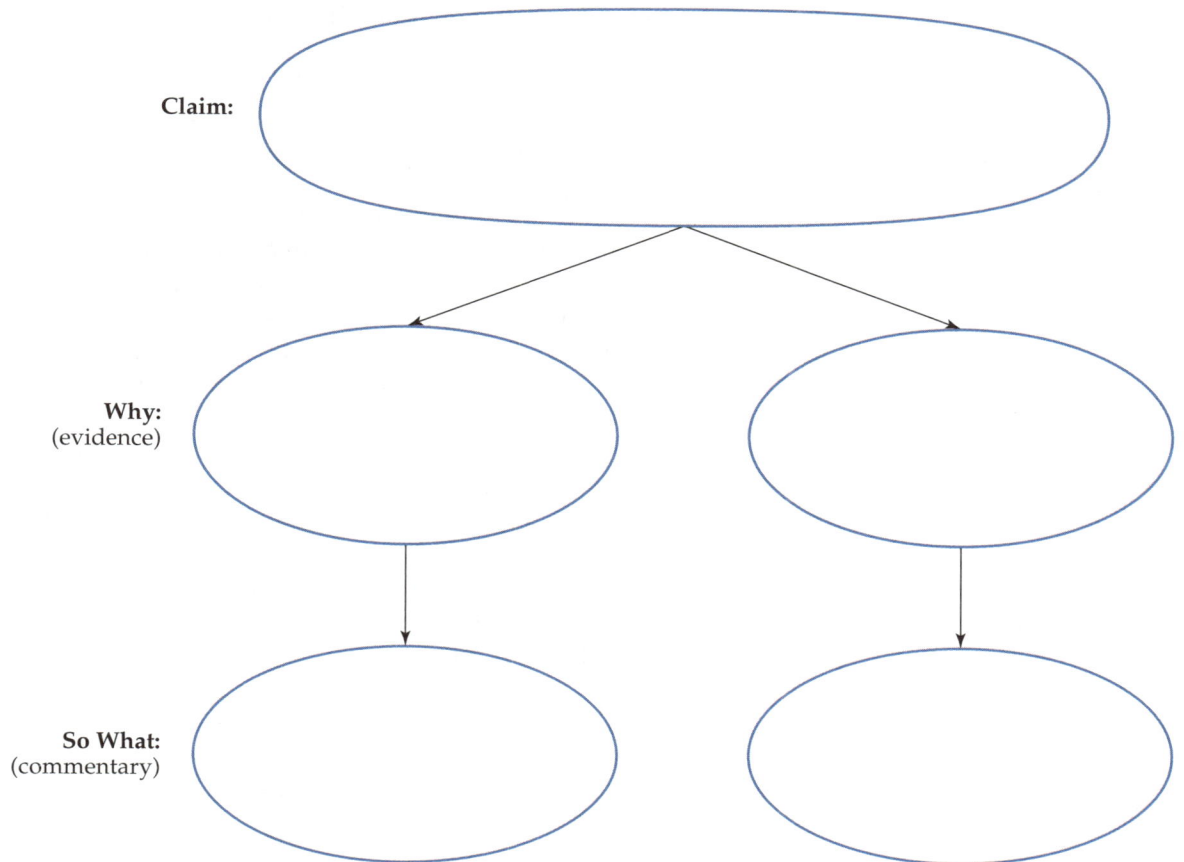

Goodheart-Willcox Publisher

Figure 12-2. A graphic organizer is a different method of planning for claim, evidence, and commentary.

Single Paragraph Structural Organizer

Below is a structure used to write a single paragraph response to a prompt. Expand your statements from the graphic organizer into complete sentences to create a paragraph. The examples given follow the prompt: Is playing a video game good for kids?

- **Thesis statement or topic sentence.** The sentence structure should include the topic and the stance or opinion that you are proving.
  Example: Playing video games is good for kids because it improves computer skills and teaches teamwork through cooperation.
- **Evidence #1.** This sentence should include the source of the information, quality of the information source, and a quotation or paraphrasing of the information from the source.
  Example: According to Mr. Duncan, behavioral scientist for interactive studies, children who play video games three to five hours a week have better computer skills than those who do not play video games.
- **Commentary.** This sentence should be a statement in your own words on how the evidence applies to the claim you are making. There may be more than one sentence of commentary.
  Example: His research implies that playing a video game has a direct impact on a child's ability to use a computer for other purposes. This is likely due to the fact that the game skills needed to load, install, and input commands for a game are similar to those needed for any other computer program.

- **Evidence #2.** The second evidence statement should begin with a transitional term to maintain flow and readability.
  Example: Furthermore, Ms. Wilkes, the author of the book *Using Video Games for Learning,* explains how playing cooperative games like the online team play in Call of Duty builds teamwork values such as cooperation, leadership, team planning, and mutual goal seeking.
- **Commentary.** This sentence should describe how the second piece of evidence applies to the claim you are making. There may be more than one sentence of commentary.
  Example: Children playing online team games use verbal communication to plan strategies with other team members. Since the team is trying to reach a mutual goal, the players cooperate and communicate effectively. They help each other and thereby help the team. Directing other players and planning tactics for each player develop the kind of leadership needed for next generation careers.
- **Closing statement.** This sentence should bring all of the thoughts together and close the paragraph. It often summarizes or draws a conclusion to support the main idea or topic of the paragraph. This is your chance to "make it real" or sell your claim. Be persuasive and confident in your closing.
  Example: These facts support having children play video games. Since computer skills and teamwork are necessary for high paying careers, letting kids play video games will help them get the best jobs in the 21st century workforce.

How to Begin

1. Review the Personal Evaluation Rubric score and comments from Lesson 11.
2. Compare your personal evaluation results with the Peer Evaluation Rubric score and comments.
3. Note any similarities and differences from your evaluation to the peer evaluation.
4. Applying what you have learned from the reading material, write a single paragraph to support a claim and counterclaim. Use Microsoft Word or other word-processing software to explain how your Personal Evaluation is more accurate than the Peer Evaluation. Cite specific examples to prove your point. Also cite specific examples to disprove the counterclaim by the peer evaluator.
5. Applying what you have learned, set up the word processor to check the Flesch-Kincaid Reading Level with spelling and grammar.
6. Check and correct any spelling and grammar errors.
7. Adjust vocabulary and sentence structure to write at your grade level or higher.
8. Save your document as *LastName_*Critique in your working folder, and submit your work for grading.

Name: _____

Vocabulary

Write a definition for each of the key terms from this lesson. You will develop a personal glossary of key terms throughout this course.

claim

_____

_____

pros

_____

_____

cons

_____

_____

evidence

_____

_____

commentary

_____

_____

Office Technology Integration

Using Word Processing Software Thesaurus

1. Launch Microsoft Excel or other spreadsheet software, and open the vocabulary spreadsheet you updated in previous lessons.
2. Applying what you have learned, add a new worksheet, and name it Lesson 12.
3. Add each of the vocabulary words and definitions from the Vocabulary section of this lesson.
4. Save the spreadsheet, and then close it.
5. Launch Microsoft Word or other word-processing software, and begin a new document.
6. Save the document as *LastName*_Thesaurus in your working folder.
7. On the first line of the document, add these sentences:
   My teacher is the best. He is very smart.
8. Check spelling and grammar with readability. This sentence has a Flesch-Kincaid Grade Level of 0.5.
9. Change the words *My teacher* to the name of your teacher.
10. Select the word *is*.
11. Click **Review>Proofing>Thesaurus** on the ribbon. The **Thesaurus** pane is displayed on the right side of the screen, as shown. Notice more complex vocabulary is displayed for the selected word.

Thesaurus

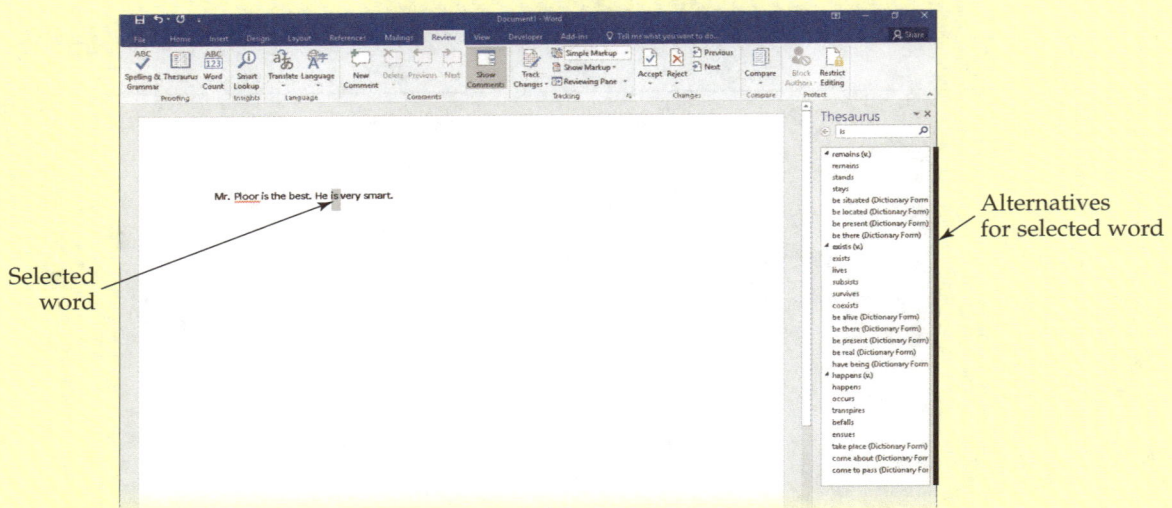

Selected word

Alternatives for selected word

Goodheart-Willcox Publisher

12. Identify an appropriate word in the thesaurus list, right-click on the word, and click Insert in the shortcut menu to replace the word *is* with the new word.
13. Use the thesaurus to find more complex vocabulary for these words: best, is, very, smart.
14. Edit the sentences so they read correctly and fit the new vocabulary.
15. Refine any additional vocabulary as needed, such as the pronoun *he,* to use more precise vocabulary.
16. Use the Flesch-Kincaid readability statistics to discover how your changes affect the readability level. For example, the following rewrite has a grade level of 10.7.
    Mr. Ploor, the video game design teacher at my school, performs at an unsurpassed level. This teacher demonstrates extraordinary genius.
17. Save your work, and submit it for grading.
18. Apply expanded vocabulary to the critique lesson.

0 1 0 0
1 1 1 0
0 0 1 1
1 1 1 1
0 0 0 1
1 1 0 1
0 0 1 0
0 1 0 0
1 0 0 1
0 0 0 1
0 1 1 1
1 0 1 0
1 1 1 0
1 0 1 1
1 0 0 0
0 0 1 0
1 1 0 0
0 1 1 1
1 0 1 1
0 0 1 1
1 0 1
0 1
1 0
1
0

Lesson 13

Proof of Concept: Launching

Learning Objectives

After completing this lesson, you will be able to:

- explain the iterative process of game design.

- compare and contrast input and output devices of a user interface.

- create frame-by-frame animation using automated settings.

- program acceleration and deceleration.

Situation

The Ugly Furniture Organization (UFO) has contacted the Awesome Game Company to develop a game that it can use on its website and distribute as a mobile app. Before starting on this project, you and your team must learn about the developmental cycles used to create video games. After obtaining this knowledge, you will be able to develop the game for the client.

Reading Materials

The process of building a game is an iterative process. Iteration means refining through repetition. An *iterative process* is one of making improvements through repetitions. In game design, that means you will build the game, test the game, get feedback, refine the game, and repeat until the game is the best it can be within the allowed time frame.

Professional designers can take a game through many iterations, or developmental cycles, of refinement until it is ready. During the process, the game is thoroughly tested. The purpose of testing is to find bugs and get feedback needed to make the game better. The first iteration of the game is a prototype. A *prototype* is a simple or basic version of the game that has most of the gameplay features, but lacks polishing. The final graphics likely will not be used, and it may not have sounds included.

A prototype is typically the first step in proof of concept. *Proof of concept (POC)* is where new ideas (concepts) are tried out to see if the technology and interactions will work. Once the concept has been proved, it is time to start polishing the game to make it successful.

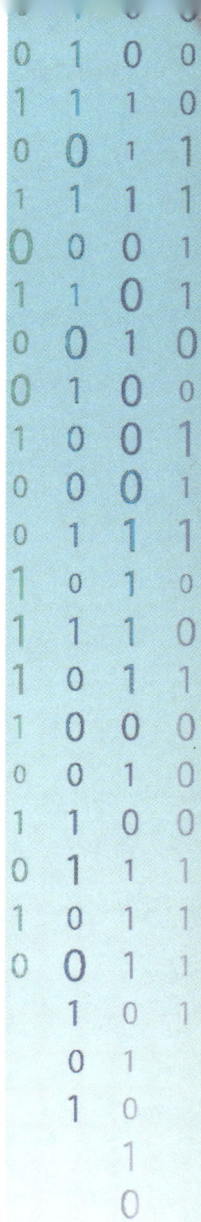

Name: _____

Date: _____

Class: _____

As the build progresses through iterations, the designer will send out copies of the game for testing. These testing versions are called beta versions. Beta is the second letter in the Greek alphabet. A **beta version** is the second major iteration of the game. All previous versions were **alpha versions.** Alpha is the first letter in the Greek alphabet. While the beta version is very close to the final release version of the game, designers will still make several changes based on the comments of the beta testers.

Someone who gets a copy of the game for testing is known as a **beta tester.** Beta testers serve a very important role in the design process. When you design a game or other software, you make it work the way in which you think and process information. Unfortunately, there are many other ways of thinking and processing information that are different from your own ways. For example, a beta tester may make lots of mistakes and send in feedback on how to make the user interface simpler. By using many beta testers, a designer can get a lot of feedback to fix all of those crazy errors and bugs that would be difficult to find without help.

A **user interface** is a way for the user to control and get feedback from the game. A user interface has input and output devices. An **input device** accepts instructions from the user and inputs them into the game. A user-interface input can be the keyboard, mouse, game pad, game controller, touchscreen, or other device to send information to the computer. A user-interface **output device** provides information from the computer to the user. Items such as the monitor and speakers send information from the computer to the user. Anything the player uses to input information and get feedback from the game is part of the user-interface system, as shown in **Figure 13-1.**

The final iteration of the game is called **ready to market (RTM).** When the designer feels there is no more that should be done to the game, then the game has been made ready to release to the market. The **market** is all of the people who are willing and able to buy the game. Through **market research,** game companies try to determine what the market wants in a game. Hopefully, the game is polished, free of bugs, and what the market is asking for, along with a market full of buyers willing to purchase the game. Good luck!

Game Build

The Ugly Furniture Organization (UFO) has contacted the Awesome Game Company to develop a game that it can use on its website and distribute as a mobile app. The client loves to make fun of the company name and the UFO acronym, so it wants a UFO-themed game. Your job is to create a proof-of-concept game that uses a UFO launching projectiles to destroy meteors. The focus of this game build is on workable gameplay. You will have to create the basic game art needed for the prototype and program the interactions to see if the concept will work.

How to Begin

1. Launch Clickteam Fusion 2.5, and begin a new application.
2. Applying what you have learned, create three frames named Title Frame, Game Frame, Winner Frame, and place them in that order.
3. Set the size for all frames to be 640 by 480.
4. Save the file as *LastName*_Meteors_POC in your working folder.

Game Frame

5. Display the Game Frame in the frame editor.
6. Applying what you have learned, insert a new active object anywhere on the frame, and name it Meteor_L.

Frame Editor

Device	Input	Output	Both
Barcode reader	X		
CD/DVD			X
Digital camera			X
Flash drive			X
Headphones		X	
Joystick	X		
Keyboard	X		
Modem			X
Monitor/screen		X	
Optical pen	X		
Plotter			X
Printer			X
Scanner	X		
Speakers		X	
Touchscreen			X

Goodheart-Willcox Publisher

Figure 13-1. A user interface consists of input and output devices. There are many types of devices that may be part of the user interface.

7. Set the position to (400, 100).
8. Set the size to 80 wide and 80 high.
9. Applying what you have learned, open the Meteor_L object in the image editor, and clear the canvas.

Clear

10. Use the **Zoom** slider to enlarge the view of the canvas so you can draw more accurately.
11. Click the **Shape Tool** button.
12. Click the **Outlined** button in the tool options. This option will create only an outline without any fill color.

Shape Tool

13. In the tool options, change the size to 2 and make sure the opacity is 100.
14. Select black as the foreground color. You can use the color palette to select the color or enter the hexadecimal number #000000 or RGB values of 0.

Outlined

15. Click and drag to draw a shape that is roughly a circle, as shown in **Figure 13-2.** This shape will be a meteor so it should not be perfectly round.
16. Change the foreground color to a dark gray of your choice, such as hexadecimal value #535353.
17. Make sure the **Shape Tool** is active, and click the **Filled** button in the tool options.
18. Draw several roughly circular shapes inside the large outline. These will simulate craters on the meteor.

Filled

19. Change the foreground color to a light gray of your choice, such as hexadecimal value #CBCBCB.
20. Click the **Fill Tool** button, and click inside the outline to fill the meteor shape with light gray, as shown in **Figure 13-3.**
21. Click the **OK** button to close the image editor and update the object.

Fill Tool

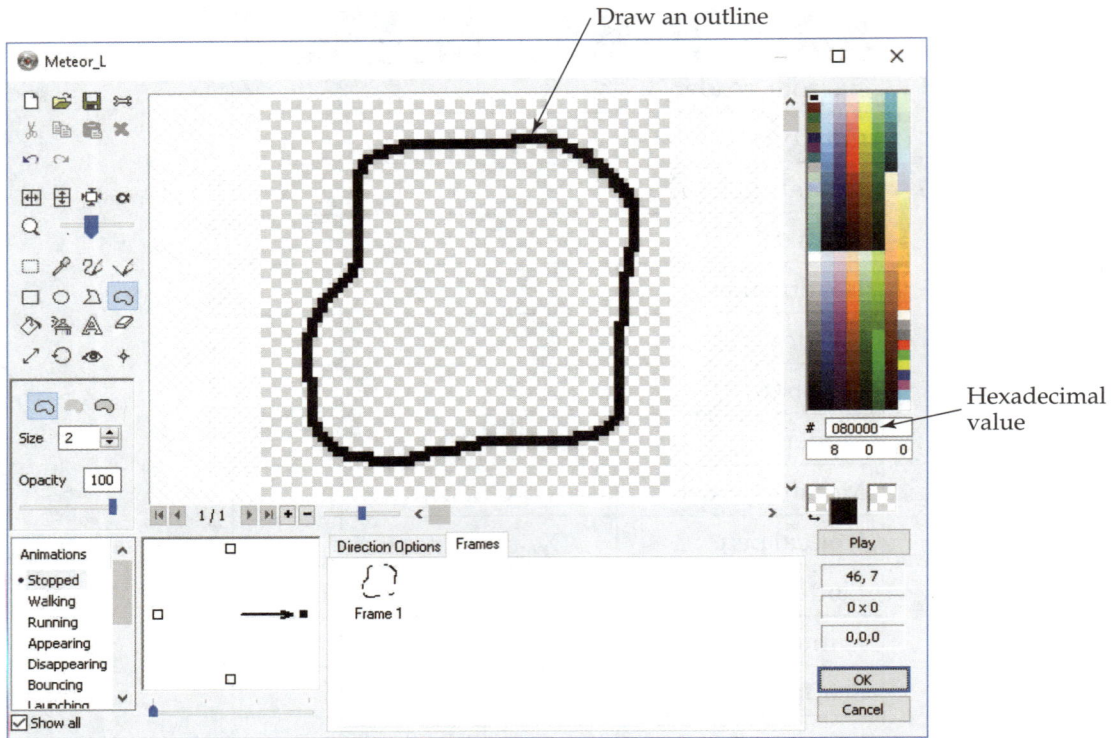

Goodheart-Willcox Publisher

Figure 13-2. The outline of the meteor is a freeform shape.

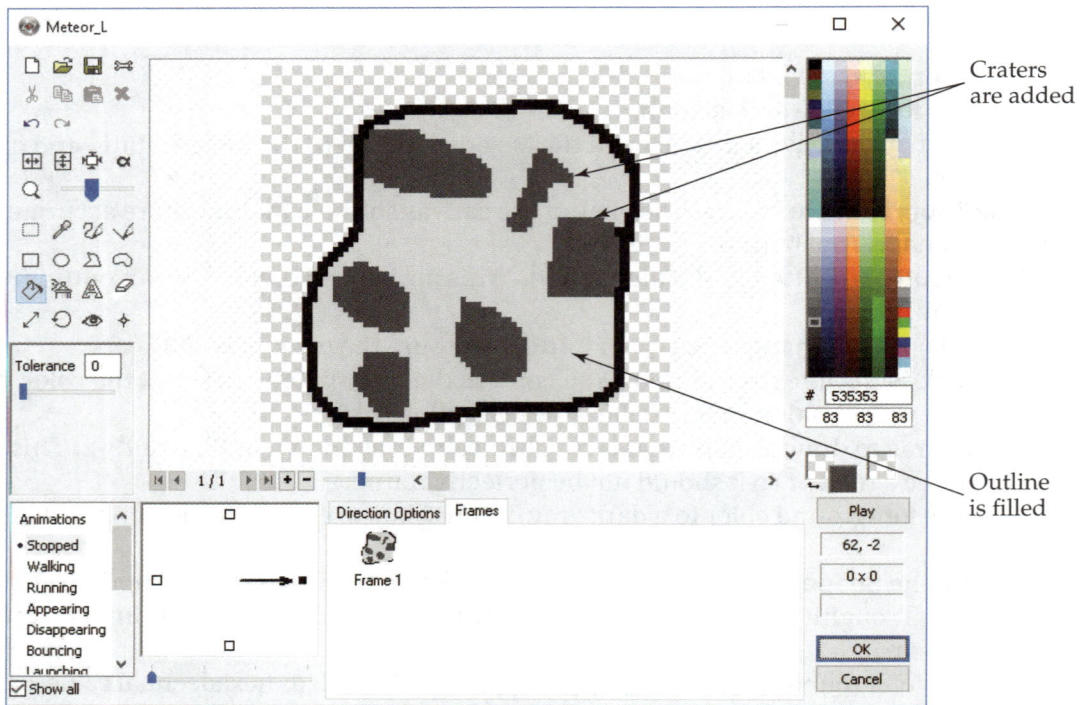

Goodheart-Willcox Publisher

Figure 13-3. Craters are added to the meteor, and the outline is filled to complete the sprite.

Cloning

The game specifications call for three sizes of meteors. To save time, the large meteor can be cloned and resized to make the other meteors.

22. Right-click on the Meteor_L object and select **Clone Object** in the shortcut menu.
23. Applying what you have learned, create clones in three rows and one column.
24. Change the name of the middle meteor to Meteor_M, and set its width and height to 45.
25. Change the name of the bottom meteor to Meteor_S, and set its width and height to 20.

Animation

The meteors will be spinning in space. Clickteam Fusion 2.5 has a feature that allows animation frames for rotation to be quickly created.

26. Open the Meteor_L object in the image editor.
27. Right-click on Frame 1, and click **Rotation** in the shortcut menu. The **Make One-Turn Rotation** dialog box is displayed, as shown in **Figure 13-4.**
28. Click in the **Number of frames in the** text box, and enter 15. This will create 14 new frames, so counting the original frame there will be a total of 15 frames.
29. Click the **Clockwise** radio button. This will set the rotation to spin in the direction in which the hands of a clock rotate. Clockwise is from the top to the right. Counterclockwise is the opposite of that.
30. Click the **OK** button to create the animation frames. Notice that the meteor rotates a bit on each frame.
31. Click the **Play** button on the right side of the image editor. A preview of the animation is displayed. Notice the meteor spins in one full rotation. Close the preview.
32. Click the **Direction Options** tab at the bottom of the image editor.
33. Click in the **Speed** text box, and enter 5. This will result in the meteor spinning slowly.
34. Check the **Loop** check box. This will keep the meteor spinning throughout the game.
35. Preview the animation again. Notice how slowly the meteor spins and that it keeps spinning beyond one rotation. Close the preview.
36. Click the **OK** button to close the image editor and update the object.
37. Applying what you have learned, create rotation animations for the Meteor_M and Meteor_S objects using the settings below.

Object Name	Animation Rotation	Number of Frames	Animation Speed	Loop
Meteor_M	Counterclockwise	10	10	Yes
Meteor_S	Clockwise	8	8	Yes

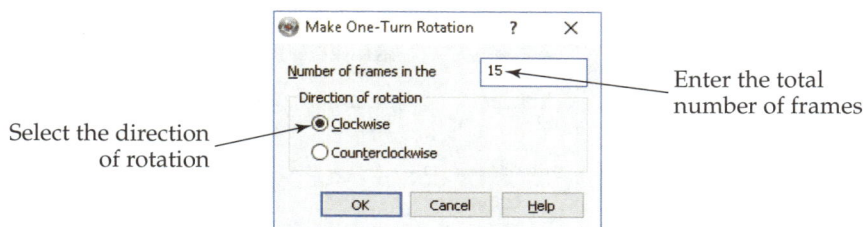

Select the direction of rotation

Enter the total number of frames

Goodheart-Willcox Publisher

Figure 13-4. Clickteam Fusion 2.5 has a feature that allows a spinning animation to be automatically created.

Photon Objects

The game specifications require a photon object that will be used to destroy the meteors. The photon should be animated to disappear as it travels. Clickteam Fusion 2.5 has a feature that allows this animation to be automatically created.

38. Insert a new active object, and name it Photon.
39. Open the Photon object in the image editor, and clear the canvas.
40. Change the foreground color to a shade of yellow of your choice.
41. Applying what you have learned, draw the outline of a circle that is one pixel thick so the circle is the size of the canvas. Tip: hold down the [Shift] key as you draw to create a perfect circle. Undo and try again if needed.
42. Change the foreground color to a shade of red of your choice.
43. Applying what you have learned, fill the yellow outline with red.
44. Right-click on Frame 1, and click **Zoom** in the shortcut menu. The **Insert Resized Frames** dialog box is displayed, as shown in **Figure 13-5.**
45. Click in the **Final width** text box, and enter 0. The **Final height** setting automatically changes to 1.
46. Click in the **Number of frames** text box, and enter 20.
47. Click the **OK** button to create the animation frames.
48. Preview the animation. Notice how the object gradually reduces in size until it almost disappears. Close the preview.
49. Applying what you have learned, change the speed to 30.
50. Click the **OK** button to close the image editor and update the object.

Player Character

Next, you need to create an avatar for the player. Recall, an avatar is the representation of the player in the game. The avatar for the player character will be a UFO. The object to which this avatar is applied will launch photons to destroy falling meteors.

51. Insert a new active object, and name it UFO.
52. Set the size of the UFO object to 36 wide and 18 high.
53. Set its position to (340, 430).
54. Open the UFO object in the image editor, clear the canvas, and zoom in to make the canvas appear larger.
55. Change the foreground color to green or another color of your choice. This color will be used for the body of the UFO.
56. Applying what you have learned, draw a filled ellipse from (0, 6) to (36, 18).

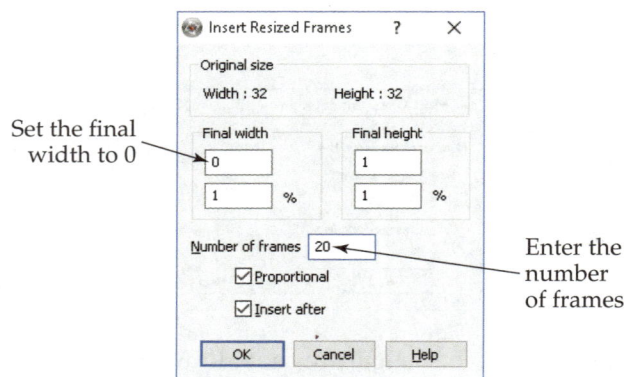

Clear

Ellipse Tool

Fill Tool

Set the final width to 0

Enter the number of frames

Goodheart-Willcox Publisher

Figure 13-5. Clickteam Fusion 2.5 has a feature that allows animating a change in size to be automatically created.

57. Change the foreground color to yellow or another color of your choice. This color will be used for the canopy or window of the UFO.
58. Draw a filled ellipse from (10, 0) to (26, 10), as shown in **Figure 13-6.**
59. Click the **OK** button to close the image editor and update the object.

Player Character Movement

60. Select the UFO object, and click the **Movement** tab in the **Properties** toolbar.
61. Change the Type property to Eight Directions.
62. Click the Directions property to display the directions window.
63. Applying what you have learned, remove all directions except direction 0 and direction 16, as shown in **Figure 13-7.**
64. Set the Initial direction property to only direction 0 and direction 16.
65. Set the Speed property to 20.
66. Set the Deceleration property to 0.
67. Set the Acceleration property to 20.
68. Run the frame. Use the arrow keys to test the left and right movement of the player character. Notice how the object keeps moving even when you release the arrow key. This is because the Deceleration property is set to 0. Close the game window when done testing.

Movement

Run Frame

Launching the Photon

The photon will not be visible during gameplay until the player launches it. You will use programming to control when the object is displayed. The following pseudocode will be used.

IF the player presses the space bar,
  THEN launch a Photon object from the UFO object in an upward direction.

69. Drag the Photon object outside the frame. This allows you to use the object, but not have it on screen when the game starts.
70. Display the event editor for the Game Frame.
71. Applying what you have learned, add a new condition for if the space bar is pressed.

Event Editor

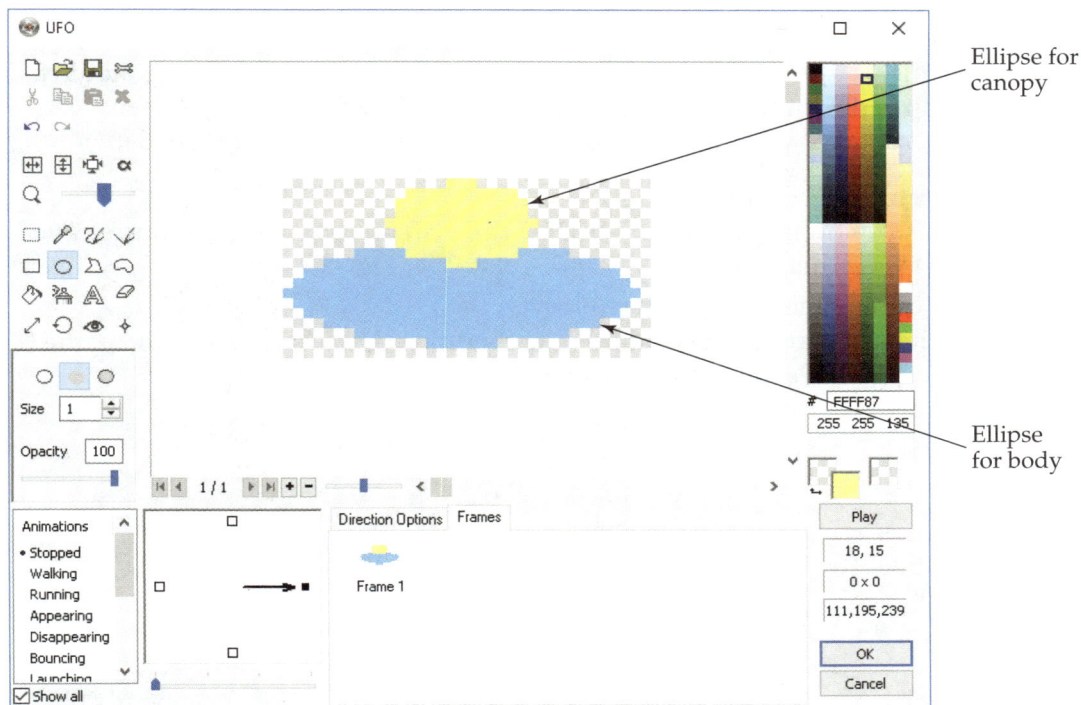

Goodheart-Willcox Publisher

Figure 13-6. The sprite for the UFO object is created with two filled ellipses.

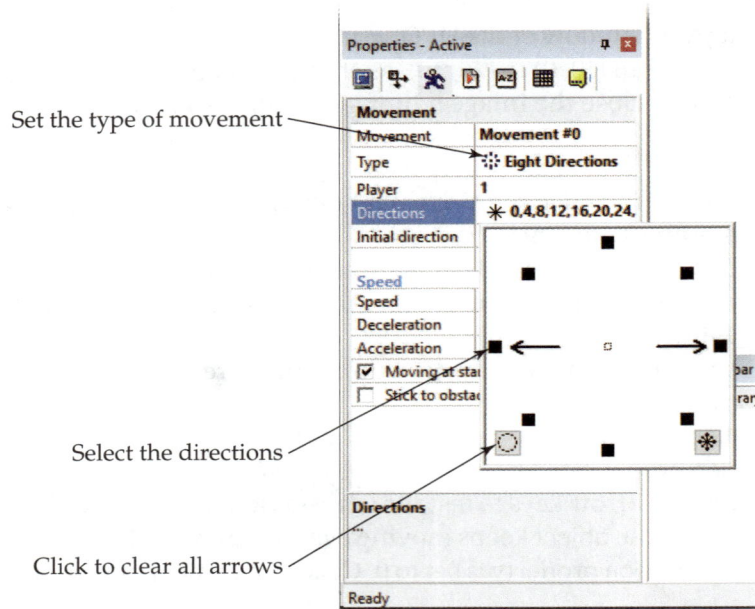

Set the type of movement

Select the directions

Click to clear all arrows

Figure 13-7. Set the movement for the UFO object to left and right.

72. Right-click in the cell below the icon for the UFO object, and click **Launch an Object...** in the shortcut menu.
73. In the **Launch an Object** dialog box, select the Photon object, and click the **OK** button. A new dialog box is displayed, as shown in **Figure 13-8.**
74. Click in the **Speed of object:** text box, and enter 50.
75. Click the **Launch in selected directions...** radio button. A dialog box is displayed in which to select a direction or multiple directions.
76. Choose only direction 8, and click the **OK** button.
77. Click the **OK** button to close the **Launch an Object** dialog box.
78. Run the frame. Try pressing the space bar to launch a photon. The photon should fade out at the top of the frame. Close the game window when done testing.

Run Frame

79. Debug any problems with the UFO movement or photon launching if needed.

Movement Wrap

When testing, you probably noticed the UFO can drift off the screen. A feature called wrap can be used to fix this issue.

80. Display the event editor for the Game Frame.
81. Applying what you have learned, add a new condition that tests the position of the UFO object to see if it leaves the frame area on the left or right.

Event Editor

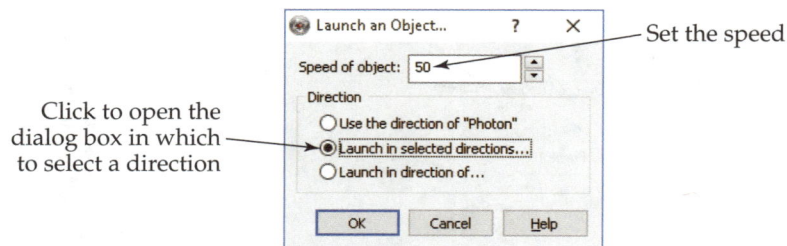

Click to open the dialog box in which to select a direction

Set the speed

Figure 13-8. When programming an object to launch, set the speed and choose the direction in which to launch it.

82. For the new condition, right-click in the cell below the icon for the UFO object, and click **Movement>Wrap Around Play Area** in the shortcut menu.

83. Run the frame. Test that the UFO exits one side of the frame and enters on the opposite side. Close the game window when done testing.

Run Frame

84. Debug any errors as needed.

Exploding the Meteors

So far, the player can move the UFO and launch photons. However, there is no way to destroy the meteors. Remember, an object looks like a real-world object, but without programming it will not function or act correctly. Relative positioning was used in Lesson 7 to position child objects in relation to a parent. The same programming can be used to properly locate the explosion to the correct position. Also, when a photon hits a meteor, the meteor and photon should both disappear.

85. Display the Game Frame in the frame editor.

86. In the **Library Toolbar**, expand the tree Local Library>Games>Explosions and drag the Explosion 1 object onto the frame outside of the visible area.

Frame Editor

87. Display the event editor for the Game Frame.

88. Create a new condition to match this pseudocode:

> **IF** the Photon object collides with the Meteor_L object

Event Editor

89. For this new condition, right-click in the cell below the **Create new objects** icon, and click **Create object** in the shortcut menu. The **Create Object** dialog box is displayed.

90. Select the Explosion 1 object, click the **OK** button. The frame editor is displayed to select a location at which to create the object.

91. Applying what you have learned, set the location at (0, 0) relative to the Meteor_L object.

92. Applying what you have learned, modify the event you just created to match this pseudocode, as shown in **Figure 13-9**.

> **IF** the Photon object collides with the Meteor_L object,
> > **THEN** create an Explosion 1 object at (0, 0) relative to the Meteor_L object
> > > **AND** destroy the Meteor_L object
> > > **AND** destroy the Photon object.

93. Display the Game Frame in the frame editor.

94. Applying what you have learned, copy and paste three of the large meteors at the top of the visible frame so there is a total of four.

Frame Editor

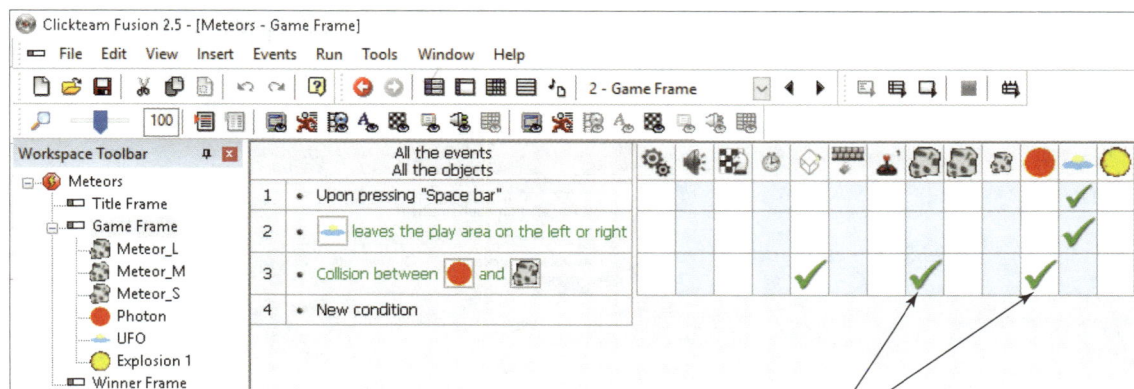

Figure 13-9. Programming to create the explosion and destroy the meteor and photon can be contained in a single event line.

Run Frame

95. Run the frame. Test to see if the explosion occurs in the correct location, which is the center of each large meteor. Close the game window when done testing.
96. Debug any errors as needed. If the explosion does not occur at the center of the meteor, adjust the hotspot on the Explosion 1 object. It will need to be adjusted on *each* frame in the animation.

Cleaning Up the Animation

During your testing, you probably noticed dirty smudges left behind when the explosion ends. This is because the last frame of animation for the Explosion 1 object is showing. The computer will continue to track these objects until they are removed. Having a large number of these leftover and unused objects can cause lag to your game. The most efficient way to change this is to destroy the object when the animation has finished. The following pseudocode removes the Explosion 1 object when it is no longer needed.

> **IF** the Explosion 1 object animation named Stopped is over,
>> **THEN** destroy the Explosion 1 object.

Event Editor

97. Display the event editor for the Game Frame, and add a new condition.
98. In the **New Condition** dialog box, right-click on the Explosion 1 object, and click **Animation>Has an animation finished?** in the shortcut menu.
99. In the dialog box that is displayed, select the Stopped animation, and click the **OK** button, as shown in **Figure 13-10.**
100. For the condition you just added, right-click in the cell under the icon for the Explosion 1 object, and click **Destroy** in the shortcut menu.

Run Frame

101. Run the frame. See if the explosion is destroyed once the animation is over.
102. Debug any errors as needed.

Copying and Editing Programming

There is more programming needed to finish the game. Much of this programming is similar to what you have already coded. Often, it is more efficient to copy and edit programming than to create it from scratch for each event.

103. Right-click on the 3 of line 3, and click **Copy** from the shortcut menu. Make sure you click the number 3, not any other part of the line. Line 3 is for the condition of a collision between the Photon object and the Meteor_L object.
104. Right-click on the number 4 of line 4, and click **Paste** in the shortcut menu. This places a copy of the line 3 programming below line 3 as line 4. The existing line 4 is renumbered as line 5.
105. Right-click on the number 5 of line 5, and click **Paste** in the shortcut menu. This adds another copy of the line 3 programming. The existing line 5 is renumbered as line 6. There should now be three identical lines of programming, as shown in **Figure 13-11.**

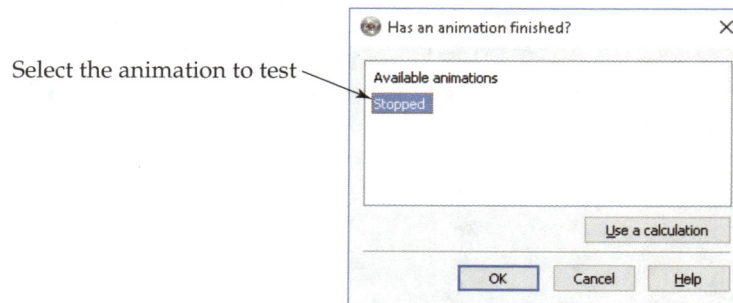

Select the animation to test

Figure 13-10. A condition can be programmed to test if a specified animation has ended.

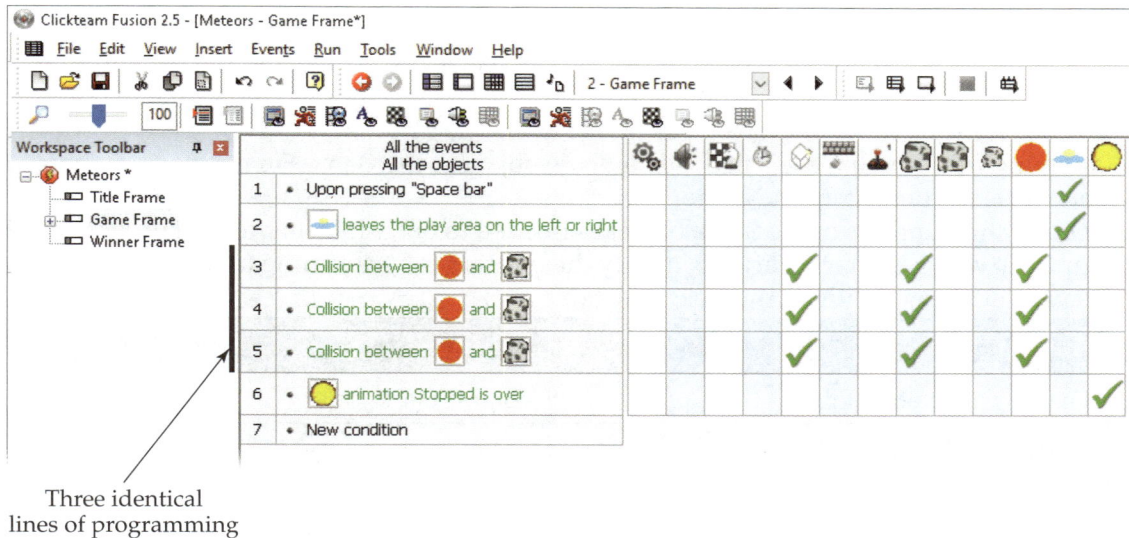

Three identical
lines of programming

Figure 13-11. Copying and pasting existing programming and then editing the copies is an efficient way to program.

106. In the condition for line 4, double-click on the icon for the Meteor_L object. This is the icon in the condition, not the icon along the top of the event editor. Once you double-click, dialog box is displayed showing the available objects that can replace the Meteor_L object.

107. Select the Meteor_M object, and click the **OK** button. The condition is updated to test for a collision between the Photon object and the Meteor_M object.

108. Applying what you have learned, edit the condition on line 5 to test for a collision between the Photon object and the Meteor_S object.

109. In line 4, right-click the check mark under the icon for the Meteor_L object, and click **Delete** in the shortcut menu. This removes the programming for destroying the Meteor_L object.

110. Delete the check mark in line 5 that is the programming for destroying the Meteor_L object.

111. In line 4, drag the check mark from the cell under the Photon object and drop it into the cell under the Meteor_M object. This copies the programming, which is a "destroy" action.

112. Copy the "destroy" action to the cell in line 5 under the Meteor_S object.

113. In line 4, right-click the check mark in the cell under the **Create new object** icon, and click **Edit** in the shortcut menu. The frame editor is displayed, and the dialog box for setting the position is opened.

114. Click the **Relative to:** radio button. In the **Choose an object** dialog box, select the Meteor_M object, and click the **OK** button.

115. Make sure the X and Y values in the **Create Object** dialog box are 0, and then click the **OK** button to complete the update of the programming.

116. Applying what you have learned, edit the programming in line 5 so the new object is created relative to the Meteor_S object.

117. Display the frame editor, and make several copies of both the Meteor_M and Meteor_S objects scattered across the screen.

Frame Editor

118. Run the frame. Make sure all objects are destroyed properly and the explosions occur in the correct locations. Close the game window when done testing.

Run Frame

119. Debug any errors as needed.

Backdrop and Scoring

120. Applying what you have learned, add a decorative backdrop object as the background to the Game Frame. Use a backdrop from the library, create your own image file in photo-editing software, or locate a free-use image using the Internet.
121. Applying what you have learned, add a Score object to the Game Frame. Place it where you feel is the best fit for the game.
122. Recolor the numbers of the Score object as needed to be visible on the background.
123. Applying what you have learned, modify the existing programming to change the Player 1 score as shown in the following table.

Action	Score
Destroy a Meteor_L object	+5 points
Destroy a Meteor_M object	+10 points
Destroy a Meteor_S object	+15 points

124. Design and create a title page that introduces the game and explains how to play it. Use the Title Frame for this. Make sure to add buttons as appropriate. This is a proof-of-concept game, so the design only needs to be enough to communicate the function of the frame.
125. Design and create a high-score page that displays the high scores of all players. Use the Winner Frame for this. Make sure to add buttons as appropriate.
126. Run the application. Fully test the game.
127. Debug all frames as needed.
128. Save your work, and submit it for grading.
129. Is this a video game? Why or why not? If not, make suggestions as how to make it into a video game.

Run Application

_____

_____

_____

_____

Vocabulary

Write a definition for each of the key terms from this lesson. You will develop a personal glossary of key terms throughout this course.

iterative process

_____

_____

prototype

_____

_____

Name: _____

proof of concept (POC)

_____

_____

beta version

_____

_____

alpha version

_____

_____

beta tester

_____

_____

user interface

_____

_____

input device

_____

_____

output device

_____

_____

ready to market (RTM)

_____

_____

market

_____

_____

market research

_____

_____

Review Questions

1. How does a prototype differ from the video game a consumer may purchase at a store?

_____

_____

_____

_____

Applied Technology

Language Arts

2. Describe why beta testers are important to game design.

_____

_____

_____

_____

Applied Technology

3. List at least two input devices that may be part of a video game console user interface.

_____

_____

_____

_____

Language Arts

4. What is the difference between clockwise and counterclockwise rotation?

_____

_____

_____

_____

Applied Technology

5. In the game build in this lesson, why would the large meteor be cloned instead of copied?

_____

_____

_____

_____

Higher-Order Thinking Strategies

Language Arts

6. Summarize how the iterative process works for game design.

_____

_____

_____

_____

Science

7. Think about how a game company would be able to determine what the market wants in a game. List ways you think the company could find this information.

_____

_____

_____

_____

Name: _____

8. Why would it be better to make the large meteor smaller instead of a small meteor larger?

_____

_____

_____

_____

Applied Technology

9. The art department requires information on the following objects to properly create a disappearing animation. Using the number of frames as the denominator for a fraction, create a fraction for the reduction value for one frame of animation. Next, express the fraction as a decimal. Lastly, express the decimal as a percentage.

Mathematics

Number of Additional Frames	Reduction Fraction	Reduction Decimal	Reduction Percentage
2	1/2	0.5	50%
8			
10			
20			
25			
32			
40			
50			

10. The movement physics of the UFO object has the Deceleration property set to 0. How does this affect the movement of the UFO? Is this realistic, and why or why not?

_____

_____

_____

_____

Science

Office Technology Integration

Using SmartArt Graphics

1. Launch Microsoft Excel or other spreadsheet software, and open the vocabulary spreadsheet you updated in the last lesson.
2. Applying what you have learned, add a new worksheet, and name it Lesson 13.
3. Add each of the vocabulary words and definitions from the Vocabulary section of this lesson.
4. Save the spreadsheet, and then close it.
5. Launch Microsoft Word, begin a new blank document, and save the file as *LastName_DevelopmentCycles* in your working folder.
6. On the first line of the document, add the text Cycles of Development, and press the [Enter] key to start a new line.
7. Select the text, and format it as typeface (font) of Tahoma, bold, size of 22 points, and centered.
8. Click on the second line to place the insertion point there. Ensure the paragraph alignment is left-aligned.
9. Click **Insert>Illustrations>SmartArt** on the ribbon. The **Choose a SmartArt Graphic** dialog box is displayed.

SmartArt

10. Click **Process** on the left side of the dialog box, and click **Alternating Flow** tile in the middle. Hover the cursor over the tiles in the middle of the dialog box to see the names in help text.
11. Click the **OK** button. This will place the SmartArt template in the document and open a dialog box to the left of the graphic in which text information can be entered in a hierarchical format.
12. Enter the information shown.

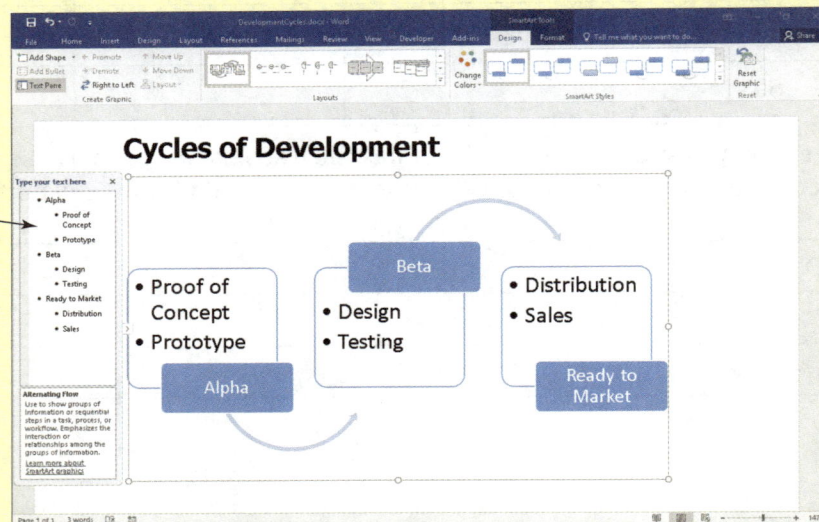

Goodheart-Willcox Publisher

13. Close the dialog box to apply the information to the graphic.
14. With the graphic selected, click the **Design** tab on the ribbon. In the **SmartArt Styles** group, click the **More** button on the style gallery to expand the gallery, and then click the Bird's Eye Scene image tile to create a three-dimensional graphic.

More

15. Click **Design>SmartArt Styles>Change Colors** on the ribbon, and select a color scheme that you like in the drop-down menu.

Change Colors

16. Applying what you have learned, insert a SmartArt graphic of your choice to describe the iterative design process. Review Lesson 6 for details of the iterative design process.
17. Submit your work for grading.

0 1 0 0
1 1 1 0
0 0 1 0
1 1 1 1
0 0 0 1
1 1 0 1
0 0 1 0
0 1 0 0
1 0 0 1
0 0 0 1
0 1 1 1
1 0 1 0
1 1 1 0
1 0 1 1
1 0 0 0
0 0 1 0
1 1 0 0
0 1 1 1
1 0 1 1
0 0 1 1
1 0 1
0 1
1 0
1
0

Lesson 14

Beta Build: Launching

Learning Objectives

After completing this lesson, you will be able to:

- simulate conservation of matter in a video game.

- describe how momentum influences object motion.

- program emitters to create random objects.

- develop bonuses and perks to enhance gameplay.

Situation

The Awesome Game Company sent the prototype game to the customer, Ugly Furniture Organization, and received some feedback. It liked the game concept, but requested some additional gameplay features be included. Your team has the task of incorporating these requested changes. The client wants to see a better application of physics in the game to make things more realistic, so first you must learn how physics is applied in a game to simulate lifelike movement.

Reading Materials

Physics is the field of science involving the study of matter and motion. In a game, real-world physics has to be simulated using programming. Some aspects of programming physics can be very advanced, while simulating other aspects can be very simple.

In the Click Ball game, the ball bounce was realistic, because a ball would naturally bounce when it hits a wall. However, the fact that the ball continued at the same speed after bouncing was not realistic. In the real world, forces like gravity and friction slow down the ball until it eventually stops. That is why when you throw a ball on the ground, it bounces, but each time it does not go as high, as shown in **Figure 14-1.** The force of gravity pushes the ball back down and the friction with the air and ground causes the ball to slow down as it travels.

A cornerstone of physics is momentum. ***Momentum*** can be thought of as the energy of movement. In the real world, momentum is calculated using the formula:

$$\text{momentum} = \text{mass} \times \text{velocity}$$

If an object with little mass, like a penny, hits you moving at a low speed (velocity), it has low momentum and does little damage. However, if you

Name: _____

Date: _____

Class: _____

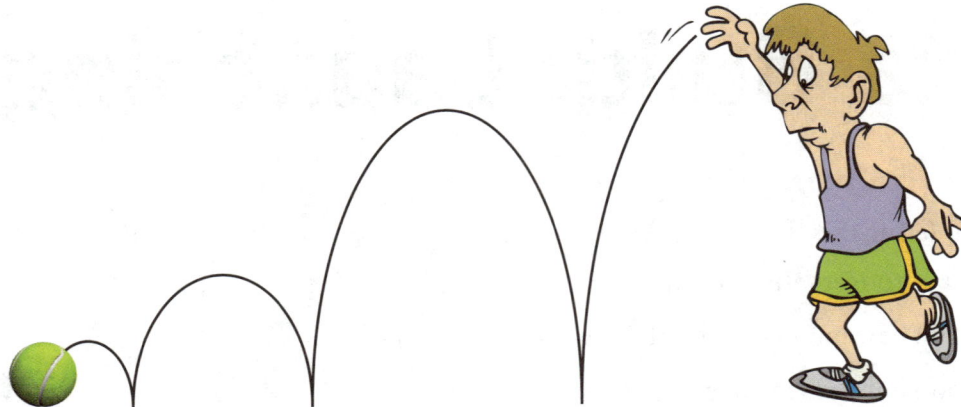

Goodheart-Willcox Publisher; line art: Clipart.com

Figure 14-1. When you drop a ball, it bounces, but because of gravity each bounce is not as high as the previous one.

speed up the penny (increase the velocity) to 30 miles an hour, it will have great momentum and will really hurt if you are hit by it. By increasing the velocity, more energy is added that must be accounted for during the collision. The mass could also be changed to add energy. A pebble slowly rolling down a hill will do little damage to anything it strikes. However, if an object with more mass, like a boulder, rolls down the same hill at the same speed, then a more powerful collision results because the object has more energy.

Another part of physics deals with the conservation of matter and energy. In a closed system, like a game world, all energy and matter will remain constant. ***Conservation of matter*** means that all of the matter (the "stuff") that exists before a collision should exist after the collision. ***Conservation of energy*** means no energy can be created or destroyed, only changed in form (electrical energy into heat energy, for example). So, if you were to weigh two large meteors before they collided, collected the shattered pieces after the collision, and weigh all the pieces, the two measured values should be the same, as shown in **Figure 14-2.**

Game Build

Your team has demonstrated the proof of concept and shown the game can work. Now, you need to incorporate more challenges to the gameplay. The Ugly Furniture Organization suggests that the meteors break apart when hit with the photon and to add power-ups to extend gameplay.

How to Begin

1. Launch Clickteam Fusion 2.5 software, and open the proof of concept game created in Lesson 13.
2. Save the file as *LastName*_Meteor_Beta in your working folder.
3. Open the Game Frame in frame editor.
4. Applying what you have learned, insert a new lives object, and place it in the top-left corner of the frame.

Frame Editor

Editing the Lives Image

Notice the default image used to display lives is a heart. It would look better if the lives used the UFO object instead.

5. Applying what you have learned, open the UFO object in the image editor.

Goodheart-Willcox Publisher; photographs: Mike Tan, Eastimages, Bragin Alexey, and JGade/Shutterstock.com

Figure 14-2. Conservation of matter means all of the pieces must weigh the same as the whole before it is broken apart, unless there is an energy conversion.

6. Click the **Selection Tool** button, and drag a selection box around the entire UFO on the canvas, as shown in **Figure 14-3.**
7. Click the **Copy** button to place the selected image on the system clipboard.
8. Click the **Cancel** button to close the image editor without making any changes.
9. Open the Lives object in the image editor.

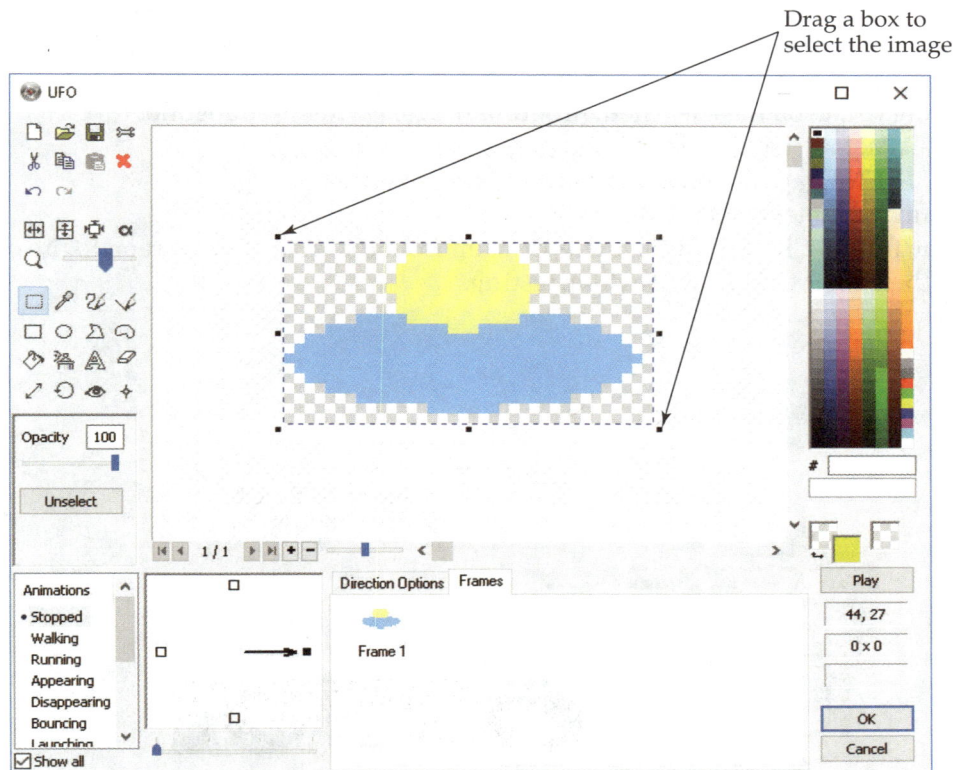

Selection
Tool

Copy

Goodheart-Willcox Publisher

Figure 14-3. Use the **Selection Tool** to select the entire image.

Clear

10. Applying what you have learned, clear the canvas.
11. Click the **Paste** button to place the copied UFO image on the canvas. A message appears indicating the clipboard image is larger than the current canvas. Click the **Yes** button to resize canvas.

Paste

12. Click the **Crop** button. This automatically removes any part of the canvas that is not being used. Removing unneeded data will help keep the file size down.
13. Click the **OK** button to update the object. Notice three UFOs are displayed on the Lives object instead of three hearts, as shown in **Figure 14-4**.

Crop

Adding Challenge

While building the proof of concept, all the meteors were static and did not move. This made it easy to test, but not very interesting to play. Making the meteors move will force the player to hit moving targets, which will add challenge to the game. If the meteors can also destroy the UFO, there will be even greater challenge to the game.

Movement

14. Select any of the Meteor_L objects, and click the **Movement** tab of the **Properties** toolbar.
15. Change the Type property to Bouncing Ball.
16. Change the Initial Direction property to only downward motion by selecting directions 18 through 30, as shown in **Figure 14-5**.
17. Change the Speed property to 8.
18. Applying what you have learned, change the movement of the Meteor_M object to bouncing ball with a speed of 15 and initial directions 0 to 5, 11 to 21, and 27 to 31.
19. Change the movement of the Meteor_S object to bouncing ball with a speed of 20 and initial directions of 0, 4, 8, 12, 16, 20, 24, and 28.
20. Run the frame to see the movement of the meteors. Close the game window when done testing.

Run Frame

Movement Wrap

You probably noticed the meteors travel off-screen, and the screen is quickly blank. Adding movement wrap will wrap the meteors around the frame when they exit.

Event Editor

21. Open the Game Frame in event editor.
22. Applying what you have learned, program the following pseudocode.
    IF the Meteor_L object leaves the play area,
        THEN wrap the movement around the play area.
23. Program the Meteor_M and Meteor_S objects to wrap as well.
24. Run the frame. Check that the meteors wrap from one side of the screen to the other. Close the game window when done testing.

Run Frame

UFOs are displayed instead of hearts

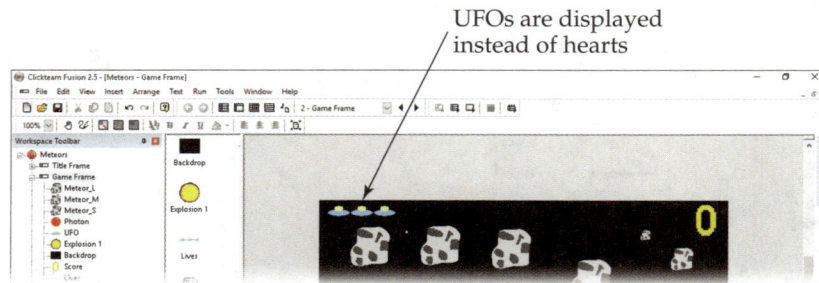

Goodheart-Willcox Publisher

Figure 14-4. The Lives object is updated to reflect the player character.

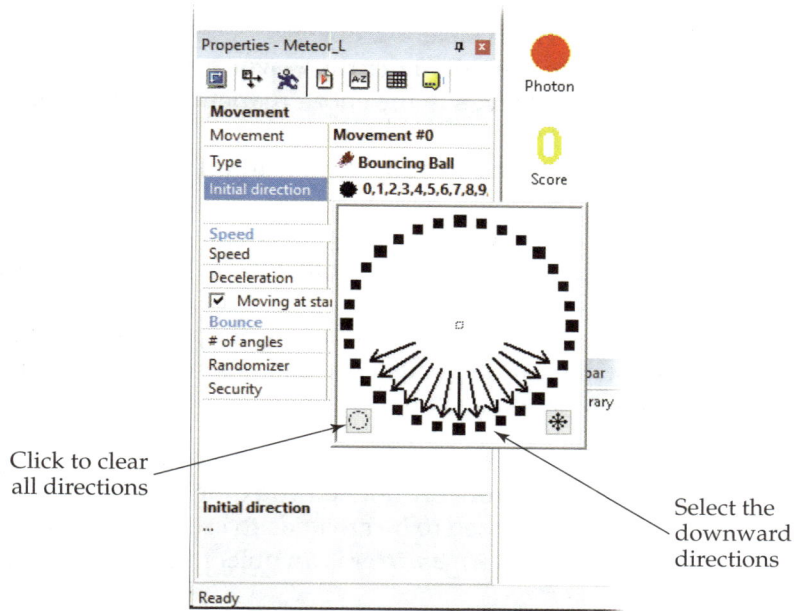

Goodheart-Willcox Publisher

Figure 14-5. The initial direction for the object will be in one of the selected directions indicated by the arrows.

Collisions

To make the game more realistic, the meteors should not be able to pass through each other. Some additional programming is needed to detect when meteors collide with each other and what happens during the collision.

25. Add a new event, and program this pseudocode:
   IF the Meteor_L object collides with the Meteor_L object,
       THEN have the Meteor_L object bounce.

26. Use the table below to program the other collisions to simulate physics in the game. The bigger meteor will not move, the smaller meteor will bounce. This simulates how the larger-mass object is less affected by the collision. Same-size objects will both bounce. Remember, you can copy and paste programming to be more efficient.

Collision	Meteor_L Movement	Meteor_M Movement	Meteor_S Movement
Meteor_L with Meteor_M	None	Bounce	None
Meteor_L with Meteor_S	None	None	Bounce
Meteor_M with Meteor_M	None	Bounce	None
Meteor_M with Meteor_S	None	None	Bounce
Meteor_S with Meteor_S	None	None	Bounce

27. Run the frame. Do not launch photons. See how the meteors react to each other when they collide.

Run Frame

Limited Lives

During development of the proof of concept, the player did not have to worry about getting hit by a meteor. If a meteor can destroy the player character, the game will be more challenging. The player will not only need to destroy meteors, but also avoid them.

28. Add a new event, and program this pseudocode to create the condition:

     IF the UFO object collides with a Meteor_L object

29. On the same line, right-click in the cell under the **Player 1** icon, and click **Number of Lives>Subtract from Number of Lives** in the shortcut menu. The expression editor is displayed.

30. In the expression editor, enter 1, and click the **OK** button. This tells the computer to remove one life from player 1.

31. Applying what you have learned, copy the event line you just programmed and paste it twice. Modify the two new lines to remove one life if the UFO object collides with either the Meteor_M or Meteor_S object.

32. Run the frame. See if the number of lives is reduced when the UFO hits any meteor. Note: the programming has not been added to destroy and spawn the UFO. Close the game window when done testing.

Run Frame

More Meteors

As you test-played the game, you probably noticed you quickly run out of meteors. To continue the game, more meteors will need to be created. To create maximum randomness, emitters will be used to spawn meteors. An *emitter* is an object that generates other objects or particles.

33. Open the Game Frame in the frame editor.

34. Insert a new active object in the top-right corner of the frame, and name it Emitter_Red.

Frame Editor

35. Open the Emitter_Red object in the image editor.

36. Applying what you have learned, clear the canvas, and fill it with any shade of red. Then, close the image editor.

37. Applying what you have learned, clone the Emitter_Red object so there is a total of three, as shown in **Figure 14-6.** Use a row spacing of 5.

38. Name one of the new emitters Emitter_Green, and change the sprite to a solid green fill.

39. Name the second new emitter Emitter_Yellow, and change the sprite to a solid yellow fill.

Movement

40. Select the Emitter_Red object, and click the **Movement** tab in the **Properties** toolbar.

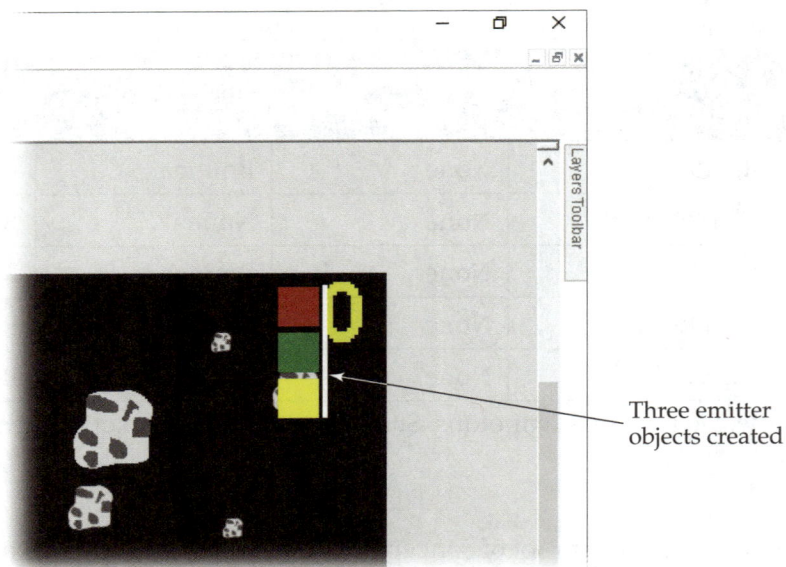

Three emitter objects created

Figure 14-6. The first emitter is cloned to create two additional emitters.

Set the path color

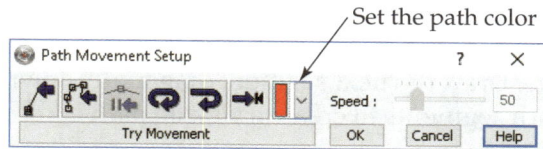

Goodheart-Willcox Publisher

Figure 14-7. The **Path Movement Setup** dialog box contains tools for creating and modifying an object's movement path.

41. Change the Type property to Path, and click the **Edit** button. The **Path Movement Setup** dialog box is displayed, as shown in **Figure 14-7.** If necessary, move the dialog box so it is not covering the frame. Hover the cursor over the buttons to show the help text.

42. Click the drop-down arrow next to the color swatch, and click the red swatch in the drop-down list. This sets the color of the path to red.

43. Click the **New Line** button. A line segment is attached to the object and the cursor. This tool allows you to draw straight-line paths for the object to follow. The path will not be visible during gameplay.

44. Click in the top-left corner of the frame to draw a straight-line path across the top of the frame, as shown in **Figure 14-8.** The red line is the path between the starting and ending nodes. Notice that the ending node is flashing. This means it is selected.

45. Click in the **Speed:** text box, and enter 20. This sets the speed of the object at the selected node, which in this case is the ending node.

46. Click the starting node in the middle of the Emitter_Red object to select the node. When the starting node is selected, the path also flashes.

47. Click in the **Speed:** text box, and enter 20 to set the speed of the object at the starting node.

48. Click the **Reverse at End** button. This will send the object back along the path when it reaches the ending node.

49. Click the **Loop the Movement** button. This will restart the movement when the object reaches the starting node.

50. Click the **OK** button in the **Path Movement Setup** dialog box to create the path for the Emitter_Red object.

51. Run the frame. Notice the Emitter_Red object traveling back and forth along the top of the screen. Close the game window when done testing.

Multiple-Node Path

A straight-line path can have more than one segment. This creates a multiple-node path. Each segment in the path is straight, but the overall path can go in different directions.

52. Applying what you have learned, change the movement of the Emitter_Green object to a path, and edit the path.

53. Change the path color to green.

New Line

Reverse at End

Loop the Movement

Run Frame

Set the speed   Selected node   Path

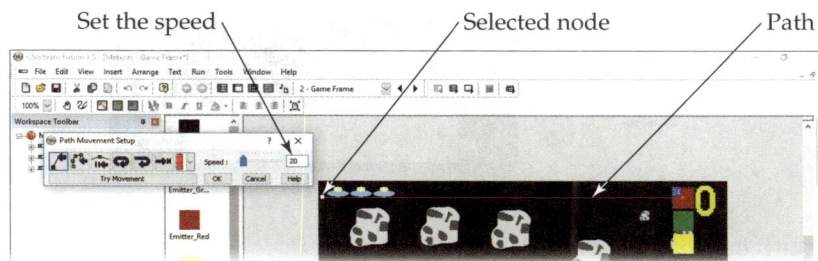

Goodheart-Willcox Publisher

Figure 14-8. A straight-line path is created, and the speed at the selected node is set.

New Line

54. Click the **New Line** button, and draw a line diagonally upward and off the frame.
55. Click the **New Line** button again. A new path segment appears connected to the cursor and the previous node. Draw the next segment diagonally downward onto the frame.
56. Continue drawing path segments to create a zig-zag path across the top of the frame, as shown in **Figure 14-9.**
57. Applying what you have learned, change the speed at each node to 30, loop and reverse the movement, and finish creating the path. If each node has the same speed setting, the object will move at a consistent speed along the entire path.
58. Run the frame. Test the movement of the Emitter_Green object. Close the game window when done testing.

Run Frame

Drawing a Path

Each node of a path does not have to be drawn in one node at a time. The tape mouse feature allows a path to be drawn following the movement of the cursor. Each path segment is still straight, but this method allows for curved paths to be approximated.

59. Applying what you have learned, change the movement of the Emitter_Yellow object to a path, and edit the path.
60. Change the path color to yellow.
61. Click the **Tape Mouse** button.
62. Position the cursor over the Emitter_Yellow object, click, and hold down the left mouse button. Drag to draw a looping path across the top of the screen, as shown in **Figure 14-10.** Release the mouse button to finish drawing the path.
63. Drag a selection box around the path. This selects all nodes in the path. The entire path should be flashing.
64. Click in the **Speed:** text box, and enter 60. Since all nodes are selected, the speed is changed for all nodes in one step.
65. Applying what you have learned, set the path to reverse and loop, and finish creating the path.

Tape Mouse

Run Frame

66. Run the frame. Check the movement of all three emitters. Close the game window when done testing.

Creating Random Meteors

When testing, you probably notice how the emitters collided at different points. This is random enough to be used to simulate a random condition. When an emitter collides with another emitter, the emitters will spawn meteors.

67. Open the Game Frame in the event editor.

Event Editor

Multinode path

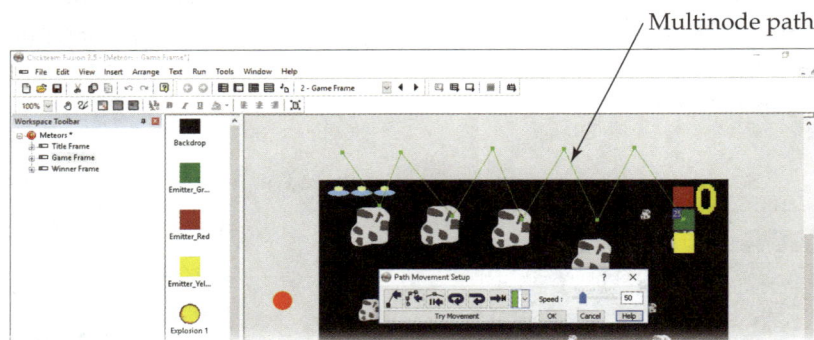

Figure 14-9. A path can consist of multiple segments.

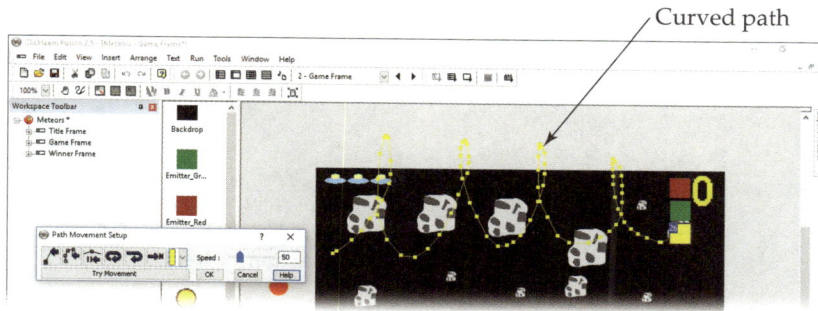

Curved path

Figure 14-10. The **Tape Mouse** tool can be used to create a curved path. However, each path segment is a straight line.

68. Applying what you have learned, program this pseudocode as a new condition:
    IF the Emitter_Red object collides with the Emitter_Green object,
        THEN create a Meteor_L object at (0, 0) relative to the Emitter_Red object.
69. Run the frame. Destroy many of the meteors to test how the Emitter_Red object spawns new Meteor_L objects. Close the game window when done testing.
70. Program this pseudocode to spawn Meteor_M objects:
    IF the Emitter_Green object collides with the Emitter_Yellow object,
        THEN create a Meteor_M object at (0, 0) relative to the Emitter_Green object.
71. Program this pseudocode to spawn Meteor_S objects.
    IF the Emitter_Red object collides with the Emitter_Yellow object,
        THEN create a Meteor_S object at (0, 0) relative to the Emitter_Yellow object.
72. Run the frame. Test to see if all three types of meteors are being created. Also check to see if enough or too many meteors are created. Close the game window when done testing.
73. Edit the path and speed of the emitters if needed to make sure more of each type are being created. To edit the path, display the frame editor, select the emitter, and click the **Edit** button in the **Properties** toolbar. The path can then be adjusted.

Simulated Physics

This game will not have real-world physics, but will have some simulated physics to make the game more realistic. Currently, the large and medium size meteors are destroyed by a photon. Instead, the large meteor can be split into smaller pieces to add a bit of realism.

74. Display the Game Frame in the event editor.
75. In the event line for a collision between the Photon object and the Meteor_L object, right-click in the cell under the **Create new object** icon, and click **Create object** in the shortcut menu. Note: there is already a check mark in that cell. This will be added to the existing programming.
76. In the **Create Object** dialog box, select the Meteor_M object, and click the **OK** button.
77. Click the **Relative to:** radio button, and select the Meteor_L object. Do *not* close the **Create Object** dialog box yet.
78. Enter 10 in the **X:** text box and 20 in the **Y:** text box, as shown in **Figure 14-11.** This sets an offset from the object where the new object will be created.
79. Click the **OK** button to finish the programming.
80. For the same condition, create a Meteor_S object with an offset of (0, –20).

Run Frame

Run Frame

Event Editor

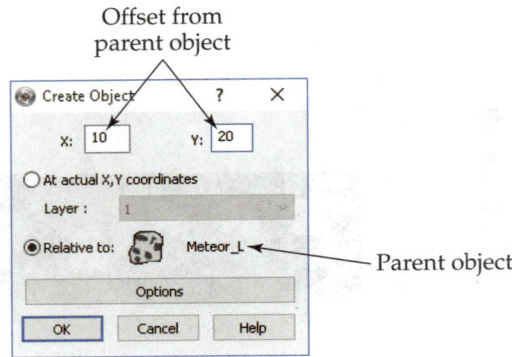

Offset from parent object

Parent object

Figure 14-11. An object can be created offset from its parent object. This can help avoid the stacking or bunching of objects in the game.

81. For the same condition, create a second Meteor_S object with an offset of (0, 10). This one event should result in creating four objects, as shown in **Figure 14-12:** Explosion 1, Meteor_M, and two of Meteor_S. Using the offsets will prevent the meteors from overlapping and getting stuck together.

82. Applying what you have learned, modify the event for a collision between the Photon object and the Meteor_M object to create two new Meteor_S objects that are offset to avoid overlap. Use an offset of your own choosing.

83. Run the frame. Take special notice on how the large meteor and the medium meteor split when hit with a photon. There should be more of the small meteors as the game progresses due to the split. Close the game window when done testing.

Run Frame

Shield Perk

Bonuses and perks are enhancements to the game that encourage the player to take risks to achieve the benefit. In this game, earning extra lives or a shield to protect against the meteors would be worth the risk to collect the reward. The first perk you will create is a shield to protect the UFO. This shield will be present from the start and can be regenerated by collecting shield perks throughout the game.

84. Display the Game Frame in the frame editor.

85. Insert a new active object outside the visible play area, name the object Emitter_Bonus, and set the movement to a path.

Frame Editor

86. Applying what you have learned, use the **Tape Mouse** function to create a path that weaves through the paths of the other emitters. The idea here is to create random collision with the other emitters.

Tape Mouse

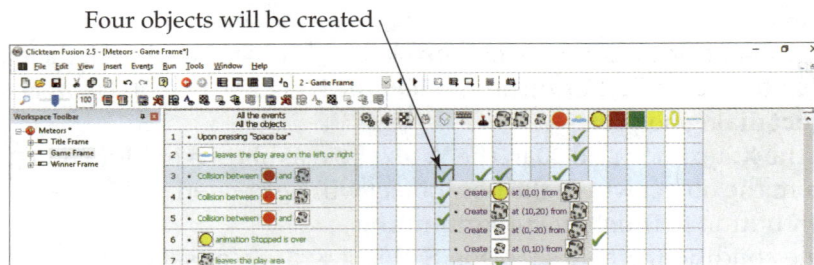

Four objects will be created

Figure 14-12. To help simulate physics, the large meteor will split into three meteors when hit with a photo. An explosion is also created.

87. Set the path to loop and reverse at end, and finish creating the path.

88. Insert a new active object outside the visible play area, name it Shield, set the width and height to 83, and open the object in the image editor.

89. Use the **Zoom** slider to make the canvas as big as possible while still being able to see the entire canvas. You may wish to change the size of the image editor or make it full screen.

90. Applying what you have learned, clear the canvas, and draw the outline of a circle (not filled) that is five pixels wide and the size of the canvas, as shown in **Figure 14-13.** Use a color of your choice that will contrast with the game frame's background color, such as yellow.

Ellipse Tool

91. Click the **OK** button to update the object.

92. Applying what you have learned, create a clone of the Shield object below it, name the clone Bonus_Shield, and open the Bonus_Shield object in the image editor.

93. Applying what you have learned, add text to the center of the circle that states Shield. Use a color, font, and size of your choice.

94. Click the **OK** button to update the object and close the image editor.

95. Select the Bonus_Shield object, and click the **Movement** tab in the **Properties** toolbar.

Movement

96. Set the Type property to Bouncing Ball.

97. Set the Initial direction property to directions 21 through 27.

98. Set the **Speed** property to 20.

Shield Perk Programming

The shield should protect the UFO from collisions with meteors. Also, when the shield is used, it should be centered on the UFO and follow the UFO as it moves. There are already several lines of programming for the Game Frame. As more and more lines are added, it is a good practice to add notes to help keep the programming organized. A *comment* is a line

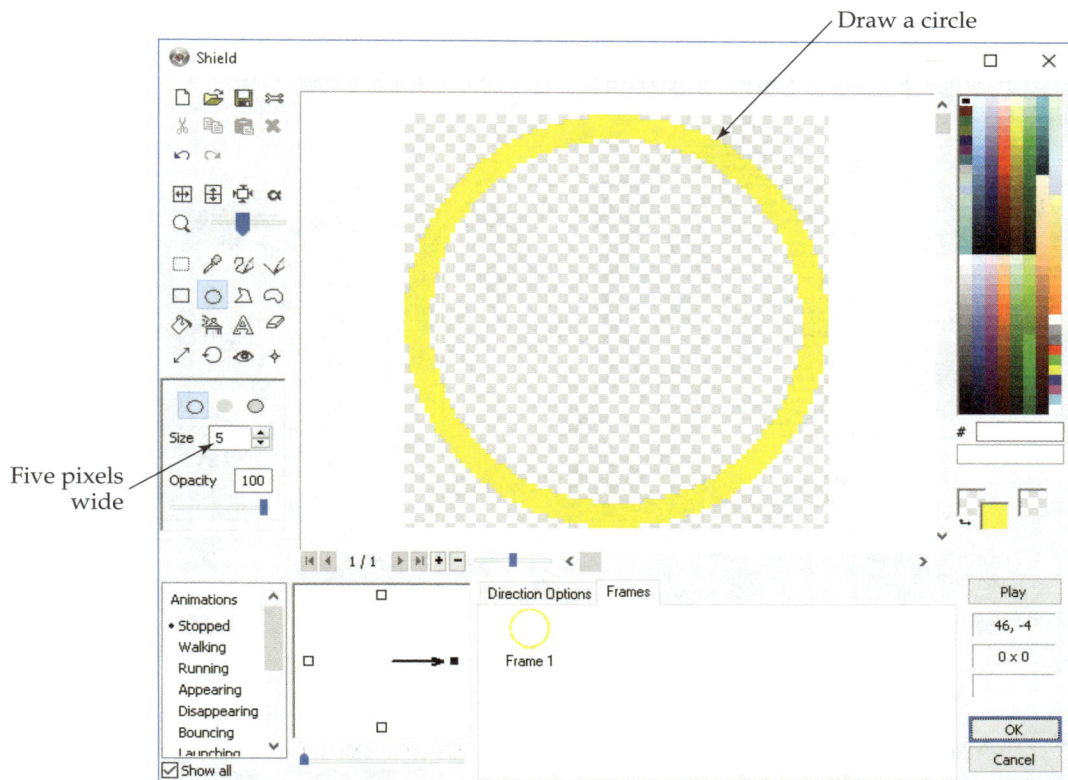

Goodheart-Willcox Publisher

Figure 14-13. The shield is a simple circle that will surround the UFO.

of text that programmers use to write notes inside their programs. It is not programming. Commenting helps you remember what you were doing with a section of programming. It also helps other programmers figure out what you were trying to do when they debug the code.

Event Editor

99. Display the event editor for the Game Frame.
100. Right-click the number next to New condition (the last line), and click **Insert>A comment** in the shortcut menu. The **Edit Text** dialog box is displayed.
101. Enter Power Up Shield. This text is the comment.
102. Click the **OK** button to create the comment. Notice how a comment line was added, as shown in **Figure 14-14.** Even though this appears to be a line in the programming, it will not be processed by the game engine.
103. Add a new condition below the comment, and program this pseudocode:
    IF the Emitter_Bonus object collides with the Emitter_Red object,
        THEN create a new Bonus_Shield object at the absolute coordinate (300, –30).
104. Add a new condition, and program this pseudocode:
    IF the UFO object collides with the Bonus_Shield object,
        THEN create a new Shield object at (0, 0) relative to the UFO object
            AND destroy the Bonus_Shield object.
105. Add a new condition, and program this pseudocode:
    IF always
106. In event line for the new condition, right-click in the cell under the icon for the Shield object, and click **Position>Select position…** in the shortcut menu.
107. Applying what you have learned, set the position at (0, 0) relative to the UFO object.
108. Run the frame. Notice that the shield appears around the UFO and follows it around, but it does not block any meteors…yet. Close the game window when done testing.

Run Frame

109. Add a new condition, and program this pseudocode:
    IF the Meteor_L object collides with the Shield object,
        THEN bounce the Meteor_L object.
110. Applying what you have learned, copy the event line you just programmed, and paste it twice. Then, edit the two new lines to bounce the medium and small meteors.

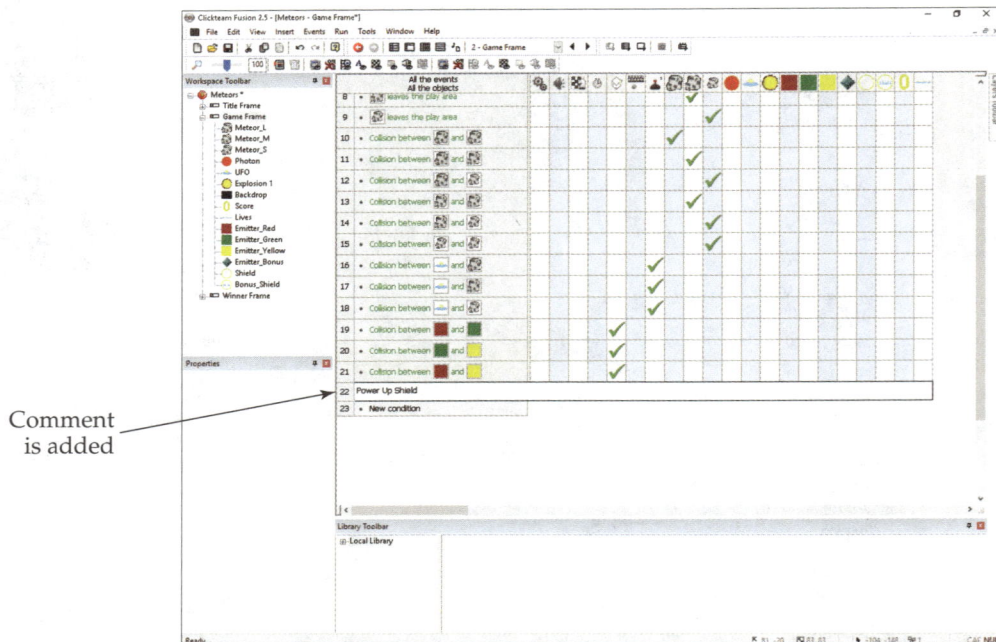

Goodheart-Willcox Publisher

Figure 14-14. Comments should be used to help group and organize the programming.

111. Run the frame. Test that all meteors bounce off the shield. Note: it may get a little buggy if there are too many meteors bouncing on the shield at the same time and some meteors may slip past the shield.

Shield Power Level

Being invincible behind the shield is nice, but does not make for much challenge. Giving the shield limited time creates a challenge for the player. To help the player, a power-level indicator will be added to show how long the shield will last. When the shield is out of power, it will be destroyed. Since this programming is for the shield, it will be added under the Power Up Shield comment to keep the programming organized.

112. Display the Game Frame in the frame editor.
113. Add a new Counter object anywhere on the frame, and name it Shield Power.
114. Select the Shield Power object, and click the **Settings** tab in the **Properties** toolbar.
115. Set the Type property to Horizontal bar, as shown in **Figure 14-15.** This changes the format from numbers to a health bar.
116. Make sure the Count property is set to From left.
117. Set the Fill type property to Gradient.
118. Click the color swatch for the Color property, and click the red color swatch in the palette.
119. Set the Color 2 property to green.
120. Set the Initial Value property to 10.
121. Set the Minimum Value property to 0.
122. Set the Maximum Value property to 10.
123. Click the **Size and Position** tab in the **Properties** toolbar.
124. Set the Width property to 40 and the Height property to 10.
125. Display the event editor for the Game Frame.
126. In the event line for **IF** the UFO object collides with the Bonus_Shield object, right-click in the cell under the icon for the Shield Power object, and click **Set Counter** in the shortcut menu.
127. In the expression editor, enter 10, and click the **OK** button. This programming will reset the power if the shield is still in place.

Frame Editor

Settings

Size and Position

Event Editor

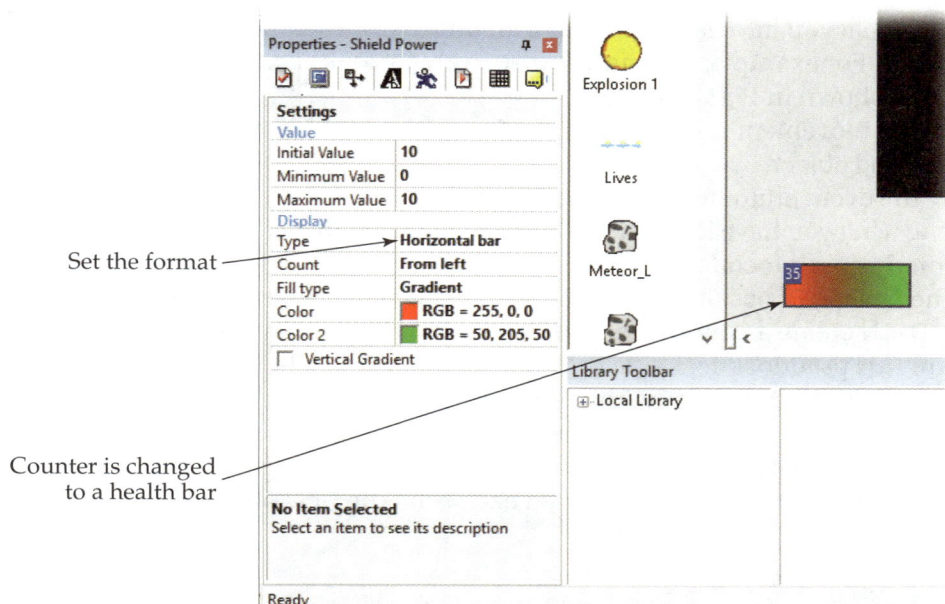

Set the format

Counter is changed to a health bar

Goodheart-Willcox Publisher

Figure 14-15. A Counter object can be set up to be a health bar instead of a number counter.

128. To make the power bar follow the UFO, add this pseudocode to the existing Always event:
THEN set position of the Shield Power object to (–20, 20) relative to the UFO object.

129. Edit the event line for **IF** the Meteor_L object collides with the Shield object by programming this pseudocode:
THEN subtract 3 from the Shield Power counter.

130. Edit the event line for **IF** the Meteor_M object collides with the Shield object by programming this pseudocode:
THEN subtract 2 from the Shield Power counter.

131. Edit the event line for **IF** the Meteor_S object collides with the Shield object by programming this pseudocode:
THEN subtract 1 from the Shield Power counter.

132. Add a new event. In the **New Condition** dialog box, right-click on the Shield Power object, and click **Compare the counter to a value...** in the shortcut menu. The expression editor is displayed.

133. Enter 0 in the expression editor, and click the **OK** button. This creates the pseudocode:
IF the Shield Power equals 0.

134. In the event line for the condition you just created, right-click in the cell under the icon for the Shield object, and click **Destroy** in the shortcut menu. This creates the pseudocode:
THEN destroy the Shield object

Run Frame

135. Run the frame. Test how the shield performs. The power bar should be below the UFO and should follow it around the screen. Bigger meteors cause more damage to the shield than smaller ones. When the shield runs out of power, it should be destroyed. Close the game window when done testing.

Bonus Lives Perk

The shield helps keep the player in the game much longer before running out of lives. However, another perk could be to add a way for the player to earn extra lives. This will also encourage the player to take risks to gain the perk.

Frame Editor

136. Display the Game Frame in the frame editor.

137. Insert a new active object, name it Bonus_Lives, and open the object in the image editor.

138. Applying what you have learned, create an image from scratch to represent a health or lives bonus. For example, you may choose to create an image that looks like a Red Cross symbol, as shown in **Figure 14-16.**

139. Change the movement to function of the Bonus_Lives object to be the same as the Bonus_Shield object.

Event Editor

140. Display the event editor for the Game Frame.

141. Applying what you have learned, add a new comment that states Power Up Lives.

142. Program this pseudocode:
    IF the Emitter_Bonus object collides with the Emitter_Green object,
        THEN create a new Bonus_Lives object at (*location of your choice*).

143. Program this pseudocode:
    IF the UFO object collides with the Bonus_Lives object,
        THEN increase Player 1 lives by 1
            AND destroy the Bonus_Lives object.

Run Frame

144. Run the frame. Test that lives are added each time the UFO object collides with the Bonus_Lives object.

145. Debug the programming as needed.

Image for lives bonus

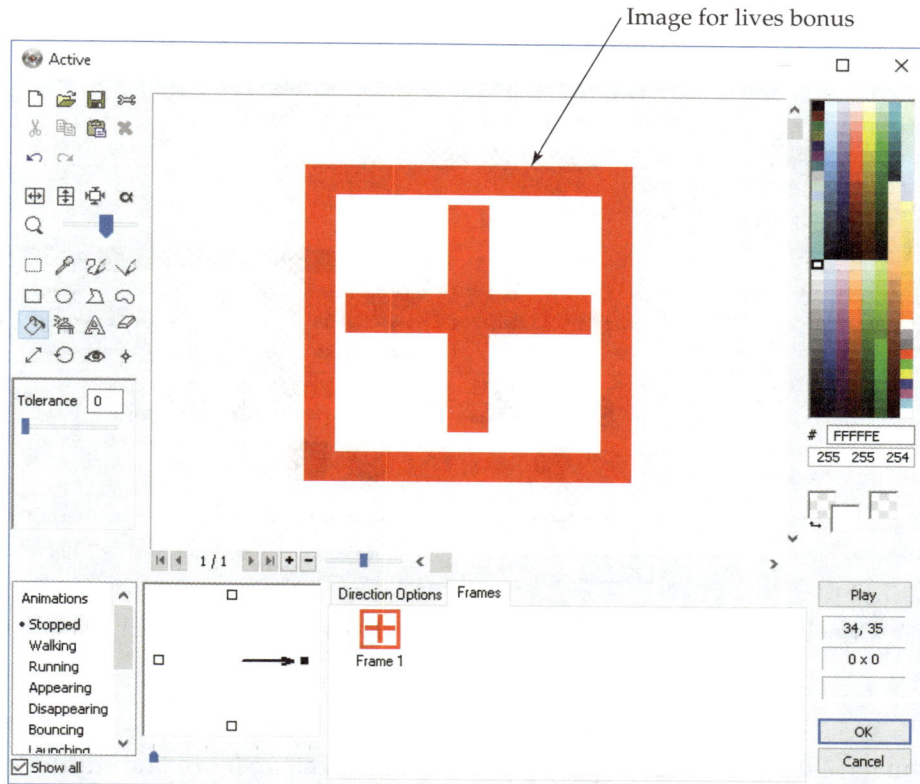

Goodheart-Willcox Publisher

Figure 14-16. The sprite for a health or lives perk should communicate to the player what collecting the object means. A red cross is a universal symbol for aid or health in a game. Most players will automatically understand what this means.

Player Lives

Testing the game to this point has been easy as the lives did not really matter. This was good for testing, but is not good for challenging gameplay. However, the game should end when the player runs out of lives.

146. Display the Game Frame in event editor.
147. Add a new condition. In the **New Condition** dialog box, right-click in the cell under the **Player 1** icon, and click **Compare to the player's number of lives** in the shortcut menu.
148. In the expression editor, set the comparison method to equal and the amount to zero, as shown in **Figure 14-17.** Then, click the **OK** button to close the expression editor. This tests to see if there are no more lives left for the player.
149. In the event line for the condition you just created, right-click in the cell under the **Storyboard Controls** icon, and click **Next Frame** in the shortcut menu. This will move the player to the next frame when the lives have reached zero.
150. Click the line number for the event line you just programmed, and drag the line up above first comment. This line of programming is not related to either the shield power up or the lives power up, so it should be grouped with the more general programming.
151. Display the Game Frame in the frame editor.
152. Delete any meteors in the visible frame. This will allow only spawned meteors to occur in the game. This will also allow the player a few moments before any meteors appear.
153. Run the frame. Test all aspects of the game. Close the game window when done testing.
154. Debug the programming as needed.

Event Editor

Run Frame

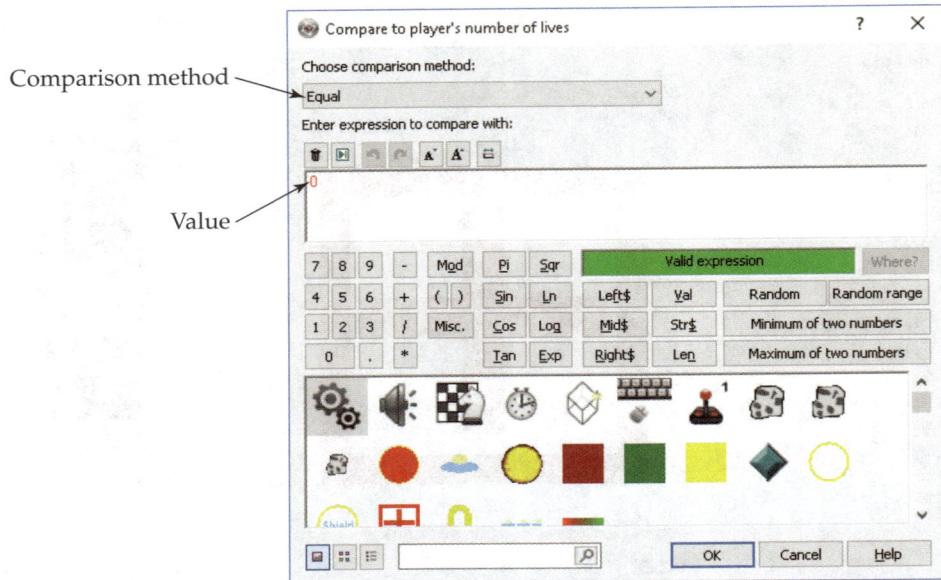

Comparison method

Value

Goodheart-Willcox Publisher

Figure 14-17. Checking to see if the number of player lives equals zero can be used to end the game.

Tuning

Once you have the game working properly, it is time to clean it up. The emitters should not be visible during gameplay. The game also needs polishing with sounds.

Event Editor

155. Display the Game Frame in the event editor.
156. Add a new condition. In the **New Condition** dialog box, right-click on the **Storyboard Controls** icon, and click **Start of frame** in the shortcut menu, as shown in **Figure 14-18.**
157. In the line for the condition you just added, right-click in the cell under the icon for the Emitter_Red object, and click **Visibility>Make Object Invisible**. This event line will hide the Emitter_Red object when the frame starts. The object will still be active in the game, but the player will not be able to see it.

Right-click

Select

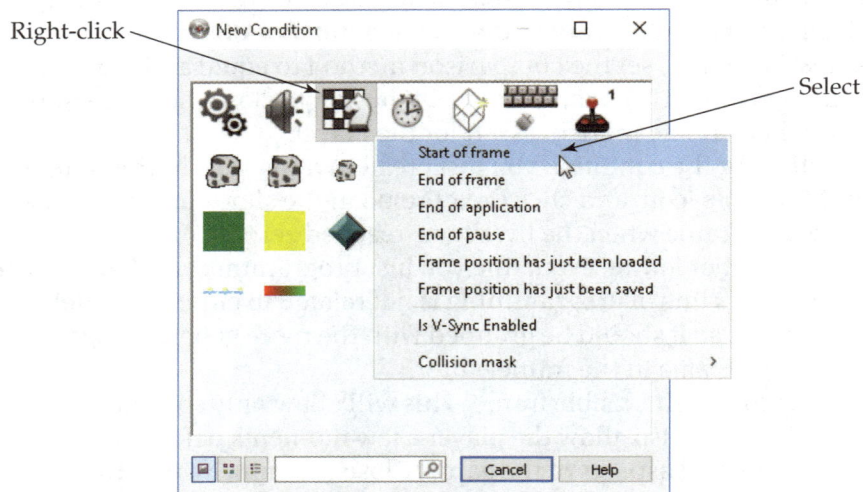

Goodheart-Willcox Publisher

Figure 14-18. The condition of when the frame starts can be used to hide objects so the player does not see them.

158. Drag the check mark you just added to the cells for the Emitter_Green and Emitter_Yellow objects.

159. Drag event line to above the first comment. This event applies to the game in general and should not be grouped under either comment.

160. Applying what you have learned, add appropriate sounds to the game interactions. Use sounds supplied in the Clickteam Fusion 2.5 Samples folder or locate your own free-use sound files.

161. Edit the UFO object to allow for more directions of motion, not just left and right movement. Be sure to update the programming to check if the object leaves the play area in any direction.

162. Design and add an additional perk that will spawn when the Emitter_Bonus object collides with the Emitter_Yellow object. Add the programming needed for the perk to function properly in the game.

163. Make other modifications that you feel would make the gameplay better.

164. Make any refinements to the Title Frame and Winner Frame as you see fit. Include your name on the Title Frame as the designer of the game.

165. Run the application. Fully test the game.

166. Debug all frames as needed.

167. Save your work, and submit your work for grading.

Run Application

Vocabulary

Write a definition for each of the key terms from this lesson. You will develop a personal glossary of key terms throughout this course.

physics

_____

_____

momentum

_____

_____

conservation of matter

_____

_____

conservation of energy

_____

_____

emitter

_____

_____

comment

_____

_____

Review Questions

1. Why would a bonus or perk be added to a game?

_____
_____
_____
_____

2. If a ball has a mass of 30 ounces and is traveling at 90 miles per hour, what is its momentum?

_____
_____
_____

3. In the game build in this lesson, how can you simulate momentum for the meteors when a large meteor collides with a small meteor?

_____
_____
_____

4. Why would a large meteor decrease the strength of the shield more than a small meteor? Refer to momentum and energy in your answer.

_____
_____
_____
_____

5. Use the momentum formula to complete the table below.

Mass (kg)	Velocity (m/s)	Momentum (kg·m/s)
0.1	5	0.5
25	4	
	10	50
0.5		25

Name: _____

Higher-Order Thinking Strategies

6. In your own words, summarize the concept of conservation of energy.

   _____

   _____

   _____

   _____

   Language Arts

7. Hypothesize what has happened when a rock weighing 2.0 pounds is smashed with a hammer and the pieces collected only weigh 1.9 pounds.

   _____

   _____

   _____

   _____

   Science

8. When playing the game created in this lesson, did you feel excited to see a perk and try to catch it? Do you think other people will feel the same way? Why or why not?

   _____

   _____

   _____

   _____

   Social Science

9. If a falling branch has a mass of 20 kilograms and a momentum of 100 kilogram-meters per second, what is the branch's velocity at the instant the measurements were taken?

   _____

   _____

   _____

   _____

   Mathematics

10. Explain the concept of conservation of matter to describe what happens when water is boiled.

   _____

   _____

   _____

   _____

   Science

Office Technology Integration

Using a Template to Write a Résumé

1. Launch Microsoft Excel or other spreadsheet software, and open the vocabulary spreadsheet you updated in previous lessons.
2. Applying what you have learned, add a new worksheet, and name it Lesson 14.
3. Add each of the vocabulary words and definitions from the Vocabulary section of this lesson.
4. Save the spreadsheet, and then close it.
5. Launch Microsoft Word or other word-processing software.
6. On the startup page, or click **File>New** on the ribbon, click in the search box at the top, and enter entry level resume. Note: you can enter just the word resume, but the list of results may be very long.
7. Select the Entry-level resume template, as shown. A *template* is already formatted and contains placeholder text for you to customize. Recording your accomplishments on a résumé will help you apply for jobs in the future.

Search phrase   Select a template

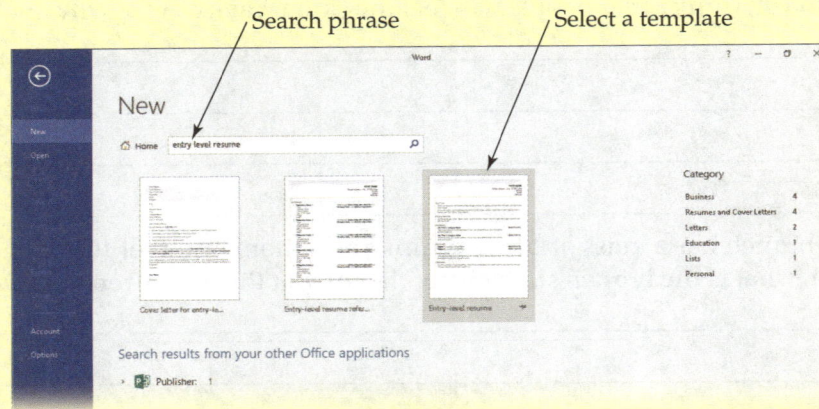

8. In the preview window, click the **Create** button to start a new document based on the template.
9. Add your personal information, such as name and address.
10. Edit the professional information to include your education and experience.
11. List your games as publications.
12. List any awards you have received.
13. Record important information such as industry certifications and other credentials you have achieved.
14. Delete any unwanted or unused placeholders.
15. Save your résumé as *LastName*_Resume in your working folder, and submit it for grading.
16. Applying what you have learned, find a thank-you card template, and create a custom thank-you card for your teacher.

Quality Assurance

Learning Objectives

After completing this lesson, you will be able to:

- evaluate the quality of your own work and the work of others.

- assess positive aspects of the playability and functionality of a game.

- provide constructive criticism to peers by suggesting possible solutions to problems.

Situation

The Awesome Game Company would like you and a colleague to review the beta-version game built in Lesson 14. The results of the review will be used to create a game critique that will be posted to the company website and blog space on the Internet. Complete an evaluation report on the playability and functionality of the game. Each member of the design team needs to evaluate the product and suggest reasons why each item achieves or does not achieve the objective. Be accurate and complete in your evaluations. The personal and peer evaluation are for the same game by the same designer. That means you must give your personal evaluation to a classmate for them to complete the peer evaluation for your game on the same page as your personal evaluation.

Quality Assurance Team

Personal Evaluator Name:

_____

_____

Total Score from Personal Evaluation Rubric:

_____

_____

Peer Evaluator Name:

_____

_____

Total Score from Peer Evaluation Rubric:

_____

_____

Name: _____

Date: _____

Class: _____

Design Reasoning: Personal Evaluation

1. Reflect on your work, and evaluate your game for each of the five key areas of design identified in the rubric.
2. Rank each key area using a scale from 0 to 5. Record the value in the Score column.
3. Complete the Personal Evaluation rubric in the Commentary and Constructive Criticism section. Explain why you gave the score you did for each area of design.
4. Suggest improvements needed for your game in the Personal Evaluation rubric in the Commentary and Constructive Criticism section.

Key Area	0	1	2	3	4	5	Score
Concept Is the idea well developed?	No main idea or theme.					Clear theme or main idea maintained on all levels.	
Aesthetics Does the look, color, contrast, and placement of objects fit the game?	Poor quality graphics, color, and contrast.					Awesome graphics and animations. Items contrasted well.	
Sound Effects Do the sounds play? Are the music and sounds appropriate?	No sound. Sound is too loud, too soft, or not related to the game.					Sounds enhance gameplay and play clearly.	
Functionality Does everything work as expected?	Unfinished. Could not play. Major errors.					Plays perfectly. No bugs, glitches, or errors.	
Replay How likely are you to play this game again?	Game solved. Too easy. Not interesting or impossible to win.					Cannot wait to play it again! Skill was challenging, but enjoyable.	
Add the values in the Score column to get a total.						**Total Score**	

Name: _____

Design Reasoning: Peer Evaluation

1. Play the game designed by the peer as assigned by your instructor.
2. Reflect on the peer's work, and evaluate the game for each of the five key areas of design identified in the rubric.
3. Rank each key area using a scale from 0 to 5. Record the value in the Score column.
4. Complete the Peer Evaluation rubric in the Commentary and Constructive Criticism section. Explain why you gave the score you did for each area of design.
5. Suggest improvements needed for the peer's game in the Peer Evaluation rubric in the Commentary and Constructive Criticism section.

Key Area	0	1	2	3	4	5	Score
Concept Is the idea well developed?	No main idea or theme.					Clear theme or main idea maintained on all levels.	
Aesthetics Does the look, color, contrast, and placement of objects fit the game?	Poor quality graphics, color, and contrast.					Awesome graphics and animations. Items contrasted well.	
Sound Effects Do the sounds play? Are the music and sounds appropriate?	No sound. Sound is too loud, too soft, or not related to the game.					Sounds enhance gameplay and play clearly.	
Functionality Does everything work as expected?	Unfinished. Could not play. Major errors.					Plays perfectly. No bugs, glitches, or errors.	
Replay How likely are you to play this game again?	Game solved. Too easy. Not interesting or impossible to win.					Cannot wait to play it again! Skill was challenging, but enjoyable.	
Add up the values in the Score column to get a total.						**Total Score**	

Commentary and Constructive Criticism

Explain why you assigned the score for each key item assessed. Provide details on what you liked in that area and what needed improvement. Cite specific examples from the game. Provide suggestions on how to improve the game.

Personal Evaluation

Key Area	Detailed Assessment
Concept	
Aesthetics	
Sound Effects	
Functionality	
Replay	
Suggested Improvements	

Peer Evaluation

Key Area	Detailed Assessment
Concept	
Aesthetics	
Sound Effects	
Functionality	
Replay	
Suggested Improvements	

Global Variables

Learning Objectives

After completing this lesson, you will be able to:

- compare and contrast global and local variables.

- evaluate multilevel gameplay navigation.

- analyze navigation for seamless gameplay.

Situation

The Awesome Game Company likes how you have progressed in learning basic programming concepts. It feels you are ready to go beyond basic concepts to construct more complex programming. You must first learn about Boolean logic. You will also need to learn about the core mechanics used in video games and the game loop.

Reading Materials

The programming behind video games uses much advanced programming. Programming is used to enforce the rules of the game. However, the foundation of programming is Boolean logic.

Boolean Logic

Boolean logic is a system of mathematical logic developed by George Boole. *Boolean logic* is a form of algebra in which an argument can be interpreted only as true or false. Much of computer programming is based on Boolean logic using the operators **IF**, **THEN**, **NOT**, **ELSE**, **AND**, and **OR**. As you have seen in previous lessons, the basic logic statement includes the operators **IF** and **THEN**. An example of a basic logic statement is:

IF the ball collides with the wall,
    THEN the ball bounces.

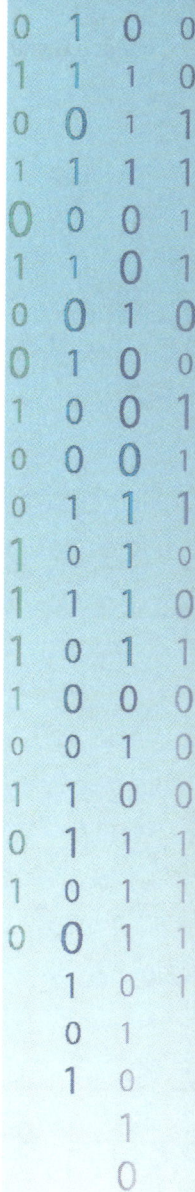

Name: _____

Date: _____

Class: _____

The **IF** side of the logic statement, which is the condition, is tested using Boolean logic. When the **IF** side of the logic statement tests true, the **THEN** side of the statement is executed, which is the action. Here is how the computer solves this logic statement when the ball is touching the wall:

    IF the ball collides with the wall,   true

       THEN the ball bounces.   make the ball bounce

This is how the computer will solve this logic statement when the ball is *not* touching the wall:

    IF the ball collides with the wall,   false

       THEN the ball bounces.   do nothing

NOT and ELSE Operators

To test if a condition is false, the logic operators of **NOT** and **ELSE** are used. An example is setting gravity if a ball is *not* moving downward. Notice in the logic statements below that the action to set gravity is only activated when the logic test is true.

    IF the ball is moving down,   true

       THEN set gravity to 5.   set gravity

    IF the ball is moving down,   false

       THEN set gravity to 5.   do nothing

The computer will only execute commands when the logic test evaluates to true. However, in this game, gravity should be set when the logic test is false. To properly set gravity, the **NOT** operator is included to create a true statement when the ball is not moving.

    IF the ball is **NOT** moving down,   true

       THEN set gravity to 5.   set gravity

    IF the ball is **NOT** moving down,   false

       THEN set gravity to 5.   do nothing

Clickteam Fusion 2.5 software uses the **Negate** command to program a **NOT** logic test, shown in **Figure 16-1.** Notice the red X in front of the condition. This is how Clickteam Fusion 2.5 indicates the **NOT** operator is applied.

Another powerful programming operator that can activate an action if the logic test is false is the **ELSE** operator. For example, suppose the player approaches a chest with a key. The pseudocode below controls the actions seen by the player.

    IF the player has the key,   true

       THEN open the chest   do this

       ELSE display message "Find the key." do not do this

Suppose the player does *not* have the key. The logic test is false, so the programming will activate the **ELSE** action:

    IF the player has the key,   false

       THEN open the chest   do not do this

       ELSE display message "Find the key." do this

AND and OR operators

To combine logic statements, the conjunction operators of **AND** and **OR** are used. These operators work exactly the same as they do in English sentence composition. They join clauses of a logic statement:

    IF the player has a key

    AND the player has a potion,

       THEN open the gate.

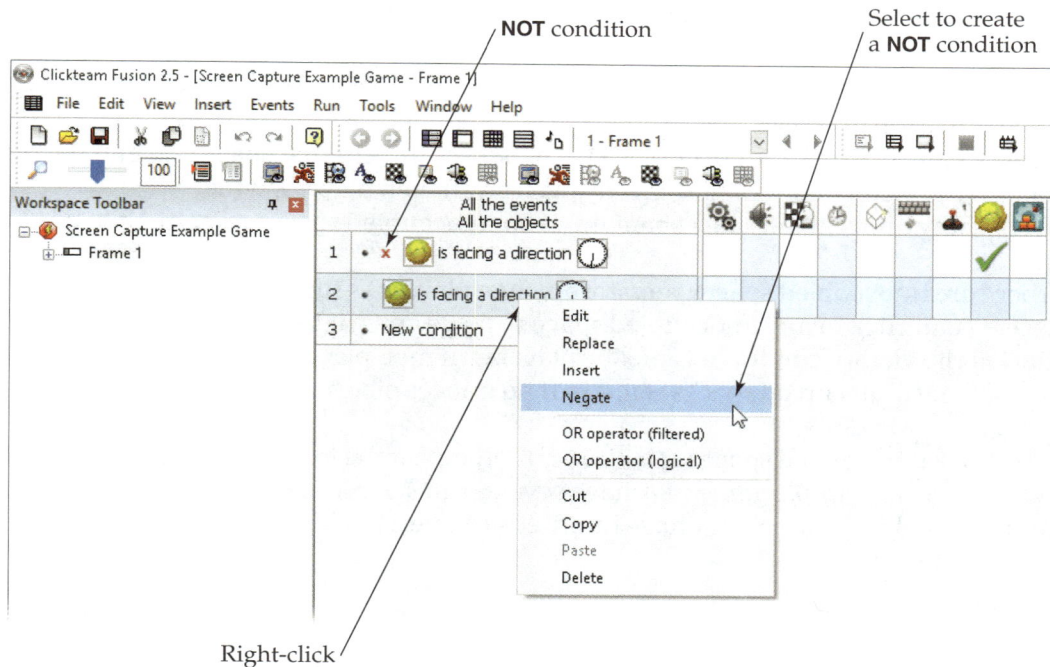

Goodheart-Willcox Publisher

Figure 16-1. In Clickteam Fusion 2.5, a **NOT** condition is indicated by a red X. To create a **NOT** condition, right-click and select **Negate** in the shortcut menu.

IF the player has a blue gem
OR the player has a green gem,
        THEN trade the gem for a potion.

Core Mechanics

The **core mechanics** is a set of programming instructions that enforces the rules required to create a video game. The rules create the game environment and all interactions in the game. When these rules are written into computer coding, the rules become the core mechanics of the game.

Once you have developed a general rule, it must be written into the programming to be part of the core mechanics. Having a general rule, such as the player can run faster than the crocodile, is good to know, but needs to be quantified by the core mechanics. The core mechanics needs to know the maximum speed of the player is 40 pixels per second and the maximum speed of the crocodile is 30 pixels per second. With this specific information, the computer can enforce the rule.

Remember, the computer does not know the graphics on a screen represent real objects. To the computer, a white line on a soccer field is just a bunch of white pixels on the screen. It does not know the white line is out of bounds. To make the out of bounds line mean something to the computer, a rule must be created for the object (graphics) and then programmed into the core mechanics of the game. Here, the rule is:

IF the ball touches the white line,
        THEN the team that did not touch it last puts the ball in play.

In this case, the line object needs to be programmed with a collision event to make the rule work. If the ball collides with the white line, test to see which team touched it last, then give the ball to the opposite team at the spot of the collision.

When designing your own games, you need to list the rules of the game. This gives you a good guide to how each object must be programmed to meet the needs of the core mechanics. As an example, listed below are the simple rules for a game of *Tic-Tac-Toe*.

1. Player X has the first turn.
2. Player X can click in any unoccupied space to place an X in that space and end the turn.
3. Check if the victory condition is met by player X. If met, player X wins.
4. Check if any unoccupied spaces remain. If no unoccupied spaces remain, then it is a tie game.
5. If there are unoccupied spaces remaining, then player O's turn begins.
6. Player O can click in any unoccupied space to place an O in that space and end the turn.
7. Check if the victory condition is met by player O. If met, player O wins.
8. Check if any unoccupied spaces remain. If no unoccupied spaces remain, then it is a tie game.
9. If there are unoccupied spaces remaining, then repeat the loop beginning at step 1.

As you can see, a very simple game may have several rules. A more-complex game, like the video games you play at home, may have hundreds of rules. Each rule must be programmed to create the core mechanics.

Game Loop

When a game programmed in Clickteam Fusion 2.5 is run, the computer starts at the first event and processes each event in turn until it reaches the last event. The program will then loop. A *loop* is a series of instructions that are repeated until the computer receives a command to stop repeating.

In a video game, the process of repeatedly beginning and processing game elements is called the *game loop.* It is the overall flow of conditions and events in the game. Due to the speed of the processor in modern computers, the game loop is repeated hundreds of times per second. The games that you have made so far are rather simple and have only a single loop to run on each frame. The game loop has consisted of the single loops on each frame.

A complex game may have many loops to run within the main game loop. These are called subroutine loops, or simply subroutines or subs. When activated, a *subroutine* is a group of code within the main game loop (or program) that controls a segment of the overall program function. It runs in a loop until instructed to return to the main program loop.

Simple turn-based games need to have a subroutine for each player. The sub will loop until that player's turn is completed. Look at the rules for the *Tic-Tac-Toe* game described earlier. The game loop would contain instructions to activate a specific subroutine loop for the player X turn and another for the player O turn. When the subroutine loop for the player X turn is activated, the loop would permit adding only one X to the game board. When player X adds an X to the board, the loop would check if player X has won. The subroutine for the player X turn would include the rules listed as step 2 and step 3 from the core mechanics.

After the check for player X winning, the player X turn subroutine would be deactivated, and the program would return to the game loop in step 4. In step 5, the game loop would activate the player O turn subroutine and run commands specific to player O as the next turn. The player O turn subroutine would run step 6 and step 7 of the rules, and then be deactivated so the program returns to the game loop on step 8. On step 9, the game loop has completed one full loop and is given instructions to restart at step 1.

Game Build

A new client, Rainforest Laser Tag, wants a game for its website. In this game, the player will have to find treasure hidden in a maze. If the player makes it to the end of the maze, a coupon can be printed for a free game of laser tag.

How to Begin

1. Launch Clickteam Fusion 2.5, and begin a new application.
2. Rename the default frame Level 1.
3. Save the file as *LastName*_Maze_Alpha in your working folder.

Tile-Based Grid

A ***tile-based game*** uses standard-size tiles to construct the scene. To help place tiles on the frame, the grid function can be used to snap each tile into place.

4. Display the Level 1 frame in the frame editor.
5. Click the **Grid Setup** button on the **Navigator Toolbar**. The Grid Setup dialog box is displayed, as shown in **Figure 16-2.**
6. Change the origin to (0, 0). This will place the origin for the grid in the top-left corner of the frame.
7. Enter 32 in the **Width** and **Height** text boxes. Each tile that will be used in this game is 32 pixels square. Setting the grid to match the tile size will allow for easy placement of the tiles.
8. Check the **Snap to** and **Show grid** check boxes to activate and show the grid.
9. Click the **OK** button to apply the grid.

Frame Editor

Grid Setup

Objects

10. In the **Library Toolbar**, expand the tree Local Library>Games>Miscellaneous, and double-click the Game Objects 1 library to display the objects it contains.
11. Place the following objects on the frame, and modify the location and setting as indicated. Try using the snap and grid features to position the objects.

Object Name	Position	Settings
Manic Miner	(36, 439)	Movement Type property: Eight Directions
Corner Wall Tile 12	(0, 32)	Runtime options Obstacle Type property: Obstacle
Corner Wall Tile 10	(0, 448)	Runtime options Obstacle Type property: Obstacle
Corner Wall Tile 9	(608, 32)	Runtime options Obstacle Type property: Obstacle
Corner Wall Tile 11	(608, 448)	Runtime options Obstacle Type property: Obstacle
Wall Tile 7	(608, 64)	Runtime options Obstacle Type property: Obstacle
Wall Tile 6	(32, 32)	Runtime options Obstacle Type property: Obstacle

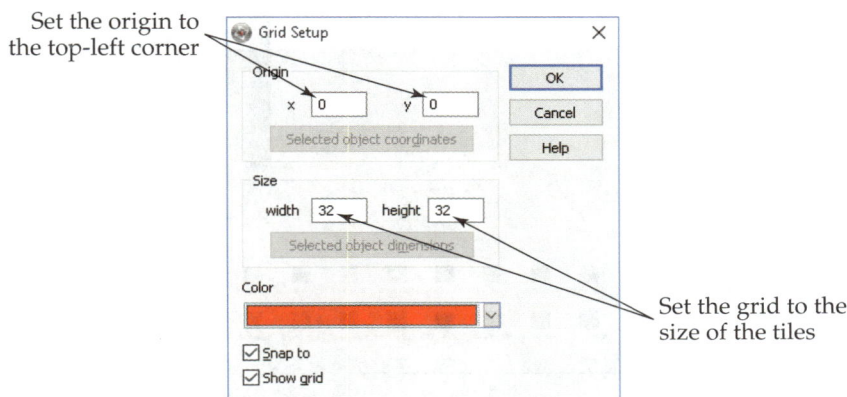

Set the origin to the top-left corner

Set the grid to the size of the tiles

Goodheart-Willcox Publisher

Figure 16-2. Setting up the grid and snap for creating a tile-based game.

Level Design

The wall tiles will need to be copied and pasted to build the design of this level. Clickteam Fusion 2.5 has a feature that allows you to quickly create a copy by dragging the original.

12. Hold down the [Ctrl] key, click and hold the Wall Tile 6 object, and drag to the right. As you drag, an outline of the object is attached to the cursor. Move the outline one grid space to the right, and release the mouse button to create a copy.

13. Continue creating copies to form a wall across the top of the maze.

14. Using the drag method, copy the Wall Tile 7 object to form a wall down the right-hand side, as shown in **Figure 16-3.**

15. Click and drag from approximately (640, 60) to approximately (590, 450) to select all of the objects in the right-hand wall except the corners. Use the coordinate indicator to help find the correct cursor locations, but the locations do not need to be exact as long as the marquee encloses all of the Wall Tile 7 objects.

16. With all of the Wall Tile 7 objects selected, click the **Copy** button on the **Standard Toolbar** to copy the entire side wall.

17. Click the **Paste** button on the **Standard Toolbar**.

18. Click at approximately (0, 60) and click to place the copied tiles. The tiles will snap into position even if they are pasted in a slightly different position. The left-hand wall is created.

19. Applying what you have learned, copy the wall tiles at the top and paste them at the bottom.

Player Movement

The player character is set for eight-direction movement. This movement needs a bit of modification to function best with this game.

20. Select the Manic Miner object, and click the **Movement** tab in the **Properties** toolbar.

Copy

Paste

Movement

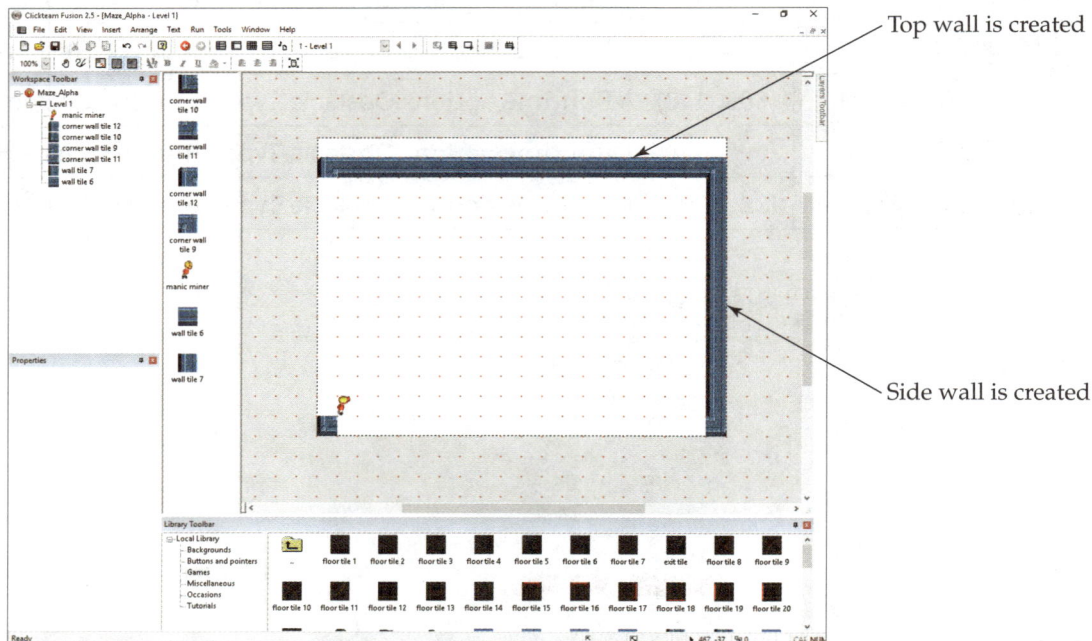

Goodheart-Willcox Publisher

Figure 16-3. Create the top and right-hand walls using the drag method to copy the original objects.

21. Applying what you have learned, modify the Directions property to only directions 0, 8, 16, and 24. This will allow the player character to move up, down, left, and right only.
22. Set the Initial direction property to the same directions.
23. Uncheck the check box for the Moving at start property.
24. Uncheck the check box for the Stick to obstacles property.
25. Change the Speed property to 25.
26. Open the frame in the event editor.
27. Program this pseudocode:
      IF the Manic Miner object collides with the backdrop,
         THEN stop the movement of the Manic Miner object.
28. Run the frame. Rest if the manic miner stops when it collides with any of the wall tiles. Close the game window when done testing.
29. Debug the obstacle type of any wall tile if the manic miner does not stop.

Level Layout

Currently, the game does not meet the definition of a video game. There is nothing for the player to do. The player would find this very boring. You will now add and remove some wall tiles to make the maze for the manic miner. The maze will also continue from one frame to the next. To do this, a new frame will need to start when the player character exits the first part of the maze.

30. Display the Level 1 frame in the frame editor.
31. Using wall tiles from the library, create the layout shown in **Figure 16-4.** The exact design can vary from what is shown, but pay attention to where the opening in the wall is. You will need to match this later. Be sure to set any tiles you add as obstacles. Leave the top row blank. This will be used to hold items such as the score.
32. Run the frame. Test moving the manic miner through the maze. Note: the manic miner may move slowly in some places, which will be fixed later during the tuning stage. Close the game window when done testing.
33. Display the storyboard editor.

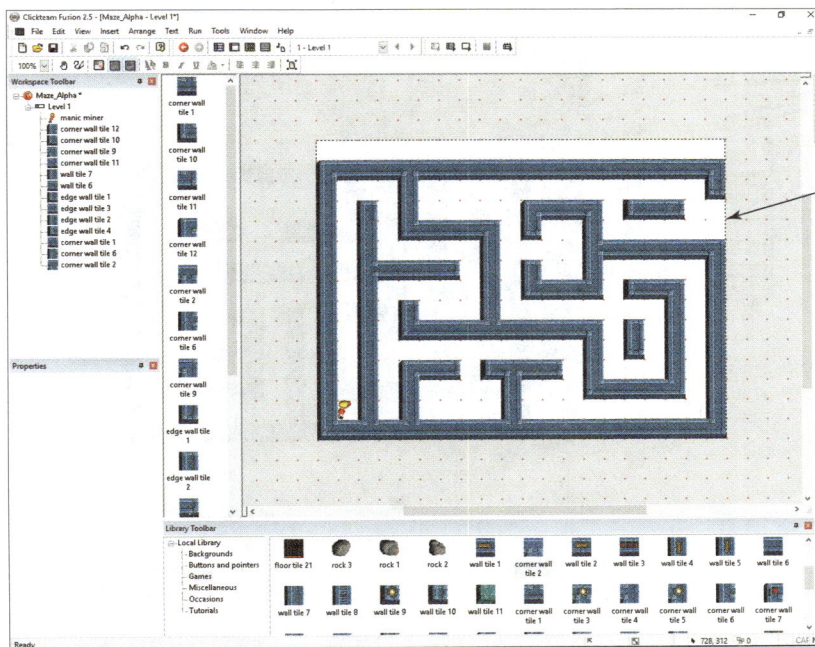

Goodheart-Willcox Publisher

Figure 16-4. Create a maze on the Level 1 frame. You can design your own maze or replicate the one shown here.

Copy

Paste

Run Frame

34. Applying what you have learned, copy and paste the Level 1 frame.
35. Rename the new frame Level 2.
36. Open the Level 2 frame in the frame editor.
37. Applying what you have learned, create a layout for the Level 2 frame similar to that shown in **Figure 16-5.** Be sure to set any objects you add as obstacles. Leave the top row blank. Make sure the opening in the wall, or doorway, on this frame matches the opening in the wall on the first frame. It is very important that the openings align. Place the Manic Miner object near this opening. Also, create another opening that will lead to a third level.
38. Run the frame. Test all wall objects in the maze to be sure they are set as obstacles. Close the game window when done testing.

Transitions Between Rooms

The player needs to be able to travel from one frame to the next using the doorways (openings). Also, the doorways should be two-way openings. The player should be able to exit one level and return to it later.

Event Editor

39. Display the event editor for the Level 1 frame.
40. Applying what you have learned, add a new condition that tests the position of the Manic Miner object to see if it leaves the play area on the right. In this case, the only way the object can leave the frame is to the right due to the position of the opening in the wall.
41. In the event line you just added, right-click in the cell under the **Storyboard Controls** icon, and click **Next frame** in the shortcut menu. This programming allows the player to move from the Level 1 frame to the Level 2 frame.
42. Run the application (not the *frame*). Test that you can exit the Level 1 frame and move to the Level 2 frame. Close the game window when done testing.

Run Application

43. The player should be able to go back to a previous part of the maze. Applying what you have learned earlier, program this pseudocode for the Level 2 frame:

IF the Manic Minor object leaves the play area to the left,
　　THEN go to the previous frame.

Opening should exactly match the one on the previous frame

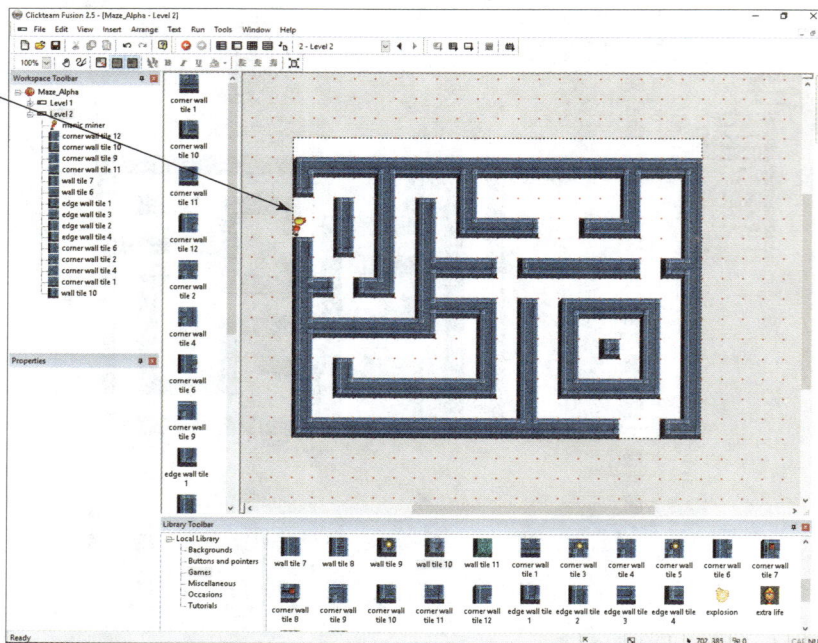

Goodheart-Willcox Publisher

Figure 16-5. Create a different maze on the Level 2 frame. You can design your own maze, but make sure the opening on the left matches the opening on the Level 1 frame.

44. Run the application. Test that you can move from the Level 1 frame to the Level 2 frame and back to the Level 1 frame. Note any bugs, and close the game window when done testing.

45. If you experience a bug where the Level 1 frame flashes, but the game does not go to Level 2, the Manic Miner object may be too close to the left exit on the Level 2 frame. The game is sending you back to the Level 1 frame as soon as the Level 2 frame loads. To fix this, set the position of the Manic Miner object on Level 2 frame further to the right, but not too far. The object should not appear to jump when entering the Level 2 frame.

Global Value

Yikes! When returning to the Level 1 frame, the manic miner jumps to the original starting point instead of the entry point. This is a serious bug that will negatively affect gameplay. Values on a frame will reset unless a global value is used to tell the game engine to remember something. Remember, all items on a frame have *local* values (with some exceptions, like the score). Local values are not stored when the frame is closed. A *global* value can be recalled and changed on every frame of the game. The score is an example of a global value. As the game progresses, the player character needs to be properly positioned when each frame is entered. A global value can be used to track the progress of the Manic Miner object and put it in the correct position on each frame.

46. Display the event editor for the Level 1 frame.

47. In the existing event line that tests if the Manic Miner object leaves the play area to the right, right-click in the cell under the **Special Conditions** icon, and click **Change a Global Value>Set** in the shortcut menu. The expression editor is displayed, as shown in **Figure 16-6.**

Event Editor

48. Click the **Choose value** drop-down arrow, and click **Global Value A** in the drop-down list. Which global value is used is not important. It could be B, C, D, or whatever. You just need to use a global value, and A is the first one.

49. Enter 1 as the expression. This will set Global Value A to 1 when the Manic Minor object leaves the room. The value can be anything so long as you remember what you want it to control. In this case, the value of 1 is used to indicate that the Level 1 frame has been completed.

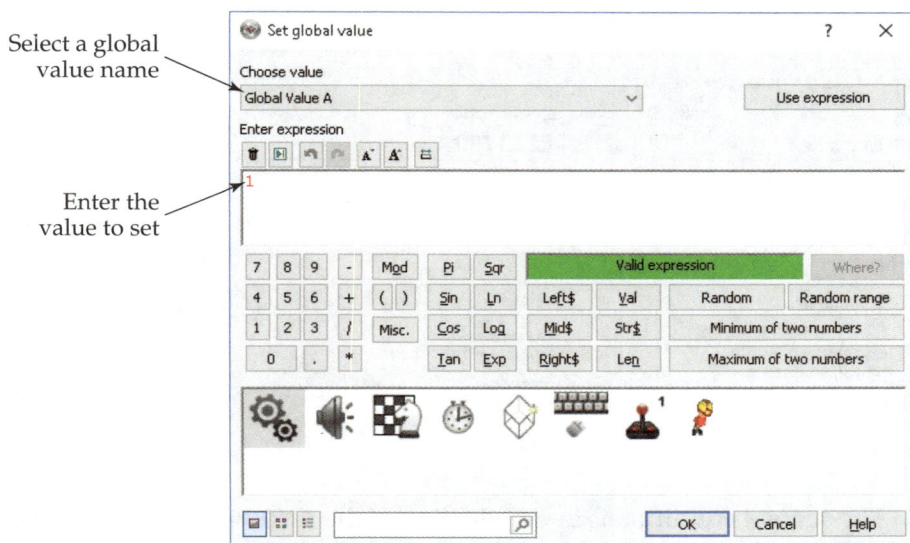

Goodheart-Willcox Publisher

Figure 16-6. A global value can be read by all frames in the application.

50. Click the **OK** button to close the expression editor and complete the action.

51. Add a new condition, and program the following pseudocode. Use the storyboard controls.

> **IF** the Level 1 frame is at the start of the frame

52. Right-click on the event line you just added, and click **Insert** in the shortcut menu. This adds the **AND** Boolean operator, which allows you to add another condition to the existing condition. This shortcut menu is also used to add a **NOT** (negate) or **OR** Boolean operator.

53. In the **New Condition** dialog box, right-click on the **Special Conditions** icon, and click **Compare to a global value** in the shortcut menu. The expression editor is displayed.

54. Enter 1 in the expression editor, and click the **OK** button. This programs the following pseudocode, as shown in **Figure 16-7**.

> **AND IF** Global Value A is equal to 1.

55. In the same event line, right-click in the cell under icon for the Manic Miner object, and click **Position>Select Position…** in the shortcut menu. The frame editor is displayed with the **Select Position** dialog box open.

56. Set the position to the absolute coordinates (623, 143), and click the **OK** button to complete the programming. This will set the position of the manic miner to match where the player character comes into the frame from the Level 2 frame.

57. Applying what you have learned, program the Level 2 frame with this pseudocode:

> **IF** at the start of the Level 2 frame
> **AND IF** Global Value A is equal to 1,
> > **THEN** set the position of the Manic Miner object to absolute coordinates (32, 128).

58. Run the application. Test how the manic miner can now go back and forth between the Level 1 and Level 2 frames. Close the game window when done testing.

Run Application

Global Values for More than Two Levels

The third part of the maze needs to be added. The same global value (A) will be used to track the manic miner going back and forth between the Level 2 and Level 3 frames as well as between the Level 1 and Level 2 frames. However, there needs to be a slight adjustment for this to work correctly.

59. Applying what you have learned, use the storyboard editor to copy and paste the Level 2 frame, and rename the copy as Level 3.

Storyboard Editor

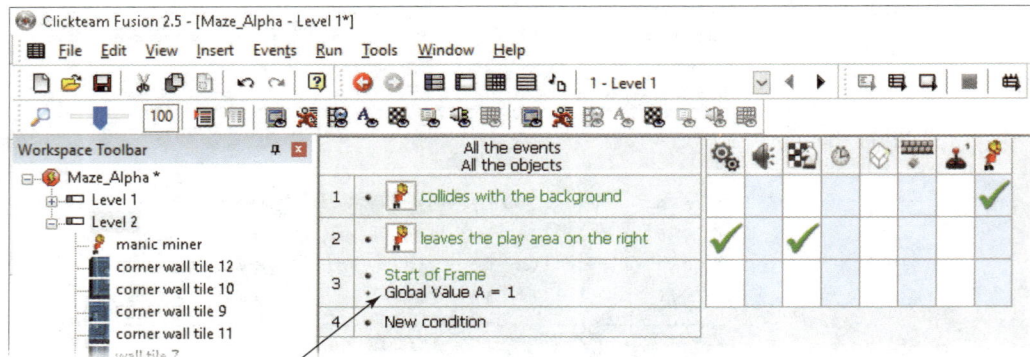

Second condition is added

Figure 16-7. The second condition is an application of the **AND** Boolean operator. Both conditions must be true for the event line to be processed.

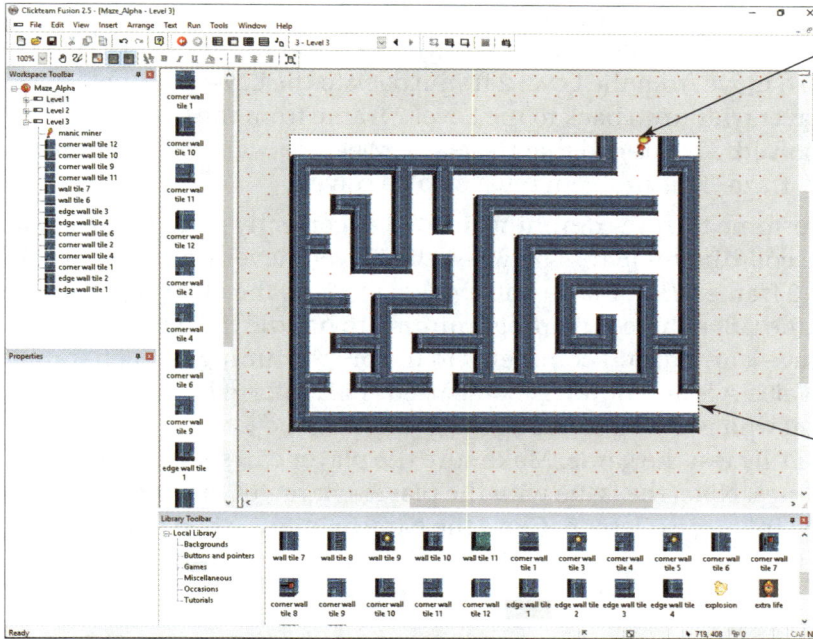

Goodheart-Willcox Publisher

Figure 16-8. Create a third maze on the Level 3 frame. Match the opening on the top to the opening on the Level 2 frame. Match the opening on the right to the starting position of the Manic Miner object on the Level 1 frame.

60. Design the maze on the Level 3 frame, shown in **Figure 16-8.** Make sure there is an opening to match the exit from the Level 2 frame. Also, include an opening that matches the starting location on the Level 1 frame. Leave the top row mostly blank.

61. Display the event editor for the Level 2 frame, add a new event line, and program this pseudocode:

> **IF** the Manic Miner object leaves the play area on the bottom,
> **THEN** set Global Value A to 2
>> **AND** go to the next frame.

62. Display the event editor for the Level 3 frame, and modify the existing event line that tests if the Manic Miner object leaves the play area on the left to match this pseudocode:

> **IF** the Manic Miner object leaves the play area on the top,
>> **THEN** go to the previous frame.

63. Modify the existing event line that tests if the frame has started to match this pseudocode:

> **IF** at the start of the frame
> **AND IF** Global Value A is equal to 2,
>> **THEN** set position of the Manic Miner object to absolute coordinates (544, 32).

64. Add a new event line, and program this pseudocode:

> **IF** the Manic Miner object leaves the play area on the right,
>> **THEN** jump to the Level 1 frame.

65. Run the application. Test that the manic miner can travel between all three frames. Note any bugs. Close the game window when done testing.

Event Editor

Run Application

Problem-Solving Issues with the Game

The player can now go from the Level 1 frame, to the Level 2 frame, and then to the Level 3 frame. The player can also move from the Level 2 frame back to the Level 1 frame. However, there is a bug when the player tries to go back to the Level 2 frame from the Level 3 frame. This serious problem must be solved. Also, recall that the Manic Miner object moves slowly to the right in some points of the maze. This problem must also be solved.

66. Problem-solve to determine the programming needed to correctly place the Manic Miner object at the absolute coordinates (544, 448) when the player moves from the Level 2 frame from the Level 3 frame. Hint: Global Value A is set to 2, so the object appears where it is placed on the frame since there is no programming to handle the positioning.

67. Applying what you have learned, add comments to the programming on each frame to explain what Global Value A is and how it is being used. This information is critical for anyone other than you who is trying to debug the game.

Run Application

68. Run the application. Fully test the game. Make sure the player can seamlessly move between all three frames. Note: the issue with the player character moving slowly to the right will be corrected in the next lesson. Close the game window when done testing.

69. Debug any errors you find.

Skill Practice

You are doing well as a new game designer and programmer. The skills needed to complete the following tasks are covered in earlier lessons. Review any previous lesson if you need help remembering how to complete these tasks. Note: the free version of Clickteam Fusion 2.5 is limited to three frames, so you will not be able to create a title page and a high score. However, be aware that these should normally be included in a game build to improve the user experience.

70. Add a new active object on Level 3 that this is off-screen. Name it Coupon. Resize it to be the same size as the entire game frame (640 × 480). Edit sprite for the Coupon object to create a coupon of your own design for a free game of laser tag. Program the coupon to appear when the player exits Level 3 to the right. The coupon should cover the entire Level 3 game map. Destroy the Manic Miner object when the coupon appears. Add a **Quit** button that also appears when the coupon appears so the player can close the game.

71. Using objects in the library, add rewards for the player to collect on each level. Resize the objects to be smaller than 32 × 32 pixels to fit the tile-based layout.

72. Add a Score object to the top row of each level.

73. Add a Lives object to the top row of each level. Note: this will be used in later versions of the game.

74. Add the programming needed to increase the score whenever the player collects a reward.

75. Add sound for when the player collects a reward.

76. Change the background color for each frame to black or other dark color of your choice.

77. Recolor the numbers for the Score object to be visible on the background.

78. Thoroughly test the game, and fix any bugs you find.

79. Save your work, and submit it for grading.

Name: _____

Vocabulary

Write a definition for each of the key terms from this lesson. You will develop a personal glossary of key terms throughout this course.

Boolean logic

_____

_____

core mechanics

_____

_____

loop

_____

_____

game loop

_____

_____

subroutine

_____

_____

tile-based game

_____

_____

Review Questions

1. A computer will only execute a command or action when a Boolean statement evaluates to which state?

   _____

   _____

   _____

   _____

Applied Technology

2. Write a few sentences to briefly describe how long a subroutine will loop.

   _____

   _____

   _____

   _____

Language Arts

Applied Technology

3. Explain how the grid and snap help to speed up scene design.

_____

_____

_____

_____

_____

Science

4. The player character in the game build in this lesson is a miner. What types of rewards would be appropriate to include in a game with a character that is a miner?

_____

_____

_____

_____

_____

Language Arts

5. Summarize why there was a bug in this game build when the miner was going to the original starting point on the game map when he reentered a room.

_____

_____

_____

_____

_____

Higher-Order Thinking Strategies

Science

6. Think about how water changes state from solid, to liquid, to gas. Write a Boolean logic statement to describe this action.

_____

_____

_____

_____

_____

7. Consider an American custom that may be unfamiliar to someone from a different country, such as tipping in a restaurant. Write core mechanics that can be used to guide someone through the custom.

Social Science

_____

_____

_____

_____

_____

8. How can global values help the game designer add rewards, such as a treasure, that should only be found once or that should not reappear if the player returns to a previous level?

Applied Technology

_____

_____

_____

_____

_____

9. The game build in this lesson has tiles based on 32 × 32 pixels. The grid settings used allowed the tiles to be placed exactly matching the grid. What if you want to be able to place tiles in partial increments of the grid? Calculate the snap settings needed to allow this in the following table.

Mathematics

Grid	Increment	Snap Setting
32	1/2	16
32	1/4	
32	1/8	
24	1/2	
24	1/4	
24	1/8	

10. Write a few sentences speculating disadvantages to using a tile-based layout for a game.

Language Arts

_____

_____

_____

_____

_____

Office Technology Integration

Using a Job Description Template

1. Launch Microsoft Excel or other spreadsheet software, and open the vocabulary spreadsheet you updated in previous lessons.
2. Applying what you have learned, add a new worksheet, and name it Lesson 16.
3. Add each of the vocabulary words and definitions from the Vocabulary section of this lesson.
4. Save the spreadsheet, and then close it.
5. Launch Microsoft Word or other word-processing software. The Awesome Game Company would like to create a job description for a position available at the company.
6. On the startup page, or click **File>New** on the ribbon, click in the search box at the top, and enter job description form.
7. Select the Job Description Form template, as shown.

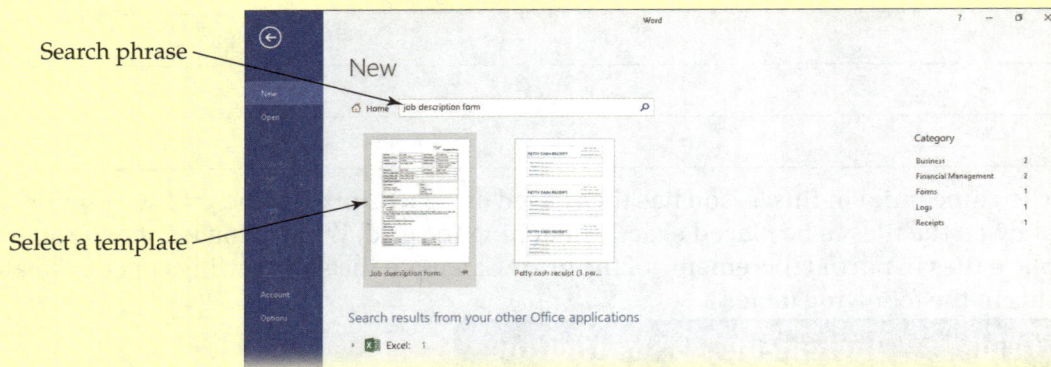

Search phrase

Select a template

Goodheart-Willcox Publisher

8. In the preview window, click the **Create** button to start a new document based on the template.
9. Review the different areas listed in the template.
10. Using the Internet, conduct the research necessary to complete the job description form for either a game programmer, game designer, or game artist. Remember to use the good researching skills you have learned in previous lessons and to evaluate the validity of sources.
11. Based on your research, complete all of the form fields in the template. Use your understanding of what the job requires and what the company should be offering to an employee who would fill that job.
12. Save the document as *LastName*_Job-Posting in your working folder, and submit it for grading.

Lesson 17

Sensory Detection and Navigation

Learning Objectives

After completing this lesson, you will be able to:

- program custom movement for tile-based gameplay.
- design a sensory-detection system.
- implement collision detection within a sensory-detection system.
- perform maintenance on programming to include proper commenting and elegant composition.
- create modular programming components and structures.

Situation

The Awesome Game Company would like you to be able to create many different types and styles of games. To do this, you will need to understand the major categories of games that are popular. Games are usually grouped by type to help players find games they are interested in playing.

Reading Materials

Different types of games are classified into major categories called *genres.* In most cases, a game will fit into one of 12 game genres:

- action
- board/card/quiz
- educational
- fighting
- music/party
- puzzle
- role-playing
- shooter
- simulation
- sports
- strategy
- toy

By classifying games, it is easier to compare and contrast the different elements of each game that make it unique from all other similar games.

Action games focus on the player moving to build skill through game difficulty. The gameplay of an action game is based upon moving the avatar through obstacles to seek an objective. Some common game *themes,* or subcategories, for action games include adventure, bat and ball, crime, fight, horror, platform, and tactical. Arcade games like *Pac-Man* and *Frogger* are other examples of action-genre games. In *Pac-Man,* the action is moving the Pac-Man character through the maze to eat the pellets; this is the primary gameplay mode.

A *gameplay mode* is a defined set of rules and actions that determine how the game is played. The *primary gameplay mode* is the most dominant set of actions the player must perform. A secondary gameplay mode for *Pac-Man* is chasing the ghosts when you eat a power pellet. Notice how the primary and secondary gameplay mode each have a different set of actions and objectives.

The *board/card/quiz games* genre is fairly straightforward. This genre involves making a physical board game, card game, or quiz show game into an electronic video game. Most of the gameplay in this genre will be the same as if the game were played in the real world.

An *educational game* is specifically designed to teach, train, or educate the player. Even if the gameplay is primarily action based, a game that intends to deliver educational content to the player falls into the education games genre.

A *fighting game* allows the player to battle other virtual characters through the use of physical moves and handheld weapons. These games are characterized by hand-to-hand combat and do not involve advanced weapons like guns, tanks, and other war devices.

A *music/party game* uses songs and rhythm as a primary game feature. Some examples of this popular genre include *Dance, Dance Revolution*; *Guitar Hero*; and *Rock Band.*

A *puzzle game* requires solving a puzzle. These games may be electronic versions of a physical puzzle. Or, the games may be puzzles that cannot exist in the physical world.

A *role-playing game (RPG)* relies on story more than any other genre. The player in an RPG typically has a human or humanoid avatar and performs quests and battles to build skill points, magic points, or other elements of status. A motivating factor for players of RPGs is to increase their status and "level up." When a player levels up, the character receives a new set of powers and abilities as a reward for achieving the elevated status. For example, when a player gains enough experience points, the character may change status from a level-three wizard to a level-four wizard.

A *shooter game* involves launching objects toward the player character or other objects as the primary gameplay mode. In some games, like an RPG, the player character may also launch objects. If this is part of a secondary gameplay mode, the game should not be categorized as a shooter game. Rather, the game should be categorized based on the primary gameplay mode.

A *simulation game* attempts to duplicate a real-world situation in the virtual world. Designers try to make these games as realistic as possible. Some simulation games, like *Microsoft Flight Simulator,* are advanced duplicates of the equipment and function of the real world. Others are more like *Rollercoaster Tycoon,* where the simulation is a business function.

A *sports game* is based on a real-world sporting event. The primary gameplay mode is the same as the sport the video game replicates. Football, soccer, hockey, golf, baseball, and basketball video games are all examples of the sports genre.

A *strategy game* focuses on gameplay that requires planning to beat the computer or human opponent. An example of a strategy game is a turn-based war game where the player can either move or shoot on his or her turn. Players compete with each other, and each player allocates game resources before the other player gets a turn. You need to plan and think what you need as part of your strategy. When players take turns making their moves, the game is a *turn-based strategy game.* Many other strategy games are played simultaneously. In a *simultaneously played strategy game,* all players can move their assets at the same time without the need to wait for other players to move. For example, in a war game, players may be able to move their tanks, planes, soldiers, and other resources at the same time as other players are moving their resources.

A **toy** does not really fit the definition of a game because it lacks rules or a victory condition. A game like a digital pet does not have a victory condition. You just train and feed your pet. The toy genre also typically includes screen savers. That realistic, 3D aquarium screen saver is also not a game, it is a toy. Even the screen savers that allow you to have the fish chase your cursor are toys because there is no victory condition.

Game Build

The client enjoyed the prototype of the maze game, but has movement requirements that need to be integrated to make the game easier to play. Currently, the Manic Miner object can get stuck when moving. The client wants the avatar to move and animate properly through all of the tile-based maze.

How to Begin

1. Launch Clickteam Fusion 2.5, and open the *LastName*_Maze_Alpha game created in the previous lesson.
2. Save the file as *LastName*_Maze_Beta in your working folder.
3. Look at the top level of the tree in the **Workspace Toolbar**. Notice that the name still says "alpha." Single-click twice on the application name to make it editable, and change the name to Maze_Beta. An asterisk (*) appears after the name as soon as you make the change. This indicates something has changed in the file, but the file had not been saved.
4. Save the file. The asterisk is removed from the name. Remember, if an asterisk appears here, it means the file has unsaved changes.

Movement Sensors

The current version of the game has movement of the player character controlled by the built-in eight direction movement. To allow for the movement the client wants, sensors will be added to the Manic Miner object. These will detect movement and allow for new custom movement.

5. Open the Level 1 frame in the frame editor.
6. Applying what you have learned, change the movement Type property of the Manic Miner object to Static.

Frame Editor

7. Applying what you have learned, insert a new active object anywhere, and name the object Avatar.
8. Change the size of the Avatar object to 32 × 32 pixels, and set its position to (47, 431). This should be directly on top of the Manic Miner object.
9. Right-click on the Avatar object, and click **Order>To Back** in the shortcut menu. This moves the object to the bottom of the stack, so the Manic Miner object will be in front of (on top of) the Avatar object.
10. Display the event editor for the Level 1 frame.
11. Right-click on the *number* for the event line that tests if the Manic Miner object collides with the background (event line 1), and click **Delete** in the shortcut menu, as shown in **Figure 17-1.**

Event Editor

12. Add a new condition. In the **New Condition** dialog box, click the **The mouse pointer and keyboard** icon, and click **The Keyboard>Repeat while key is pressed** in the shortcut menu.
13. Press the right arrow key to complete the condition.

Right-click to
delete the line

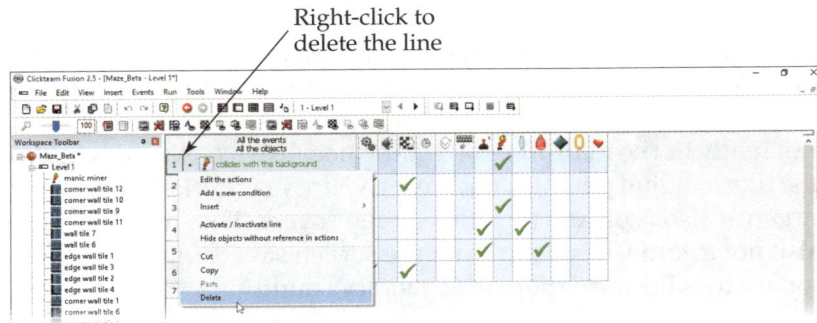

Goodheart-Willcox Publisher

Figure 17-1. The programming that handles a collision between the Manic Miner object and the background is no longer needed as the movement will be controlled in a different way.

14. In the event line for the condition you just added, right-click in the cell under the icon for the Avatar object, and click **Position>Set X Coordinate…** in the shortcut menu. The expression editor is displayed.

15. At the bottom of the expression editor, right-click on the icon for the Avatar object, and click **Position>X Coordinate** in the shortcut menu. This adds X("Avatar") to the expression, which means to retrieve the current X coordinate value from the Avatar object.

16. Click at the end of the expression, and add +32, as shown in **Figure 17-2.** The entire expression now means add 32 to the current X coordinate value of the Avatar object. Since this action will be initiated whenever the right arrow key is pressed, pressing that key will move the Avatar object 32 pixels in the positive X direction (right).

17. Click **OK** to close the expression editor and complete programming the action.

Programming Custom Movement

The Avatar object is now programmed to move to the right when the right arrow key is pressed. It still needs to be programmed to move in the other directions. Copying, pasting, and modifying the existing programming is more efficient than starting from scratch.

18. Applying what you have learned, copy the event line you just programmed, and paste it once. There should be two identical lines.

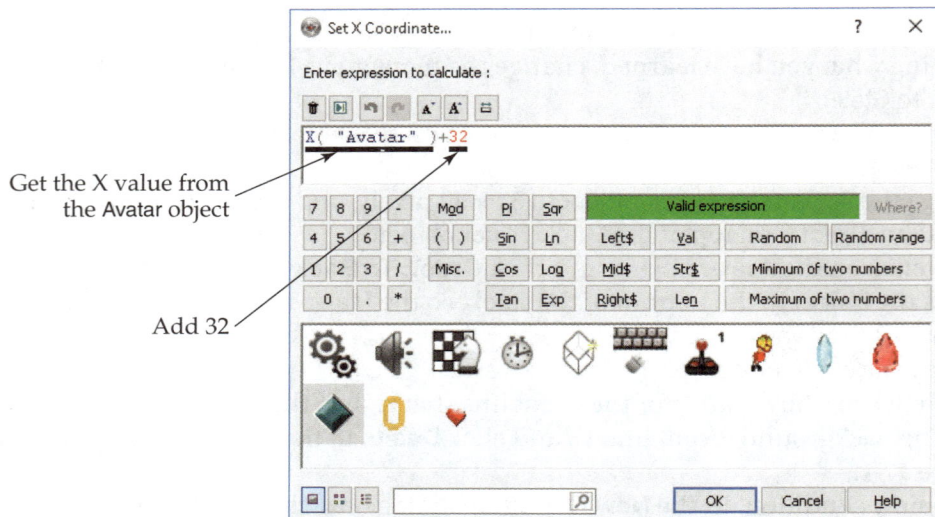

Get the X value from
the Avatar object

Add 32

Goodheart-Willcox Publisher

Figure 17-2. A value can be obtained from other objects and used as the basis for an expression.

19. Modify the pasted event lines to match this pseudocode:
   IF the player holds down the left arrow key,
      THEN position the Avatar object 32 pixels to the left of where it was before.

20. Run the frame. Test if the Avatar object correctly moves to the left and right. Note: you are only testing movement at this point, not collisions. Close the game window when done testing.

21. Debug the new programming as needed.

22. Applying what you have learned, copy and paste the programming, and then edit it to move the Avatar object up 32 pixels when the up arrow is held down and down 32 pixels when the down arrow is held down, as shown in **Figure 17-3.**

23. Run the frame. Test the movement of the Avatar object in all four directions. Close the game window when done testing, and debug the programming as needed.

Run Frame

Collision Sensors

Collision sensors are objects that follow another object to detect when there is a collision without the main object having to make the collision. In this case, you will use sensors to detect if the tile next to the Avatar object is *not* filled with a wall. If a wall is not next to the Avatar object, then the object can move into the open space. If the space is already filled with a wall, then the Avatar object will not be able to move into that tile on the game board.

24. Display the Level 1 frame in the frame editor, and insert a new active object anywhere outside the visible game frame.

25. Name the object Sensor_Top, and set its size to 10 × 10 pixels.

26. Open the Sensor_Top object in the image editor.

27. Applying what you have learned, clear the canvas, and fill it will a shade of blue of your choice. The color is not important to the programming. It is only used to help identify which sensor is which.

28. Click the **OK** button to close the image editor. The Sensor_Top object now appears as a small blue rectangle.

29. Applying what you have learned, create three clones of the Sensor_Top object, and edit the clones to match the table below.

Frame Editor

Name	Color
Sensor_Bottom	Black
Sensor_Right	Red
Sensor_Left	Green

30. Position the sensors outside of the visible play area in a plus sign (+) pattern, as shown in **Figure 17-4.** This will help you correctly identify and edit each sensor.

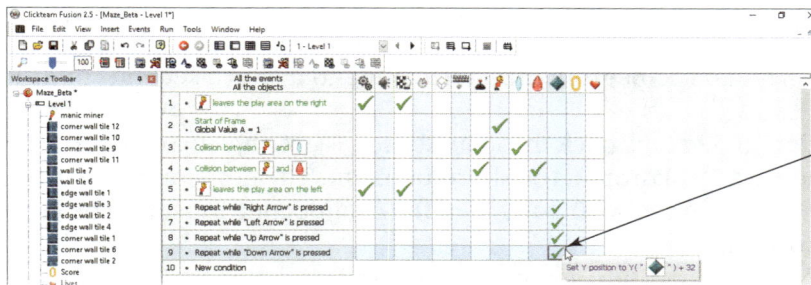

Modify to set the Y value

Goodheart-Willcox Publisher

Figure 17-3. Be sure to modify the programming for up and down movement to Y values.

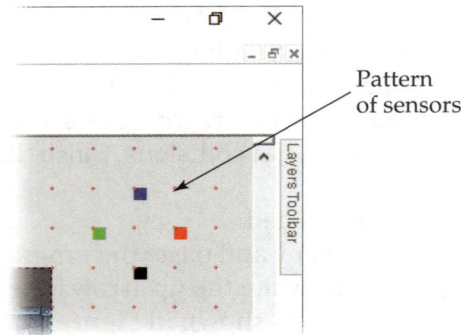

Pattern of sensors

Figure 17-4. Four sensors are created to use for controlling the movement of the Avatar object.

Programming Relative Positioning for the Sensors

In Lesson 8, you learned how parent and child objects work together. Relative positioning was used to have the child object always follow the parent object. The sensors will be programmed as child objects of the parent Avatar object.

Event Editor

31. Display the event editor for the Level 1 frame, and program a new event line to match this pseudocode:

> **IF** always,
>> **THEN** set the position of the Sensor_Top object to 32 pixels above the Avatar object
>>> **AND** set the position of the Sensor_Bottom object to 32 pixels below the Avatar object
>>> **AND** set the position of the Sensor_Left object to 32 pixels left of the Avatar object
>>> **AND** set the position of the Sensor_Right object to 32 pixels right of the Avatar object.

Run Frame

32. Run the frame. Test that the sensors follows the Avatar object. Close the game window when done testing.

33. Debug the programming for positioning the sensors as needed.

Programming a NOT Condition

Until now, you have been programming the computer to look for conditions that are true. Programming can also be done using a **NOT** operator to test when conditions are false. The **NOT** operator is sometimes called the **NULL** operator. The **NOT** operator is used in this pseudocode:

> **IF** the player holds down the right arrow key,
>> **AND** the Sensor_Right object is **NOT** overlapping the wall background,
>>> **THEN** move the Avatar object to the right by 32 pixels.

Once the movement of the Avatar object is working properly, it is no longer necessary to see the sensors. The sensors should be invisible to the player.

34. Locate the event that tests for if the right arrow is pressed, right-click on the condition portion of the line 5, and click **Insert** in the shortcut menu to add a second condition (**AND**).

35. In the **New Condition** dialog box, click the icon Sensor_Right object, and click **Collision>Overlapping a Backdrop** in the shortcut menu. The new condition is added to the event line. Notice that the **AND** portion of the pseudocode must first be created without the **NOT** portion.

36. Right-click on the second condition you just added, and click **Negate** in the shortcut menu. An X appears before the conditional statement to make a **NOT** condition, as shown in **Figure 17-5**. The second condition must be false for the action to be executed.

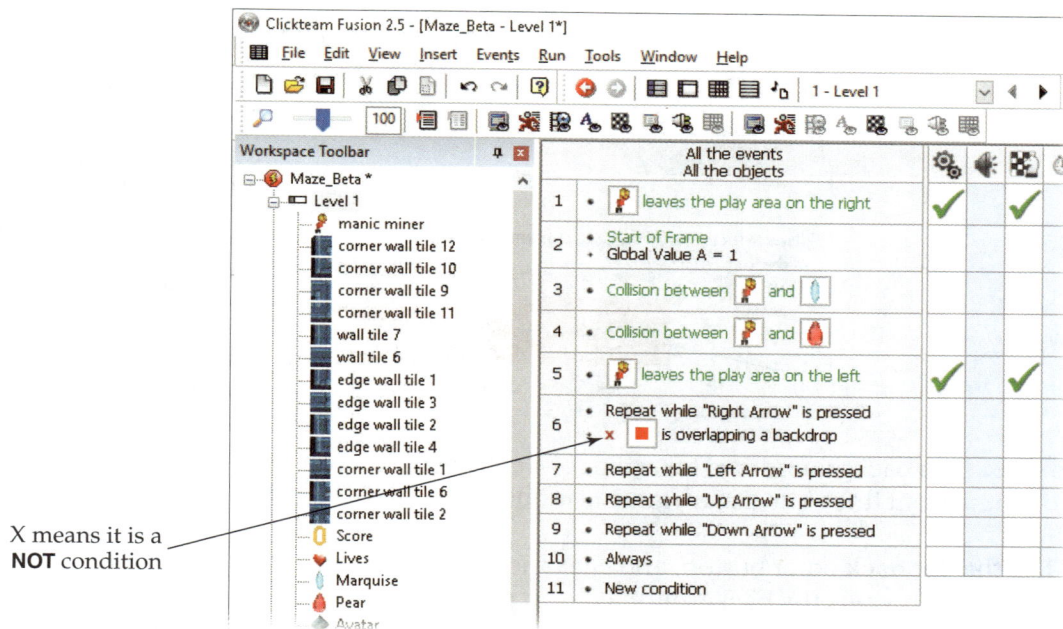

Goodheart-Willcox Publisher

Figure 17-5. Negating a condition applies the **NOT** operator to the condition.

37. Applying what you have learned, add the programming to check that the other sensors are **NOT** overlapping a backdrop object.
38. Run the frame. Test that the Avatar object can only move in the direction of an opening where the correct sensor is not overlapping a wall. You should be able to navigate through the maze on the first level. Close the game window when done testing.
39. Debug the movement as needed.
40. Add a new condition, and program this pseudocode:
    IF at the start of the frame,
        THEN make the Sensor_Top object invisible.
41. Copy the check mark to all other sensors to apply the programming to them as well.
42. Run the frame. Test that the sensors are invisible and that the Avatar object can still navigate the maze. Close the game window when done testing.
43. Debug the sensors and movement as needed.

Modular Programming

Recall, comments are statements that a programmer adds to help describe what is happening in a section of code. This makes it easier to remember what you are doing when you go back and edit the programming. Adding modules to the program is another way to help other programmers quickly and easily understand what you intend the code to do. *Modular programming* separates each function of the program into sections. Each function is programmed into a module and later linked to or added to the main program script.

44. Locate the event line for moving sensors with the Avatar object. Click the line number for this event, drag to the top of the list of events, and drop to move the event line to the top.
45. Drag the event line for setting the sensors invisible to the top. This cleans up the organization of the programming.
46. Right-click on the number for event line 3, and click **Insert>A comment** in the shortcut menu. The **Edit Text** dialog box is displayed for adding the comment text, as shown in **Figure 17-6.** Notice that you can also format the appearance of the comment.
47. Add the text Frame Navigation in the edit box.

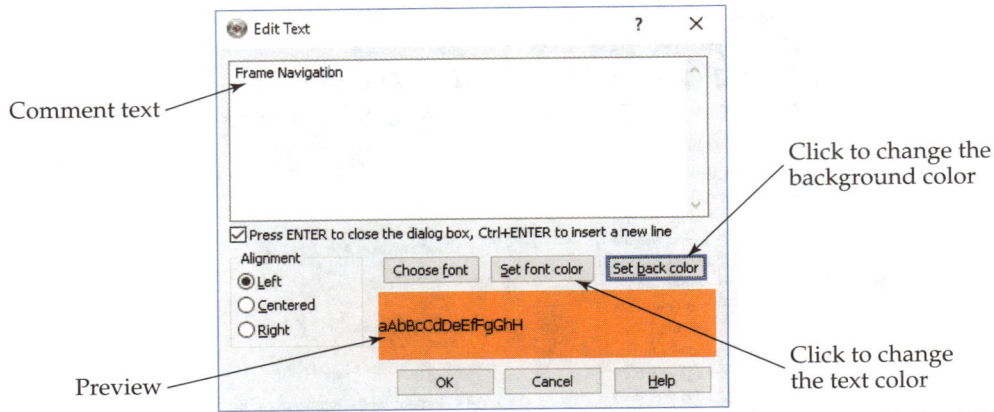

Goodheart-Willcox Publisher

Figure 17-6. The background and text color of a comment can be customized. This can be done to group event lines into programming modules.

48. Click the **Set back color** button, and click the yellow color swatch in the palette that is displayed. This sets the background color of the comment.

49. Click the **OK** button to add the comment. Notice how it appears as a yellow bar. This helps to visually identify the comment. Different colors can be used to identify different programming modules.

50. Applying what you have learned, move the programming lines for testing if the Manic Minor object leaves the play area and any global values to be directly under the comment you just added.

51. Add comments to create modules using the information in the table below, as shown in **Figure 17-7.**

Event Line	Text	Background Color	Font Color
Tests for collision with a reward object	Rewards	Orange	Black
Tests for the right arrow key pressed	Right Movement	Red	Black
Tests for the left arrow key pressed	Left Movement	Green	Black
Tests for the up arrow key pressed	Up Movement	Blue	White
Tests for the down arrow key pressed	Down Movement	Black	White

Attaching the Miner to the Avatar

Currently, the Avatar object moves within the maze, but the Manic Miner object does not. This is because you removed the object's ability to move when it was changed to a static object. The Manic Miner object needs to be programmed to follow the Avatar object.

52. In the event line for the start of the frame, add a new action that sets the position of the Manic Miner object to (0,0) relative to the Avatar object. This will align the Manic Miner object to the movement of the Avatar object, but only when the frame starts.

53. Applying what you have learned, copy the action you just added into the event line for always. This will always align the Manic Miner object to the movement of the Avatar object, not just when the frame starts.

54. Run the frame. Test how the manic miner moves differently from the previous version of the game. Notice that the manic miner does not walk or face in the direction of movement except when moving to the right. There is no animation of the sprite at all. Close the game window when done testing.

Run Frame

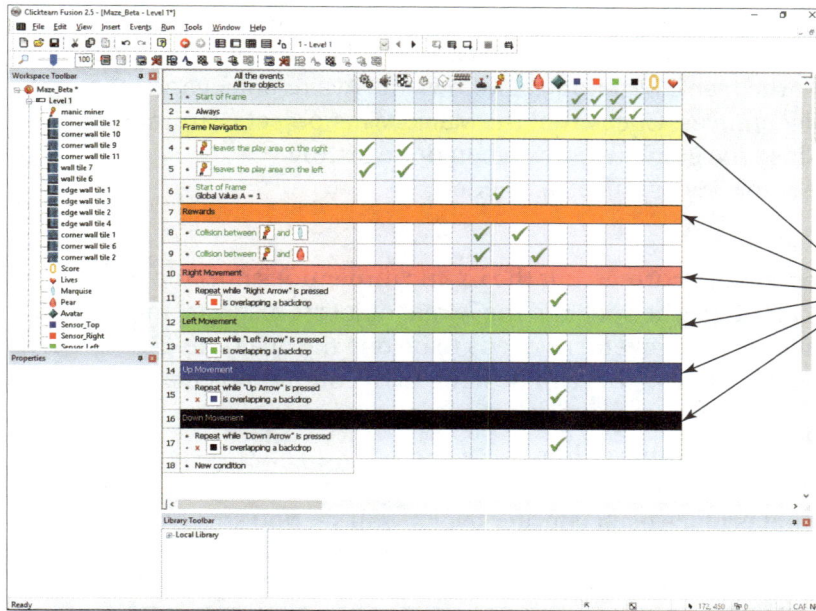

Goodheart-Willcox Publisher

Figure 17-7. Comments have been used to group event lines into programming modules.

55. In the event line in the Left Movement programming module, right-click in the cell below the icon for the Manic Miner object, and click **Direction>Select Direction...** in the shortcut menu. The **Select Direction** dialog box is displayed to allow you to choose the direction the character will face, as shown in **Figure 17-8.**

56. Applying what you have learned, clear the existing direction, select direction 16 (left), and close the dialog box.

57. Right-click in the same cell, and click **Animation>Change>Animation Sequence...** in the shortcut menu. A dialog box is displayed containing a list of the animation sets for the Manic Miner object.

58. Select the Walking animation, and click the **OK** button to close the dialog box.

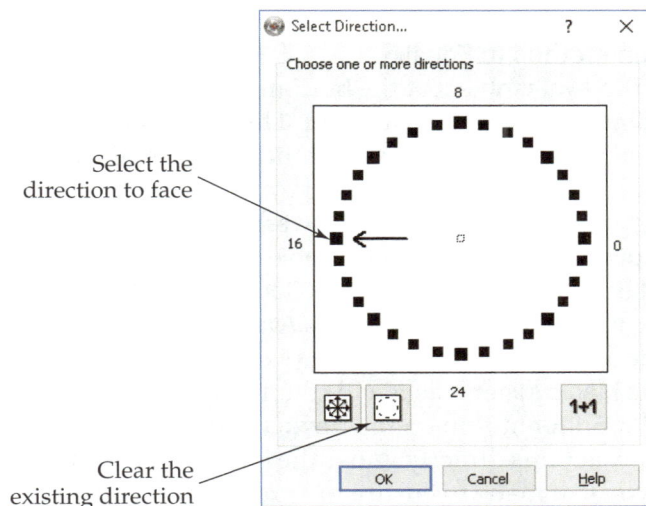

Goodheart-Willcox Publisher

Figure 17-8. Setting the direction the character will face determines how the sprite will appear on the object.

Run Frame

59. Using these skills, add the correct direction for the Up, Down, and Right movement modules. Change the animation sequence to walking for all movement modules.

60. Run the frame. Test that the Manic Miner object follows the Avatar object and faces the direction the Avatar object moves. Check that the Manic Miner object is animated walking in all four directions. Close the game window when done testing.

61. Debug the facing of the Manic Miner object as needed.

Tuning Animation

The animation and direction are correct, but the manic miner does not stop walking when the Avatar object stops moving. The speed of the Avatar object is also way too fast. To better match the tile-based game, the movement needs to be one tile at a time. To correct the movement, you will need to store values. This can be done with counter objects or with an array. For this application, you will use a counter object.

Frame Editor

62. Display the Level 1 frame in the frame editor.

63. Applying what you have learned, insert four new counter objects using the data in the table below. The coordinates place each counter over a wall section so it can be seen during programming and testing. If your maze layout differs from what is shown, adjust the coordinates as needed to place the counters over walls.

Name	Position	Width	Height
Counter_Right	(372, 382)	20	30
Counter_Left	(212, 382)	20	30
Counter_Up	(308, 318)	20	30
Counter_Down	(308, 478)	20	30

Event Editor

64. Display the event editor for the Level 1 frame.

65. In the event line that tests for always, delete the check mark under the icon for the Manic Miner object. This action sets the position of the Manic Miner object to the position of the Avatar object. It is no longer needed as you will be programming a new movement action for the Manic Miner object.

66. In the Right Movement programming module, add a new condition to the existing event line. In the **New Condition** dialog box, click on the icon for the Manic Miner object, and click **Position>Compare X Position to a Value** in the shortcut menu. The expression editor is displayed.

67. Set the comparison method to Equal.

68. Click the icon for the Avatar object at the bottom of the expression editor, and click **Position>X Coordinate** in the shortcut menu. The expression should read X("Avatar").

69. Click the **OK** button to close the expression editor. The condition should be:
    IF the player holds down the right arrow key,
      AND the Sensor_Right object is **NOT** overlapping a backdrop
      AND the X position of the Manic Minor object equals the X position of the Avatar object.

70. In the same event line, add an action for the Counter_Right object to set the counter to 32. The value 32 is to record the 32 pixels the Avatar object has moved. Later, you will program the Manic Miner object to move one pixel at a time until the counter returns to zero. That way, the Manic Miner object will catch up with the Avatar object.

Event List Editor

71. Click the **Event List Editor** button on the **Navigate Toolbar**. This changes the view in the event editor to show actions directly under the conditions, as shown in **Figure 17-9**.

72. Review the edits you just made to ensure the programming matches this pseudocode:
    IF the player holds down the right arrow key,
      AND the Sensor_Right object is **NOT** overlapping a backdrop
      AND the X position of the Manic Minor object equals the X position of the Avatar object

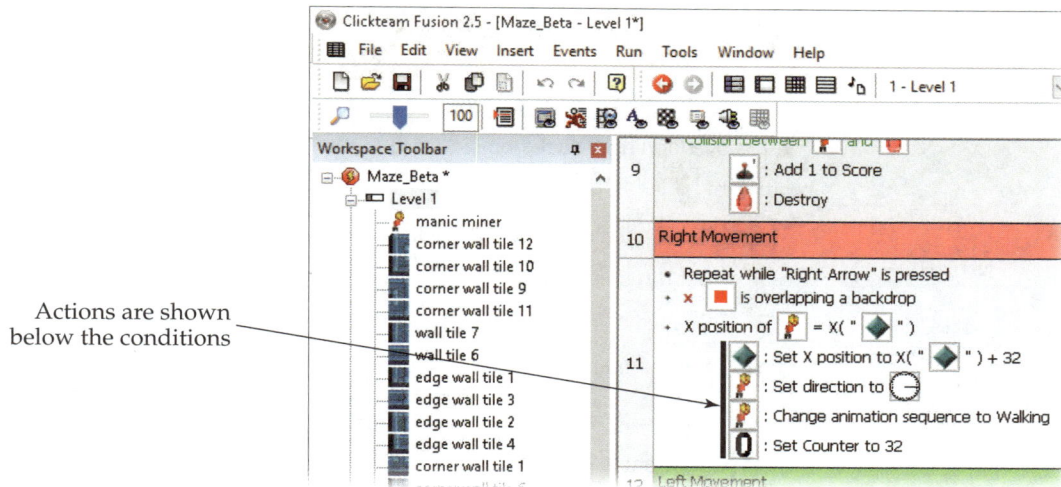

Actions are shown
below the conditions

Goodheart-Willcox Publisher

Figure 17-9. The view in the event editor can be changed so actions are displayed directly under conditions instead of as check marks in cells to the right of the conditions.

> **THEN** set the direction of the Manic Miner object to direction 0 (right)
> > **AND** change the animation sequence for the Manic Miner object to Walking
> > **AND** move the Avatar object 32 pixels to the right relative to itself
> > **AND** set the Counter_Right object to 32.

73. Right-click on the *number* for the event line in the Right Movement module, and click **Insert>A new event** in the shortcut menu. This will start the process of adding a new event line by displaying the **New Condition** dialog box. Once the new condition is programmed, the new event line will appear above the line you right-clicked.

74. Applying what you have learned, program this pseudocode to complete the new event line:
> **IF** the X position of the Manic Miner object is lower than the X position of the Avatar object,
> > **THEN** increase the X position of the Manic Miner object by 1
> > > **AND** subtract 1 from the Counter_Right object.

75. Drag the event line you just programmed to the bottom of the Right Movement module, and then compare the programming in the module to **Figure 17-10.** Edit the programming as needed to match the figure. Note: the order of the actions may be different than what is shown, but as long as the actions match the conditions, everything should be okay.

76. Applying what you have learned, insert additional programming in the Left Movement, Up Movement, and Down Movement modules to move the Manic Minor object. Remember to use the correct coordinate position, X or Y, and the correct direction, positive or negative, for the movement to work properly.

77. Run the frame. Test the movement of the Manic Miner object. The character should walk to the position of the Avatar object. Take note of the counters when testing. If a counter is going crazy and the manic miner is walking in the wrong direction, then you have likely mixed up the X and Y positions or the plus or minus sign in the expression editor. Close the game window when done testing.

78. Debug any programming as needed to get the movement to perform correctly.

79. Display the list view in the event editor, and compare your programming to **Figure 17-11.**

Run Frame

Bug Testing

You may have noticed when testing that the Avatar object can move diagonally when two of the arrow keys are pressed at the same time. Even worse, in some cases, the object can end

Event List Editor

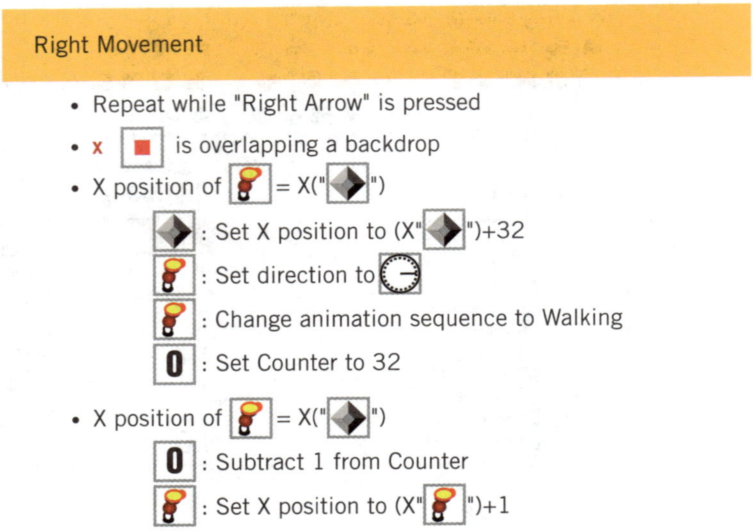

Right Movement

- Repeat while "Right Arrow" is pressed
- x ▦ is overlapping a backdrop
- X position of 🔦 = X("◆")
  - ◆ : Set X position to (X"◆")+32
  - 🔦 : Set direction to ◷
  - 🔦 : Change animation sequence to Walking
  - 0 : Set Counter to 32
- X position of 🔦 = X("◆")
  - 0 : Subtract 1 from Counter
  - 🔦 : Set X position to (X"🔦")+1

Figure 17-10. Check your programming for the Right Movement module to ensure it matches what is shown here.

up on top of a wall tile due to this bug. The programming needs to be modified to prevent the diagonal movements.

80. Applying what you have learned, locate the event line in the Right Movement module that tests for when the right arrow is pressed, and add a new condition. Program the new condition to match this pseudocode:

    IF the up arrow key is **NOT** held down (repeat)

81. Add another condition in that same line to match this pseudocode:

    IF the down arrow is **NOT** held down (repeat)

82. Applying what you have learned, drag the conditions to rearrange them with all of the "arrow key" conditions together. This does not affect the function of the code, but it makes it easier to read when you are looking for bugs.

83. Modify the programming in the Left Movement, Up Movement, and Down Movement modules to prevent diagonal movement.

84. Run the frame. Test pressing two arrow keys at the same time for diagonal movement.

85. Debug as needed.

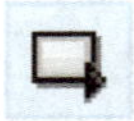

Run Frame

Stop Animation Debug

The manic miner moves well, but never stops walking, even when standing in one place. The existing counters can be used to detect if the Manic Miner object is not moving since they will all read 0 when the object is stopped.

86. Right-click on the number next to **New Condition**, and insert a comment that states Stop Animation. Set the background color to a light color of your choice, and change the text color if needed.

87. Add a new condition in the Stop Animation module, and program the following pseudocode, as shown in **Figure 17-12.**

    IF the Counter_Right object equals 0

        AND the Counter_Left object equals 0

        AND the Counter_Up object equals 0

        AND the Counter_Down object equals 0,

          THEN change the animation sequence for the Manic Miner object to Stopped.

88. Modify event line 1 to make the Avatar object invisible at the start of the frame.

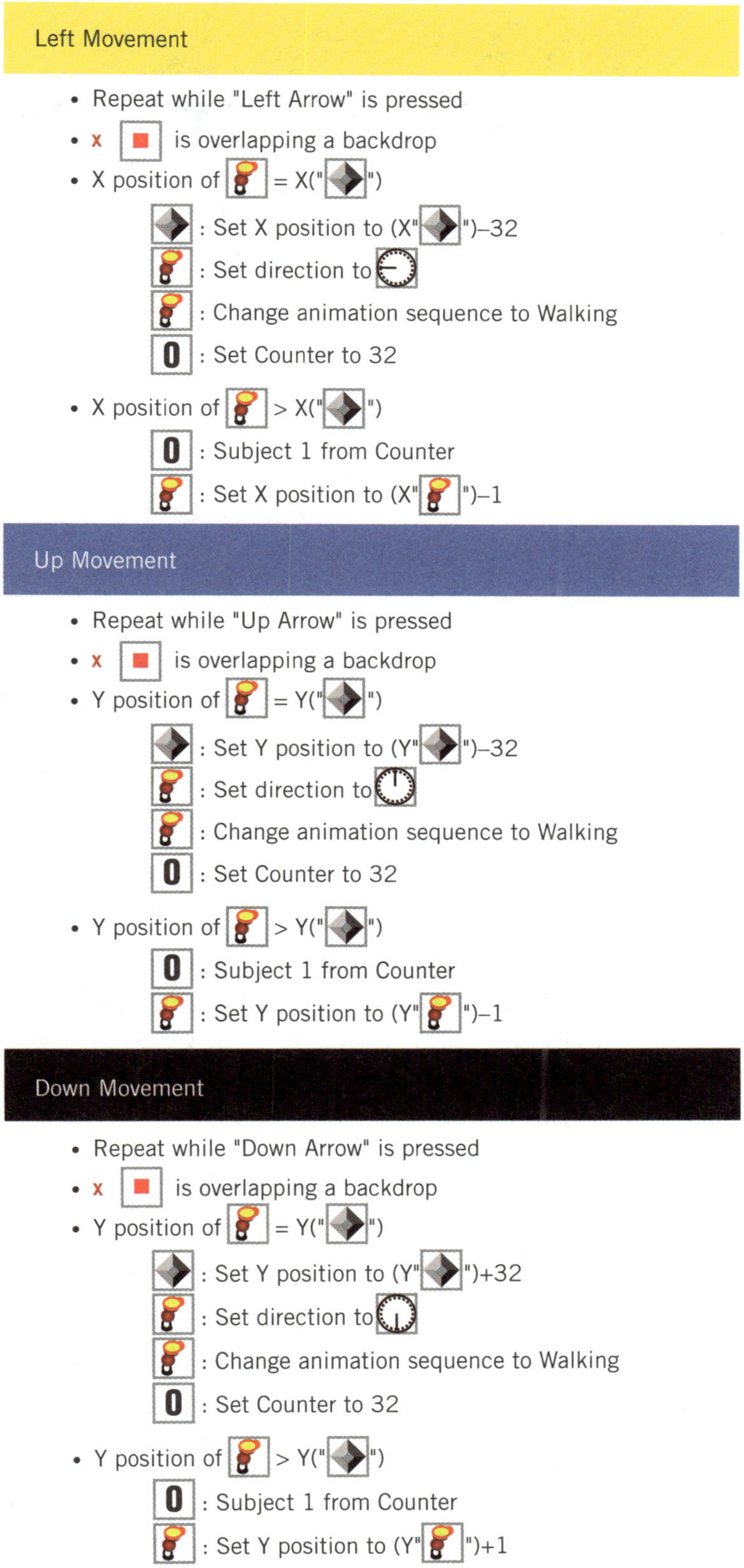

Left Movement

- Repeat while "Left Arrow" is pressed
- x [■] is overlapping a backdrop
- X position of [🔦] = X("[◆]")
    - [◆] : Set X position to (X"[◆]")–32
    - [🔦] : Set direction to [⊖]
    - [🔦] : Change animation sequence to Walking
    - [0] : Set Counter to 32
- X position of [🔦] > X("[◆]")
    - [0] : Subject 1 from Counter
    - [🔦] : Set X position to (X"[🔦]")–1

Up Movement

- Repeat while "Up Arrow" is pressed
- x [■] is overlapping a backdrop
- Y position of [🔦] = Y("[◆]")
    - [◆] : Set Y position to (Y"[◆]")–32
    - [🔦] : Set direction to [🕛]
    - [🔦] : Change animation sequence to Walking
    - [0] : Set Counter to 32
- Y position of [🔦] > Y("[◆]")
    - [0] : Subject 1 from Counter
    - [🔦] : Set Y position to (Y"[🔦]")–1

Down Movement

- Repeat while "Down Arrow" is pressed
- x [■] is overlapping a backdrop
- Y position of [🔦] = Y("[◆]")
    - [◆] : Set Y position to (Y"[◆]")+32
    - [🔦] : Set direction to [🕕]
    - [🔦] : Change animation sequence to Walking
    - [0] : Set Counter to 32
- Y position of [🔦] > Y("[◆]")
    - [0] : Subject 1 from Counter
    - [🔦] : Set Y position to (Y"[🔦]")+1

Goodheart-Willcox Publisher

Figure 17-11. Check your programming for the Left Movement, Up Movement, and Down Movement modules to ensure it matches what is shown here.

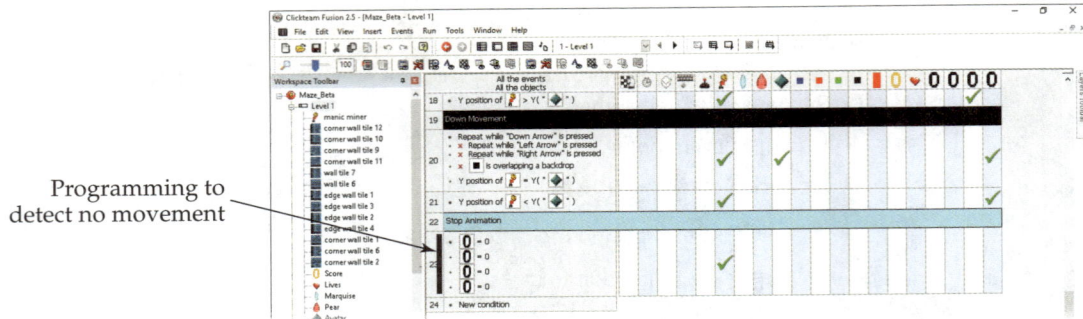

Programming to
detect no movement

Goodheart-Willcox Publisher

Figure 17-12. When the counters are all equal to zero, the Manic Miner object is not moving and the Stopped animation set should be displayed.

Frame Editor

89. Display the Level 1 frame in the frame editor.
90. Move all of the counter objects to outside the visible play area. They no longer need to be visible while testing the game.

Run Application

91. Run the application. Fully test the movement on the Level 1 frame. Also test moving between frames. Close the game window when done testing.

Frame Navigation Bug

You should have seen during testing that the navigation from one level to the next no longer functions properly. This is because the computer is having a hard time tracking when the Manic Miner object exits the frame. To make it easier for the computer to detect, a collision will be used to trigger the exit.

92. Insert a new active object, and change its properties as shown below. The position will be just outside the visible frame area where the exit to the Level 2 frame is, and the object should match the size of the opening. If needed, adjust the position and size to match your maze design.

Name	Position	Width	Height
Exit_1to2	(655, 126)	32	64

93. Open the object in the image editor, clear the canvas, and fill it with the color of your choice. The object will appear as a solid block of color.
94. Display the event editor for the Level 1 frame.

Event Editor

95. Locate the event line that tests for the Manic Miner object leaving the play area on the right, right-click on the condition, and click **Replace** in the shortcut menu.
96. Change the condition to match this pseudocode:
    IF the Manic Miner collides with the Exit_1to2 object

Run Application

97. Run the application. Test moving back and forth between the Level 1 and Level 2 frames. Make note of any bugs. Close the game window when done testing.

Final Tuning

When the manic miner reenters the Level 1 frame from the Level 2 frame, it is dragged across the screen to the starting location. This bug is due to the placement of the event line setting the global values. The action on this line is to occur at the start of the frame, but the line is not at the top of the script. This results in other events interfering with the correct placement of the Avatar object. Remember, the Manic Miner object is following the Avatar object.

98. Locate the event line that sets the global value, and drag this line to the top of the list so it is the number 1 line.

99. Modify the programming on event line 1 so it sets the position of the Avatar object instead of the Manic Miner object.

100. Run the application. Test moving back and forth between the Level 1 frame and the Level 2 frame. Close the game window when done testing.

101. Debug the existing programming as needed.

102. Applying what you have learned, add comments to the programming for the Level 2 and Level 3 frames to create the same modules created on the Level 1 frame. Note: comments and programming can be copied and pasted between frames.

103. Problem-solve to create the same movement used on the Level 1 frame on the other two levels.

104. Problem-solve to modify the navigation between all levels. Create new exit objects as needed. If the character "freezes" from one frame to the next and cannot move, you may need to adjust the starting position of the Avatar object on the frame. The object position should match the 32-pixel tile-based grid.

105. Save your work, and submit it for grading.

Run Application

Vocabulary

Write a definition for each of the key terms from this lesson. You will develop a personal glossary of key terms throughout this course.

genre

_____

_____

action game

_____

_____

theme

_____

_____

gameplay mode

_____

_____

primary gameplay mode

_____

_____

board/card/quiz game

_____

_____

educational game

_____

_____

fighting game

_____

_____

music/party game

_____

_____

puzzle game

_____

_____

role-playing game (RPG)

_____

_____

shooter game

_____

_____

simulation game

_____

_____

sports game

_____

_____

strategy game

_____

_____

turn-based strategy game

_____

_____

simultaneously played strategy game

_____

_____

toy

_____

_____

collision sensor

_____

_____

modular programming

_____

_____

Review Questions

1. In which genre would a game require the user to operate equipment identical to real-world equipment, such as an airplane yoke, as part of the user interface?

_____

_____

_____

_____

Applied Technology

2. Write a few sentences comparing and contrasting turn-based strategy games and simultaneously played strategy games.

_____

_____

_____

_____

Language Arts

3. Compare and contrast a game genre and a game theme.

_____

_____

_____

_____

Language Arts

4. Consider an educational game to teach someone from another country about American football. What cultural differences do you think need to be considered?

_____

_____

_____

_____

Social Science

5. What is another name for the **NOT** Boolean operator?

_____

_____

_____

_____

Applied Technology

Higher-Order Thinking Strategies

Science

6. Think about how your body defends itself from bacterial and viral infections. Summarize how you could create a game in the simulation genre to represent this. List the avatar and enemies and how they would interact in the simulation.

_____

_____

_____

_____

Social Science

7. Select four countries, including the United States, and research popular spectator sports. Select a sports genre game for each country, and explain why you think that game would be a good game to sell in that country.

_____

_____

_____

_____

Applied Technology

8. Briefly describe how sensors are used in the game build in this lesson.

_____

_____

_____

_____

Language Arts

9. Write a few sentences explaining the concept of modular programming.

_____

_____

_____

_____

Mathematics

10. The object for the player character is 25 pixels wide and 30 pixels high. There are four collision sensors to be used, each four pixels square. If the player character is placed at (150, 240) and there should be a space of seven pixels between the player character and any obstacle, what are the coordinates of each sensor? Assume the coordinates are in the center of the player character and each sensor.

_____

_____

_____

_____

Office Technology Integration

Using Mouse-Over Commands

1. Launch Microsoft Excel or other spreadsheet software, and open the vocabulary spreadsheet you updated in previous lessons.
2. Applying what you have learned, add a new worksheet, and name it Lesson 17.
3. Add each of the vocabulary words and definitions from the Vocabulary section of this lesson.
4. Save the spreadsheet, and then close it.
5. Launch Microsoft PowerPoint, start a new blank presentation, and save the file as *LastName*_Maze_POC in your working folder.
6. Change the layout so the slide is blank with no text boxes.
7. Add a rectangle that covers the entire slide. Fill it with red, and remove the outline.
8. Draw a rectangle in the top-left corner of the slide that is approximately 1.5 inches high and 3.0 inches wide. Fill it with yellow, and change the outline to black.
9. With the yellow rectangle, enter the text Click Here to START. Format the text color as black and make it bold.
10. Draw a rectangle in the bottom-right corner of the slide that is approximately 1.5 inches high and 3.0 inches wide. Fill it with green and change the outline to black. Add the text GOAL in white.
11. Draw a rectangle that is .3 inches high and 12 inches wide. Position it so it is centered in the slide. Fill it with blue, and remove the outline.
12. Draw a rectangle that is 3.5 inches high and .3 inches wide. Position it so it overlaps the yellow rectangle and the blue rectangle in the center. Fill it with the same blue used for the horizontal rectangle, and remove the outline.
13. Copy and paste the vertical blue rectangle, and position it such it overlaps the blue rectangle at the center and the green rectangle, as shown. Note: there must be no red space along the path created from the start to the goal.

Layout

Rectangle

Position the rectangles to create a continuous path

Goodheart-Willcox Publisher

14. Right-click on the yellow rectangle, and click **Bring to Front** in the shortcut menu to place the rectangle above the blue rectangle overlapping it. Do the same for the green rectangle.

15. Applying what you have learned, copy and paste the slide.

16. Insert a new title slide as slide 3, and enter the text Try Again.

17. Insert a new title slide as slide 4, and enter the text Winner.

18. Display slide 2, and select the red rectangle.

19. Click **Insert>Links>Action** on the ribbon.

20. In the **Action Settings** dialog box, click the **Mouse Over** tab. Mouse-over commands do not require a click to activate, only that the mouse is over an object.

21. Click the **Hyperlink to:** radio button, and select **Next Slide** in the drop-down list. Then, click the **OK** button. Anytime the cursor is touching the red rectangle during the slideshow, the presentation will jump to the next slide.

22. Applying what you have learned, add a mouse-over action to the green rectangle to hyperlink to the last slide.

23. Play the slideshow from the beginning. Click the yellow rectangle to start, and move the cursor along the blue path to the green goal. If you touch the red, you will be told to try again. If you make it all the way through the path and touch the green goal, you will be the winner.

24. Applying what you have learned, add a button to slides 3 and 4 to restart the game. Link the button to the first slide.

25. Submit your work for grading.

Action

From Beginning

Challenges Using Variables

Learning Objectives

After completing this lesson, you will be able to:

- implement elegant programming solutions.

- evaluate existing programming for errors or refinement possibilities.

- build a playable video game.

Situation

The Awesome Game Company has reviewed your beta game build of the maze game. The maze functions well, but the game needs more immersion. You have been assigned the task of learning about game immersion and challenges versus rewards within games. Then, you will improve the game.

Reading Materials

A game with little challenge quickly becomes boring for the player. In the maze game, there is very little challenge. **Challenge** is difficulty. This makes it simple to play, but not very interesting to play after the first time. By adding difficulty, objectives, missions, tasks, and obstacles, the player can get more immersed in the action of the game. **Immersion** is the degree to which a player connects with the game world.

Critical to immersion and the success of any game is the association of risk to reward. **Risk** is making a move that could cause damage to the player's character. For example, a player takes a risk when jumping over a hole. If the player jumps too soon, the character will fall in the hole and lose a life. In this way, the player takes a risk in jumping over the hole.

For every risk, there must be a reward. A **reward** is a benefit given to the player. In the case of the hole, the game programmer might place a coin or other token on the opposite side of the hole that the player must collect to score points. Without the reward, the player would probably just avoid the hole and find another path. When creating an obstacle or hazard, like a hole or enemy, the programmer must always balance the risk with the reward. Jumping a hole might get the player a coin. Defeating an enemy might give the player a

new ability. The reward must be great enough to make the player take the risk of injury to the character or defeat.

Another element that needs to be planned when designing a game is the skill level of the player. Part of the approval process for a game idea is to select a target audience. A *target audience* is the typical player that might purchase the game. Usually, a target audience is separated from everyone else by specific demographics. *Demographics* are observable features of a person, including age, gender, income, education, cultural background, and so on. If the target audience is 8-year-old boys, a cartoon-style game based on the popular Scooby Doo character may be appropriate. On the other hand, if the target audience is 20-year-old college students, the game would likely need to require greater skill and have more action than the game designed for a younger age group. The age and skill of the target audience help determine the amount of challenge and action needed in a game.

A successful game must also have skill progression. *Skill progression* describes how a game starts easy and gets harder as the player progresses through levels. By increasing the skill required to complete higher levels, the game presents increasing challenges to the player. Skill progression also helps teach the player how to play properly. The first level is easy so the player can get used to the controls and learn the moves needed to play the game. In the second level, more challenges are added, and the level is slightly more difficult than the first. Each level continues to add more difficult challenges until the final level, which should be the most difficult to complete.

When creating difficulty, remember the ultimate goal of the player is to defeat the game by achieving the victory condition. There is a progression of challenges that lead to the victory condition. *Atomic challenges* are the smallest possible challenges. This term comes from the atom, which is the smallest particle of an element. Atomic challenges are simple, like jumping a hole or hitting a target. By combining atomic challenges, sub-missions are created. *Sub-missions* are tasks that need to be completed in the game. A sub-mission might be navigating the level from beginning to end, collecting 100 coins, or other small in-game challenges. All of the sub-missions combine to form a game mission. A *mission* is a combination of sub-missions needed to complete a major set of tasks within the game. For example, a mission might be to destroy all enemies on the level and collect supplies needed for advanced levels. After completing all of the missions, the game is over and the player is victorious. This is the final victory condition that ends the game.

In addition to skill progression and challenges, the designer must understand the emotion of the player. In some cases, the player might get frustrated trying to defeat an enemy or overcome an obstacle. The player will likely stop playing if the character repeatedly dies and the player has to start over from the beginning. Repeating the same tasks over and over gets boring. Additionally, the feeling of joy from defeating a powerful enemy might be short-lived if the player later does something that requires battling the same enemy again. To avoid these conditions, designers use checkpoints and bonus lives. A *checkpoint* is a saved location in the game from where the player can restart if the character dies. A bonus life is often used as a reward for the player taking the risk of battling powerful enemies or achieving a certain score. Together, checkpoints and lives allow the player to test different strategies in the game through trial and error. Eventually, the player can learn the correct choices to achieve victory.

A designer needs to understand how to properly build challenge throughout the game. Each atomic challenge, sub-mission, and mission must meet the needs of the game and provide adequate reward. Taken together, these challenges must also be appropriate to the age and skill of the target audience. Finally, these challenges must build throughout the game to teach the player and allow for skill-building. Every game should be made so a player can eventually build enough skill to make it to the end and achieve the victory condition. In the end, the player should have enjoyed the game and not felt frustrated.

Game Build

The client has approved the player movement, but would like to see some gameplay challenges. The game is going to need some obstacles to overcome. Suggestions include adding enemies, rocks, doors, keys, and explosions to make the game more fun to play.

Before beginning this lesson, go to the student companion website (www.g-wlearning.com), and download the asset files for this lesson. Place the downloaded files in your working folder.

How to Begin

1. Launch Clickteam Fusion 2.5, and open the *LastName*_Maze_Beta game created in the previous lesson.
2. Save the file as *LastName*_Maze_Challenges in your working folder.
3. Display the Level 1 frame in the frame editor.
4. Applying what you have learned, add or create the objects in the table below, as shown in **Figure 18-1.** You may need to adjust the position of the objects based on your maze design.

Frame Editor

Name	Location	Position	Width	Height
Key	Treasure.mfa file	(176, 391)	32	14
Treasure Chest	Treasure.mfa file	(384, 169)	32	25
springer (purple)	Local Library>Games>Miscellaneous> Game Objects 1	(326, 278)	21	28
rock 3	Local Library>Games>Miscellaneous> Game Objects 1	(399, 431)	31	31
1 stick dynamite	Local Library>Games>Miscellaneous> Game Objects 1	Off frame	32	32
3 stick dynamite	Local Library>Games>Miscellaneous> Game Objects 1	(112, 440)	32	32
Explosion 4	Local Library>Games>Miscellaneous> Explosions	Off frame	26	26
Counter_Key	New Counter object	(320, 64)	32	32
Counter_ Dynamite	New Counter object	(160, 480)	32	32
Counter_ Explosives	New Counter object	(320, 480)	32	32

5. Applying what you have learned, edit the Key object to move the hotspot to the center of the sprite.

Creating Custom Objects

The art department has provided you with many of the items you need for this game. However, there are some items you will need to create on your own.

6. Applying what you have learned, insert a new active object, set the size to 32 × 32, position it at (239, 271), and name it TNT_Plunger.

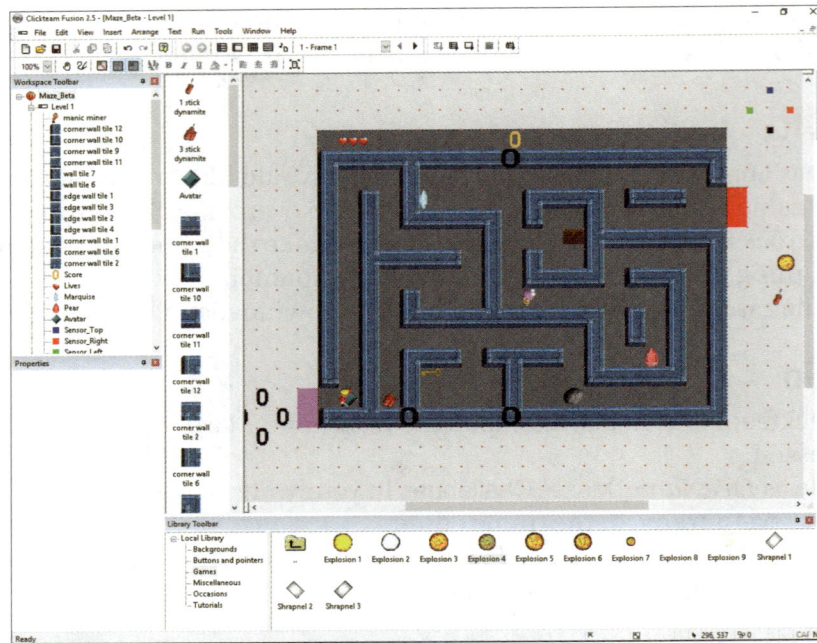

Goodheart-Willcox Publisher

Figure 18-1. Obstacles, rewards, an enemy, and counters are added to the Level 1 frame.

Clear

Rectangle Tool

Line Tool

Fill Tool

Ellipse Tool

7. Open the TNT_Plunger object in the image editor.
8. Clear the canvas and zoom in.
9. Set the foreground color to yellow and the background color to red.
10. Applying what you have learned, draw a filled rectangle with a 1 pixel outline, as shown in **Figure 18-2.** Leave a little room on the right and left edges, and a little more on the top.
11. Applying what you have learned, add the text TNT centered on the rectangle.
12. Change the foreground color to green.
13. Applying what you have learned, draw a T-shaped handle above the rectangle. Make sure the lines are wide enough to be seen in the game.
14. Right-click on Frame 1 in the **Frames** tab at the bottom of the image editor, and click **Copy** in the shortcut menu.
15. Click the box for direction 16 (left) in the animation direction area. Notice the canvas is now blank. This is because there currently are no animation frames for this direction.
16. Right-click in the **Frames** tab, and click **Paste** in the shortcut menu.
17. Select direction 0 (right).
18. Set the foreground color to transparent.
19. Using the **Fill Tool**, change the T-shaped handle to transparent. This will erase the handle. Direction 0 now has an image without a handle, and direction 16 has an image with a handle.
20. Click the **OK** button to update the object and close the image editor.
21. Insert a new active object, set the size to 32 × 32, position it at (399, 367), and name it Door. Adjust the position as needed to match your maze design. It should be positioned to block a passageway.
22. Open the Door object in the image editor, and clear the canvas.
23. Change the foreground color to a light brown. Select a color that will help make the object look like a wooden door.
24. Draw a filled ellipse in the upper third of the canvas, as shown in **Figure 18-3.**

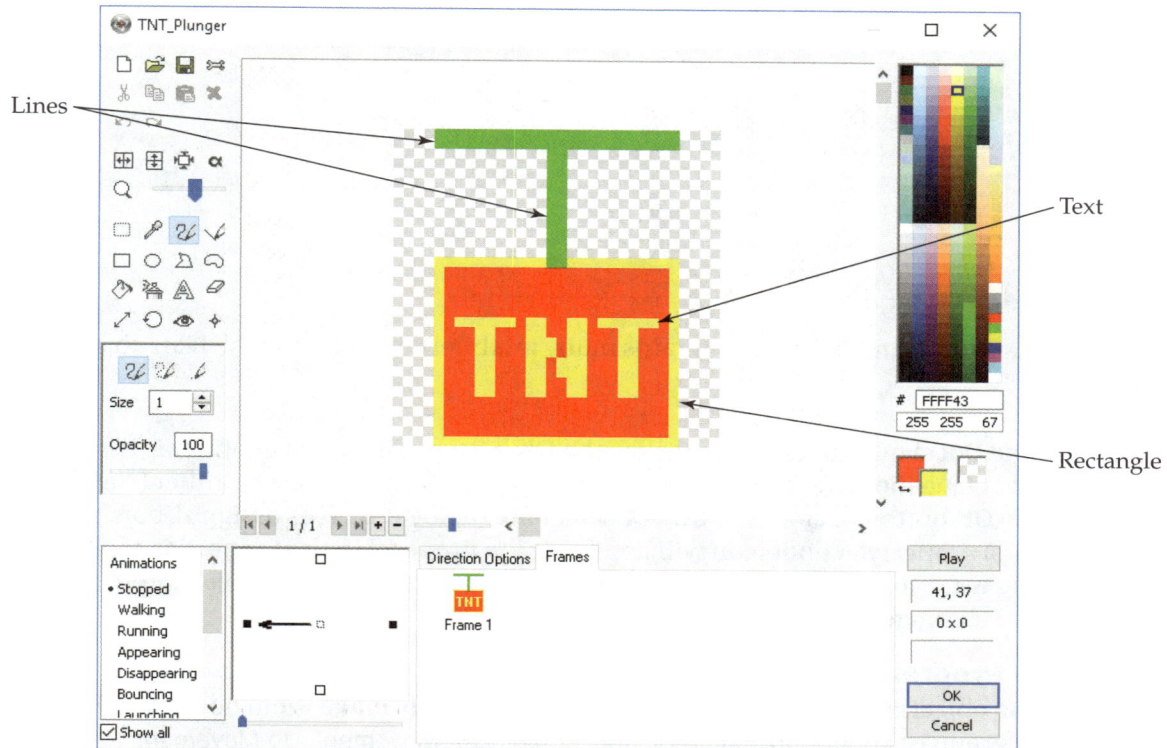

Figure 18-2. Creating a custom sprite for the TNT_Plunger object.

25. Draw a filled rectangle in the bottom portion of the canvas up to the midpoint of the oval. This forms the shape of the door.
26. Add a black line to separate the image into left and right doors.
27. Add rectangles or ellipses to create door handles.
28. Click the **OK** button to update the object and close the image editor.

Object Classes

An object can be assigned a class such as Good or Bad. A **class** is a named group of objects. By assigning a class, the programmer does not need to code an interaction for each possible "bad" object. Instead, the programmer can code one interaction for the Bad class. Then, any "bad" object can be assigned to that class and the programming will automatically be applied. To create an object class in Clickteam Fusion 2.5, a qualifier needs to be added to each object that is part of the class.

29. Select the Door object, and click the **Events** tab in the **Properties** toolbar.
30. Click the blank space for the Qualifier(s) property, and click the **Edit** button that appears. The **Object Qualifiers** dialog box is displayed.
31. Click the **Add** button in the **Object Qualifiers** dialog box. Another dialog box is displayed for selecting the qualifier (class), as shown in **Figure 18-4.**

Events

Goodheart-Willcox Publisher

Figure 18-3. A custom sprite for the Door object is created from an ellipse (left), rectangle (middle), and lines (right).

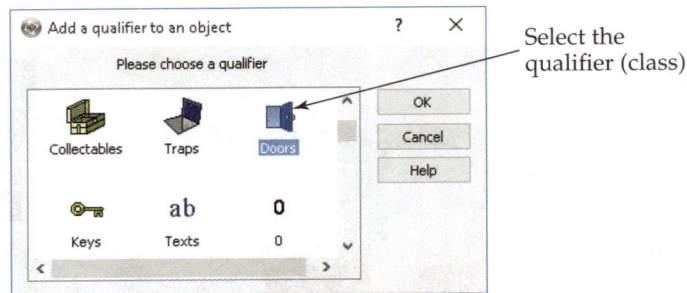

Select the qualifier (class)

Goodheart-Willcox Publisher

Figure 18-4. Clickteam Fusion 2.5 contains many qualifiers (classes) to which an object can be assigned.

32. Select the Doors qualifier icon, and click the **OK** button. The Doors qualifier is listed in the **Object Qualifiers** dialog box. An object can have more than one qualifier (class).
33. Click the **OK** button to close the **Object Qualifiers** dialog box. This assigns Doors to the Qualifier(s) property. A door icon will appear in the property in the **Properties** toolbar.
34. Applying what you have learned, add the Door qualifier to the rock 3 object. Rocks will block the character's path just like a door.

Navigation Programming

Assigning objects to the Door class does not automatically make them obstacles. A class is just a named group or collection. The Right Movement, Left Movement, Up Movement, and Down Movement modules all need to be modified to create the obstacle interaction.

Event Editor

35. Display the event editor for the Level 1 frame.
36. Right-click on the condition in the first line of the Right Movement module, and click **Insert** in the shortcut menu.
37. In the **New Condition** dialog box, click the icon for the Sensor_Right object, and click **Collisions>Overlapping another object** in the shortcut menu.
38. In the **Test a Collision** dialog box, select the Group.Doors icon. This indicates any object that has the Doors qualifier. Click the **OK** button to finish programming the condition.
39. Applying what you have learned, modify the condition you just created to match this pseudocode:
     IF the Sensor_Right object is **NOT** overlapping a Group.Doors object.
40. Drag and drop the conditions so the **NOT** conditions are grouped together, as shown in **Figure 18-5.** This does not affect the programming, but makes the code easier to read.
41. Applying what you have learned, modify the programming in each movement module to check for the sensor not overlapping a Door-class object.
42. Run the frame. Test if the Manic Miner object stops at the Door object. Close the game window when done testing.

Run Frame

Opening the Door

The player will need to collect a key to open the door. The Counter_Key object will be used to record when the player has collected the key. Since a door can also be placed in any direction on the frame, the **OR** operator must be used to test if any of the sensors are overlapping the door.

43. Applying what you have learned, add a comment at the bottom of the programming to create a module called Key Unlocking. Change the background and text colors as needed.
44. In the Key Unlocking module, add a new event, and program this pseudocode:
     IF the Manic Miner object collides with the Key object,
         THEN destroy the Key object
             AND create a new object Key at position (140, 16)
             AND add 1 to the Counter_Key object.

Right Movement

- Repeat while "Right Arrow" is pressed
- **x** Repeat while "Down Arrow" is pressed
- **x** Repeat while "Up Arrow" is pressed
- **x** [■] is overlapping [🚪]
- **x** [■] is overlapping a backdrop
- X position of [🔦] = X("[◆]")
  - [◆] : Set X position to (X"[◆]")+32
  - [🔦] : Set direction to [↻]
  - [🔦] : Change animation sequence to Walking
  - [0] : Set Counter to 32
- X position of [🔦] = X("[◆]")
  - [0] : Subtract 1 from Counter
  - [🔦] : Set X position to (X"[🔦]")+1

Figure 18-5. Grouping the **NOT** conditions together makes the code easier to read, but does not affect the function of the programming.

45. Run the frame. Test if a key appears at the top when you collect the Key object. Check that the counter is increased by 1. Close the game window when done testing.

Run Frame

46. In the Key Unlocking module, add a new event, and program this pseudocode.
    IF the Counter_Key is greater than 0
    AND the Sensor_Right object is overlapping a Door-class object.

47. Right-click on the second condition you just added, and click **OR operator (filtered)** in the shortcut menu. An **OR** statement is added to the condition.

48. Right-click on the **OR** operator, click **Insert** in the shortcut menu, and program this pseudocode:
    IF the value of the Counter_Key object is greater than 0
    AND the Sensor_Left object is overlapping a Door-class object.

49. Continue modifying the same condition by adding the following pseudocode, as shown in **Figure 18-6.**
    OR
        IF the Counter_Key object is greater than 0
        AND the Sensor_Top object is overlapping any Door-class object
    OR
        IF the Counter_Key object is greater than 0
        AND the Sensor_Bottom object is overlapping any Door-class object
    THEN destroy the Door-class object
    AND destroy the Key object
    AND subtract 1 from the Counter_Key object.

50. Display the Level 1 frame in the frame editor.

51. Applying what you have learned, copy the Key object, and place the copy at (272, 391). Adjust the position as needed to fit your maze.

Frame Editor

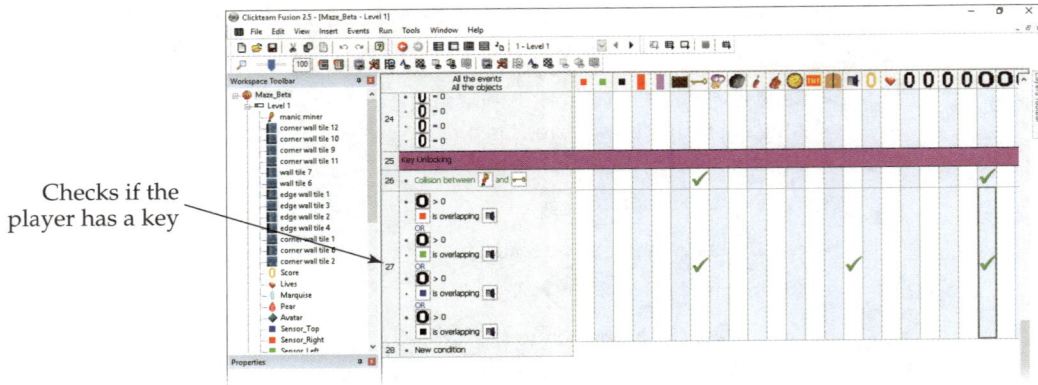

Checks if the player has a key

Goodheart-Willcox Publisher

Figure 18-6. The four **OR** statements check of the player has a key when touching the door.

Run Frame

52. Run the frame. Test the items indicated in the following chart. You will need to run the frame twice to complete all tests. Close the game window when done testing.

Test	Pass	Fail
Collect only one key, and the door will open (disappear)		
Collect the second key and the rock will be destroyed		
Player can navigate the entire maze on the Level 1 frame		

Level A Bug

You should have noticed a *huge* bug in the operation of the game. A **Level A** bug is one that would prevent the game from being released to the public. This may include game crashes, features not working, legal issues, or anything else that would cause the game to be a failure. When the rock 3 object was removed, the Manic Miner object was stuck in place. This bug crashes the game. The reason for the bug is when the last Door-class object is destroyed, all of the conditions to test if any sensor is overlapping a Door-class object can no longer be tested.

53. Create a copy of the rock 3 object.
54. Move the copy outside of the visible play area. This will allow there to always be at least one Door-class object on the frame even if it is not visible to the player.

Run Frame

55. Run the frame. Test that the player can continue once the rock is destroyed. Close the game window when done testing.

Placing Dynamite

The manic miner should also be able to use dynamite to blow up obstacles and enemies. To do this, the player will need to collect a stick of dynamite from the supply stack, place the stick in a location, and use the TNT plunger to set off the explosion. The Counter_Dynamite object will be used to track if the player has picked up a stick of dynamite.

56. Display the event editor for the Level 1 frame.

Event Editor

57. Applying what you have learned, add a new module at the end of the programming named Dynamite Controls. Change the background and text colors as needed.

58. In the Dynamite Controls module, program this pseudocode:

> **IF** the Manic Miner object collides with the 3 stick dynamite object,
>> **THEN** destroy the 3 stick dynamite object,
>>> **AND** create a 1 stick dynamite object at location (175, 25)
>>> **AND** add 1 to the Counter_Dynamite object.

59. Add a second event in the Dynamite Controls module, and program the following pseudocode, as shown in **Figure 18-7**.

> **IF** the Counter_Dynamite object is greater than 0
>> **AND** the space bar is pressed,
>>> **THEN** subtract 1 from the Counter_Dynamite object
>>>> **AND** create a 1 stick dynamite object at the exact location of the Manic Miner object
>>>> **AND** create a 3 stick dynamite object at (112, 440)
>>>> **AND** add 1 to the Counter_Explosives object.

60. Run the frame. Test if you can collect dynamite and place it one stick at a time around the game map. Close the game window when done testing.

Run Frame

Exploding the Dynamite

The manic miner will need to use the TNT plunger to blow up the dynamite sticks placed in the maze. For safety purposes, the manic miner will be limited to placing only one stick of dynamite at a time. Additionally, to prevent disaster, the dynamite cannot be set off if the manic miner is holding it. The Counter_Explosives object will be used to test if there is any dynamite placed on the map. The Counter_Dynamite object will be used to test if the manic miner is holding any dynamite.

61. Add a new event in the Dynamite Controls module, and program this pseudocode:

> **IF** the Counter_Explosives object is greater than 0
>> **AND** the Counter_Dynamite object is equal to 0,
>>> **THEN** change the direction for the TNT_Plunger object to direction 16 (left).

62. Add a new event in the Dynamite Controls module, and program this pseudocode:

> **IF** the direction for the TNT_Plunger object is direction 16 (left)
>> **AND** the Manic Miner object collides with the TNT_Plunger object,
>>> **THEN** destroy the 1 stick dynamite object
>>>> **AND** set the Counter_Explosives object to 0
>>>> **AND** change the direction for the TNT_Plunger object to direction 0 (right)
>>>> **AND** create an Explosion 4 object at the exact location of the 1 stick dynamite object.

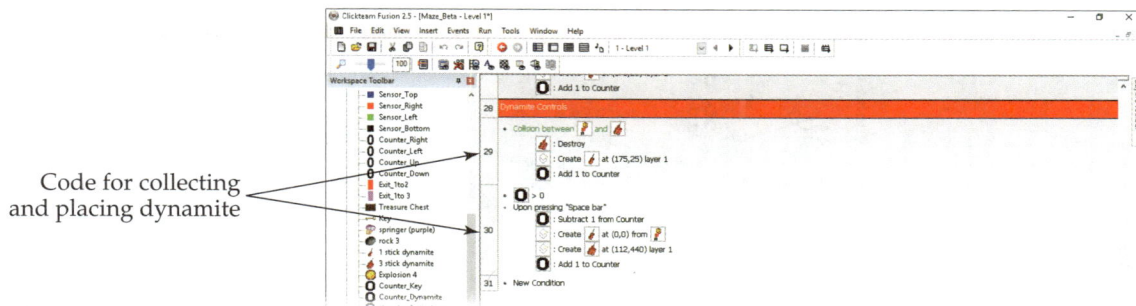

Code for collecting and placing dynamite

Goodheart-Willcox Publisher

Figure 18-7. The Dynamite Controls module contains the programming for collecting and placing the dynamite.

Event List Editor

63. Display the event list view. Notice the condition Collision between Manic Miner object and TNT_Plunger object is red. This means there is an error in that condition and it will not work.
64. Drag the red condition up so it is the first condition tested within the event, as shown in **Figure 18-8.** It will turn green to indicate the condition can now be solved.

Run Frame

65. Run the frame. Test that the plunger changes when dynamite is collected. Test that dynamite cannot be set off if the manic miner is carrying any. Close the game window when done testing.

Problem Solving

Everything should work good at this point, but your programming is not elegant. *Elegant programming* means that the number of steps are at a minimum and the code is a clean and efficient order of operation.

Event List Editor

66. Examine the Dynamite Controls module in the event list view.
67. Analyze the order of operations for the actions in each event. Think about which action should occur before another. Are there any actions that if they occurred before another would prevent the second action from being performed correctly?
68. Using only reordering of the existing actions, find an elegant solution.

Multiple Classes for an Object

Remember how the Door object is part of the Doors qualifier (class)? Each object can be a member of multiple object classes. This can help your programming become more elegant by reducing "code clutter."

Frame Editor

69. Display the Level 1 frame in the frame editor.
70. Select the Door object, and click the **Events** tab in the **Properties** toolbar.
71. Click the Qualifier(s) property, and click the **Edit** button.

Events

72. In the **Object Qualifiers** dialog box, click the **Add** button.
73. In the next dialog box, select the Obstacles qualifier, and click the **OK** button. This is the same process you used earlier to add the first qualifier.
74. Click the **OK** button in the **Object Qualifiers** dialog box. Notice that there are now two qualifiers for this object, as shown in **Figure 18-9.**

Event Editor

75. Display the event editor for the Level 1 frame.

Drag the condition to the top

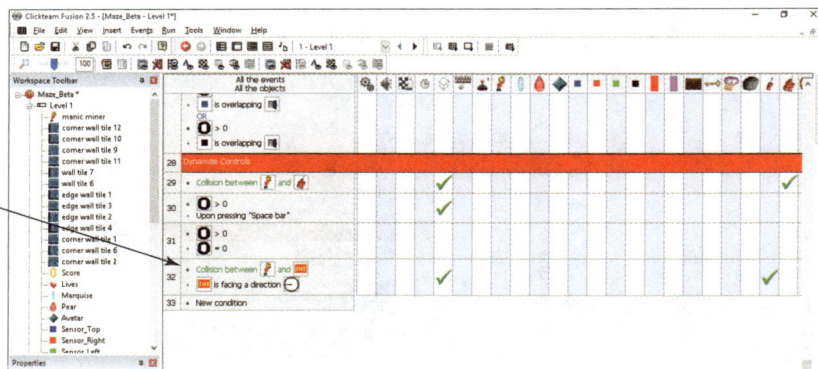

Figure 18-8. If a condition is displayed in red, it means the condition cannot be tested. In this case, dragging the condition to the top corrects the problem.

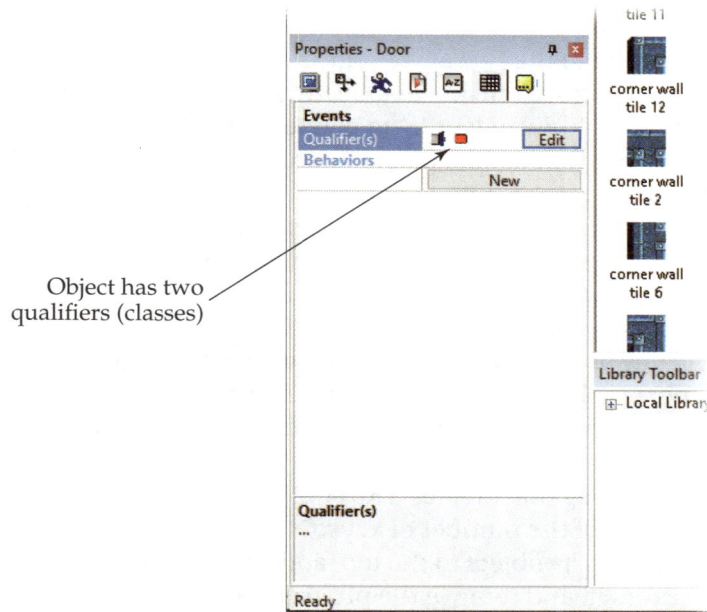

Goodheart-Willcox Publisher

Figure 18-9. An object can be a member of more than one class (qualifier).

76. Applying what you have learned, add a new comment to create a new programming module named Exploding Objects at the bottom of the programming. Change the text and background colors as needed.

77. In the Exploding Objects module, program this pseudocode:

    IF the Explosion 4 object collides with an object in the Obstacles class,

      THEN destroy the Obstacles-class object.

78. Run the frame. Test if an explosion destroys the door. Close the game window when done testing.

79. Display the Level 1 frame in the frame editor.

80. Applying what you have learned, assign the rock 3 and springer (purple) objects to the Obstacles class.

81. Run the frame. Test that each object in the Obstacles class is destroyed with an explosion. Close the game window when done testing.

Run Frame

Frame Editor

Tuning the Game

The mechanics of the game are complete, only the tuning or refining process of the game design remains. The enemy should be programmed to move around the maze to add challenge to the level. The counters need to be repositioned to be more useful. You also probably noticed the explosions did not completely disappear. This will need to be cleaned up to make the game look better.

82. Delete one of the Key objects from the Level 1 frame.

83. Set the movement Type property for the springer (purple) object to Bouncing Ball.

84. Add the programming needed to make the springer (purple) object bounce off the walls of the maze. Place the programming near the top of the script before the first programming module.

85. Adjust the speed of the springer (purple) object as needed to fit with the game.

86. Add programming to give the player a reward when the Treasure Chest object is opened (collision). Add the code to the Rewards programming module.

87. Add programming to remove one life and destroy the Manic Miner object if it collides with an enemy or an explosion. Use object classes to your advantage to create elegant programming. Be sure to spawn the player character, and remember the character follows the Avatar object.

88. Add programming to end the game if there are no lives remaining.

89. Move the Counter_Explosives object outside the visible game frame. This counter does not need to be seen during gameplay.

90. Move the Counter_Key object to the top near the Lives object.

91. Right-click on the Key object, click **Create**>**Backdrop Object** in the shortcut menu, and click in the area next to the Counter_Key object. This will act as the identifier for the counter. Since it is a backdrop object, it will be unaffected by programming associated with the Key object.

92. Remove the programming that creates a Key object. The counter will be visible during gameplay to keep track of the number of keys.

93. Move the Counter_Dynamite object to the top, add a backdrop object of the 1 stick dynamite object next to it, and remove the programming that creates a 1 stick dynamite object at the top of the frame. Be sure to remove only the programming that creates the object at the top.

94. Open the Explosion 4 object in the image editor, right-click in the **Frames** tab at the bottom, and click **New Frame** in the shortcut menu. This should place a blank frame as the last frame of the animation. If the new frame is not the last frame, drag it to the last frame position. The blank frame will clean up the explosion. This is another way to approach this problem in addition to the programming method you learned in a previous lesson.

95. Test and debug the Level 1 frame as needed. Once this level is completely error free, you can tune the other levels.

96. Add enemies and obstacles to the other levels of the game.

97. Add rewards to the other levels of the game.

98. Save your work, and submit it for grading.

Vocabulary

Write a definition for each of the key terms from this lesson. You will develop a personal glossary of key terms throughout this course.

challenge

_____

_____

immersion

_____

_____

risk

_____

_____

reward

_____

_____

target audience

_____

_____

demographics

_____

_____

skill progression

_____

_____

atomic challenge

_____

_____

sub-mission

_____

_____

mission

_____

_____

checkpoint

_____

_____

class

_____

_____

Level A

_____

_____

elegant programming

_____

_____

Review Questions

Applied Technology

1. List four of your favorite games and describe how the game designers used checkpoints to help the player during gameplay.

_____

_____

_____

_____

Social Science

2. Research the demographics of your town. List five demographics that you feel are key to describing your community. Describe what you think the statistics say about your community in comparison to other communities.

_____

_____

_____

_____

Language Arts

3. Write an explanation of what role you feel immersion plays in video game addiction.

_____

_____

_____

_____

Social Science

4. During gameplay, what must accompany every risk?

_____

_____

_____

_____

Science

5. How is physics part of the interaction of a player character jumping over a hole?

_____

_____

_____

_____

Name: _____

Higher-Order Thinking Strategies

6. All game interactions are composed of atomic challenges just as all matter is composed of atoms. Research atomic structure, and describe the parts of an atom.

_____

_____

_____

_____

_____

Science

7. In this lesson, you created an event consisting of four **OR** statements in the Key Unlocking module. How can these statements be eliminated using a qualifier (class) to make the programming elegant?

_____

_____

_____

_____

_____

Applied Technology

8. Suppose the target market is teenagers interested in engineering. Speculate what game elements would appeal to this market. Use your knowledge of game genres to propose a game concept.

_____

_____

_____

_____

_____

Social Science

9. Describe how skill progression helps a player learn how to play the game.

_____

_____

_____

_____

_____

Language Arts

Mathematics

10. Suppose a game rewards the player with a bonus life at 1000 points. Each additional bonus life is rewarded after scoring another 1000 points plus 10% of the previous reward level. For example, the second bonus life is rewarded at a score of 2100 points. Complete the following table to show what score must be achieved to obtain the next bonus life.

Extra Life	Score Plus 1000	10% of Previous Score	Total Score Needed
1	1000	0	1000
2	2000	100	2100
3	3100	210	
4			
5			

Office Technology Integration

Using Animation Presets

1. Launch Microsoft Excel or other spreadsheet software, and open the vocabulary spreadsheet you updated in previous lessons.
2. Applying what you have learned, add a new worksheet, and name it Lesson 18.
3. Add each of the vocabulary words and definitions from the Vocabulary section of this lesson.
4. Save the spreadsheet, and then close it.
5. Launch Microsoft PowerPoint and open the *LastName*_Maze_POC presentation created in Lesson 17. Save the file as *LastName*_Maze_Challenge in your working folder.
6. Display slide 1, and delete the horizontal blue rectangle.
7. Replace the deleted rectangle with three smaller rectangles. Place them end to end in the same location as the deleted rectangle. Make sure there is no red between the rectangles.
8. Select the centermost rectangle, and click the **Animations** tab on the ribbon.
9. In the **Animation** group, locate the Spin animation in the gallery, and click it to apply the animation to the center rectangle. The rectangle should spin as the animation is previewed.
10. Click **Animations>Advanced Animation>Animation Pane** on the ribbon. The **Animation Pane** is displayed on the right-hand side of the screen.

Animation Pane

11. Select the rectangle name in the **Animation Pane**, and click the drop-down arrow on the right of the animation tile. Click **Effect Options…** in the drop-down menu to open the **Spin Animation** dialog box, as shown.

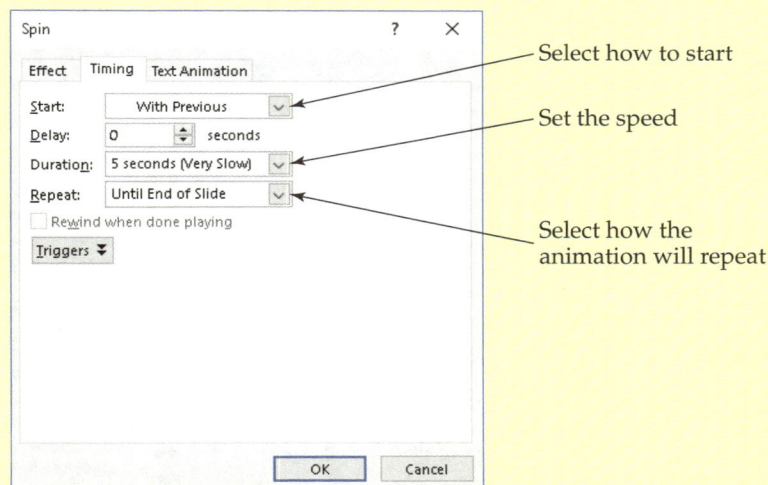

Goodheart-Willcox Publisher

12. Click the **Timing** tab, change the **Start:** setting to **With Previous**, change the **Duration:** setting to **5 seconds (Very Slow)**, change the **Repeat:** setting to **Until End of Slide**, and click the **OK** button.
13. Insert a smiley face shape that is 1 inch tall and 1 inch wide. Fill it with yellow, and position it between the green rectangle and center path.
14. Add a Lines animation to the smiley face shape. This will create a vertical line path for the shape to follow. A faded-out shape appears at the end of the path.
15. Click the handle at the end of the path, and drag it so the path crosses the final blue rectangle before the goal.
16. Select the smiley face name in the **Animation Pane**, click the drop-down arrow, and click **Effect Options…** in the drop-down menu.

17. Click the **Effect** tab, and check the **Auto-reverse** check box.

18. Click the **Timing** tab, change **Start:** setting to **With Previous**, change the **Duration:** setting to **3 seconds (Slow)**, change the **Repeat:** setting to **Until End Slide**, and click the **OK** button.

19. Applying what you have learned, apply a mouse-over action to the smiley face shape to jump to the last slide. This turns the smiley face into an obstacle.

20. Select all three horizontal blue rectangles and the smiley face, and copy them.

21. Display slide 2, and delete the center blue rectangle. Then, paste the copied objects from slide 1. Each shape should be automatically positioned in the same place it was on slide 1. All properties of each object are inherited from the original shape that was copied.

From
Beginning

22. Play the presentation from the beginning. Try to complete the maze with the new obstacles in place.

23. Modify the obstacles as needed to successfully navigate the maze.

24. Explore the animation settings and redesign the maze to include a more complex maze design with different obstacles.

25. Submit your work for grading.

Two-Dimensional Game Art

Learning Objectives

After completing this lesson, you will be able to:

- evaluate images using the elements of art and the principles of design.
- explain how visual perspective, lighting, and shadows help create the illusion of 3D space.
- create custom colors using the RGB color model.
- compose complex shapes from primitive shapes.
- generate custom gradients to create lighting, shadow, and illusion of depth.
- apply textures and pictures to object surfaces.
- simulate 3D objects using 2D shapes.
- rotate objects in 3D space around the X, Y, and Z axes.

Situation

The Awesome Game Company has a new management program to develop team members as project managers and directors. The company hopes to expand business with a new division to handle more work in the app-development marketplace. Since the company is always looking to promote current employees, you could be up for a promotion soon. To develop the skills the company is looking to hire, you will need to develop more knowledge and skills related to game art. Begin by learning the foundations of artwork and design, and then apply your knowledge to develop the game art needed for an exciting new app.

Reading Materials

To develop the skills needed to create game artwork, the elements of art and the principles of design must be applied. The *elements of art* deal with the individual features needed to compose artwork. Each individual feature or element is constructed and arranged to create artwork. Artwork is an artistic work developed using a combination of art elements to create a visual scene, character, volume, or image. Artwork should

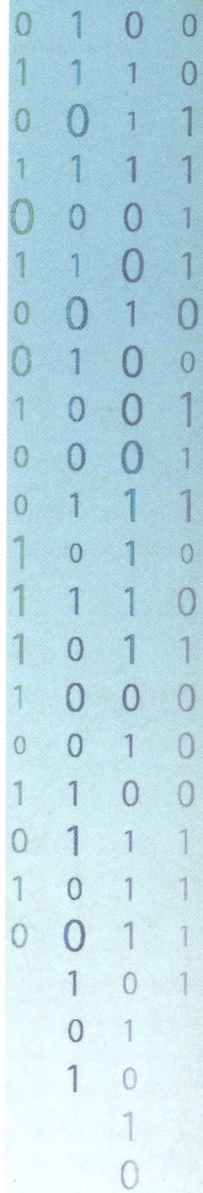

also be developed following the principles of design. The ***principles of design*** govern how to effectively combine the elements of art to compose a pleasing work of art. Together, the elements of art and principles of design are used to create game art and artistic scenes.

Traditional artwork is created without the use of computer technology. Examples of traditional artwork include paintings, drawings, sculptures, pottery, and so on. ***Digital artwork*** is created using a computer. The artist inputs information into a computer program that helps create the artwork. The final artwork can be displayed in physical form or in virtual form. Digital artwork can be output in physical form, such as a printed page or an object produced by molding, rapid prototyping machine, computer-guided lathe, or other computer-controlled output. Digital artwork in virtual form may be digital pictures or animations displayed on a computer screen.

Elements of Art

There are seven elements of art: shape, form, line, color, value, space, and texture. Each of these elements details an aspect of a single attribute of an object. These elements are universal and apply to both traditional and digital art. Below are brief descriptions of each element of art.

Shape

The black circle shown in **Figure 19-1** is a shape defined by the edges of the black ink on the paper. ***Shape*** is a defined area in two-dimensional (2D) space. Shapes come in two different varieties: geometric and organic.

Geometric shapes are regular figures, like a square, circle, triangle, octagon, or trapezoid. Geometric shapes are also known as 2D primitives. ***Primitives*** are regular shapes and objects that are used to assemble more complex shapes or objects. For example, the robotic character shown in **Figure 19-1** is constructed from 2D primitives: three circles, five rectangles, and one trapezoid.

Irregular shapes are known as ***organic shapes.*** Organic shapes describe things like a cloud, tree, blowing steam, or even an ergonomic computer mouse. Mostly, organic shapes are used to describe things in nature. In practice, organic shapes describe natural and unnatural shapes that have curved or irregular edges.

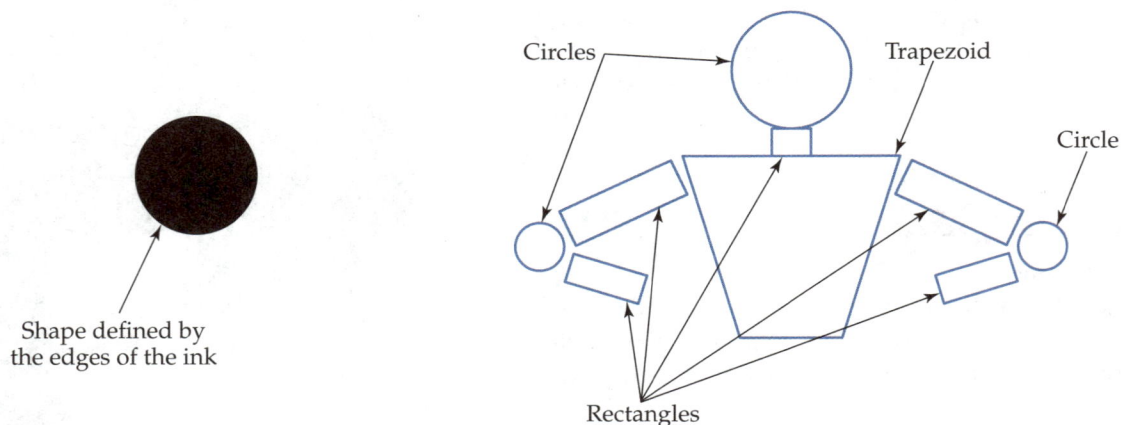

Figure 19-1. Shape is a defined area in 2D space. The circle on the left is a shape defined by the edges of the black ink. The character on the right is composed of several 2D primitives, which are geometric shapes.

Form

The assembly of 2D shapes to represent a third dimension is *form.* Form shows measurable dimensions of length, width, and depth for an object. A traditional sculpture has form, but a computer-modeled character also has form.

Line

If you look at the basic robot in **Figure 19-1,** each shape is defined by the boundary created by a solid black line. *Line* is the path between two points and most often used as a boundary to create a shape. Lines can be straight, curved, looping, or organic and can be solid or composed of dashes or other marks. When a line is composed of dashes or other marks, it is an implied line. An *implied line* is the path the viewer's eye takes to connect the two endpoints of the line when it is not continuous. Basically, the viewer's eye connects the dots with an invisible (implied) line to complete the line path, as shown in **Figure 19-2.**

Color

The hue applied to a line or shape is its *color.* A fill is color applied to the area enclosed by lines or shapes. Colors are defined using a color model, which is a way of mixing base colors to create a spectrum of colors. The RGB color model is the most common color model used in game design. The name comes from the three base colors used in the color model: red, green, and blue. All of the colors you see on your computer screen are made by mixing these three base colors. Other color models include hue, saturation, luminescence (HSL) and cyan, magenta, yellow, and key (CMYK). Hue is the pigment color, saturation is how dark or rich the color is, and luminescence is how much light is shining on the color. Cyan, magenta, and yellow are process colors. The most detail in a printed image appears in the key color, which is almost always black.

The model used for a project is typically based on the required output. For example, CMYK is the color model used when the output is a printed product. A printing press uses four colors to create the colors seen on the printed page. These colors are cyan, magenta, yellow, and the key. An artist creating something to be printed needs to use the CMYK color model to match the requirements of the printing press. Since most computer monitors use red, green, and blue pixels to create color, an artist creating something that will be displayed on a computer or television as the final output needs to use the RGB color model.

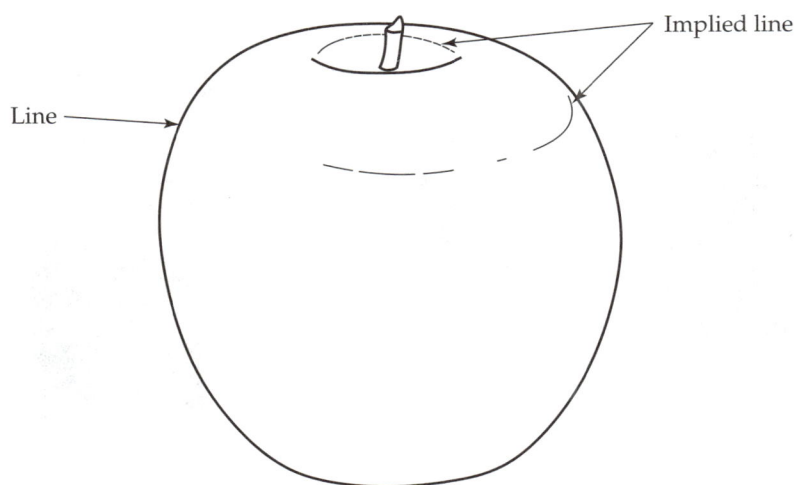

Goodheart-Willcox Publisher

Figure 19-2. A line is a path between two points, while an implied line is the path the viewer's eyes take if the line is not continuous.

Figure 19-3. This apple and its shadow are created by varying value, or light and dark.

Value

Value is the use of light and dark to add highlight, shading, or shadows. If you look at a black-and-white image, the entire image is created based on the principle of value. Look at the image of the apple shown in **Figure 19-3.** Depth is created around the stem by darkening that area. Near the top of the apple, depth is created by lightening the part of the apple that is closest to the light.

Value can be used in a scene to create depth by adding shadow and light to create contrast between objects. In game design, artists use pixel shading to create the illusion of depth. Pixel shading is the use of lighter and darker colors, or changes in value, to create light and shadow. *Pixel shading* is used to create the illusion of 3D by darkening images as they get farther from the light source. It also helps in applying overlap.

Look at **Figure 19-4.** Pixel shading is used on the cube to color the different faces based on the light source. This shows the left-hand face closest to the light source and, therefore, the lightest. The right-hand face is farthest from the light source and, therefore, the darkest. Notice how pixel shading is used on the cylinder as well. Also, notice how shadows are added

Figure 19-4. Pixel shading is used to create the illusion of three dimensions. The farther an object or surface is from a light source, the darker it should appear.

to ground the objects on an imaginary plane, as opposed to the light object, which appears to float in space.

Space

The area or volume in a scene is the *space.* Space may be physical or virtual. A sculpture occupies physical space. You actually cut into the block of marble and create a statue with physical length, width, and depth. However, using a computer, you can create in virtual space. The object you create in a 3D modeling program has virtual length, width, and depth. In 2D art, whether physical or virtual, space must be represented with illusion.

Positive and negative space apply emphasis to the design. *Positive space* is the area or volume occupied by the primary objects. *Negative space* is the area or volume around or between the primary objects. An example of these is your yearbook photo. You are the positive space in the portrait. The volume between you and the background is the negative space. The amount of negative space in a design can help provide contrast and emphasis to the primary objects. Imagine your yearbook photo is taken as a panoramic view in a stadium. While you are still a primary object, you are surrounded by hundreds of other objects. You are hard to identify as the primary object in the photo. This is because there is little negative space to separate you from everything else in the photo. Without any negative space, your picture has less emphasis than it did in the portrait of just you in front of a background. Likewise, in game design, a scene can become cluttered if there is not enough negative space.

In three-dimensional space, length, width, and depth dimensions are used to create an object. When working with a 2D surface like a sheet of paper or a computer screen, the artist must trick the eye to create the illusion of 3D space. In computer rendering, artists apply both pixel shading and vertex shading to help create the illusion of 3D. *Vertex shading* is moving the points on an object to resize it such that the object appears smaller in the distance. The principle of visual perspective is applied during vertex shading.

Visual perspective is the proportional scaling of objects as they move toward a vanishing point. In **Figure 19-5,** notice how the parallel lines of the road angle inward until the lines meet in the distance. Of course, the sides of the road remain parallel. It is just the principle of visual perspective that makes the sides of the road appear to converge. Also, notice how the tree trunks appear to get thinner in the distance. Each object is scaled down as it moves toward the vanishing point. The point where parallel lines meet is the *vanishing point,* as shown in **Figure 19-6.** There may be one, two, or three vanishing points, but one- and two-point perspectives are the most common.

Texture

Variations in form and color create *texture,* which is an uneven surface. *Tactile texture* is an irregular surface that can be physically felt, like sandpaper. When you touch it, you feel the surface is bumpy or rough. This texture is a variation in surface depth to create a coarse physical sensation. *Optical texture* is creating variation in what you see. Look at **Figure 19-7.** The skin of the orange has an optical texture because the color changes around the orange. The surface of the orange is not a single solid color. Additionally, the orange has tactile texture because the surface has physical bumps that can be felt.

Principles of Design

The principles of design are the set of rules or guidelines used to create artwork. The principles of design are specific to make sure you are creating effective layouts or art. Depending on the type of design (web, game, fine art, or other), the number of principles will change. For game design, the principles of design are movement, emphasis, harmony, variety, balance, contrast, proportion, pattern, and unity.

Figure 19-5. In real life, these trees are approximately the same size, but the trees in the distance appear smaller because they are farther away from the viewer. Also notice how the edges of the road appear to converge at a point in the distance, but in reality the edges stay the same distance apart.

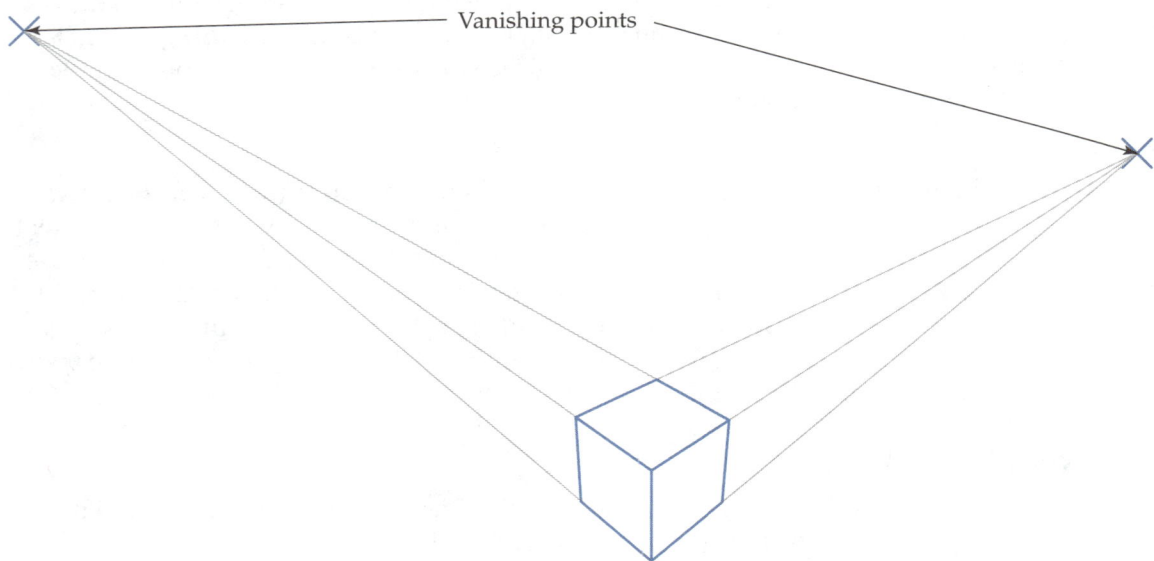

Vanishing points

Figure 19-6. In perspective drawing, the edges of objects will, if extended, converge at vanishing points. This is a two-point perspective because there are two vanishing points.

Figure 19-7. Optical texture is created by visual variation in a surface, such as the skin on this orange. The skin also has tactile texture because if you were to touch it, you would feel the texture of the surface.

Movement

Applied action is ***movement.*** In traditional art forms, a static picture must convey movement. In game art, movement is typically done through animation. A game artist must understand and apply the movement principle, even if the object is going to be animated.

Look at **Figure 19-8** and see how movement is represented in the illustration. The tassels on the jacket are drawn to the right instead of straight down. This implies the snowboarder is moving to the left. Additionally, bits of snow are drawn to the right of the snowboarder, which also imply movement to the left. Lines are added to imply movement. Straight lines imply the leftward movement, while curved lines imply the legs and outstretched arm are moving. Finally, the position of the snowboarder implies movement. For the snowboarder to be in that pose, it is logical to interpret movement, and the fact that the character is looking to the left implies leftward movement. A game artist can use some of these same visual cues to help improve the movement of a character as it runs, jumps, draws a sword, or performs some other action.

Communicate movement

Figure 19-8. The artist has used lines and the placement of shapes to communicate that the snowboarder is moving.

Emphasis

When a designer draws attention to an object, the object is given *emphasis.* In game design, emphasis is typically accomplished by making an object larger, brighter, repeated, or moving. Having the object make noise is another way to add emphasis. The idea behind adding emphasis is that the player will understand the object is special in some way. The object may be a reward or it could be an obstacle that needs to be avoided. For example, if tokens are gold coins almost as large as the player, the tokens are being emphasized. In this way, emphasis is giving a clue to the player.

Harmony

Using similar elements is the principle of *harmony.* Harmony helps hold the image or scene together. Imagine a dirty character dressed in old raggedy clothes, but wearing a gold crown. The gold crown just does not fit with the way the character is dressed. The design of this character is not demonstrating harmony.

Likewise, the elements of a scene need to have harmony. Objects that are out of place detract from the game. If you are creating a medieval game, all characters, buildings, vehicles, language, etc., need to match the medieval setting. A scene in which knights are sitting around a table with a computer on it lacks harmony. Harmony also needs to be maintained between levels in a game. Some characters, tools, and other game elements should move with the player to the next level to give the game a sense of harmony.

Variety

The purposeful absence of harmony to create visual or contextual interest is the principle of *variety* (also known as alternation). This differs from emphasis in that the design is less obvious. Here the designer might want a clue that makes the player think or explore options. Imagine the classic dilemma of the two doors. Behind one door is a princess and behind the other is a tiger. To keep the player from making a guess, the designer may apply the principle of variety to the doors. Maybe the correct door has a few specs of glitter on the handle or the incorrect door handle has teeth marks. Possibly, one door is metal and the other is wood. Unlike applying emphasis, the clue is not obvious. It takes keen observation or thinking by the player to discover the clue.

Another application of variety is to change shape or color for meaning. For example, in a game a red apple may increase health, and a green apple may increase strength, as shown in **Figure 19-9.** A great use of variety is the use of color or sound to indicate a change of state of an object. You have already seen an application of this in the health bar you programmed in previous lessons. As the character's health decreases, the bar changes from green, to yellow, to red. A sound, such as a heartbeat, could be assigned to the health and variety applied to the sound. For example, as the character's health decreases, not only does the color of the health bar change, but the heartbeat becomes louder or faster. Applying variety helps the player understand the use of each object.

In game design, variety is not limited to just visual or audio elements. Variety may be changing the movement pattern of an enemy or using random elements. Random movement or obstacle generation also adds variety to the game. Randomness or chance adds unpredictability to the game. This might be something as simple as shuffling the cards in a game of *Solitaire* to make each game different.

Balance

Objects arranged such that no one section overpowers any other part is called *balance.* When constructing a work of art, the artist needs to divide the canvas into equal parts to measure balance. Balance can be established as either symmetrical or asymmetrical, as shown in **Figure 19-10.**

Red apples
increase health

Green apples
increase strength

NonStock/Shutterstock.com

Figure 19-9. Variety in the coloring of objects can provide meaning in a game. For example, red apples may give the player character an increase in health, while green apples may increase strength.

When the right and left sides, top and bottom, or all sides are equal, *symmetrical balance,* or formal balance, is created. If you split the image down the middle, both halves have the same number and size of objects. An example of symmetrical balance is your eyes on your face. Your nose is in the center and one eye on each side of your nose provides symmetrical balance. Since the right side of your face is a mirror image of the left side, this is called *horizontal symmetry.* Symmetry can also be established from a center point and radiate equally from that center. *Radial symmetry* is equal in length from a center point. An example of radial symmetry is the rings created by dropping a pebble into a puddle.

Asymmetrical balance, or informal balance, is the use of similar objects to create balance, or the use of color and light balance instead of object balance. Unlike symmetrical balance in which the right and left sides may be mirror images, asymmetrical balance can be seen in something like a bookshelf. The shelves balance the amount of space taken up by the books, but the size, shape, color, and arrangement of the books differ on each shelf. The concept is that a lot of something small can balance a little of something big. A swarm of small bees provides asymmetrical balance to a single large beehive. This can work with color as well, where a small area of a vibrant color provides asymmetrical balance to a large area of a neutral color.

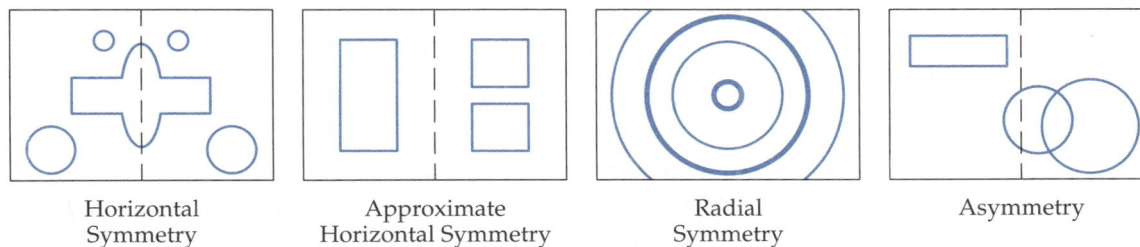

| Horizontal Symmetry | Approximate Horizontal Symmetry | Radial Symmetry | Asymmetry |

Goodheart-Willcox Publisher

Figure 19-10. Symmetry is part of the principle of balance. There are different types of symmetry.

Asymmetrical balance is often confused with asymmetry. *Asymmetry* means that the work is not at all balanced. Placing objects off-center or heavy to one side of a work can draw the viewer to an area of attention.

The final element of balance is proximity. *Proximity* is how closely objects are arranged. In a social setting, placing characters close to each other conveys a meaning such as friendship, family, or camaraderie. Conversely, placing characters far apart conveys a meaning such as enemy, stranger, or rival. Proximity can help create tension. Placing an object such as a stick of dynamite near an open fire creates tension as these two elements will cause an explosion. Proximity can also help show scale or relative size. Placing a character next to a building provides scale to the height of the character. If the character is taller than a tree, for example, the player understands the character is a giant.

Contrast

The variation of color and brightness to make objects stand out from each other is *contrast.* Contrast is very important in game design. Imagine using blue text on a blue background. Players could not read the letters. As a designer, you need to select a color, such as yellow or orange, that contrasts with the blue background. Alternately, you could vary the brightness of the blue used for either the text or background to provide contrast. A light blue text on a dark blue background may provide enough contrast for the player to read the words. This same principle applies to game objects. Imagine using a red ball on a red background. The ball needs to contrast with the background to be seen easily.

Proportion

Proportion is the size of an object in relation to the other objects around it. In game design, proportion may be exaggerated to make something more noticeable or prominent. A boss character may be much larger than the player character to communicate that the character is more prominent or more powerful. In other cases, the size of the game objects in relation to the player character may be reduced. In some games, the player character may be almost as large as the buildings. This exaggerated proportion is used to make the game easy to navigate and to show the character detail. If the player character is shown in proper proportion to the buildings, the character would be a small dot on the game map. When possible, a designer tries to show objects in proper proportion to the other objects in the scene. This gives the game a realistic look.

Proportion is also used to give the illusion of depth, or a third dimension. The concept of visual perspective states that an object looks smaller in the distance and gets larger as it approaches the viewer. In the Renaissance period of art, the concept of trompe l'oeil was applied to art. *Trompe l'oeil* translates to "fool the eye." Art of this type uses perspective, depth, and shadow to create ultrarealistic scenes. **Figure 19-11** shows the painting Escaping Criticism by Pere Borrell del Caso (1874). The artist has made it appear as if the boy is climbing out of the painting. A painting of the trompe l'oeil type appears to the viewer as if looking out of a window at a real landscape. In a similar manner, game designers attempt to create realistic game art.

Pattern

When an element is repeated, a *pattern* is created. In game design, patterns occur in both visual layout and in gameplay. Visually, pattern is applied in one of three ways: regular, flowing, and progressive.

A regular pattern has repeating objects of similar size and spacing, such as seen on a checkerboard. Flowing patterns have more organic shapes than regular patterns and mimic movement, **Figure 19-12.** A simple example of flowing pattern is an arrow or curve that leads to a point. The eye follows the curve from the thickest end to the point, which provides a feeling of movement or motion. Progressive patterns display a sequence or series of steps. This is a dominant visual pattern used in game design, since it is used in animations, **Figure 19-13.** In static (non-animated) art, a progressive pattern can simulate continuing motion or progression within a single frame.

Public Domain

Figure 19-11. This painting uses the concept of trompe l'oeil to make the boy look as though he is real and climbing out of the picture.

FreshStock/Shutterstock.com

Figure 19-12. This static 2D organic shape communicates not only movement, but depth.

Frame 1 ◄─────────────────────────────────────► Frame 8

Goodheart-Willcox Publisher

Figure 19-13. Progression in pattern from one static image to another can imply animated movement.

In gameplay, objects move in patterns. This patterned movement allows the player to navigate hazards that require timing. For example, a player may need to recognize the pattern of a swinging vine and jump at the right time to catch the vine and swing to the next platform. Pattern can also help set the pace of a game. For an animation of a running character, the artist must balance the pace of the animation with the movement of the background. If these are not synchronized, the animation will appear odd to the player.

Unity

All of the elements and principles of art work together to create unity. When something has *unity,* it appears as a single piece and not an assembly of different parts. The easiest way to explain this is to look at a character. A game character might have a hat, whip, leather jacket, dark hair, large muscles, mustache, jeans, and boots. Each of these pieces is one part of the whole. When these pieces come together, a single character is created that has a sense of unity.

Additionally, unity can be applied to the entire game or project. Maintaining unity across the game involves keeping buttons and controls in the same location on different levels or screens. Unity of color involves using the same colors or color palette to help tie together the entire game. Drastically changing colors on each game level or having buttons look different each time would distract the user and make the game feel jumbled and disorganized.

Game Build

The Awesome Game Company wants you to try building and importing your own game art from other programs. You will start by using Microsoft PowerPoint to build game assets. This software can be used to create basic 2D art from primitives.

How to Begin

1. Launch Microsoft PowerPoint. Note: these instructions are based on PowerPoint 2016. If using a different version, the instructions may need to be modified.
2. Start a new blank presentation or create a blank slide, and delete any existing placeholder text boxes.
3. Click **Insert>Illustrations>Shapes>Oval** on the ribbon.
4. Hold down the [Shift] key, and draw a circle of any size. Holding down the [Shift] constrains the shape to a circle instead of allowing an oval.
5. With the circle selected, click the **Format** on-demand tab. You can also double-click the shape to display the tab.
6. Locate **Height:** and **Width:** text boxes in the **Size** group on the far-right side of the **Format** tab, as shown in **Figure 19-14.**
7. Change the size to 2 inches high and 2 inches wide. As long as both values are identical, the shape will be a circle.
8. Save the file as *LastName_*Art in your working folder.

Oval

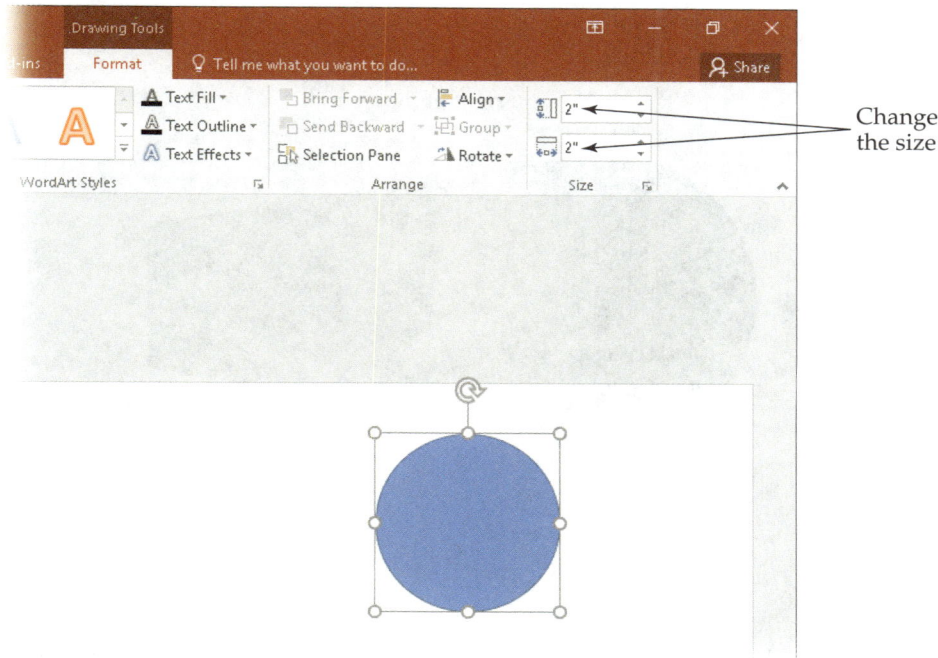

Goodheart-Willcox Publisher

Figure 19-14. If the height and width of an elliptical shape are identical, the shape is a circle.

Assembling Primitives

The art department has requested a cartoon-style cannon. You will need to combine three primitives to make the barrel of this object.

9. Click **Insert>Illustrations>Shapes>Trapezoid** on the ribbon. Insert a trapezoid of any size on the slide.

10. Applying what you have learned, change the size of the trapezoid to 2 inches wide and 3 inches high.

11. Click **Format>Arrange>Rotate>Rotate Right 90°** in the ribbon.

12. Click and hold on the trapezoid, and drag it so the widest section is slightly to the right of the center of the circle, as shown in **Figure 19-15.** The angle of the trapezoid should blend with the curve of the circle to make the shape of a cartoon cannon.

13. With the trapezoid selected, click the drop-down arrow next to **Format>Shape Styles>Shape Fill**, and click the black swatch in the drop-down menu.

14. Click the drop-down arrow next to **Format>Shape Styles>Shape Outline**, and click **No Outline** in the drop-down menu.

15. Applying what you have learned, fill the circle with black and remove the outline.

16. Applying what you have learned, draw a circle, set its size to .3 inches high and wide, fill it with black, and remove the outline.

17. Drag the small circle to the back of the cannon. Alignment guides will appear when the circle is in the correct position, as shown in **Figure 19-16.**

18. With the small circle selected, press the right arrow key two times. This will nudge the shape two pixels to the right and make the small circle appear attached to the cannon as a handle. To *nudge* is to move a shape a small distance. In this case, a nudge is one pixel.

19. Hold down the [Shift] key, and click each of the three shapes to select all of them. The [Shift] key allows you to select multiple items.

20. Click **Format>Arrange>Group** or press the [Ctrl][G] key combination to join the primitives so they act as one object.

Trapezoid

Rotate

Shape Fill

Shape Outline

Group

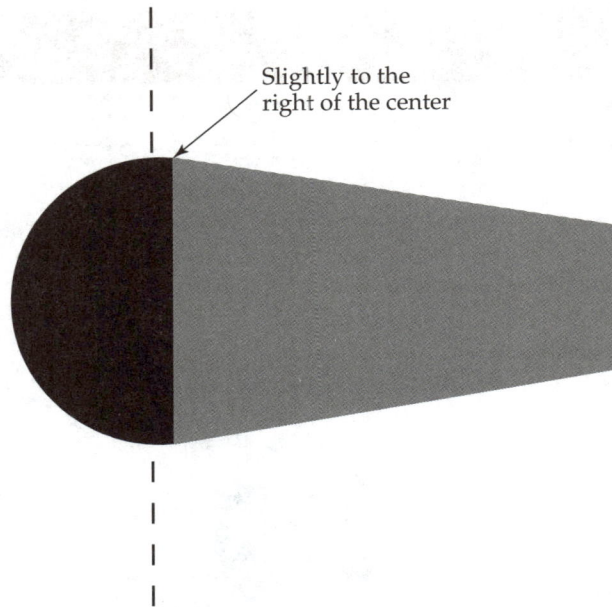

Slightly to the
right of the center

Goodheart-Willcox Publisher

Figure 19-15. Move the trapezoid so it is vertically aligned with the center of the circle, but place its left-hand edge slightly to the right of the circle's vertical centerline.

Gradients

A *gradient* is a gradual change from one color to another. For the cannon, a gradient will be added to make the cannon appear more rounded. By adding a lighter section, the illusion of depth is created to make it appear rounded. A *gradient ramp* is used to blend the colors of a gradient. The color on the ramp will begin where a *gradient stop* is placed on the ramp. The computer will blend the colors from one gradient stop to another on the gradient ramp.

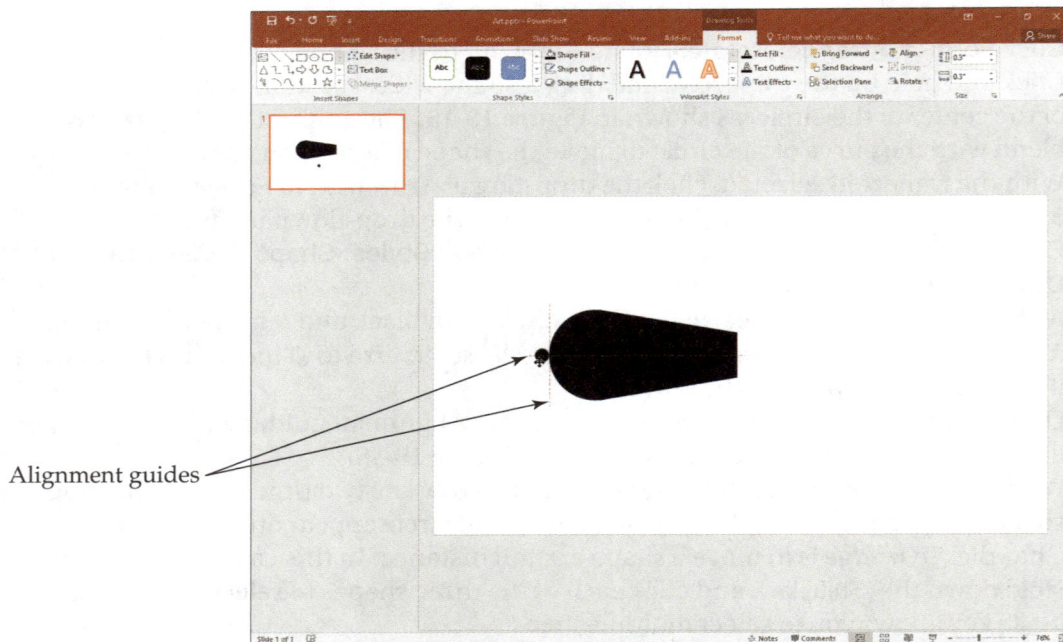

Alignment guides

Goodheart-Willcox Publisher

Figure 19-16. Alignment guides in PowerPoint can be used to precisely locate a shape in relation to other shapes.

21. Select the cannon grouped object.
22. Click **Format>Shape Styles>Shape Fill**, and click **Gradient>More Gradients...** in the drop-down menu. The **Format Shape** pane is displayed on the right-hand side of the screen, as shown in **Figure 19-17**.

Shape Fill

23. Click the **Fill & Line** button at the top of the pane, and then click the **Gradient fill** radio button.
24. Click the **Type** drop-down arrow, and click **Linear** in the drop-down list. *Linear* means in a straight line.
25. Click the **Direction** drop-down arrow, and click the **Linear Down** swatch in the drop-down list. Hover the cursor over each swatch to display the name as help text.
26. Click in the **Angle** text box, and enter 90.
27. Locate the **Gradient stops** section. This displays the gradient ramp as a bar and the gradient stops as triangular tabs on the ramp. There should be a gradient stop on each end of the ramp and one or two stops in the middle of the ramp. At least two gradient stops are required.
28. Select any of the middle gradient stops so it is highlighted with an orange outline, and click the **Remove gradient stop** button to delete the stop from the gradient ramp.

Remove gradient stop

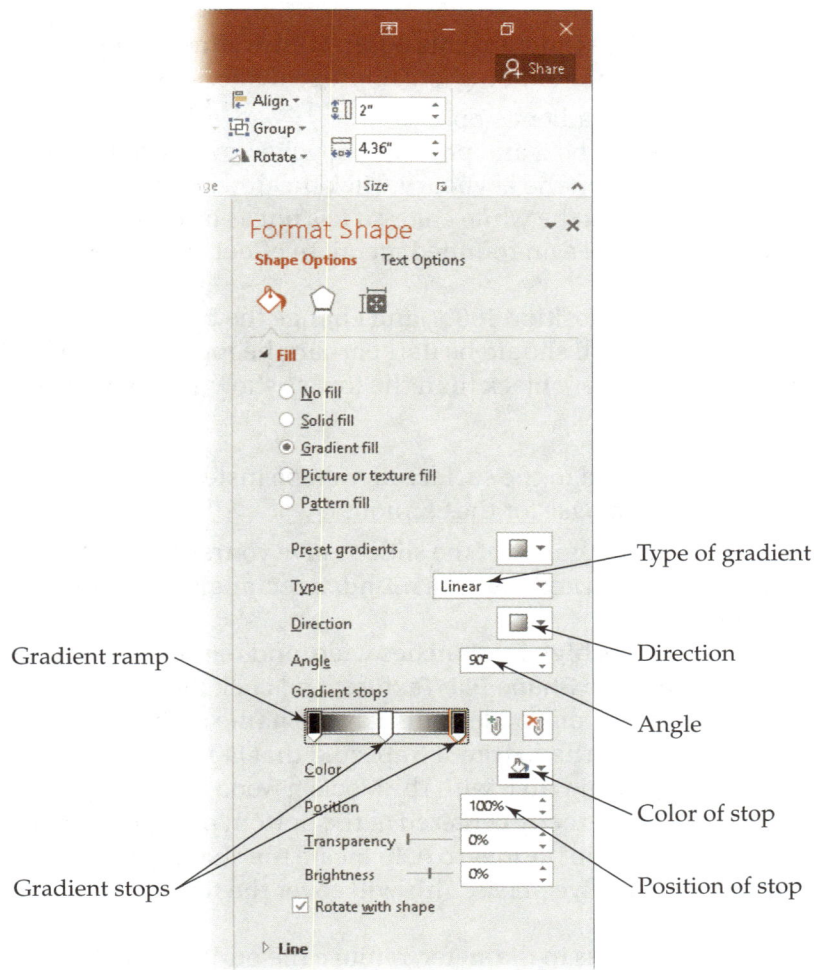

Goodheart-Willcox Publisher

Figure 19-17. A gradient is a gradual transition from one color to another. There are many options when creating a gradient in PowerPoint.

29. Remove all gradient stops from the middle of the ramp so only the stops on the ends remain.

30. Look at how the gradient is applied to the shapes. Select the gradient stop where the gradient ramp matches the color on the top of the shapes. This is probably the left-hand stop.

31. Click the **Color** drop-down arrow, and click the black color swatch in the drop-down menu.

32. Applying what you have learned, select the other gradient stop, and change the color to white. Notice how the cannon is black on top and white on the bottom to match the blending of the gradient ramp.

33. Slowly drag the white gradient stop toward the black gradient stop. Notice how the gradient ramp changes and the color on the cannon changes.

34. With the white gradient stop selected, click in the **Position** text box, and enter 50. This moves the stop to the middle of the ramp.

Add gradient stop

35. Click the **Add gradient stop** button. A new gradient stop is added halfway between the existing stops. The color of the ramp at that point is also assigned to the stop.

36. Drag the new gradient stop to the end of the ramp, and change the color to black. The gradient now starts as black on the top of the cannon, transitions to white at the middle of the cannon, and transitions to black on the bottom of the cannon.

Blending and Shading

The gradient is not very convincing at this point. Some refinement needs to take place to better blend the colors to make the shading look more realistic.

37. Select the middle (white) gradient stop.

38. Click in the **Brightness** text box, and press the down arrow to adjust the setting to −50%. You can use the arrow key on the keyboard, click the down arrow button, or directly enter the value. This softens the white color so it is not as bright, which will help produce a highlight like you would see on rounded metal. In effect, you have changed the color from white to gray.

39. Select the gradient stop at position 100%, and change the position to 75%. This is the bottom of the cannon, which should be darker than the top due to shadowing. Notice how the bottom now has more black than the top, as shown in **Figure 19-18.**

Textures

A texture is an image applied to the surface of a shape instead of a solid color. A texture will be used to create a wooden base for the cannon.

40. Move the cannon object to the top of the slide to give yourself room to draw the base.

41. Applying what you have learned, insert a rounded rectangle shape of any size in the middle of the slide.

Rounded Rectangle

42. Change the size to 2 inches high by .5 inches wide, and remove the outline.

43. Click **Format>Shape Styles>Shape Fill>Texture**, and click the Medium wood image tile. Hover the cursor over each image tile to display the name of the texture as help text.

Shape Fill

44. Applying what you have learned, draw a trapezoid that is 1.8 inches high and 3.5 inches wide, remove the outline, and fill it with the Medium wood texture.

45. Move the trapezoid so it is exactly centered at the bottom of the rounded rectangle. Remember, use the alignment guides to help locate the shape.

46. Nudge the trapezoid up by five pixels. This will cover the rounded corners on the rectangle with the trapezoid.

Trapezoid

47. Draw a circle that is .2 inches in diameter, remove the outline, and fill it with black.

48. Move the circle so it is centered at the top of the rounded rectangle, as shown in **Figure 19-19.** This will be the pivot point for the cannon on the base.

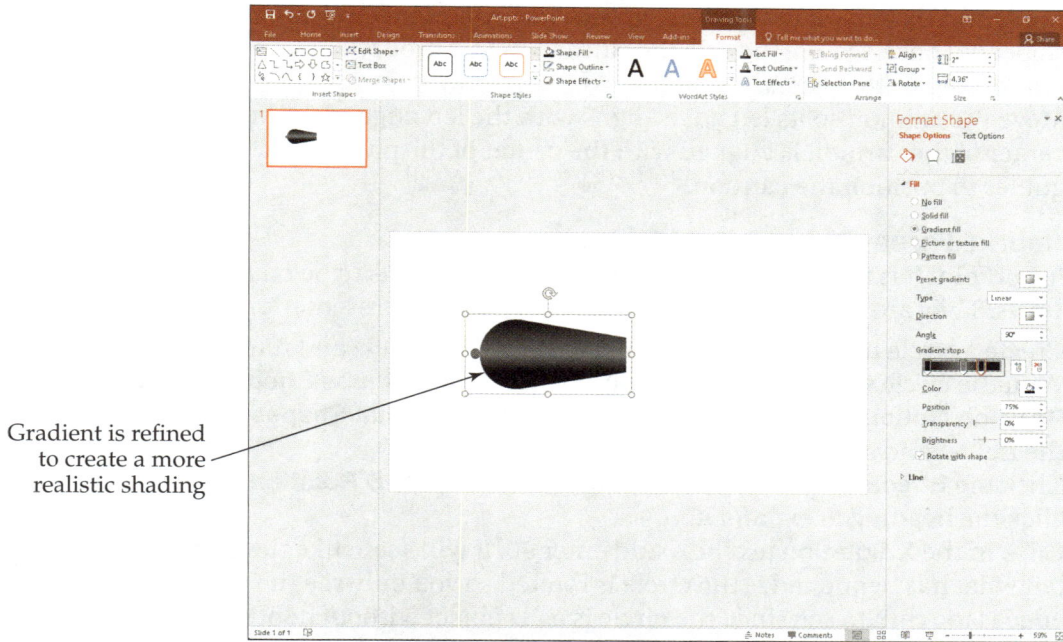

Figure 19-18. A gradient can be used to simulate a three-dimensional object from two-dimensional shapes.

Gradient is refined to create a more realistic shading

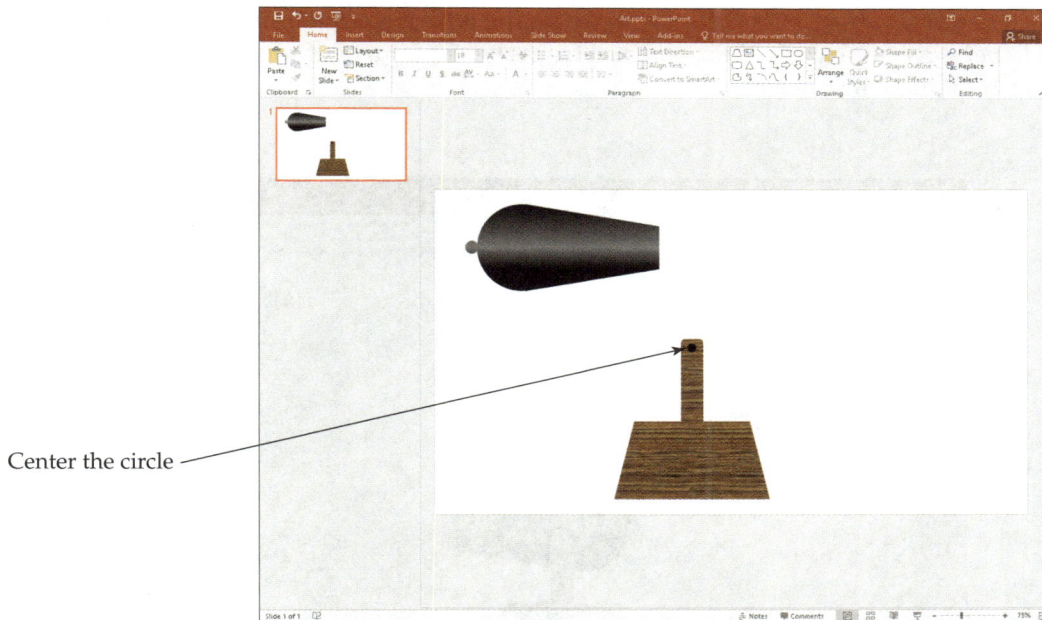

Figure 19-19. A small circle centered near the top of the vertical rectangle will represent a pivot point.

Center the circle

49. Applying what you have learned, group the pivot point circle, rounded rectangle, and trapezoid base. Do *not* include the cannon in this group. The cannon and base must remain separate objects.

50. Move the cannon so its left edge aligns with the left edge of the base and the vertical center of the cannon is aligned with the center of the pivot point. Use the alignment guides to position the cannon.

Simulating Three-Dimensional Objects

PowerPoint has features that allow simulated 3D objects to be created. These are not true 3D models. They are 2D shapes, but they are acceptable representations of 3D shapes.

51. Create a circle that is 1 inch in diameter, fill it with black, and remove the outline.

Shape Effects

52. With the circle selected, click **Format>Shape Styles>Shape Effects>3-D Rotation>3-D Rotation Options…** in the drop-down menu. The **Format Shapes** pane is displayed on the right-hand side of the screen.

53. Click the **Effects** button at the top of the pane. If the **3-D Rotation** area is not expanded, click the heading to expand it.

54. Click in the **X Rotation** text box, and enter 90. It will seem like the circle has disappeared, but what has happened is the circle is rotated so you only see the edge view. However, the edge is too thin to see since the circle is a 2D object without depth.

55. With the circle still selected, click the **3-D Format** heading in the pane **Format Shape** pane to expand that area, as shown in **Figure 19-20**.

56. Locate the **Depth** area, click in the **Size** text box, and enter 36. Note that this measurement is in points (pt). There are 72 points per inch, so 36 points is 1/2 inch. Entering 36 adds 1/2 inch of depth to the circle. From the side view, the circle now appears as a rectangle because you have just simulated a cylinder.

57. Locate the **Top bevel** area, click in the **Width** text box, and enter 36. Also enter 36 in the **Height** text box. This will produce a shape with a rounded tip and cylindrical base. A *bevel* is a curve applied to a surface from the center to the edge. This will round the depth to make it spherical.

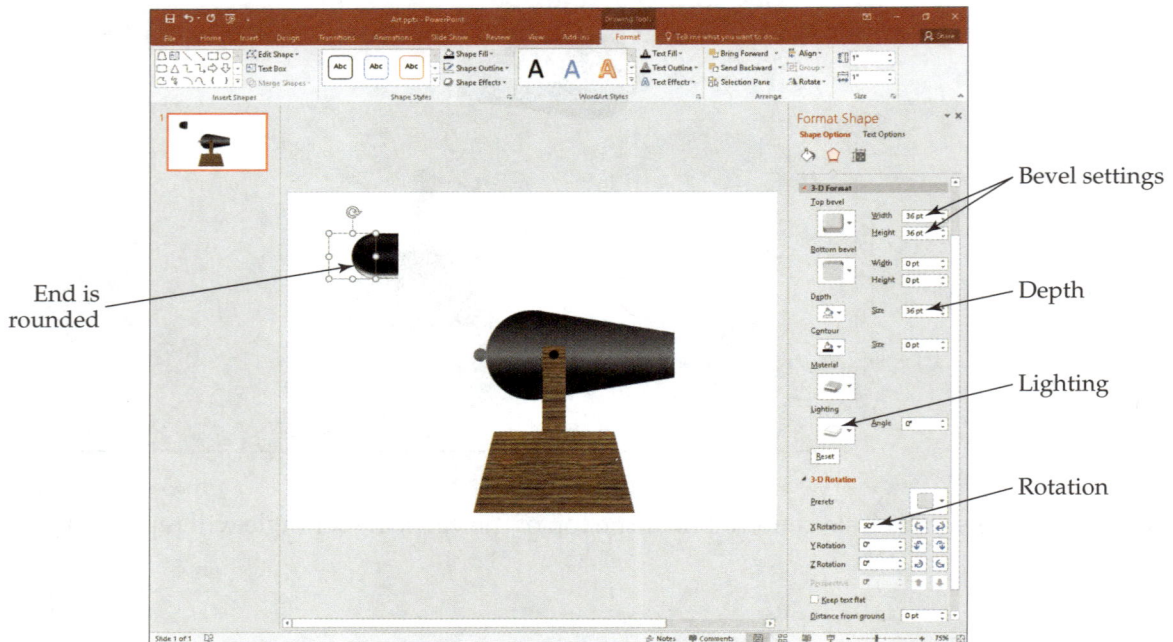

Goodheart-Willcox Publisher

Figure 19-20. A 3D bevel effect can be used to simulate a rounded end on a cylinder.

58. Click the **Lighting** drop-down arrow, and click the **Flat** image tile in the drop-down menu. This will produce lighting highlights on the shape to make it more visible from different angles.

59. Use the **X Rotation**, **Y Rotation**, and **Z Rotation** text boxes under the **3-D Rotation** heading to twist and turn the shape to see it displayed in many different views.

60. Enter 90 in the **X Rotation** and 0 in the **Y Rotation** and **Z Rotation** text boxes to return to the previous settings.

61. Locate the **Bottom bevel** area, and enter 36 in the **Width** and **Height** text boxes. This will round the bottom to create a capsule shape.

62. Locate the **Depth** area, and enter 0 in the **Size** text box to create a sphere.

63. Change the shape fill color to dark gray instead of pure black to better display shadows on the sphere. Use your judgment to decide which shade of gray best represents shadows.

Shape Fill

64. Use the **Material** and **Lighting** settings under the **3-D Format** heading in the **Format Shape** panel to refine the look of the sphere to suit you.

Photographic Textures

Textures are not limited to basic images. A photograph can also be used as a texture. This may be a photograph you have taken or one you located as a free-use image on the Internet. Be sure you have permission to use the photograph.

65. Click **Insert>Images>Online Pictures** on the ribbon. This command is used to insert clip art onto the slide.

Online Pictures

66. In the **Insert Pictures** dialog box, click in the search box, enter face, and click the search button, as shown in **Figure 19-21.** This will search Bing for images matching the term that have a Creative Commons license attached. A Creative Commons license generally allows for reuse of the image, but it is still your responsibility to ensure you comply with the usage rights for an image.

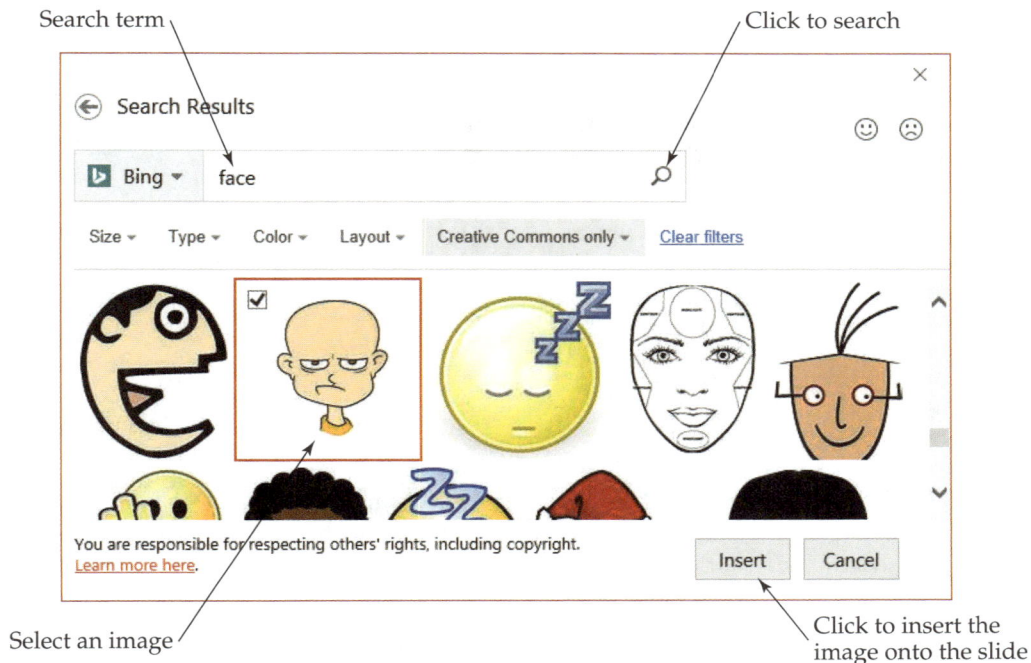

Goodheart-Willcox Publisher

Figure 19-21. An image can be used as a fill for a shape. PowerPoint allows you to search Bing for images.

67. Scroll through the results, and select an image you like. Then, click the **Insert** button to place the image on the slide.

68. Resize the face image to 1 inch by 1 inch. Clip art is resized in the same way a shape is resized.

69. Right-click on the face image, and click **Save As Picture...** in the shortcut menu. A standard save-type dialog box is displayed.

70. Navigate to your working folder, and save the image as Face. You can accept the default file type.

71. Delete the clip art from the slide. It was only used to save the image file and is no longer needed.

72. Draw a 1-inch diameter circle, and change the outline color to black.

73. With the circle selected, click **Format**>**Shape Styles**>**Shape Fill**>**Texture**>**Picture...** on the ribbon.

Shape Fill

74. In the **Insert Pictures** dialog box, click the **Browse** link to the right of **From a file**, navigate to your working folder, and select the Face image file you saved earlier. Click the **Insert** button to add the image as a texture to the circle, as shown in **Figure 19-22.**

Assembling Primitives to Create Objects

The game requires two buttons. One will raise the cannon. The other will lower the cannon. You need to create the artwork that will be used for each of these buttons, as shown in **Figure 19-23.** The art department also needs you to create a box object with rounded corners for the game. The box needs to be constructed with different textures, fills, and line weights.

75. Draw two rounded rectangles, each .5 inches square with a black outline.

76. Fill one of the rectangles with green and the other with yellow.

77. Insert an up arrow shape.

78. Resize the arrow to .3 inches by .3 inches, fill it with black, and remove the outline.

Up Arrow

79. Drag the arrow shape to the center of the green-filled rectangle. Use the alignment guides to locate the arrow in the exact center of the rectangle.

80. Group the arrow and the green-filled rectangle.

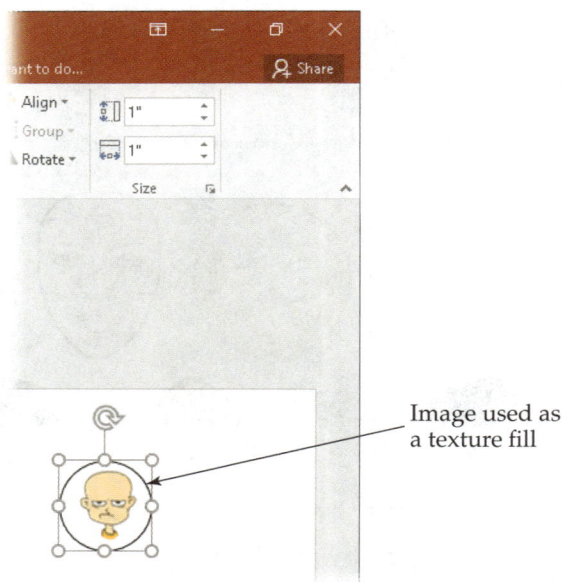

Image used as a texture fill

Figure 19-22. An image located with Bing has been applied as a fill for this circle shape.

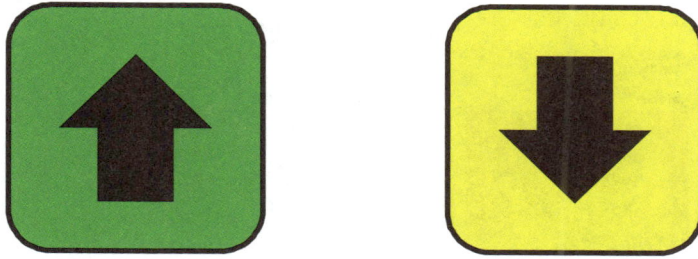

Figure 19-23. These buttons are created from primitives in PowerPoint.

81. Applying what you have learned, add a similar down arrow shape to the center of the yellow-filled rectangle, and group the arrow and rectangle.

Down Arrow

82. Draw a rounded rectangle, size it to .5 inch square, fill it with the Walnut texture, and remove the outline. This is the first part of the box you need to create. The completed box is shown in **Figure 19-24.**

83. Draw a rectangle (not rounded), size it to .1 inch high by .6 inch wide, fill it with the Oak texture, and remove the outline.

84. With the rectangle selected, click **Format>Arrange>Rotate>More Rotation Options…** on the ribbon. The **Format Shape** pane is displayed with the **Size & Properties** button automatically selected.

Rotate

85. Click in the **Rotation** text box, and enter 45. This places the rectangle on an angle.

86. Copy and paste the rectangle.

87. Click **Format>Arrange>Rotate>Flip Horizontal** on the ribbon.

88. Drag the pasted rectangle to the center of the original rectangle to create an X. Use the alignment guides to locate the shapes.

89. Group the rectangles to form a single X-shaped object.

90. Copy and paste the rounded rectangle with the Walnut texture.

91. Remove the fill color from the copy.

92. With the copy selected, click the arrow next to **Format>Shape Styles>Shape Outline** on the ribbon, and click **More Outline Colors…** in the shortcut menu. The **Colors** dialog box is displayed, which allows you to select or create a custom color.

93. Click the **Custom** tab in the **Colors** dialog box, as shown in **Figure 19-25.**

94. Click the **Color Model:** drop-down arrow, and click **RGB** in the drop-down list.

95. Click in the **Red:** text box, and enter 198.

96. Click in the **Green:** text box, and enter 140.

97. Click in the **Blue:** text box, and enter 82. This creates a color close to the color of the Oak fill image.

98. Click the **OK** button to apply the color to the outline.

99. Click the arrow next to **Format>Shape Styles>Shape Outline** on the ribbon, and click **Weight>6 pt** in the drop-down menu. This sets the outline to be six points thick.

Figure 19-24. This game art of a box is created in PowerPoint from four different primitives.

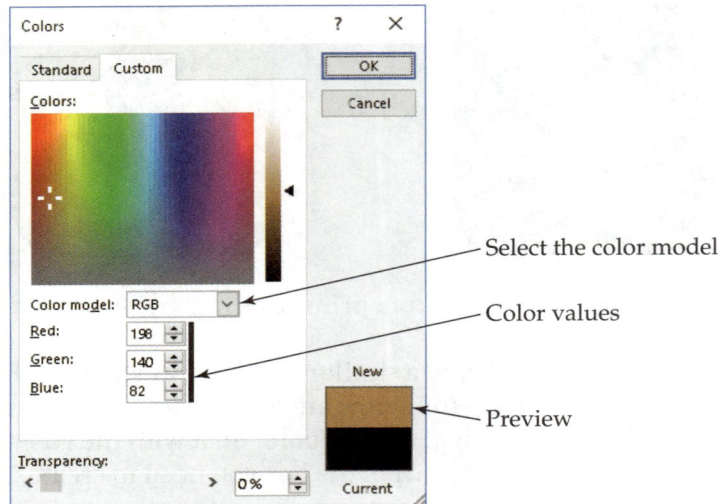

Figure 19-25. Custom colors can be created in PowerPoint and used as fill or line colors.

100. Assemble both rounded rectangles and the X-shaped object to make the box. Group the objects.

Going Beyond

101. Use a single primitive to create a .5 inch by .5 inch plus sign (+). Add a green fill and a black outline. Note: you can use the yellow handle on the primitive to adjust the width of each leg of the plus sign.
102. Create a minus sign (–) that would fit in a .5 inch by .5 inch rectangle (do not draw the rectangle). Add a red fill and a black outline. Make the height of the minus sign match the width of the legs on the plus sign you just created.
103. Draw a .7 inch by .7 inch rectangle, fill it with the Cork texture, and remove the outline.
104. Draw additional shapes and place them over the Cork-filled rectangle to form an object similar to the one shown in **Figure 19-26.** This will be used as a tile for ground objects in a tile-based video game.
105. Draw a 1-inch diameter circle. Fill the circle with an image. If you have a digital camera available, use a photograph of your face as the image.
106. Change the circle shape to create it as a 3D ball object with no outline. Rotate the object to see how the software handles the picture applied to the surface.
107. Save your work, and submit it for grading.

Green-filled rectangle

Cork-filled rectangle

Green-filled triangles

Goodheart-Willcox Publisher

Figure 19-26. This image is created from four separate images and will be used as a ground tile in a tile-based video game.

Vocabulary

Write a definition for each of the key terms from this lesson. You will develop a personal glossary of key terms throughout this course.

elements of art

_____

_____

principles of design

_____

_____

digital artwork

_____

_____

shape

_____

_____

geometric shape

_____

_____

primitive

_____

_____

organic shape

_____

_____

form

_____

_____

line

_____

_____

implied line

_____

_____

color

_____

_____

value

_____

_____

pixel shading

_____

_____

space

_____

_____

positive space

_____

_____

negative space

_____

_____

vertex shading

_____

_____

visual perspective

_____

_____

vanishing point

_____

_____

texture

_____

_____

tactile texture

_____

_____

optical texture

_____

_____

movement

_____

_____

emphasis

_____

_____

harmony

_____

_____

variety

_____

_____

balance

_____

_____

symmetrical balance

_____

_____

horizontal symmetry

_____

_____

radial symmetry

_____

_____

asymmetrical balance

_____

_____

asymmetry

_____

_____

proximity

_____

_____

contrast

_____

_____

proportion

_____

_____

trompe l'oeil

_____

_____

pattern

_____

_____

unity

_____

_____

nudge

_____

_____

gradient

_____

_____

gradient ramp

_____

_____

gradient stop

_____

_____

linear

_____

_____

bevel

_____

_____

Review Questions

1. Explain how the trees in **Figure 19-5** create an implied line.

_____

_____

_____

_____

_____

Applied Technology

2. How do alignment guides help in organizing shapes in PowerPoint?

_____

_____

_____

_____

_____

Applied Technology

3. Compare and contrast a texture fill with a picture fill in PowerPoint.

_____

_____

_____

_____

_____

Language Arts

Language Arts

4. Compare and contrast positive space with negative space.

_____

_____

_____

_____

_____

Applied Technology

5. Summarize how to add a linear gradient to a shape in PowerPoint that is red on the left, yellow in the middle, and black on the right.

_____

_____

_____

_____

_____

Higher-Order Thinking Strategies

Social Science

6. Applying only the principles of design, speculate why a game designer would create characters that have different types of clothing and skin tones.

_____

_____

_____

_____

_____

Science

7. Observe your hand. Describe how to draw a hand object using only primitive shapes.

_____

_____

_____

_____

_____

8. Observe and describe how the human body displays symmetry and balance. Cite specific examples from the reading material in this lesson as well as specific references to the human body. For example, facial symmetry would refer to position of eyes, nose, mouth, and other features.

Science

_____

_____

_____

_____

_____

9. Research the concept of trompe l'oeil as it applies to art. What impact did this concept have on art of the Renaissance period?

Social Science

_____

_____

_____

_____

_____

10. Assume that a screen displays 72 points per inch. Complete the table needed to create the correct size sphere. Remember, bevel applies to only one-half of the shape at a time.

Mathematics

Circle Diameter	Top Bevel Height	Top Bevel Width	Bottom Bevel Height	Bottom Bevel Width
1 inch	72 pt ÷ 2 = 36 pt	36 pt	36 pt	36 pt
2 inches				
	90 pt	90 pt	90 pt	90 pt
				234 pt

Office Technology Integration

Setting Object Order, Scale, and Position

1. Launch Microsoft Excel or other spreadsheet software, and open the vocabulary spreadsheet you updated in previous lessons.
2. Applying what you have learned, add a new worksheet, and name it Lesson 19.
3. Add each of the vocabulary words and definitions from the Vocabulary section of this lesson.
4. Save the spreadsheet, and then close it.
5. Open the *LastName_*Art PowerPoint file created in this lesson, and save it as *LastName_* Scene in your working folder.
6. Click the drop-down arrow next to **Home>Slides>New Slide**, and click **Title Slide** in the drop-down menu. A new slide is added after the current slide.
7. In the slide sorter on the left side of the screen, click the mini slide for the new title slide, hold, and drag it to the top.
8. On the title slide, click in the top text box, and enter Cannon Scene.
9. Click in the bottom text box, and enter your name, class, and period.
10. Click the second slide in the slide sorter to make it active.
11. Arrange the objects to create a game scene similar to the one shown. Demonstrate proper alignment, nudge, and ordering to place objects. Copy and paste objects as needed. The scene should depict a cannon firing cannon balls to knock over boxes. Resize objects as needed.

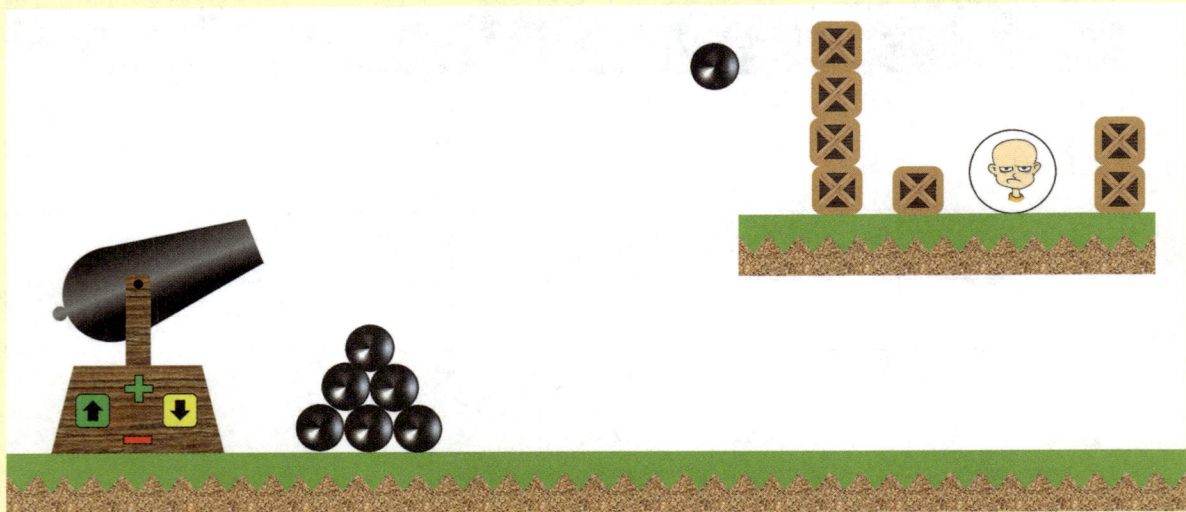

Goodheart-Willcox Publisher

12. Save your work, and submit it for grading.

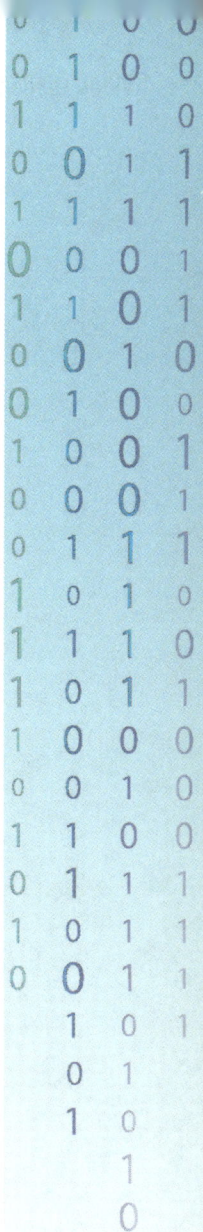

Lesson 20

Gravity and Ballistics

Learning Objectives

After completing this lesson, you will be able to:

- determine gravity and balancing forces.

- explain how vectors determine the direction of speed and forces.

- calculate acceleration, velocity, and distance.

- program using a physics engine.

- create realistic ballistic trajectories within a video game.

Situation

The Awesome Game Company would like to train you to make games using simulated gravity. You will first need to understand how gravity is simulated in a game. With that understanding, you can then build game elements that use physics to simulate gravity.

Reading Materials

The concept of gravity is a dominant programming feature of many games. Games that allow the player to jump, fall, throw, or launch projectiles all need some programming to simulate gravity.

Some programming challenges to having a character jump are the concepts of acceleration and deceleration. When you jump in the real world, you accelerate from a position of zero vertical speed to a vertical speed that lifts you from the ground, as shown in **Figure 20-1.** Your leg muscles cause your body to accelerate, or create a positive change in speed. To get off of the ground, your legs must accelerate your body fast enough to overcome the downward force of gravity.

Gravity is an attractive force that pulls objects together. For large masses (like planets) the attraction is toward the center of the mass. As planets are of different sizes, gravity varies from planet to planet. The gravity on Jupiter (larger than Earth) is much stronger than on Earth, while the gravity on Mercury (smaller than Earth) is much less. On Earth, when an object is dropped, its downward speed created by gravitational attraction increases exponentially as a function of time at 9.81 meters per second per second (9.81 m/s^2). The formula for calculating how fast an object is traveling as it accelerates is:

instantaneous velocity = acceleration × time

Name: _____

Date: _____

Class: _____

The jumping force is greater than gravity, so you can momentarily float above the ground.

The normal force is equal to gravity, so you do not float or fall through the ground.

Goodheart-Willcox Publisher; photos: Naluwan/Shutterstock.com

Figure 20-1. When you jump, your legs provide the force needed to accelerate you to overcome gravity.

For example, if you drop a ball off of a bridge, after one second the ball has a travel acceleration of 9.81 m/s², a speed of 9.81 m/s, and it has fallen a distance of 9.81 meters (approximately 32 feet). If the ball fell for two seconds, its speed would have increased to 19.62 m/s and it would have traveled a distance of 29.43 meters:

$$(9.81 \times 1) + (9.81 \times 2) = 29.43$$

The ground you are standing on is currently exerting a force equal to the force of gravity acting on your body. When the ground is not holding you up, you fall. This is clearly demonstrated when you step off of the end of a diving board into a swimming pool. You fall into the water, and you do so at an acceleration of 9.81 m/s². Additionally, you sink into the water until the buoyancy force on your body is equal to the downward force on your body from gravity. At that point, you stop sinking.

On a jump, once your legs stop providing upward acceleration, you begin to slow down, or decelerate, as the acceleration due to gravity counteracts the acceleration due to your leg muscles. The instant your feet leave the ground, your muscles are no longer providing acceleration and you start slowing down. You decelerate until your speed reaches zero.

When your upward speed reaches zero, gravity will pull you downward and your speed will increase as you travel down to the ground. It takes the same amount of time to fall back down as it did to reach the top of your jump. Additionally, your speed when you hit the ground will be the same as your speed when you jumped. The only difference is the direction of the speed. The direction of movement is called a *vector.* The vector of the speed determines if you are moving up or down. To simplify this, associate the vector direction with the game coordinates to create positive and negative speed. In a 2D video game, the upward movement is associated with a –Y vector. This makes upward speed negative speed. Downward speed is positive since the vector is in the +Y direction down.

In the virtual world, you need to program gravity to provide the same function as Earth's gravity, although the force and acceleration may not be the same. Usually, game designers give the player the ability to jump very high in comparison to real-world physics. In platform games, for example, designers have to give the player a large leaping ability to clear obstacles. Because of the screen size, the avatar may be displayed an inch tall, for example. In this case, a leap of two feet high in the real world would only be 1/3 of an inch, which is only slightly greater than the height of the capital letters in this paragraph, as shown in **Figure 20-2.** That is usually too small to notice the jump. Additionally, the obstacles would need to be very small.

In a *Mario* platform game, the obstacles are almost the same size as Mario himself. Mario must have the ability to jump more than his own height to get on the next platform or over an obstacle. That is because Mario is jumping in "Mario world." The gravity in a game world can differ from that on Earth, much like in the real world it differs from planet to planet.

The gravity of a planet applies to all objects, not just the jumping ones. When you throw a ball, the ball will return to Earth due to gravity. The **trajectory** is the curved path the ball

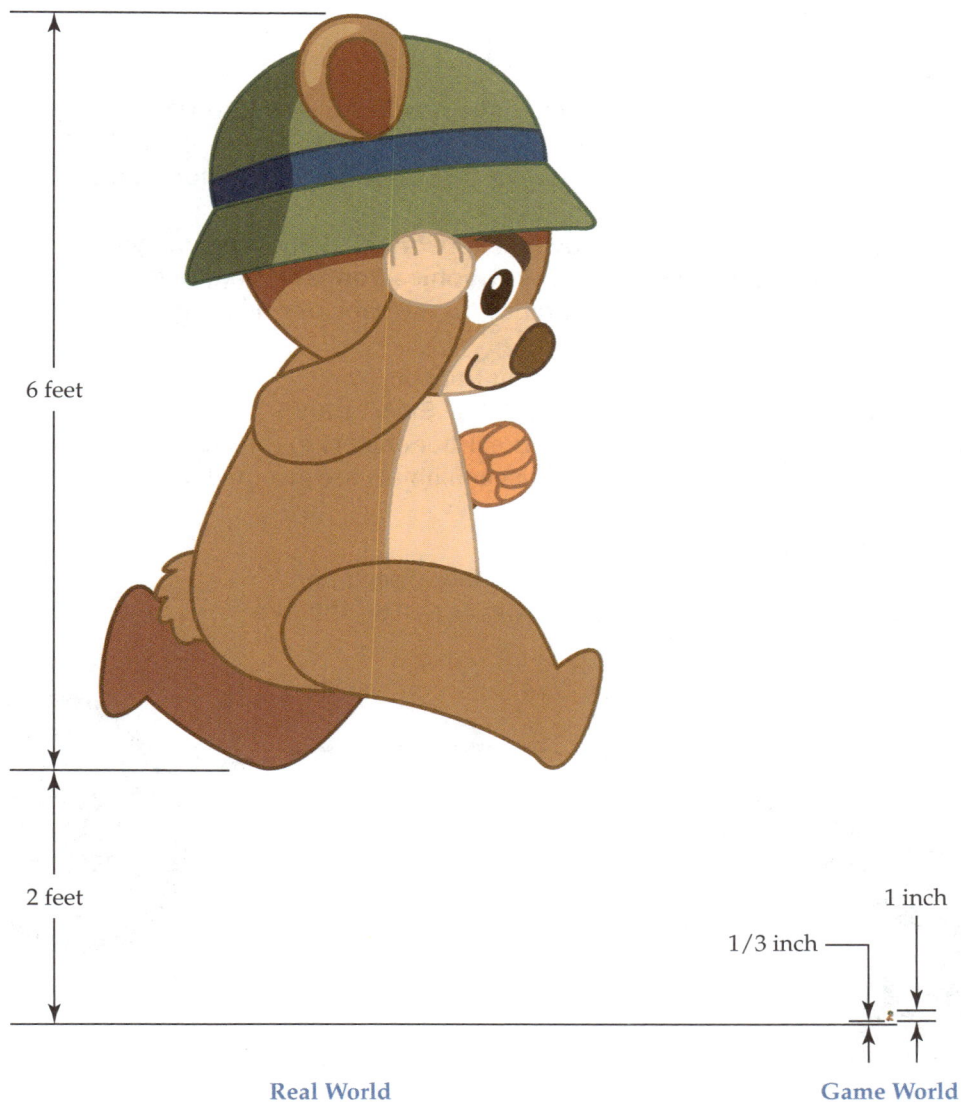

6 feet

2 feet

1/3 inch

1 inch

Real World

Game World

Goodheart-Willcox Publisher; character: BlueRingMedia/Shutterstock.com

Figure 20-2. In the game world, player characters usually have exaggerated abilities to compensate for the limitations of the world.

travels, as shown in **Figure 20-3.** This is also called a ballistic arc. ***Ballistics*** is the science of launching, flight, and behavior of projectiles. A ***projectile*** is an object that reacts to forces applied to it, but does not generate any force from itself. So, a basketball or baseball is a projectile. The ball is acted on by force from your arm throwing it, but the ball itself generates no force. A rocket is *not* a projectile because the rocket itself provides the force to make it move. In a video game such as the popular Angry Birds series, the game is programmed to move a launched bird in an arc to simulate gravity in the game world. Other game objects topple and fall as a result of the in-game gravity settings.

Game Build

The Awesome Game Company wants you to use the two-dimensional game assets that you created in Lesson 19 in a gravity-based game. The basic concept is a cannon launches cannonballs into boxes and other objects. The cannonballs must have ballistic movement, and the force of impact will provide motion to other objects. This will be a proof-of-concept build. In this build, you will use a physics engine to create realistic in-game interactions and movements.

How to Begin

1. Launch Microsoft PowerPoint, and open the *LastName_*Art PowerPoint file you saved in your working folder in Lesson 19.
2. Right-click on the grouped cannon object, and click **Save as Picture…** in the shortcut menu.
3. In the standard save-type dialog box that appears, click the **Save as type:** drop-down arrow, and click **PNG Portable Network Graphics Format (*.png)** in the drop-down list. The PNG file type allows for transparency, so the background in the image file will be transparent.
4. Click in the **File name:** text box, and enter Cannon.
5. Navigate to your working folder, and click the **Save** button.
6. Applying what you have learned, save the other objects in the PowerPoint file as PNG image files. Make sure the primitives in each object are grouped. Refer to **Figure 20-4** for the objects and file names.
7. Close PowerPoint.
8. Launch Clickteam Fusion 2.5, and start a new application.
9. In the storyboard editor, set the frame size to 640 by 480.

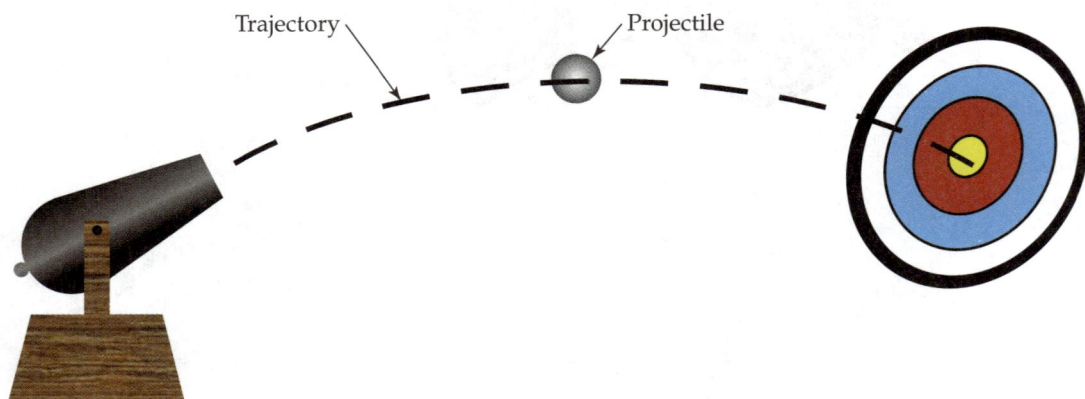

Trajectory   Projectile

Goodheart-Willcox Publisher

Figure 20-3. Ballistic arc occurs as the projectile reaches a high point (apogee) and curves back to Earth.

Object	File Name
	Base
	Box
	Button_Down
	Button_Up
	Cannon
	Cannonball
	Face Ball
	Ground
	Minus
	Plus

Goodheart-Willcox Publisher

Figure 20-4. Export these graphics from the PowerPoint file and save them as PNG image files under the names indicated.

10. Rename Frame 1 as Game_POC.
11. Save the file as *LastName*_Physics_POC in your working folder.

Scene Construction

12. Open the Game_POC frame in the frame editor. If the grid and snap are active, turn them off.
13. Applying what you have learned, insert a new active object anywhere on the frame, and name the object Cannon.
14. Applying what you have learned, open the active object in the image editor, and clear the canvas.
15. Click the **Import** button.

Frame Editor

Clear

Import

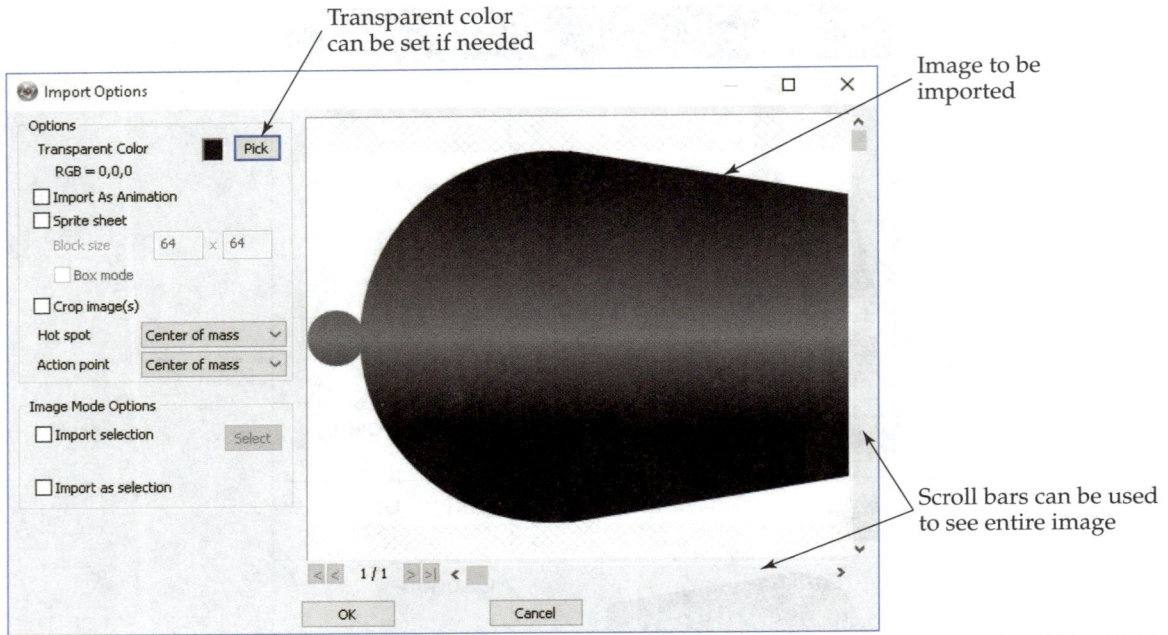

Transparent color can be set if needed

Image to be imported

Scroll bars can be used to see entire image

Figure 20-5. When importing an image file into the image editor, you have the option to select a color in the image that will be transparent in the game.

16. Navigate to your working folder, select the Cannon.png image file, and click the **Open** button. The **Import Options** dialog box is displayed, as shown in **Figure 20-5.** The **Pick** button in this dialog box can be used to choose a color to be transparent. However, since the image was exported as a PNG file, the background is already transparent, even though it may look white in this dialog box.

17. Click the **OK** button to place the image on the canvas in the image editor.

18. Click the **OK** button to close the image editor and update the object. The hotspot for the object must be adjusted, but before doing that, the object must be resized. If the hotspot is adjusted first, it may move when the object is resized.

19. Applying what you have learned, resize the object to 180 wide by 80 high.

20. Open the object in the image editor, and click the **View hot spot** button.

View hot spot

21. In the tool options area, click in the **X** text box, and enter 60. Also, enter 40 in the **Y** text box. This should place the hotspot slightly to the right of the center of the large circular part of the cannon. If not, adjust the coordinates as needed. Note: the hotspot indicator may be hard to see on the dark image. Later you will set the Cannon object to rotate about the hotspot.

22. Click the **OK** button to close the image editor and update the object.

23. Using the following table, place active objects and configure the assets as listed. Resize each object before adjusting the hotspot. Use the button indicated in the tool options area for the **View hot spot** tool. Note: the **G** button moves the hotspot to the center of mass, or center of gravity, for the object, which may or may not be the visual center of the object.

Object and File Name	Width	Height	Position	Hotspot
Base	150	170	(75, 380)	Quick Move center button
Box	48	48	(480, 207)	Quick Move **G** button
Button_Down	25	25	(120, 430)	Quick Move center button
Button_Up	25	25	(30, 430)	Quick Move center button
Cannon	180	80	(70, 305)	(60, 40)
Cannonball	32	32	(–50, 500)	Quick Move **G** button
Face Ball	32	32	(525, 215)	Quick Move **G** button
Ground	48	48	(475, 255)	Quick Move **G** button
Minus	32	12	(75, 450)	Quick Move center button
Plus	32	32	(75, 405)	Quick Move center button

Quick Backdrop

24. Applying what you have learned, duplicate the Ground object in one row and three columns. This will create a platform under the Box and Face Ball objects. Note: the spacing of the Ground objects may need to be modified as the game is tuned.
25. If there are gaps between the Ground objects, use the arrow keys to nudge the objects so there is no space between objects.
26. Copy and paste the Ground object. Paste the object anywhere on the frame.
27. Set the position of the pasted object to (0, 487). This places it at the bottom of the frame under the cannon base.
28. Applying what you have learned, duplicate the Ground object in one row and 14 columns along the bottom of the frame, as shown in **Figure 20-6.**

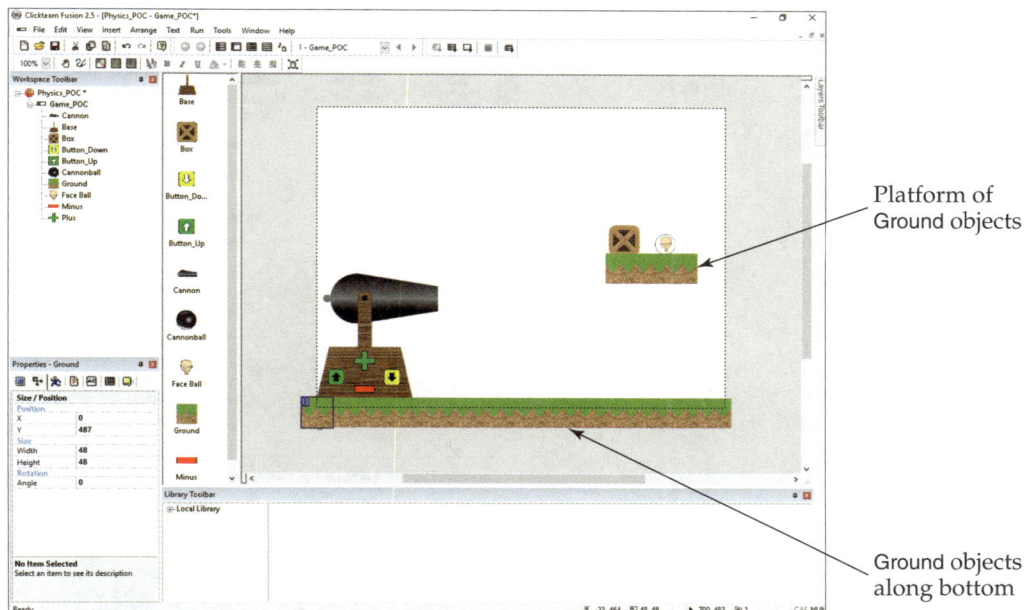

Goodheart-Willcox Publisher

Figure 20-6. Duplicate the Ground object to create a platform and the ground level.

29. Copy and paste the Box object to create a stack of three boxes on each side of the Face Ball. Do not overlap the boxes!

30. Applying what you have learned, use the **Properties** toolbar to change background color of the Game_POC frame to light blue to simulate the sky.

Movement

Clickteam Fusion 2.5 has built-in movement types based on a physics engine. These movement types will be used to control the physics of the objects. Before any physics-based movement can be added, a Physics Engine object must be added to the frame to provide control.

31. Click **Insert>New Object** in the pull-down menu.

32. In the **New Object** dialog box, click **Physics** on the left, click **Physics Engine** on the right, and click the **OK** button to add the object, as shown in **Figure 20-7**. Place the object anywhere outside of the visible game frame.

33. Select any one of the Ground objects, and click the **Movement** tab of the **Properties** toolbar.

34. Change the Type property to Physics – Background.

35. Enter 100 for the Friction property.

36. Change the Obstacle property to Obstacle.

37. Select any one of the Box objects, and click the **Movement** tab in the **Properties** toolbar.

38. Change the Type property to Physics – Static movement.

39. Enter 30 for the Density property.

40. Enter 80 for the Friction property.

41. Enter 100 for the Gravity Scale property.

42. Change the Collision shape property Box.

43. Make sure the Auto rotation and Smooth rotations properties are checked. If not, check them.

44. Select the Face Ball object, and click the **Movement** tab in the **Properties** toolbar.

Movement

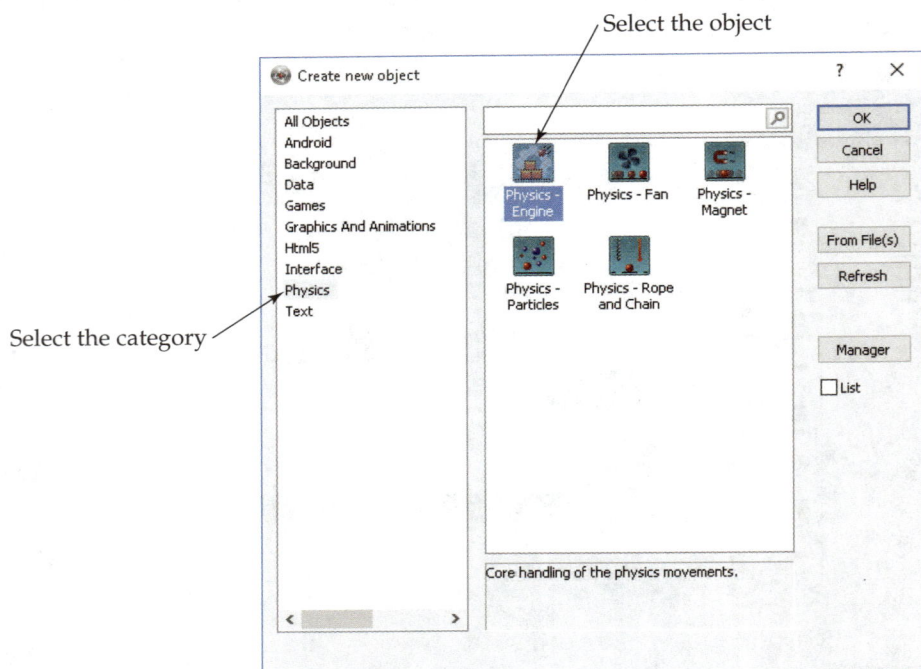

Goodheart-Willcox Publisher

Figure 20-7. In order to use the physics built into Clickteam Fusion 2.5, a physics-related object must be added to the frame.

45. Change the Type property to Physics – Bouncing Ball movement.
46. Change the Initial Direction property to direction 270 (down).
47. Enter 0 for the Initial speed property.
48. Enter 20 for the Density property.
49. Enter 40 for the Elasticity property.
50. Change the Collision shape property to Circle.
51. Make sure the Auto rotation property is checked.
52. Applying what you have learned, modify the Cannonball object with the movement settings in the table below.

Tab	Property	Setting
Movement	Type	Physics – Bouncing Ball movement
	Initial speed	150
	Deceleration	7
	Density	30
	Friction	100
	Elasticity	40
	Gravity scale	100
	Collision shape	Circle
	Auto rotation	checked
	Smooth rotations	checked
RunTime Options	Create at start	checked
	Follow the frame	checked
	Destroy object if too far from frame	unchecked
	Use fine detection	checked

53. Run the frame to see what happens. Woops! Some programming is needed to fix the bug and keep the objects from falling through the ground. Close the game window.

Run Frame

Platform Programming

A platform must apply a force equal to that of gravity to keep an object from falling through it. This balancing force can be simulated by programming the movement of the objects to stop when they collide with the Ground object.

54. Display the event editor for the Game_POC frame.
55. Applying what you have learned, add a new event, and program this pseudocode:
    IF a Box object collides with the backdrop,
       THEN stop the movement of the Box object.

Event Editor

56. Run the frame. Notice the boxes stop moving when they hit the platform. However, they did not stop when they hit each other and collapsed into only one visible box on each side. The Face Ball object also did not stop when it hit the platform and fell right through it. Close the game window.

Run Frame

57. Add a new event, and program this pseudocode:
    IF a Box object collides with another Box object,
       THEN stop the movement of the Box object.

58. Run the frame. Test that the boxes do not collapse into each other. They may move slightly if there is a vertical gap between the boxes. Close the game window when done testing.

59. Add a new event, and program this pseudocode:
    IF the Face Ball object collides with the backdrop,
        THEN stop the movement of the Face Ball object.

60. Add a new event, and program the following pseudocode. Refer to **Figure 20-8.**
    IF the Face Ball object collides with a Box object,
        THEN stop the movement of the Face Ball object
            AND stop the movement of the Box object.

61. Run the frame. Test that all boxes and the Face Ball object stop when they hit the Ground objects. Close the game window.

62. Display the Game_POC frame in the frame editor.

63. Copy and paste the Face Ball object. Place the copy above a Box object. This will allow you to check if the Face Ball object will properly interact with the Box object.

64. Run the frame. Check the interactions. Close the game window when done testing.

65. Debug if needed.

Cannonball Balancing Force

The scene has been set and the target objects are performing correctly. Now, the Cannonball object needs balancing elements programmed to react properly in the scene.

66. Display the event editor for the Game_POC frame.

67. Add a new event, and program this pseudocode:
    IF the Cannonball object collides with the backdrop,
        THEN stop the movement of the Cannonball object.

68. Add a new event, and program this pseudocode:
    IF the Cannonball object collides with a Box object,
        THEN stop the movement of the Cannonball object
            AND stop the movement of the Box object.

69. Add a new event, and program this pseudocode:
    IF the Cannonball object collides with the Face Ball object,
        THEN stop the movement of the Cannonball object
            AND stop the movement of the Face Ball object.

70. Display the Game_POC frame in the frame editor.

71. Applying what you have learned, copy and paste the Cannonball object, and place the copy at (400, 140).

72. With the copy selected, click the **Movement** tab in the **Properties** toolbar.

73. Applying what you have learned, set the initial direction property to direction 0 (right), as shown in **Figure 20-9.**

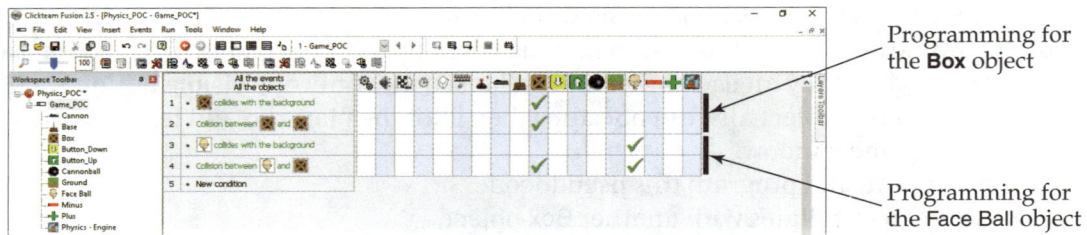

Programming for the **Box** object

Programming for the Face Ball object

Goodheart-Willcox Publisher

Figure 20-8. Programming is added to control the interaction of the **Box** and Face Ball objects.

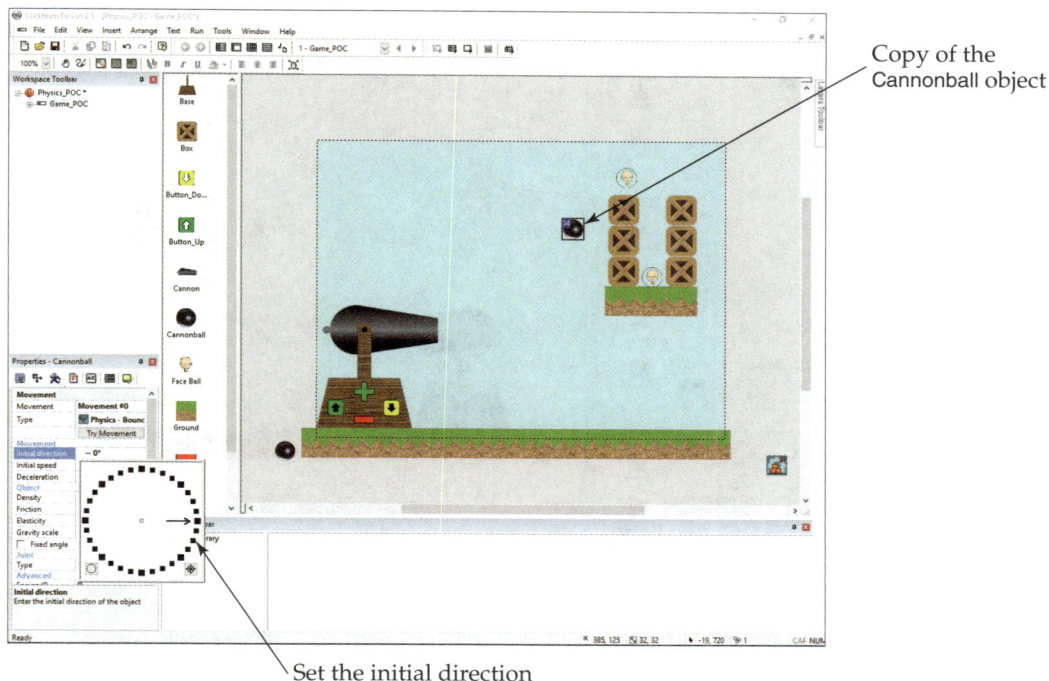

Copy of the Cannonball object

Set the initial direction

Figure 20-9. Setting the initial direction of the Cannonball object.

74. Run the frame. Test that the cannonball drops, rolls, and stops when it hits the background or another object. The cannonball may roll past the cannon base and off the screen, which is okay. Close the game window when done testing.

75. Debug if needed.

User Interface

A **Launch** button is needed to launch the cannonball projectile from the cannon. A standard Clickteam Fusion 2.5 Button object will be used for this. A power bar will also be used to show how much force the cannon will generate. This will be a gradient-bar version of a standard Counter object. The programming will be added to a programming module to create elegant programming and to help others understand what the code is doing. Other parts of the user interface will be finalized later.

76. Insert a new Button object anywhere on the frame.

77. Change the displayed text on the button to Launch. Also, change the name of the object to Button_Launch.

78. Position the button at (16, 140).

79. Insert a new Counter object anywhere on the frame, and name the object Power Bar.

80. Click the **Settings** tab in the **Properties** toolbar, as shown in **Figure 20-10.**

81. Enter 100 for the Initial Value property.

82. Enter 0 for the Minimum Value property.

83. Enter 255 for the Maximum Value property.

84. Change the Type property to Vertical bar.

85. Change the Count property to Up.

86. Change the Fill type property to Gradient.

87. Change Color property to yellow.

88. Change Color 2 property to red.

89. Make sure the Vertical Gradient property is checked.

90. Set the size to 32 × 100 and position the object at (32, 25).

Settings

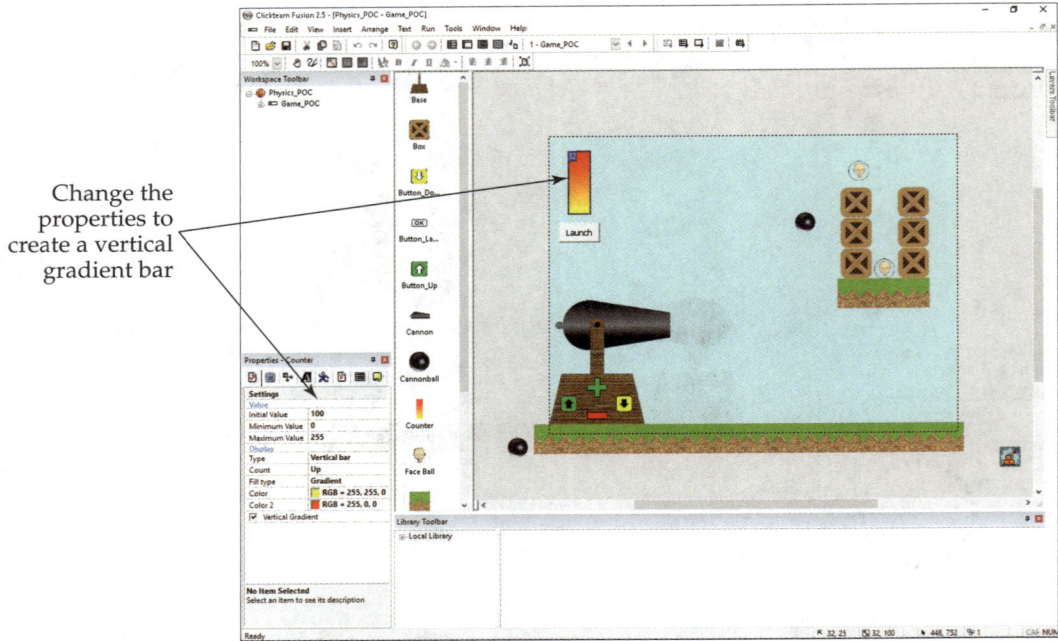

Change the
properties to
create a vertical
gradient bar

Goodheart-Willcox Publisher

Figure 20-10. Creating a vertical power bar using a counter object set to a vertical gradient.

91. Delete the copy of the Cannonball and Face Ball objects.
92. Display the event editor for the Game_POC frame.

Event Editor

93. Applying what you have learned, insert a new comment as the last line. Enter User Interface Programming as the text and format the background color as dark blue, as shown in **Figure 20-11.**
94. Select the text, and click the Choose font button. In the **Font** dialog box that is displayed, set the size to 16, select Arial as the typeface, and change the color to white. Then click the **OK** button to update the text formatting.
95. Click the **OK** button to close the **Edit Text** dialog box and add the comment. This will be the start of the User Interface Programming module.
96. Add a new event line, and program this pseudocode:
    IF the Button_Launch object is clicked,
      THEN create a new Cannonball object at absolute coordinates (200, 200).

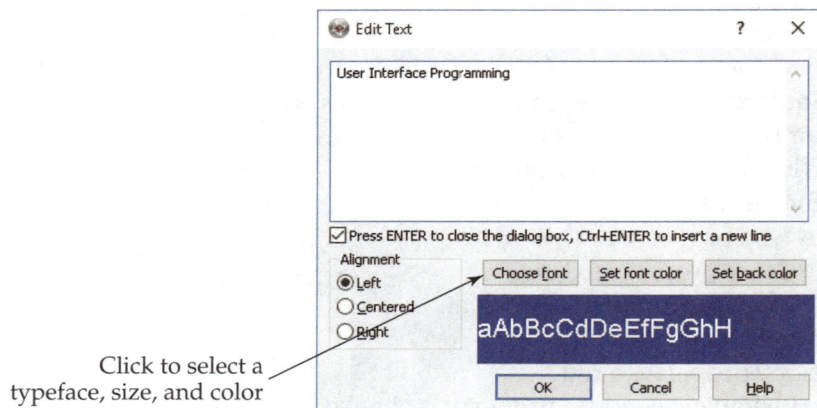

Click to select a
typeface, size, and color

Goodheart-Willcox Publisher

Figure 20-11. Create a programming module for the user interface by adding a comment.

97. Add a new event line, and program the following pseudocode. In the **New Condition** dialog box, click **The mouse pointer and keyboard>The mouse>User clicks on an object**. In the dialog box that appears, click the **Left button** radio button, the **Single click** radio button, and then click the **OK** button, as shown in **Figure 20-12.** Applying what you have learned, complete the programming for the condition and the rest of the event.

> **IF** the mouse is used to click the Button_Plus object,
> > **THEN** add 2 to the Power Bar counter.

98. Add a new event line, and program this pseudocode:

> **IF** the mouse is used to click the Button_Minus object,
> > **THEN** subtract 2 from the Power Bar counter.

99. Run the frame. Test that clicking the **Launch** button spawns a cannonball from a location above the cannon. Test that clicking the plus and minus buttons adjusts the power bar. Observe how the physics works to knock over the boxes. Close the game window when done testing.

Run Frame

Cannonball Speed

Currently, the plus and minus buttons change the power bar, but this has no effect on the speed of the cannonball. To change the speed, the Cannonball object needs to get the data from the Power Bar counter.

100. In the event line that tests for **IF** the Button_Launch object is clicked, right-click in the cell below the icon for the Cannonball object, and click **Movement>Set Speed…** in the shortcut menu. The expression editor is displayed.

101. Delete any existing value or expression.

102. Click the icon for the Power Bar object at the bottom of the expression editor, and click **Current value** in the shortcut menu. The expression value ("Power Bar Counter") is added to the expression editor, as shown in **Figure 20-13.**

103. Click the **OK** button to close the expression editor.

104. Run the frame. Test to see if the speed of the cannonball changes as you increase and decrease the power bar setting. Close the game window when done testing.

Run Frame

User Interface Tuning

In your testing, you probably noticed you have to click the plus and minus buttons quite a few times to make any significant change in the power level. A user would likely find this very frustrating. A better way to handle changing the power level is to allow the user to hold down the button to quickly increase or decrease the power level.

105. In the event line that tests for **IF** the user clicks with the left button on the Button_Plus object, right-click on the condition, and click **Replace** in the shortcut menu.

106. In the **New Condition** dialog box, click the **The mouse pointer and keyboard** icon, and click **The mouse>Check for mouse pointer over an object** in the shortcut menu.

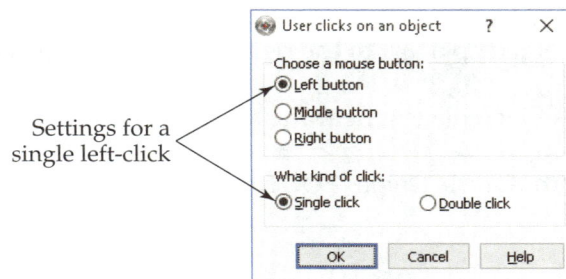

Settings for a single left-click

Goodheart-Willcox Publisher

Figure 20-12. Programming the **Launch** button to react to a left-click from the player.

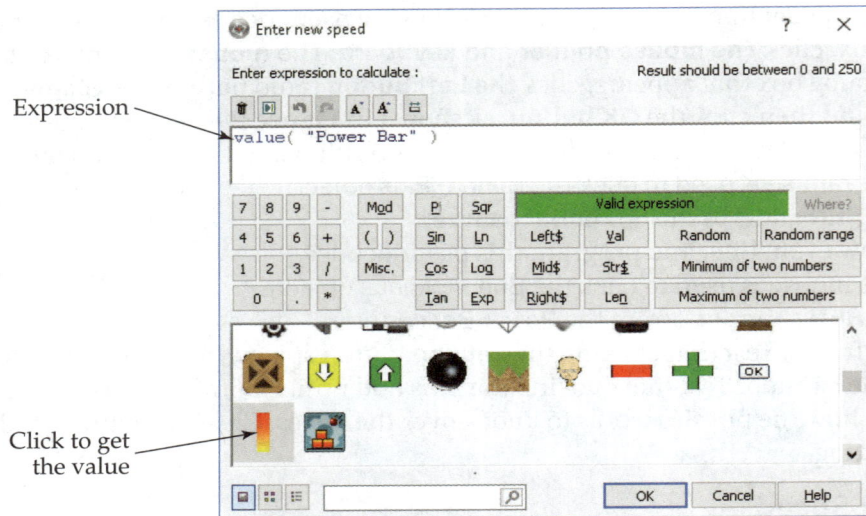

Goodheart-Willcox Publisher

Figure 20-13. The speed of the cannonball bar will be controlled by the value of the power bar.

107. In the next dialog box, select the Button_Plus object, and click the **OK** button. The new condition is:

   IF the mouse pointer (cursor) is over the Button_Plus object

108. Applying what you have learned, add an **AND** condition to the same event line. In the **New Condition** dialog box, click the **The mouse pointer and keyboard** icon, and click **The mouse>Repeat while mouse-key is pressed** in the shortcut menu.

109. In the next dialog box, click the **Left button** radio button, and click the **OK** button. The condition is now the following, as shown in **Figure 20-14.**

   IF the mouse pointer (cursor) is over the Button_Plus object
   AND the left mouse button is held down

110. Applying what you have learned, edit the event line that tests for **IF** the user clicks with the left button on the Button_Minus object to match this pseudocode:

   IF the mouse pointer is over the Button_Minus object
   AND the left mouse button is held down,
   THEN subtract 2 from the Power Bar counter.

111. Run frame. Test that holding down either the plus or minus button adjusts the power level. Close the game window when done testing.

Run Frame

Cannon Tilting and Aiming

Currently, the cannon does not tilt and the cannonballs are spawned in a location that is not realistic. The tilt angle and cannonball direction will be controlled by counters. The actual movement of the cannon will be achieved with animation.

112. Display the Game_POC frame in the frame editor.

Frame Editor

113. Insert a new Counter object, place it to the right of the Base object, and name it Counter_Tilt.

114. Insert a new Counter object, place it near the top-center of the frame, and name it Counter_Direction.

Event Editor

115. Display the event editor for the Game_POC frame.

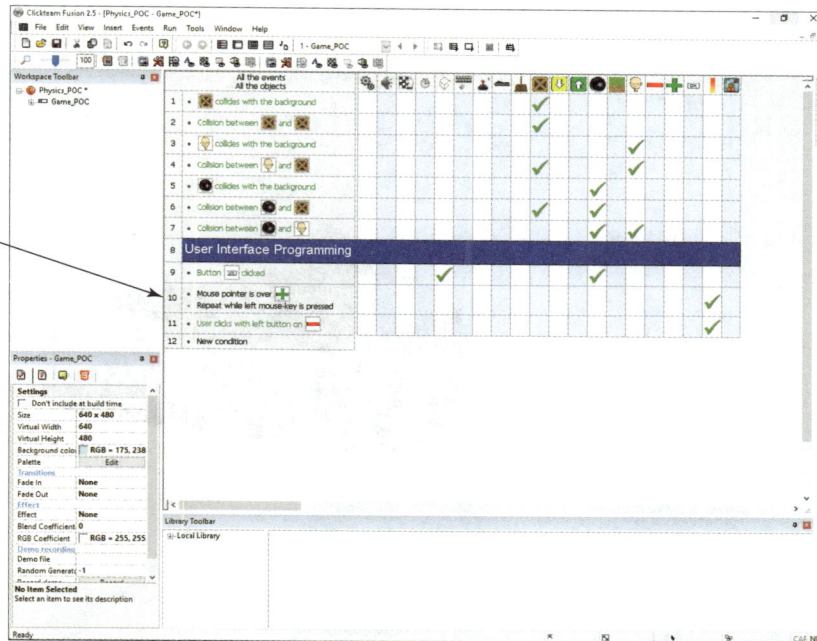

Programming updated to allow the user to hold down the button

Goodheart-Willcox Publisher

Figure 20-14. Allowing the player to hold down the button to make adjustments is a better user experience than having to click multiple times.

116. Add a new event line, and program this pseudocode:
　　　IF the mouse pointer is over the Button_Up object
　　　　　AND the left mouse button is held down,
　　　　　　　THEN add 1 to the Counter_Tilt object
　　　　　　　　　AND add 0.1 to the Counter_Direction object.

117. Add a new event line, and program this pseudocode:
　　　IF the mouse pointer is over the Button_Down object
　　　　　AND the left mouse button is held down,
　　　　　　　THEN subtract 1 from the Counter_Tilt object
　　　　　　　　　AND subtract 0.1 from the Counter_Direction object.

118. Run the frame. Test that the counter values change properly when the buttons are clicked or held down. Close the game window when done testing.

Cannon Animation

　　A rotation animation will be used to display the tilt of the cannon. The value of the Counter_Tilt object will determine which animation frame is displayed. The cannon will be programmed to tilt in one-degree increments.

119. Display the Game_POC frame in the frame editor, and open the Cannon object in the image editor.

120. Change the foreground color to red. The actual color is not important as long as it contrasts with the dark colors in the cannon.

121. Click the **Ellipse Tool** button, and click the **Filled** button in the tool options area.

122. Draw a small circle from approximately (55, 35) to approximately (65, 45), as shown in **Figure 20-15.** Use the coordinate indicated to assist in locating the points. This red marker will be used as the pivot point for the cannon.

Run Frame

Frame Editor

Ellipse Tool

Filled

Draw a small circle to use as the pivot point

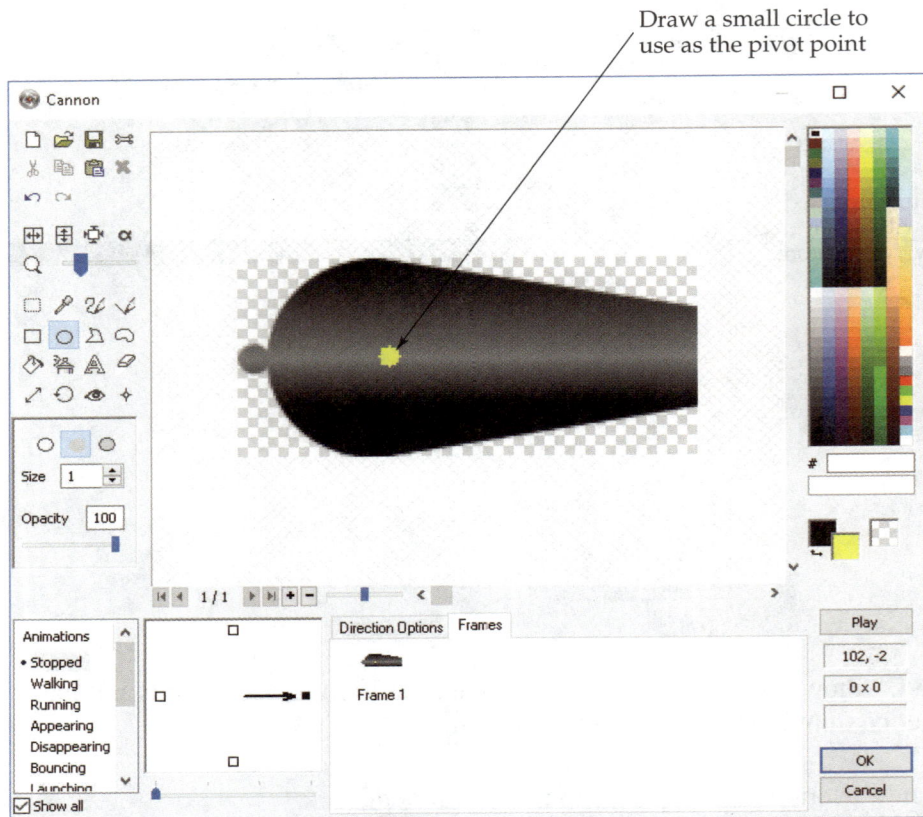

Figure 20-15. A small circle will be used as reference for setting the pivot point. It will be hidden by the Base object.

View hot spot

123. Click the **View hot spot** button, and click in the middle of the small circle you just drew.
124. Fine-tune the hotspot position to (60, 40) using tool options. This should be the exact center of the circle you drew. If not, adjust the X and Y values as needed to place the hotspot indicator in the exact center.

View action point

125. Click the **View action point** button. The *action point* is a location on the object that can be used for an action, such as spawning an object. This is where the cannonball will be set to spawn when launched. The hotspot, on the other hand, is the center of rotation for the object.
126. Click the middle-center button in the Quick Move matrix to place the action spot at the front of the cannon, as shown in **Figure 20-16.**
127. Click the **Selection Tool** button. You will not be using this tool, but activating it will prevent you from accidentally clicking and changing the action point.
128. Click the **Frames** tab at the bottom of the image editor.
129. Right-click on Frame 1, and click **Rotation** in the shortcut menu. The **Make One-Turn Rotation** dialog box is displayed, as shown in **Figure 20-17.**
130. Enter 360 in the **Number of frames in the** text box. Since there are 360 degrees in a circle, this will create a frame for each degree of rotation.
131. Click the **Counterclockwise** radio button, and click the **OK** button. All of the frames needed to rotate the cannon in a complete circle in one-degree increments are created.
132. Click the **Play** button in the image editor. Check that the cannon rotates in a complete circle, starting pointing to the right and moving upward. Notice that the point of rotation is the hotspot. Close the preview window when done checking the animation.
133. In the **Frames** tab, locate Frame 56, and click it once to select it.

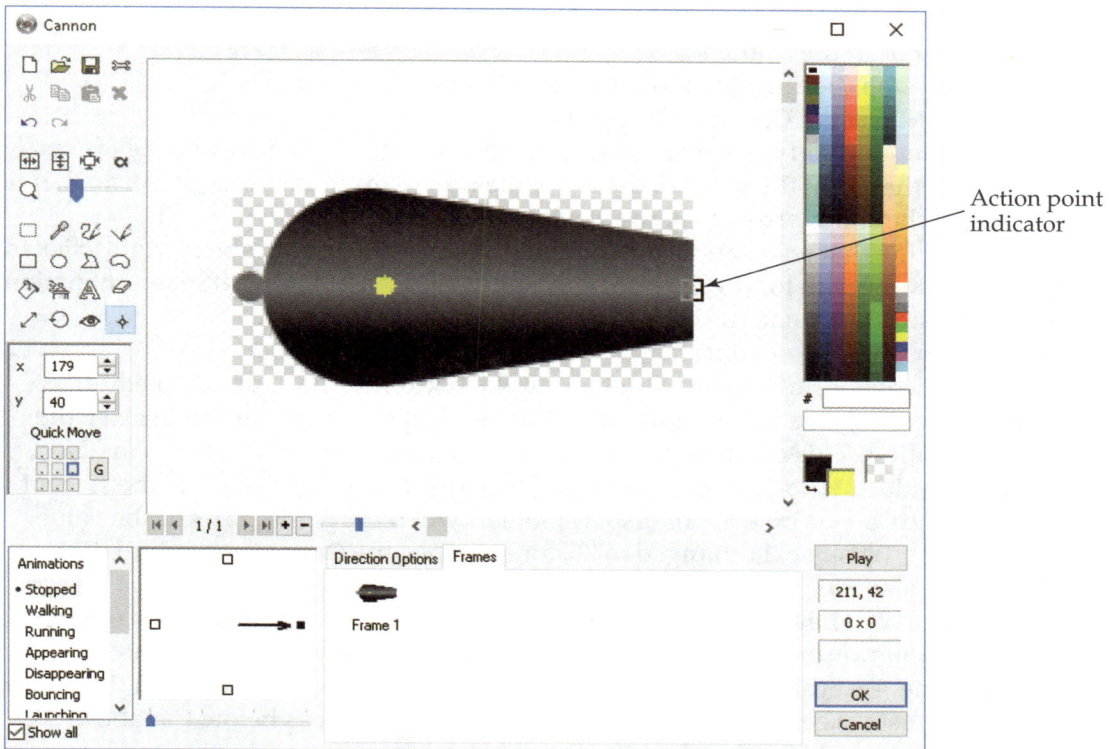

Goodheart-Willcox Publisher

Figure 20-16. The action point is a location on the object that can be used as the reference point for generating other objects.

134. Hold down the [Shift] key, and click once on Frame 360. All frames from Frame 55 to Frame 360 are selected. The cannon does not need to rotate all the way around, only up to 55 degrees, so the frames you selected can be deleted.
135. Press the [Delete] key, and when prompted, click the **Yes** button to confirm the deletion.
136. Close the image editor.
137. Run the frame. Check that the cannon elevates. Close the game window when done testing.
138. If needed, reposition the Cannon object so the red circle is aligned with the black circle on the Base object. Note: if the cannon does not rotate properly, check each frame in the image editor to see if the hotspot is over the red circle.

Run Frame

Programming Cannon Animations

Currently, the cannon rotates upward without using the buttons. The buttons need to be programmed to display the correct animation frame for the cannon.

139. Display the event editor for the Game_POC frame.

Event Editor

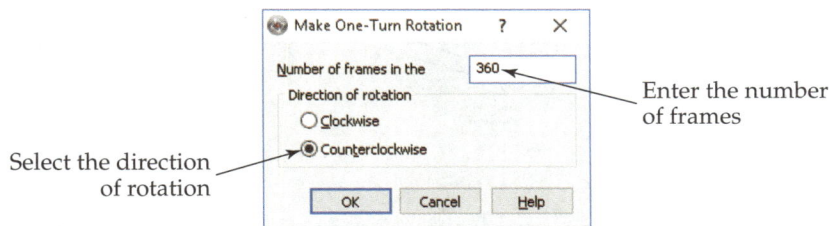

Goodheart-Willcox Publisher

Figure 20-17. By creating a rotation animation consisting of 360 frames, each frame represents a change in rotation of one degree.

140. Add a new event line, and program this pseudocode:

> **IF** at the start of the frame,
>> **THEN** stop the animation on the Cannon object
>>> **AND** set the Counter_Tilt object to 1.

141. Drag the event line you just programed to position it as line 1. Start-of-frame events should be at the top of the stack as these are the first items that will be performed. If not at the top of the stack, errors may result when the code is processed.

142. In the event line that tests for the cursor being over the Button_Up object, right-click in the cell below the icon for the Cannon object, and click **Animation>Change>Animation Frame...** in the shortcut menu. The expression editor is displayed.

143. Delete any existing expression.

144. Click on the icon for the Counter_Tilt object at the bottom of the expression editor, and click **Current value** in the shortcut menu. Then, click the **OK** button to close the expression editor. This creates programming to set the animation frame to match the current value of the Counter_Tilt object. Since this counter is set to 1 at the start of the frame, the Cannon object will display Frame 1 when the game starts. If the value of the Counter_Tilt object is changed to 20, for example, the Cannon object will display animation Frame 20.

145. Applying what you have learned, copy the action check mark for the Cannon object to modify the programming for the Button_Down object, as shown in **Figure 20-18.**

146. Run the frame. Test that the Cannon object tilts up and down properly when the buttons are clicked. Test to see if the value of the Counter_Tilt object goes below 1 or above 55. Close the game window when done testing.

Run Frame

Debugging the Tilt and Direction Counters

The Counter_Tilt and Counter_Direction objects need to have limits to perform correctly. Currently, these counters can have negative values. Additionally, they can have positive values that exceed the maximum usable value. Remember, the animation frames for the

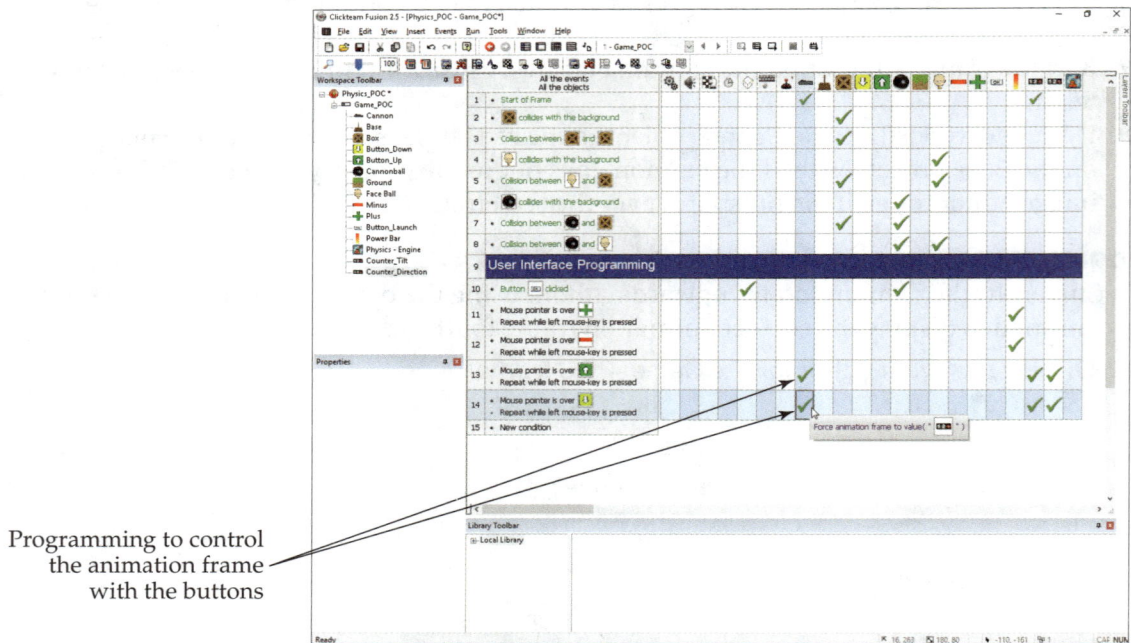

Programming to control the animation frame with the buttons

Goodheart-Willcox Publisher

Figure 20-18. The player will use the up and down buttons to set the tilt (elevation) of the cannon, which is displayed by different animation frames.

Cannon object go from Frame 1 to Frame 55. The settings for the Counter_Tilt object should be limit values to only those that correspond to the animation frame numbers.

147. Display the Game_POC frame in the frame editor.

148. Select the Counter_Tilt object, and click the **Settings** tab in the **Properties** toolbar.

149. Enter 1 for the Initial Value property.

150. Enter 1 for the Minimum Value property.

151. Enter 55 for the Maximum Value property.

152. Select the Counter_Direction object. This counter will be used to set the direction of the cannonball and must display values only from 0 to 6.

153. Applying what you have learned, change the Initial Value, Minimum Value, and Maximum Value properties for the Counter_Direction object to properly limit its values.

154. Run the frame. Test that the counters cannot have negative values or exceed the set maximum. Close the game window when done testing.

155. Debug as needed.

Modifying the Launch Point

The cannonball is spawned in the middle of the screen and does not appear to be launched from the cannon. The cannonball needs to be programmed to spawn from the action point of the Cannon object to appear as if it is being launched from the cannon no matter what the tilt.

156. Display the event editor for the Game_POC frame.

157. In the event line that checks if the **Launch** button is clicked, right-click on the action (check mark) that spawns the Cannonball object, and click **Edit** in the shortcut menu. The frame editor is displayed with the **Create Object** dialog box open.

158. Applying what you have learned, set the object to be created relative to the Cannon object, but leave the **Create Object** dialog box open.

159. Click the **Options** button in the **Create Object** dialog box. Another dialog box is.

160. Click the **Action Point** radio button, and then click the **OK** button, as shown in **Figure 20-19.** This tells the computer to spawn the object at the action point on the Cannon object.

161. Make sure the values in the **X:** and **Y:** text boxes are 0 so the object will be created exactly at the action point. Then, click the **OK** button to close the **Create Object** dialog box and return to the event editor.

162. Run the frame. Test if the Cannonball object is spawning properly by launching at different elevations of the cannon. Notice that the cannonball appears on top of the cannon. To look correct, the Cannonball object should spawn inside the Cannon object. Close the game window when done testing.

Frame Editor

Settings

Event Editor

Run Frame

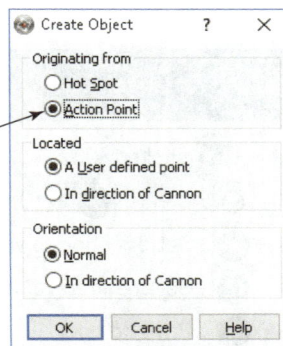

Select to create the object at the action point

Goodheart-Willcox Publisher

Figure 20-19. The cannonball should be generated at the action point set on the cannon to make it look like the cannonball is being launched from the cannon.

163. In the event line that checks if the **Launch** button is clicked, right-click in the cell under the icon for the Cannonball object, and click **Order>Bring to Back** in the shortcut menu. This places the Cannonball object behind all overlapping objects.

164. Run the frame. Test that the cannonball appears to be coming out of the end of the cannon. Notice how the cannonball moves when launched. Close the game window when done testing.

Direction Tuning and Programming

Currently, the cannonball travels awkwardly from the tip of the cannon. It does not move in a way that suggests it has come out of the cannon. To correct this, the direction of travel needs to be specified through programming. The Counter_Direction object holds the correct direction the Cannonball object should travel.

165. In the event line that checks if the **Launch** button is clicked, right-click in the cell under the icon for the Cannonball object, and click **Direction>Select Direction...** in the shortcut menu. The **Select Direction** dialog box is displayed. Notice that the right-facing direction is 0 and the up-facing direction is 8. The cannonball should be able to launch between direction 0 and direction 6 to match the maximum tilt angle of 55 degrees.

166. Locate and click the **Calculate direction** button, which is labeled **1+1**. The expression editor is displayed.

167. Applying what you have learned, create an expression that gets the current value of the Counter_Direction object. Then, close the expression editor.

168. Display the event list view in the event editor.

169. Drag the action you just added to the top of the stack just below the "create" action, as shown in **Figure 20-20.**

170. Display the Game_POC frame in the frame editor.

171. Move the Counter_Direction and Counter_Tilt objects so they are outside of the visible frame.

172. Run the frame. Test launching cannonballs from different tilt angles. Check the movement of the cannonballs. Close the game window when done testing.

173. Debug as needed.

Scoring

To enhance the gameplay, some type of scoring should be used to help the players understand they are doing well. This will also be the victory condition by allowing a high score.

174. Insert a new score object on the frame. Place it in a location that you feel best fits with the other objects in the scene.

175. Display the Game_POC frame in the event editor.

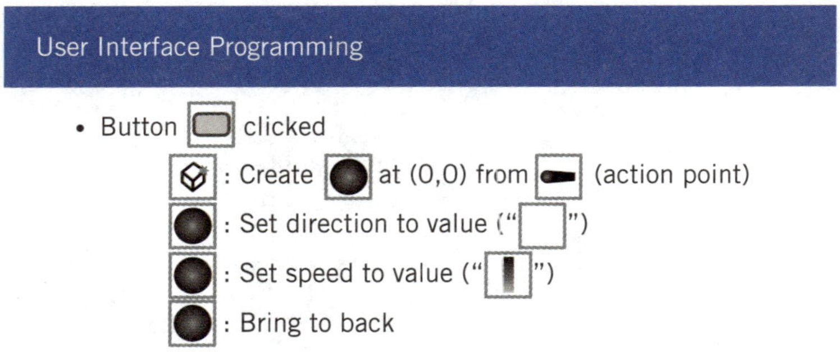

Event List Editor

Frame Editor

Run Frame

Event Editor

User Interface Programming

- Button [ ] clicked
  - : Create ⬤ at (0,0) from ▬ (action point)
  - : Set direction to value ("___")
  - : Set speed to value ("___")
  - : Bring to back

Goodheart-Willcox Publisher

Figure 20-20. To prevent a glitch in the processing of the programming, place the action that sets the direction second in the stack.

176. Add a comment to create a programming module named Scoring. Modify the background color to a color of your choice, and format the text to be bigger.

177. Add a new event line, and program this pseudocode to control what happens when a Box object leaves the screen:

   IF the Box object leaves the play area in any direction,
   > **THEN** destroy the Box object
   >> **AND** add 10 to the score for Player 1.

178. Add a new event line, and program this pseudocode to control what happens when the Face Ball object leaves the screen:

   IF the Face Ball object leaves the play area in any direction,
   > **THEN** destroy the Face Ball object
   >> **AND** add 20 to the score for Player 1.

179. Add a new event line, and program this pseudocode to control what happens when the Box object hits the ground:

   IF the Y position of the Box object is greater than 400
   > **AND** the Box object collides with the backdrop,
   >> **THEN** destroy the Box object
   >>> **AND** add 10 to the score for Player 1.

180. Add a new event line, and program this pseudocode to control what happens when the Face Ball object hits the ground:

   IF the Y position of the Face Ball object is greater than 400
   > **AND** the Face Ball object collides with the backdrop,
   >> **THEN** destroy the Face Ball object
   >>> **AND** add 20 to the score for Player 1.

181. Add a new event line, and program the following pseudocode to control what happens when all objects have been destroyed. To perform the check, select **Pick or count>Compare to the number of** "*object*" **objects**.

   IF all Box objects have been destroyed
   > **AND** all the Face Ball objects have been destroyed,
   >> **THEN** go to the next frame.

182. In the event line that checks **IF** the **Launch** button is clicked, add programming to subtract 1 from the Player 1 score. This will subtract 1 each time the player clicks the **Launch** button and spawns a cannonball. The victory condition is to destroy all objects using the fewest number of cannonballs.

183. Display the Game_POC frame in the frame editor.

184. Copy and paste a Box object, and place the copy near the top of the frame so it will fall and hit the ground when the game starts.

185. Run the frame. Test that the Box and Face Ball objects can be destroyed and the score changes. Note any bugs. Close the game window when done testing.

Frame Editor

Run Frame

Debug

The objects are not destroyed when they hit the ground. There is a glitch in how the program is reading the script. In this case, the order of operation is not able to test for a collision between the objects and the background. The built-in debugger indicates this error in the event editor, as shown in **Figure 20-21.** Red text indicates a condition is not valid. Green or black text means the programming has no errors.

186. Display the event editor for the Game_POC frame.

187. Locate the event lines that display red text. There should be two, one related to the Box object and one related to the Face Ball object.

188. In each of these event lines, drag the condition for the object colliding with the background above the condition checking for the Y position of the object. The text should change to green to indicate valid programming.

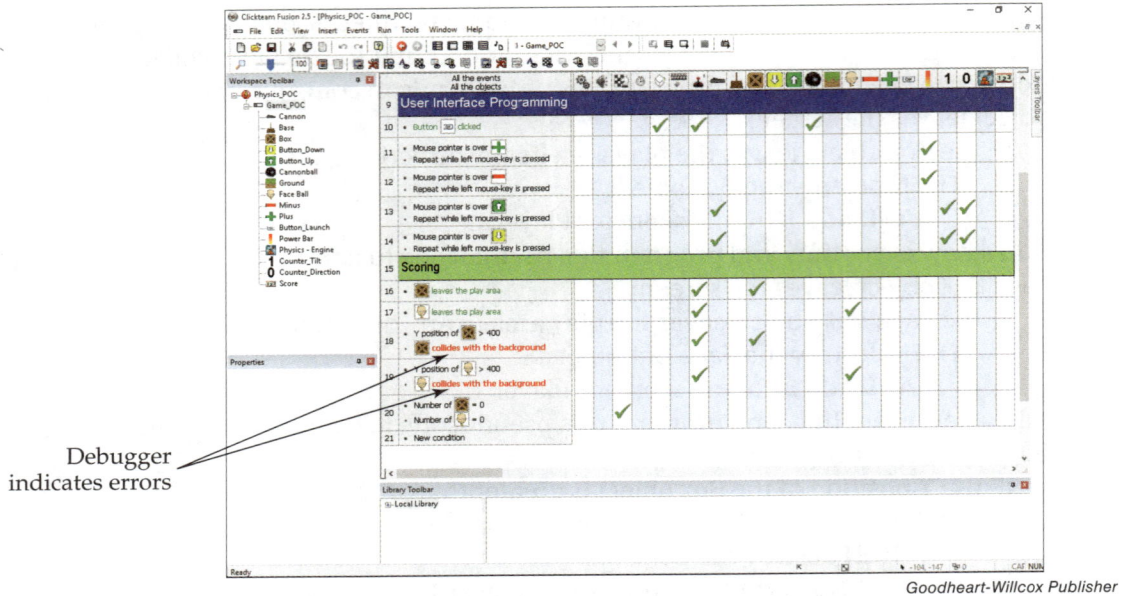

Debugger
indicates errors

Goodheart-Willcox Publisher

Figure 20-21. The built-in debugger in Clickteam Fusion 2.5 displays invalid programming in red text.

189. Run the frame. Test that the Box and Face Ball objects are destroyed when they hit the ground. Check that the score changes. Close the game window when done testing.
190. Debug as needed. Be sure to delete the box you added to test the falling as it should not appear in the final game.

Finishing

191. Applying what you have learned, create a title frame before the Game_POC frame. Think up a creative name for your game. Be sure to explain any controls or features the user will need to understand to play the game.
192. Applying what you have learned, create a high score page after the Game_POC frame.
193. On the Title and Winner frames, create the buttons and controls needed to begin play, replay, or quit the game.
194. Thoroughly test and debug the game as needed.
195. Save your work, and submit it for grading.

Vocabulary

Write a definition for each of the key terms from this lesson. You will develop a personal glossary of key terms throughout this course.

gravity

_____

_____

vector

_____

_____

Name: _____

trajectory

_____

_____

ballistics

_____

_____

projectile

_____

_____

action point

_____

_____

Review Questions

1. Why would a game in which the player character must jump have a low gravity setting?

_____

_____

_____

Applied Technology

2. In Clickteam Fusion 2.5, in which Y direction would gravity be pulling if an object falls from the top of the screen to the bottom of the screen?

_____

_____

_____

Applied Technology

3. If an alien could jump two feet high on its own planet and the moon had 1/2 the gravity of the planet, how high could the alien jump on the moon? Explain how you came to this answer.

_____

_____

_____

_____

Mathematics

4. Describe why an arrow is a projectile while a high-speed train is not.

_____

_____

_____

_____

Language Arts

Higher-Order Thinking Strategies

Mathematics

5. If the acceleration due to gravity in Clickteam Fusion 2.5 is equal to that of Earth, how long will it take a falling object to reach a speed of 29.4 meters per second, starting from a speed of zero (velocity = gravity × time)?

_____

_____

_____

Science

6. On Earth, what would be the mimimum upward buoyancy force needed to keep a boat from sinking in the ocean?

_____

_____

_____

Mathematics

7. About how long (in seconds) do you think it would take a ball to hit the ground on Earth if you dropped if from the top of a three-story building (30 feet)?

_____

_____

_____

Social Science

8. Consider the style of the graphics in the game you built in this lesson as well as the mechanics of the gameplay. What age group do you feel would be appropriate to play this game? Do you feel the region in which the player lives would affect the age range appropriate for this game? Why or why not?

_____

_____

_____

Mathematics

9. Suppose a character is jumping from an airplane. The player can set the character's parachute to automatically open at a specific speed or distance traveled. Complete the table below so the player can make the proper setting.

Seconds Falling (s)	Instantaneous Velocity (m/s) acceleration × time = velocity	Accelerated Distance Traveled (m) velocity × time = distance	Total Distance Traveled (m) initial + new = total
1	9.81 m/s^2 × 1 s = 9.81 m/s	9.81 m/s × 1 s = 9.81 m	0 m + 9.81 m = 9.81 m
2	9.81 m/s^2 × 2 s = 19.62 m/s	19.62 m/s × 1 s = 19.62 m	9.81 m + 19.62 m = 29.43 m
3			
4			
5			

Office Technology Integration

Using Data in Tables

1. Launch Microsoft Excel or other spreadsheet software, and open the vocabulary spreadsheet you updated in previous lessons.
2. Applying what you have learned, add a new worksheet, and name it Lesson 20.
3. Add each of the vocabulary words and definitions from the Vocabulary section of this lesson.
4. Save the spreadsheet, and then close it.
5. Begin a new blank workbook, and save the file as *LastName*_ExcelTable in your working folder.
6. In cell A1, enter the text Meteor Data Table.
7. In cell A3, enter the text Month.
8. In cell B3, enter the text Total.
9. In cell A4, enter the text January.
10. Select cell A4, and hover the cursor over the block in the bottom-right corner of the cell. When the cursor is over this block, it changes from a fat cross to a skinny cross. This block is the *series fill* block and can be used to automatically complete a series. In this case, the names of the months can be added in order from January.
11. With the skinny cross cursor displayed, click, drag downward to cell A15, and release. The month names are filled in.
12. A study was done to observe the number of visible meteors that entered Earth's atmosphere in a specific location near the Mojave Desert in Nevada. Below are the results recorded for one year. Using these data, complete the data table in Excel.

Month	Total
January	118
February	102
March	84
April	80
May	106
June	144
July	169
August	202
September	248
October	178
November	141
December	128

13. Select the range A3:B15.
14. Click **Home>Styles>Format as Table** on the ribbon to display a drop-down menu. Click the **Table Style Light 8** style in the menu. The **Format As Table** dialog box is displayed.
15. Check the **My table has headers** check box, make sure the range displayed is the same as the one containing your data, and then click the **OK** button. Headers are the titles at the top of each column of data, such as Month and Total in this example.

Format as Table

16. Make sure the table is selected or any cell within it is selected so the **Design** on-demand tab is displayed in the ribbon.

17. In the **Table Style Options** group of the **Design** on-demand tab, check the **Total Row** check box. This automatically adds a row at the bottom of the table that contains the total number of meteors seen for the year.

18. Click the drop-down arrow next to the Total header in cell B3, and click **Sort Smallest to Largest** in the drop-down menu. The rows in the table are reordered so the lowest number of meteors is at the top.

19. Select cell B16, which is where the total number has been calculated. A drop-down arrow is displayed in the cell.

20. Click the drop-down arrow, and click **Average** in the menu. Instead of showing the total number of meteors for the year, the value in the cell now shows the average number of meteors per month.

21. Edit the text in cell A16 to state Average.

22. Submit your work for grading.

Game Mod: Particle Physics

Learning Objectives

After completing this lesson, you will be able to:

- explain particles and particle physics use in a game.
- set up particle physics to simulate an explosion.
- create particle generation from destroyed objects.

Situation

The Awesome Game Company is impressed with your progress as a developer. It would like you to learn about programming advanced animation techniques. The first technique to learn is particle animation. After you have an understanding of this technique, you will mod a game to add particle animation.

Reading Materials

Computer animation allows for many means of creating images for each frame. One of the most interesting and useful of these techniques is particle animation. ***Particle animation*** is the use of a cluster of objects to simulate objects or actions that would be difficult to create from a single object. The objects in the cluster, or particles, are typically very small. Particle animation is used for many effects that are difficult to draw. Sparks, rain, snow, flowing water, falling leaves, and other small objects that move are best created with a particle animation. An example of flowing water is shown in **Figure 21-1.** When rendered, the particle animation is captured one frame at a time, just like any other animation.

An ***emitter*** is an object that generates particles in a particle animation. The emitter has settings for the particles it generates. The specific settings vary based on the software used, but typically include rate of generation, size, color, disbursement, and lifetime. The table in **Figure 21-2** shows typical settings for a particle system. Generally, depending on the software, each particle setting can be animated. Throughout the lifetime of a particle, it is controlled by whatever environmental physics have been assigned to it. Environmental physics simulate gravity and wind. These settings control how the particle interacts with the virtual environment.

Name: _____

Date: _____

Class: _____

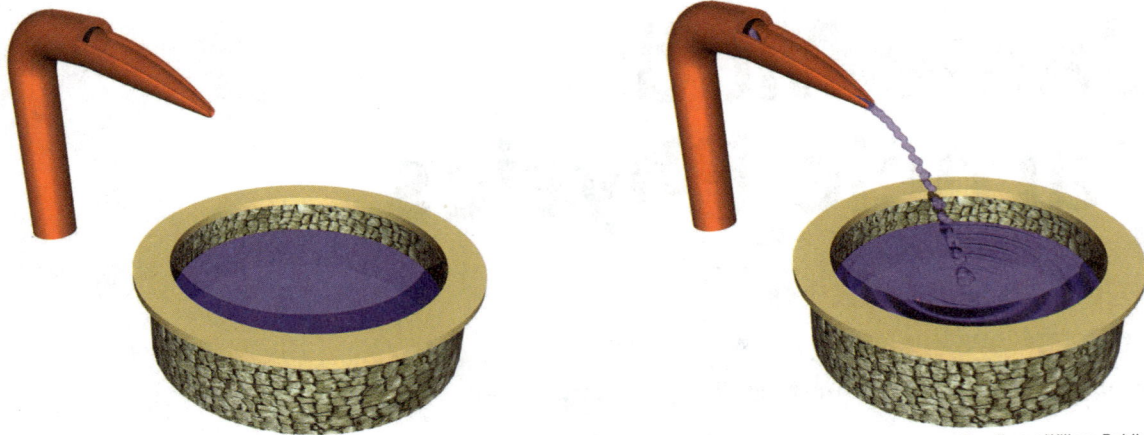

Goodheart-Willcox Publisher

Figure 21-1. A particle system is used to simulate water flowing from the fountain.

Particle Settings	Description
Initial Position	How far from the emitter the particles will be created
Initial Speed	How fast particles travel when created
Initial Vector	What direction particles travel when created
Initial Size	How big particles are when created
Initial Color	What color particles are when created
Initial Opacity	How transparent particles are when created
Shape	What shape the particles are when created
Lifetime	How long each particle will be displayed

Goodheart-Willcox Publisher

Figure 21-2. These are typical settings for a particle system. The specific setting will vary by software.

For example, to create sparks, the particles might be set as orange, a size of two, a random initial vector, and a rate of four per second. The spark may have a lifetime of about one second. The color and opacity of the particles may be animated from an initial opaque red particle to semitransparent gray to simulate a transition from glowing particle to smoke. In terms of particle systems, sparks are larger particles. Something like smoke will have much smaller particles, longer lifetime, and be disbursed over a larger area to make it realistic.

Some programs have emitter settings specifically to simulate liquids, as shown in **Figure 21-1.** However, liquid can be simulated using basic particles as well. For example, the emitter can be placed at the top of a fountain. Gravity can be set to pull the particles down toward a basin, where they can pool together. As the basin fills with particles, some spill over the edge. Or, to prevent spillover, set the lifetime of the particles so they are removed before the basin fills up. To make the water appear realistic and not just a single stream of water that follows the same path, vary the rate, direction, and lifespan of the particles. In most software, varying settings is not totally random. Generally, a setting contains a randomizing constraint, such as ±20 percent. This allows for a 40 percent variance (–20 percent to + 20 percent) for all particles emitted.

Particle animations can also be used to simulate solid objects. Usually the default is to render particles as points moving along a path or vector. However, *static particles* are rendered simultaneously along the entire vector. This is called a *strand.* The lifespan of the static particles determines the length of the strand. Static particles allow realistic simulation of fur, hair, grass, and other similar materials. The benefit of animating these with particles is that physics can be applied to material. This means that the wind will blow each of the static particle strands to create movement of the fur.

A *mod* is an alteration of the gameplay of an existing game, typically done by players, not the game studio. *Modding* is the act of creating a mod. A *partial-conversion mod* only adds content to the game. These mods can be as simple as providing a new weapon, character, enemy, or music to the existing gameplay. Advanced partial-conversion mods create a new game level or gameplay mode. Some mods result in an entirely new game. When a mod exists as a new game it is referred to as a *total-conversion mod.*

Game Build

The Awesome Game Company wants you to create an advanced partial-conversion mod of the Physics game you created in Lesson 20. This should be achieved by adding a new level to the game. This new level should incorporate particle animation.

How to Begin

1. Launch Clickteam Fusion 2.5, and open the *LastName*_Physics_POC file saved in Lesson 20.
2. In the storyboard editor, delete the title frame.
3. Copy the Game_POC frame, and paste it as the second frame.
4. Rename the copied frame as Particle_POC.
5. Save the file as *LastName*_Physics_Alpha in your working folder.

Storyboard Editor

Expanding the Play Area

6. Open the Particle_POC frame in the frame editor.
7. Applying what you have learned, change the size of the frame to 1250 wide by 480 high. You will be creating a game level that is a side-scroller.

Frame Editor

8. Applying what you have learned, extend the ground-level tiles to cover the entire bottom of the frame.
9. Applying what you have learned, select the Ground objects in the platform, all of the Box objects, and the Face Ball object.
10. Copy the selected objects, and paste them in the empty space created by extending the game map. Be sure the Box and Face Ball objects are placed above the Y = 400 pixel line (Y value less than 400) or they will be destroyed based on the programming you created in Lesson 20.
11. Insert a new Button object, place it at (16, 180), name it Button_Scroll, and change the Text property to Scroll.
12. Insert a new active object at (100, 540), and name it Scroll_Marker. This object will be used to control the scrolling of the frame.
13. Applying what you have learned, change the movement Type property of the Scroll_ Marker object to Path, and edit the path to draw a single line from the object to (900, 540), as shown in **Figure 21-3.**

New Line

14. Select the first node of the path (the entire path will flash), and enter 10 in the **Speed:** text box in the **Path Movement Setup** dialog box.

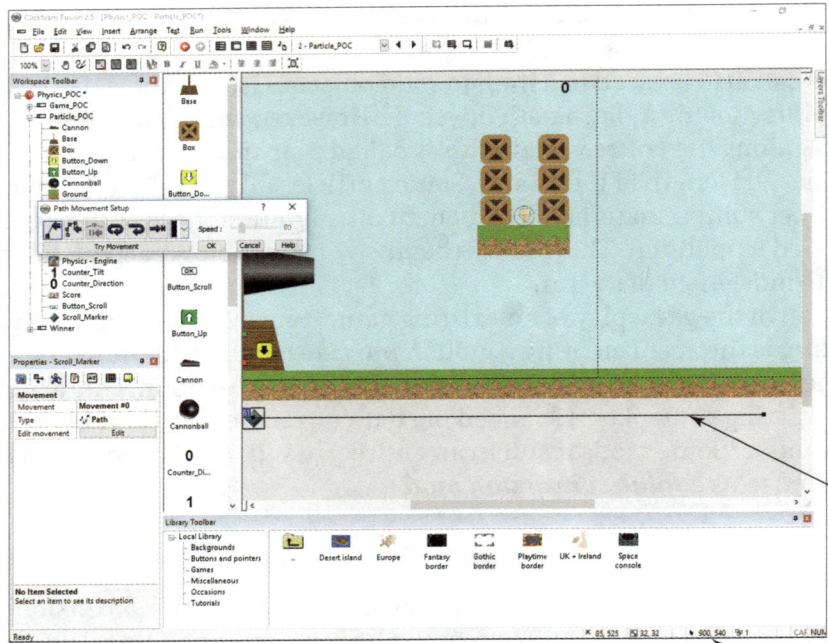

Single-line path

Use the indicator to
locate the end point

Figure 21-3. The Scroll_Marker object will follow the path, which will be used to control the scrolling of the game frame.

Reverse at End

15. Click the **Reverse at End** button.
16. Click the **OK** button to close the **Path Movement Setup** dialog box.
17. Display the event editor for the Particle_POC frame.

Event Editor

18. Create a new programming module by inserting a comment at the bottom that states Scrolling Controls. Change the color of the background and text as needed.
19. Add a new event line in the Scrolling Controls module for the condition: **IF** always.
20. In the new event line, right-click in the cell under the **Storyboard Controls** icon, and click **Scrollings>Center window position in frame** in the shortcut menu. In the dialog box that appears, set the position at (0, 0) relative to the Scroll_Marker object, as shown in **Figure 21-4.**

Run Frame

21. Run the frame. Test if the frame scrolls back and forth. The scrolling is needed so the player can view the entire game map and set up the cannon shot without resizing the map. Note: the power bar may not scroll. Close the game window when done testing.
22. If the power bar does not scroll, display the Particle_POC frame in the frame editor.
23. Select the Power Bar object, and click the **RunTime Options** tab in the **Properties** toolbar.

RunTime Options

24. Check the Follow the frame property. When this property is checked, the object will move to maintain its position within the entire game frame, not within the visible game frame.

Scroll Button Function

The game map can now scroll so the player can see more of the map. This is needed so the player can plan for destroying objects that are not in view when the cannonball is launched. Having to destroy objects that cannot be seen when the cannonball is launched increases the challenge. The **Scroll** button and Cannonball object need to be programmed to allow for screen scrolling. The first step is to edit the path settings to assign a name to the path nodes.

Frame Editor

25. Display the Particle_POC frame in the frame editor.

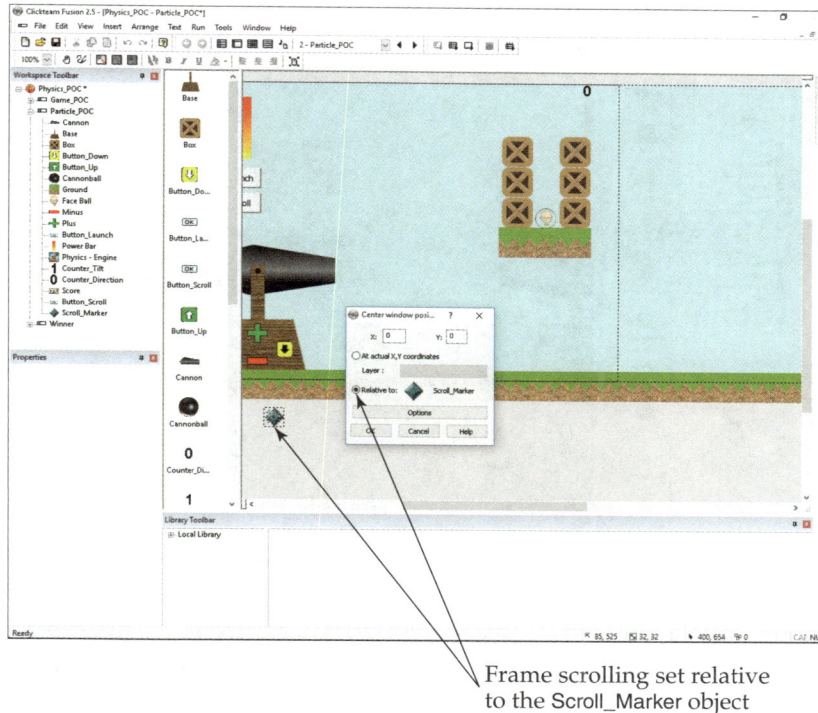

Frame scrolling set relative
to the Scroll_Marker object

Figure 21-4. Set the frame scrolling relative to the Scroll_Marker object.

26. Select the Scroll_Marker object, click the **Movement** tab in the **Properties** toolbar, and click the **Edit** button for the Edit movement property to display the **Path Movement Setup** dialog box.

27. Right-click on the first node, which is on top of the object, and click **Set name** in the shortcut menu.

28. In the **Node name** dialog box, enter Home in the text box, as shown in **Figure 21-5.** Then, click the **OK** button.

29. Click the **OK** button to close the **Path Movement Setup** dialog box.

30. Display the event editor for the Particle_POC frame.

31. Add a new event line in the Scrolling Controls module. In the **New Condition** dialog box, click on the icon for the Scroll_Marker object, and click **Movement>Path Movement>Path movement of "Scroll_Marker" has reached a named node** in the shortcut menu. The expression editor is displayed, as shown in **Figure 21-6.**

32. In the expression editor, enter "Home", and then click the **OK** button to create the expression. Be sure to include the quotation marks. Since the name is text, it must be enclosed in quotation marks or an error will be generated. The pseudocode you just programmed is:

    IF the path movement of the Scroll_Marker object has reached the node named Home

33. Complete the event line with this pseudocode:

    THEN destroy the Scroll_Marker object

34. Add a new event line in the Scrolling Controls module, and program this pseudocode:

    IF the Button_Scroll object is clicked,

    THEN create a new Scroll_Marker object at absolute coordinates (100, 540)

    AND start movement of the Scroll_Marker object.

35. Run the frame. Test if the **Scroll** button is working properly. Close the game window when done testing.

Movement

Event Editor

Run Frame

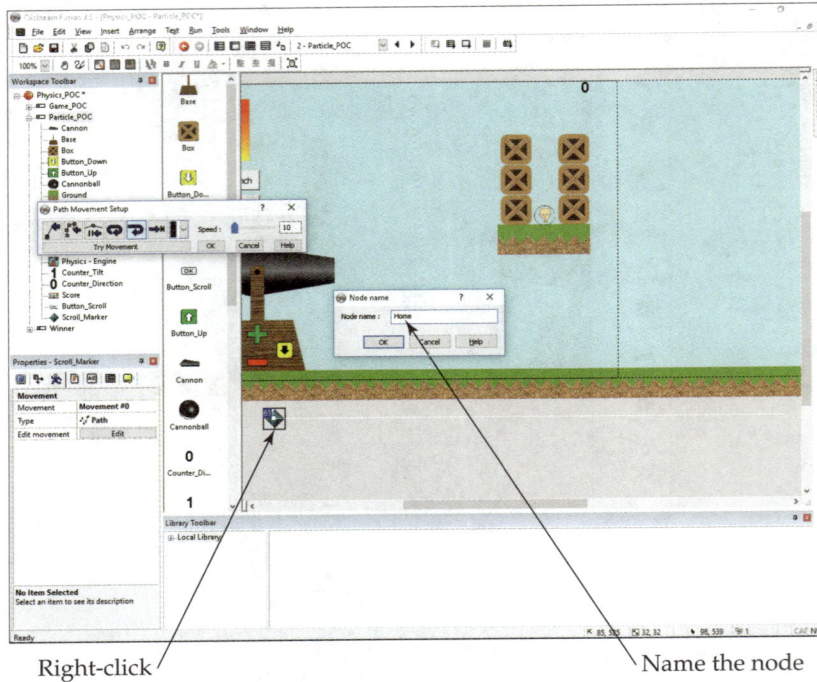

Right-click   Name the node

Figure 21-5. Path nodes can be named and the name referenced in programming.

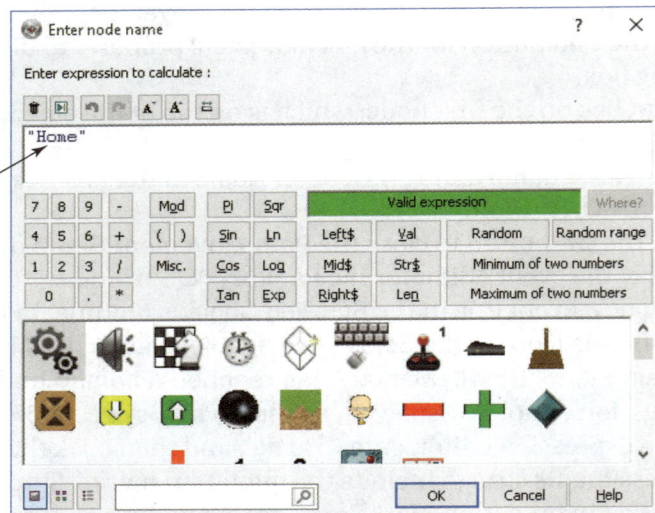

Enclose the node name within quotation marks

Figure 21-6. Referencing a node name in programming. Be sure to enclose the name in quotation marks since it is text.

Debugging the Scroll

You should have noticed that the game map no longer scrolls back to the initial position. This bug occurs as there is only one functioning node on the path. To repair the bug, the path needs to be edited and a segment added to the end.

36. Applying what you have learned, edit the path for the Scroll_Marker object.
37. Select the endpoint node.

Frame Editor

38. Click the **New line** button.

39. Draw a straight-line segment from the endpoint node to (950, 540). Note: you cannot name the endpoint node on a path, so a short segment must be added to create a third node. The length of this segment will determine how much of a pause there is before the screen scrolls back.

40. Set the speed of the node that is now in the middle of the path to 10, and name the node End.

41. Verify the **Reverse at End** button is still active (depressed). Then, close the **Path Movement Setup** dialog box.

42. Run the frame. Test that the game map scrolls in both directions. Test that clicking the **Scroll** button will send the game map through one more scrolling cycle. Close the game window when done testing.

43. Debug as needed.

Scrolling Gameplay

The player can now scroll the game map to see the objects that are outside of the initial view. The next task is to create scrolling gameplay so the frame follows the cannonball and the player can see the result of launching.

44. Display the event editor for the Particle_POC frame.

45. Edit event line 1, and add programming for the following pseudocode. This code is needed to avoid a possible conflict with the scrolling programming.

   THEN destroy the Cannonball object

46. In the event line that tests for **IF** the **Launch** button is clicked, right-click in the cell under the icon for the Cannonball object, and click **Flags>Set On** in the shortcut menu.

47. In the dialog box that is displayed, select Flag 1, and click the **OK** button, as shown in **Figure 21-7.**

48. In the same event line, add the programming needed to destroy the Scroll_Marker object.

49. Applying what you have learned, add an action for the Cannonball object in event line 1, which tests for the start of the frame, to set Flag 1 off.

50. Create a new programming module by inserting a comment at the end that states Scrolling Gameplay to Cannonball. Change the text and background color as needed.

51. Add a new event line to the Scrolling Gameplay to Cannonball programming module. In the **New Condition** dialog box, click the icon for the Cannonball object, and click **Alterable Values>Flags>Is flag on?** in the shortcut menu. In the dialog box that is displayed, select Flag 1, and click the **OK** button.

52. In the event line you just added, right-click in the cell under the Storyboard icon, and click **Scrollings>Center horizontal position of window in frame** in the shortcut menu. The expression editor is displayed.

New Line

Run Frame

Event Editor

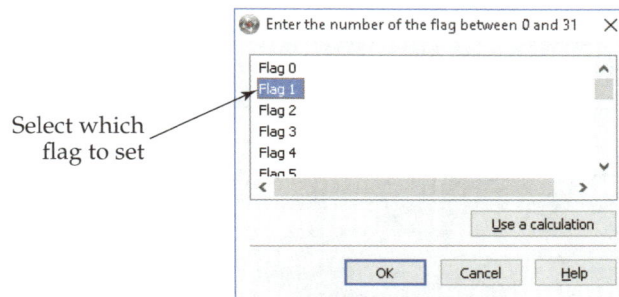

Goodheart-Willcox Publisher

Figure 21-7. Set a flag to use for controlling screen scrolling when the cannonball moves.

Run Frame

53. Applying what you have learned, create an expression that gets the X coordinate value of the Cannonball object. Then, close the expression editor.
54. Run the frame. Test that when you launch a cannonball, the frame scrolls to follow the object. Close the game window when done testing.

Creating Game Challenge

As of now, the player has an unlimited number of cannonballs to shoot the targets. To add more challenge, the gameplay can be modified to limit the number of shots and to reset the gameplay for each shot. A series of delays for the physics needs to be created to fully stop movement. Timers will be used to allow the next cannonball to be launched.

Frame Editor

55. Display the Particle_POC frame in the frame editor.
56. Insert a new active object below the **Scroll** button.
57. Name the object Sensor_Delay, set its position to (25, 225), and change its size to 10 wide and 10 high.
58. Insert a new active object next to the previous object in the empty space above the **Scroll** button, and name the object Timer_Pause. To achieve the effect of a timer, you will create an animated object to act as a countdown timer.

Clear

59. Open the Timer_Pause object in the image editor, and clear the canvas.
60. Click the **Line Tool** button, and set the size to 6.
61. Set the foreground color to a dark color of your choice.
62. Draw a diagonal line from the top-right to the bottom-left of the canvas, as shown in **Figure 21-8.**

Line Tool

63. Click the **Frames** tab of the image editor, right-click on Frame 1, and click **Rotation** in the shortcut menu.
64. Applying what you have learned, create 20 frames of rotation in the clockwise direction.
65. Click the **Direction Options** tab at the bottom of the image editor.

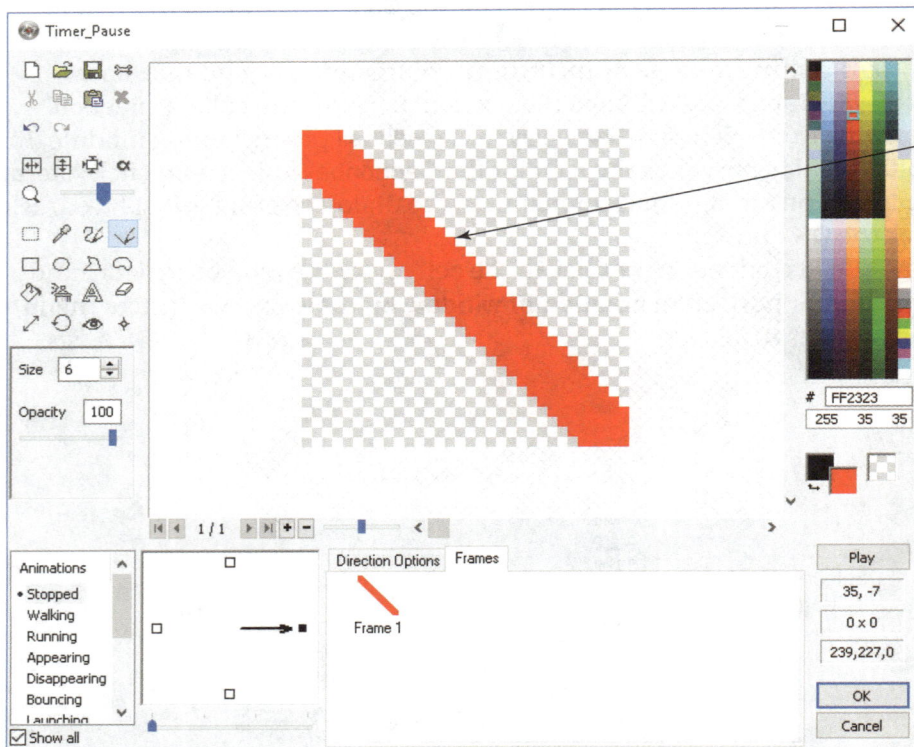

Draw a thick diagonal line

Figure 21-8. Creating a sprite for the Timer_Pause object.

66. Set the speed to 10 and the repeat to 2.
67. Click the **OK** button to close the image editor and save the animation.
68. Applying what you have learned, close the Timer_Pause object, place the clone to the side of the original, and name the clone Timer_Reset.
69. Display the event editor for the Particle_POC frame.
70. Create a new programming module by inserting a new comment that states Reset Gameplay. Change the text and background color as needed.

Event Editor

71. In the Reset Gameplay module, program this pseudocode:
    IF the X coordinate of the Cannonball object is greater than 1250
    AND Flag 1 is off,
        THEN create a Timer_Reset object at (0, 0) relative to the Cannonball object
        AND make the Timer_Reset object invisible
        AND destroy the Cannonball object.
72. Copy the event line you just programmed and paste it as the second line in the Reset Gameplay module.
73. Double-click the condition in the pasted event line to edit the condition.
74. In the event editor, modify the expression to be less than or equal to 100, and click the **OK** button to update the condition. Note: you will need to make sure the Cannonball object that is outside the visible play area is positioned someplace where its X coordinate value is greater than 100, but less than 1250.
75. Add a new event line to the Reset Gameplay module, and program the following pseudocode. Refer to **Figure 21-9.**
    IF the speed of the Cannonball object movement is equal to 0,
        THEN create a new Sensor_Delay object at (0, 0) relative to the Cannonball object.
76. Run the frame. Test how the Sensor_Delay object is positioned by launching a cannonball at very low power. Close the game window when done testing.

Run Frame

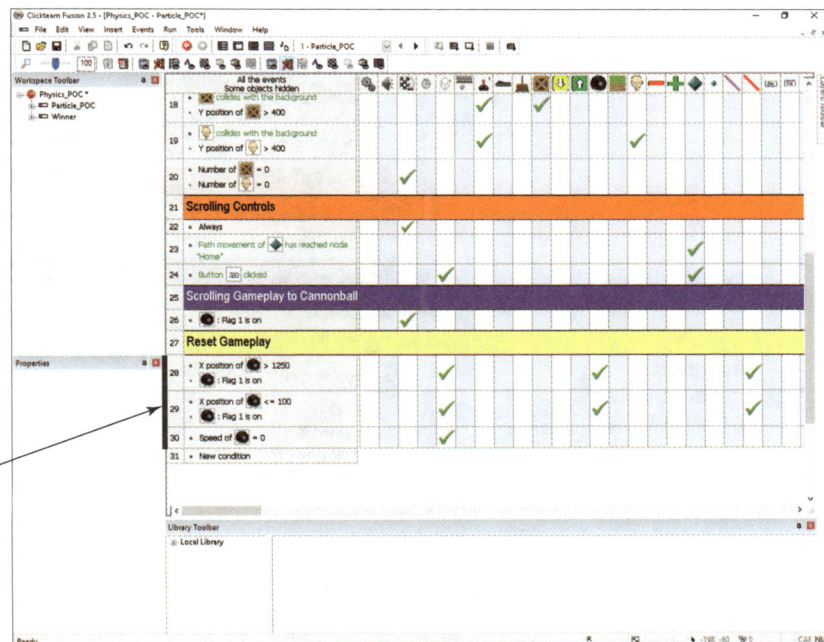

Programming to create Timer_Reset objects

Goodheart-Willcox Publisher

Figure 21-9. Programming is added to control resetting of the gameplay.

Delay for Physics-Based Action

Notice how there are several delay sensors that appear. In this section, you will program a few events to make sure only one timer is active. The timer will be used to make sure all of the physics objects have enough time to settle into place and that the cannonball has fully stopped moving.

77. Add a new event line to the Reset Gameplay module, and program this pseudocode:
    IF the Sensor_Delay object is overlapping the Cannonball object,
    >   **THEN** create a Timer_Pause object at (0, 0) relative to the Cannonball object
    >   **AND** make the Sensor_Delay object invisible
    >   **AND** make the Timer_Pause object invisible.

78. Add a new event line to the Reset Gameplay module, and program this pseudocode:
    IF the count of the number of Timer_Pause objects is greater than 1,
    >   **THEN** destroy the Sensor_Delay object.

79. Add a new event line to the Reset Gameplay module, and program this pseudocode:
    IF the Sensor_Delay object is not overlapping the Cannonball object,
    >   **THEN** destroy the Timer_Pause object.

80. Add a new event line to the Reset Gameplay module, and program the following pseudocode. Refer to **Figure 21-10.**
    IF the Stopped animation for the Timer_Pause object has finished,
    >   **THEN** create a new Timer_Reset object at (0, 0) relative to the Cannonball object
    >   **AND** destroy the Cannonball object
    >   **AND** destroy the Timer_Pause object,

81. Using the event list editor, in the event line you just programmed, move the action to destroy the Timer_Pause object to the top of the stack.

82. Run the frame. Test if the cannonball is destroyed and the Timer_Reset object is animated by launching a cannonball at very low power. The timer should spin. This object will eventually be set to hidden so it is not visible in the final game. Close the game window when done testing.

Event List Editor

Run Frame

Additional programming for the timer

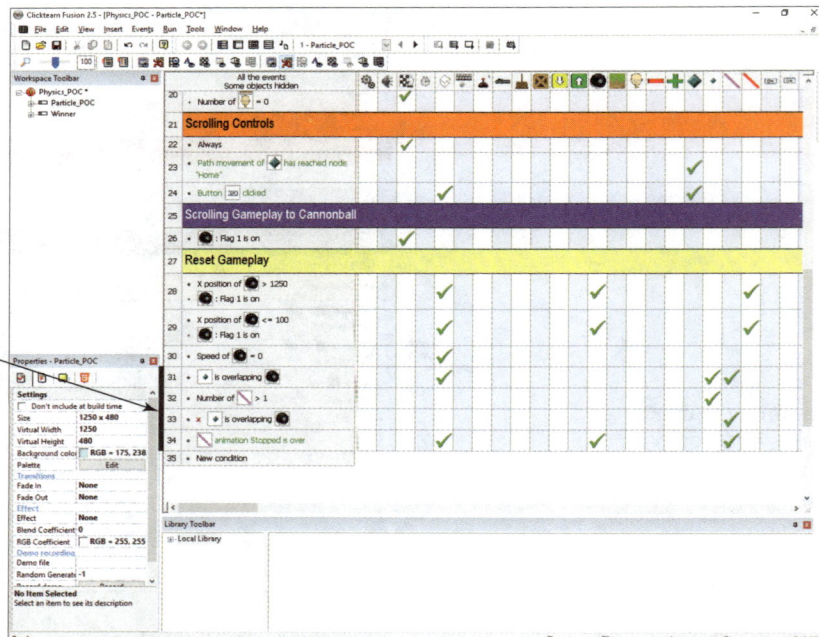

Figure 21-10. Additional programming is added to the Reset Gameplay module.

Cannon Firing Modifications

Programming needs to be added to handle when the cannon angle is too high and the cannonball leaves the play area on the top. Programming also needs to be added to limit the player to launching a single cannonball at a time.

83. Display the event editor, and create a new programming module by inserting a new comment that states Cannonball Limiting. Change the text and background color as needed.

Event Editor

84. Add a new event line in the Cannonball Limiting module, and program this pseudocode to allow the player to manually destroy a cannonball:

    IF the player left-clicks on a Cannonball object,

        THEN create a Timer_Reset object at (0, 0) relative to the Cannonball object

           AND destroy the Cannonball object.

85. Add a new event line in the Cannonball Limiting module, and program this pseudocode to perform a timeout reset if the cannonball goes off the screen:

    IF the Cannonball object leaves the play area to the top,

        THEN create a new Timer_Reset object at absolute coordinates (340, 30).

86. Add a new event line in the Cannonball Limiting module, and program this pseudocode to handle when the cannonball reenters the play area.

    IF the Cannonball object enters the play area from the top,

        THEN destroy the Timer_Reset object.

87. Add a new event line in the Cannonball Limiting module, and program this pseudocode to allow launching another cannonball when the timer has finished:

    IF the Stopped animation for the Timer_Reset object has finished,

        THEN center the display on the Cannon object

           AND subtract 1 from the number of lives for Player 1

           AND destroy the Timer_Reset object

           AND destroy the Timer_Pause object

           AND enable the Button_Launch button.

88. In the User Interface Programming module, locate the line that tests for the Button_Launch button clicked, right-click in the cell under the icon for the Button_Launch object, and click **Disable** in the shortcut menu.

89. Edit event line 1, and add programming to destroy the Timer_Pause and the Timer_Reset objects at the start of the frame. Refer to **Figure 21-11.**

Interactions for the Face Ball Object

The Face Ball object should be destroyed when it collides with another Face Ball object. It should also be destroyed if a Box object hits it on the top, but only on the top. A sensor will be used to control collision with a Box object. The programming needs to be modified to handle these situations.

90. Display the Particle_POC frame in the frame editor.

Frame Editor

91. Add a new active object, name it Sensor_Crush, and move it outside of the visible play area.

92. Resize the object to 15 pixels wide and 10 pixels high.

93. Modify the sprite for the Sensor_Crush object so it is a red square.

94. Display the event editor for the Particle_POC frame.

95. Edit event line 1, and add programming to create a Sensor_Crush object at (0, –15) relative to the Face Ball object when the frame starts. This will place the sensor on the top of and slightly over any existing Face Ball objects.

Event Editor

96. Create a new programming module by inserting a new comment that states Face Ball Interactions. Change the text and background color as needed.

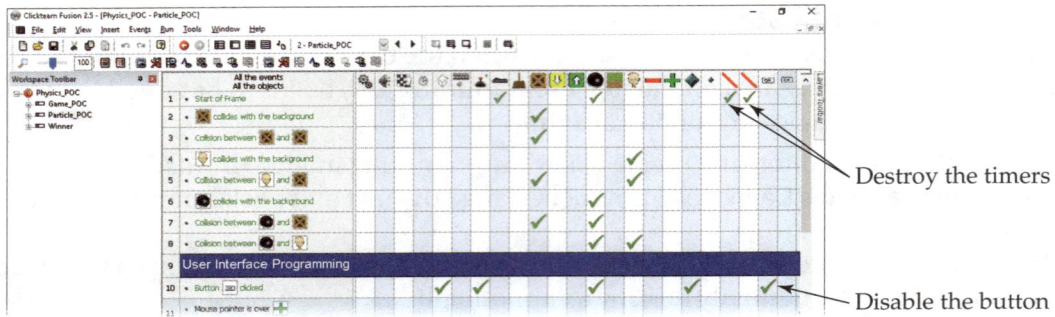

Destroy the timers

Disable the button

Goodheart-Willcox Publisher

Figure 21-11. The timers need to be destroyed when the frame starts to prevent a conflict.

97. Add a new event line in the Face Ball Interactions module, and program this pseudocode to keep a Sensor_Crush object above each Face Ball object:

> **IF** always,
>> **THEN** set the position of the Crush_Sensor object at (0, –15) relative to the Face Ball object.

Run Frame

98. Run the frame. Test if all Face Ball objects have a Sensor_Crush object slightly overlapping at the top. Test that the sensors stay with the objects as the screen scrolls and the objects move. Close the game window when done testing.

99. Add a new event line in the Face Ball Interactions module, and program this pseudocode to destroy Face Ball objects that collide with each other:

> **IF** a Face Ball object collides with another Face Ball object,
>> **THEN** destroy the Face Ball object
>>> **AND** add 20 points to the Player 1 score.

100. Add a new event line in the Face Ball Interactions module, and program this pseudocode to handle when a Box object hits the top of a Face Ball object:

> **IF** a Box object is overlapping a Sensor_Crush object
>> **AND** the Sensor_Crush object is overlapping a Face Ball object,
>>> **THEN** destroy the Face Ball object
>>>> **AND** add 20 points to player 1 score.

101. Add a new event line in the Face Ball Interactions module, and program the following pseudocode to remove any Sensor_Crush object that is no longer needed. Refer to **Figure 21-12.**

> **IF** the Sensor_Crush object is not overlapping the Face Ball object,
>> **THEN** destroy the Sensor_Crush object.

Frame Editor

102. Display the Particle_POC frame in the frame editor.
103. Copy and paste some Face Ball objects and place them on top of Box objects.
104. Run the frame. Test if Box objects will crush Face Ball objects. Also test that if one Face Ball object is destroyed they all are not destroyed. Close the game window when done testing.

Run Frame

105. Debug as needed. Note: if all Face Ball objects are destroyed when one is crushed, check that programming matches **Figure 21-12.**

Checking for Gameplay Completion

There needs to be a condition on how victory is achieved. This will be the player has only three lives to destroy all of the Face Ball objects. The victory condition is having the high score when the Face Ball objects are all destroyed. The game needs to be programmed to inspect the objects to determine if the player has destroyed all Face Ball objects. The programming has already been added to subtract one life each time the player uses a cannonball.

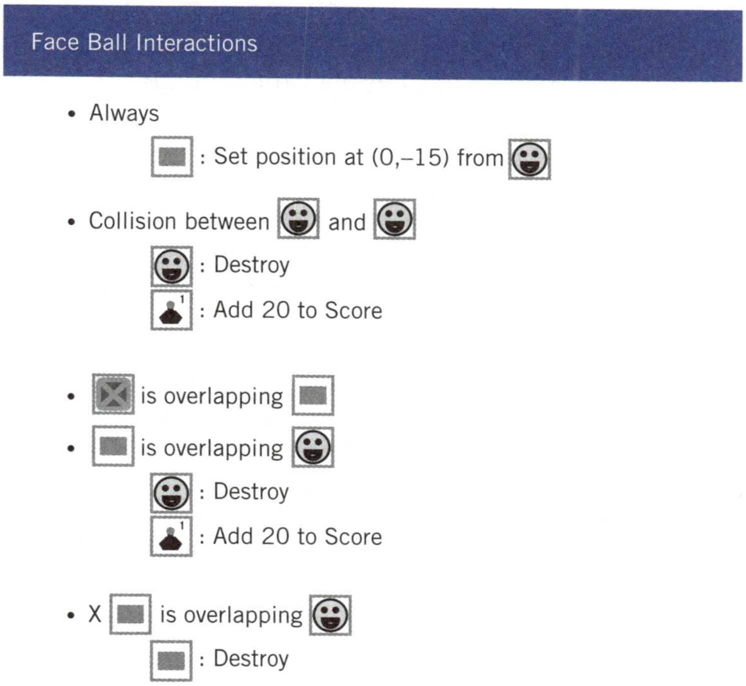

Face Ball Interactions

- Always

     ▪️ : Set position at (0,–15) from 😀

- Collision between 😀 and 😀

     😀 : Destroy

     👤¹ : Add 20 to Score

- ⊠ is overlapping ▪️

- ▪️ is overlapping 😀

     😀 : Destroy

     👤¹ : Add 20 to Score

- X ▪️ is overlapping 😀

     ▪️ : Destroy

Goodheart-Willcox Publisher

Figure 21-12. The Sensor_Crush object is used to tell when a box collides with the top of a Face Ball object.

106. Insert a new Lives object at (295, 0). Also, ensure the Cannonball object that is outside the visible play area is positioned someplace where its X coordinate value is greater than 100, but less than 1250.
107. Display the event editor for the Particle_POC frame.
108. Create a new programming module by inserting a new comment that states Storyboard Navigation. Change the text and background color as needed.

Event Editor

109. Add a new event line in the Storyboard Navigation module, and program this pseudocode to advance the player to the Winner frame on successfully completing the level:
       IF the count of the Face Ball objects shows all have been destroyed,
            THEN go to the next frame.
110. Add a new event line in the Storyboard Navigation module, and program this pseudocode to handle when the player has used up all of the lives:
       IF the Player 1 lives equals 0,
            THEN restart the application.
111. Applying what you have learned, delete the Game_POC frame. This will leave the Particle_POC and Winner frames.
112. Run the application. Test that the Winner frame is displayed once you have destroyed all Face Ball objects. Test that the game restarts if you run out of lives before destroying all Face Ball objects. Close the game window when done testing.

Run Application

Particle Physics

The game is fully functional at this point. However, recall the Awesome Game Company wants particle systems to be incorporated into the game. Clickteam Fusion 2.5 has a feature that will automatically create particle physics for certain objects. In this game, instead of just destroying the objects, particles can be used to make the object look like it explodes.

113. Display the Particle_POC frame in the frame editor.

Frame Editor

Settings

114. Insert a new Physics Particles object anywhere in the visible play area, and name it Face Ball Particles. Later, you will move this object outside the visible area.

115. With the Face Ball Particles object selected, click the **Settings** tab in the **Properties** toolbar. This tab contains properties related to how the particles are generated, as shown in **Figure 21-13.**

116. Set the Emission property to From a point.

117. Check the Create particles at start of frame property. Later, you will change this setting so particles are generated only when a specific event occurs.

118. Select the images in the Particle image property, and then click the ellipsis button (...) that appears to display the image editor.

119. Clear the canvas.

Clear

120. Applying what you have learned, import the Face Ball image from your working folder. Accept the default settings in the **Import Options** dialog box.

121. Click the **Size** button, and check the **Proportional**, **Stretch**, and **Resample** check boxes in the tool options area.

Import

122. Click in the **w** (width) text box in the tool options area, enter 20, and click the **Apply** button, as shown in **Figure 21-14**. The value in the **h** (height) text box automatically changes to match so the image is proportionally resized.

123. Zoom in on the image. Note: the image size is very small, so it will be blurry and pixelated.

Size

124. Click the **View hot spot** button, and click the center button in the Quick Move grid. Note: do *not* click the **G** button or the particles will collapse *toward* the center instead of exploding *from* the center.

125. In the **Frames** tab, delete all animation frames other than Frame 1.

View hot spot

126. Right-click on Frame 1, and click **Zoom** in the shortcut menu.

127. In the **Insert Resized Frames** dialog box, enter 1 in the **Final width** and **Final height** text boxes, enter 20 in the **Number of frames** text box, and click the **OK** button, as shown in **Figure 21-15.**

128. Close the image editor.

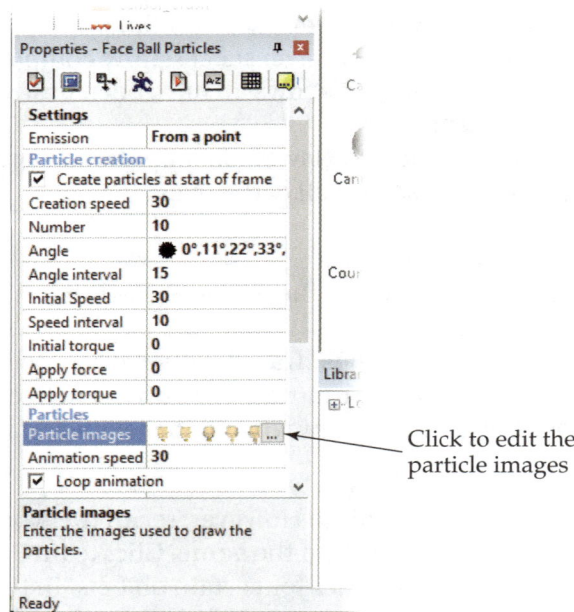

Goodheart-Willcox Publisher

Figure 21-13. Setting the properties for the particle system. The sprites used for the particles can be edited to change the effect simulated by the particle system.

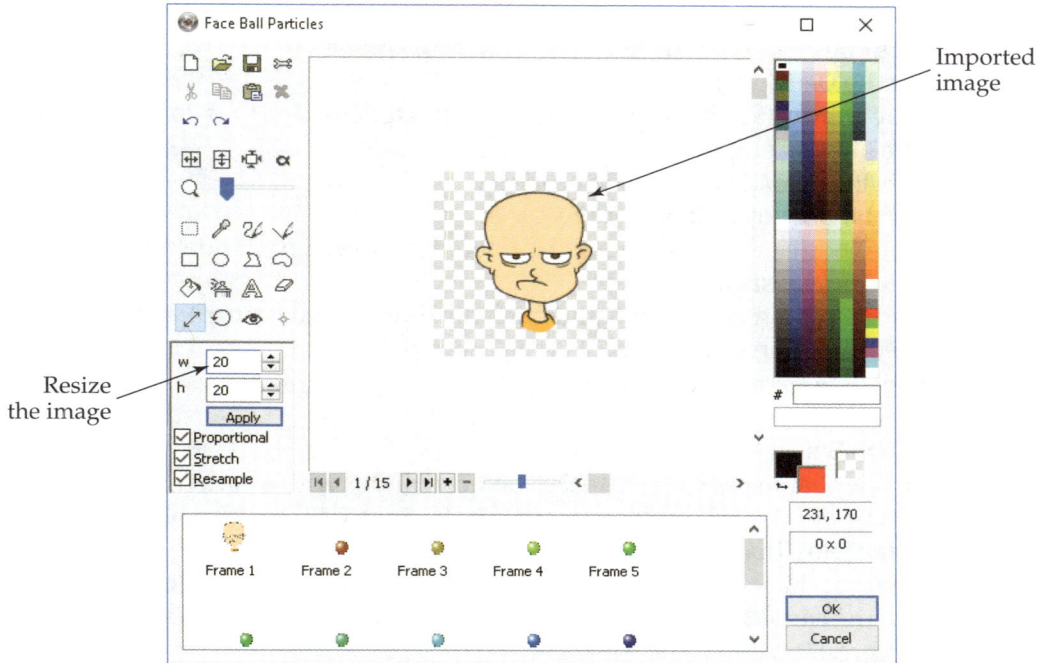

Goodheart-Willcox Publisher

Figure 21-14. An image can be imported and modified as needed to be used as the sprite for the particles.

129. Run the frame. See how the particles are generated. Close the game window when done testing.

Run Frame

Particle Tuning

To represent the Face Ball object exploding, the particles should fly out of the emitter in all different sizes and directions. However, the particles are drawn downward by gravity in the physics engine. Also, the emitter is always generating particles. Additional settings need to be made to refine the particle generation.

130. Select the Face Ball Particles object, and click the **Settings** tab in the **Properties** toolbar.
131. Uncheck the Loop animation property. This will limit the number of particles created.
132. Enter −5 for the Scale property.
133. Enter 0 for the Friction property. This will create particles that do not react to friction in the physics engine.

Settings

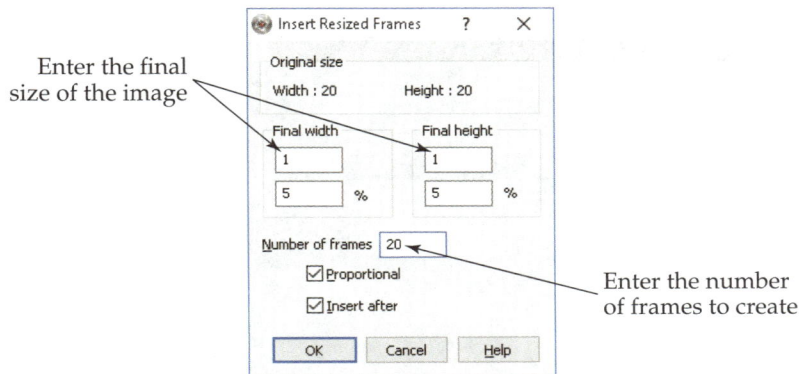

Goodheart-Willcox Publisher

Figure 21-15. Creating multiple frames for the particle sprite to reduce the image size, which in turn reduces the size of each particle as it is animated.

134. Enter 0 for the Elasticity property. This will create particles that do not react to elasticity in the physics engine.
135. Enter 100 for the Density property.
136. Enter 0 for the Gravity factor property. This will create particles that do not react to gravity in the physics engine.
137. Check the Destroy at end of animation property.
138. Enter 100 for the Destroy distance property.
139. Run the frame. Notice the difference the updated settings have made. Close the game window when done testing.

Run Frame

140. Select the Face Ball Particles object, and click the **Settings** tab in the **Properties** toolbar.
141. Uncheck the Create particles at start of frame property.
142. Move the Face Ball Particles object outside the visible play area.

Settings

143. Display the event editor for the Particle_POC frame.
144. Locate the Face Ball Interactions programming module.
145. In the event line that tests **IF** the Face Ball object collides with another Face Ball object, right-click in the cell under the icon for the Face Ball Particles object, and click **Position>Select Position…** in the shortcut menu.

Event Editor

146. Applying what you have learned, set the position to (0, 0) relative to the Face Ball object.
147. Right-click in the same cell, and click **Create/Destroy>Create Particles** in the shortcut menu. The expression editor is displayed.
148. Enter 20 in the expression editor, and click the **OK** button.
149. Using the event list editor, move the destroy action to the bottom of the stack so the create particles action occurs first. This prevents a conflict by moving the emitter before destroying the object.

Event List Editor

150. Display the event editor, and copy the check mark for the programming you just coded into the cell for the Face Ball Particles object in the event line that tests **IF** a box collides with a Sensor_Crush object, as shown in **Figure 21-16.**

Event Editor

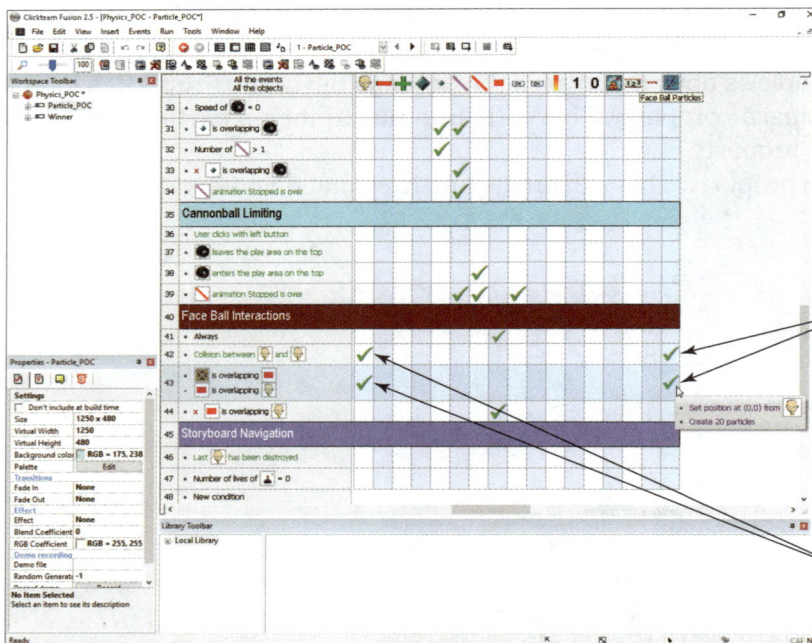

Goodheart-Willcox Publisher

Figure 21-16. Programming is added to move the particle system emitter to the location of the Face Ball object and for it to generate 20 particles.

151. Locate all other event lines that contain an action to destroy the Face Ball object, and copy the check mark into the cell for the Face Ball Particles object. Anytime the Face Ball object is destroyed, 20 particles should be generated at the location of the Face Ball object. There are four total events in which the Face Ball object is destroyed.
152. Locate the Scrolling Controls programming module.
153. Modify the event line that tests for **IF** always. Add programming to make the Timer_Pause, Timer_Reset, Sensor_Delay, and Sensor_Crush objects invisible.
154. Using the event list editor, rearrange the actions for the **IF** always condition so the action to center the display is at the bottom of the stack.

Run Application

155. Run the application. Fully test all elements of the game. Close the game window when done testing.
156. Debug all errors discovered. If the programming is correct, but an error remains, try changing the order of actions in the stack using the event list editor. Sometimes the order in which actions are processed affect gameplay. If there is a bug where lives are continuously subtracted, ensure the Cannonball object that is outside the visible play area is positioned someplace where its X coordinate value is greater than 100, but less than 1250.
157. Save your work, and submit it for grading.

Vocabulary

Write a definition for each of the key terms from this lesson. You will develop a personal glossary of key terms throughout this course.

particle animation

_____

_____

emitter

_____

_____

static particles

_____

_____

strand

_____

_____

mod

_____

_____

modding

_____

_____

partial-conversion mod

_____

_____

total-conversion mod

_____

_____

Review Questions

Applied Technology

1. What type of object contains settings for controlling particle generation?

_____

_____

_____

Language Arts

2. Write a brief description of how hair or fur can be simulated with particles.

_____

_____

_____

Science

3. Which real-world force can be simulated with a physics engine to pull particles in a specific direction?

_____

_____

_____

_____

Mathematics

4. If a randomizing constraint is +10 percent to –20 percent, what is the variance allowed? How likely is the percentage to be negative?

_____

_____

_____

_____

Applied Technology

5. Suppose you have modded a game to provide new tools for the player character to use. What type of mod is this?

_____

_____

_____

_____

Higher-Order Thinking Strategies

6. Communities often develop around modding a specific game. Speculate what would drive the development of a modding community.

_____

_____

_____

_____

Social Science

7. Describe how particles can be used to simulate a continuous stream of flowing liquid.

_____

_____

_____

Language Arts

8. Identify the setting in Clickteam Fusion 2.5 that allows the frame to be centered on a given object.

_____

_____

_____

Applied Technology

9. Particles can be used to simulate tall grass, such as you may see in a meadow or prairie. Think about what forces and other factors act on the grass that need to be replicated to produce a realistic effect.

_____

_____

_____

_____

Science

10. A particle system is set up to generate particles at a specified initial size and reduce to a second specified size over the lifespan of the particle. The size of each particle will change by one each second. Based on this information, complete the following table.

Mathematics

Initial Size	Final Size	Lifespan
10	0	10 seconds
	10	5 seconds
5	3	
10		5 seconds
20	11	

Office Technology Integration

Creating Spreadsheet Charts

1. Launch Microsoft Excel or other spreadsheet software, and open the vocabulary spreadsheet you updated in previous lessons.
2. Applying what you have learned, add a new worksheet, and name it Lesson 21.
3. Add each of the vocabulary words and definitions from the Vocabulary section of this lesson.
4. Save the spreadsheet, and then close it.
5. Open the *LastName*_ExcelTable file created in Lesson 20, and save it as *LastName*_ExcelCharts in your working folder.
6. Select the range A3:B15.
7. Click **Insert>Charts>Insert Column or Bar Chart** on the ribbon, and click **3D Clustered Column** in the drop-down menu. A chart is placed in the spreadsheet based on the selected data, as shown.

Insert Column or Bar Chart

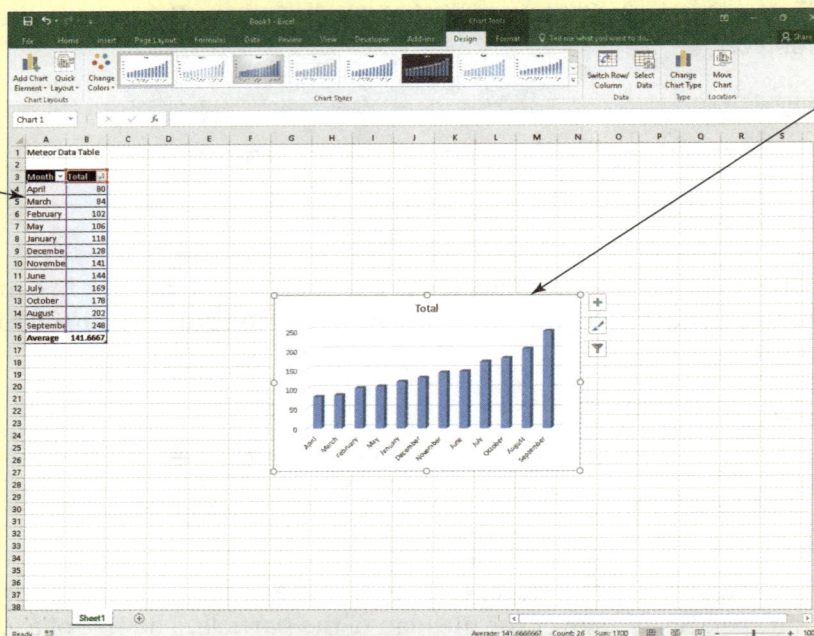

Data on which the chart is based

Chart is added

Goodheart-Willcox Publisher

8. Drag the chart so it is aligned next to the data table.
9. In the **Chart Styles** group on the **Design** tab of the ribbon, select **Style 6** in the gallery.
10. Applying what you have learned, use the data from the range A3:B15 to create a 3D pie chart.
11. With the pie chart selected, notice the three buttons that appear to the top-right side of the chart.
12. Click the **Chart Elements** button to display a menu. Uncheck the **Chart Title** check box, and check the **Data Labels** check box.

Chart Elements

13. Click the **Chart Styles** button, scroll through the list in the menu that appears, and click the **Style 6** thumbnail.
14. Evaluate which of the two charts you feel best represents the data. Enter the text Column or Pie in cell A23 to record your choice.

Chart Styles

15. In cell A24, enter text to explain your choice. Include specific details to support your claim.
16. Submit your work for grading.

Quality Assurance

Learning Objectives

After completing this lesson, you will be able to:

- evaluate the quality of your own work and the work of others.

- assess positive aspects of the playability and functionality of a game.

- provide constructive criticism to peers by suggesting possible solutions to problems.

Situation

The Awesome Game Company would like you and a colleague to review the alpha version of the physics game built in Lesson 21. The results of the review will be used to create a game critique that will be posted to the company website and blog space on the Internet. Complete an evaluation report on the playability and functionality of the game. Each member of the design team needs to evaluate the product and suggest reasons why each item achieves or does not achieve the objective. Be accurate and complete in your evaluations. The personal and peer evaluation are for the same game by the same designer. That means you must give your personal evaluation to a classmate for them to complete the peer evaluation for your game on the same page as your personal evaluation.

Quality Assurance Team

Personal Evaluator Name:

_____

_____

Total Score from Personal Evaluation Rubric:

_____

_____

Peer Evaluator Name:

_____

_____

Total Score from Peer Evaluation Rubric:

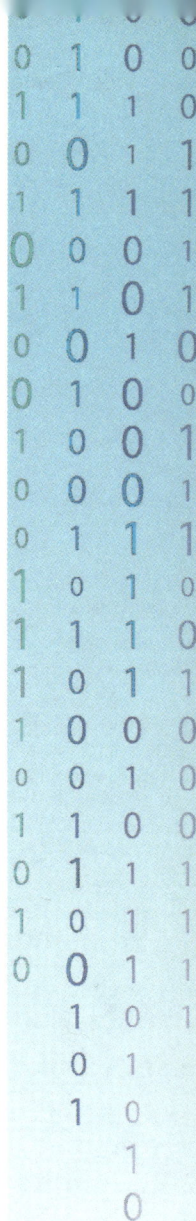

_____

_____

Design Reasoning: Personal Evaluation

1. Reflect on your work, and evaluate your game for each of the five key areas of design identified in the rubric.
2. Rank each key area using a scale from 0 to 5. Record the value in the Score column.
3. Complete the Personal Evaluation rubric in the Commentary and Constructive Criticism section. Explain why you gave the score you did for each area of design.
4. Suggest improvements needed for your game in the Personal Evaluation rubric in the Commentary and Constructive Criticism section.

Key Area	0	1	2	3	4	5	Score
Concept Is the idea well developed?	No main idea or theme.					Clear theme or main idea maintained on all levels.	
Aesthetics Does the look, color, contrast, and placement of objects fit the game?	Poor quality graphics, color, and contrast.					Awesome graphics and animations. Items contrasted well.	
Sound Effects Do the sounds play? Are the music and sounds appropriate?	No sound. Sound is too loud, too soft, or not related to the game.					Sounds enhance gameplay and play clearly.	
Functionality Does everything work as expected?	Unfinished. Could not play. Major errors.					Plays perfectly. No bugs, glitches, or errors.	
Replay How likely are you to play this game again?	Game solved. Too easy. Not interesting or impossible to win.					Cannot wait to play it again! Skill was challenging, but enjoyable.	
Add the values in the Score column to get a total.						**Total Score**	

Name: _____

Design Reasoning: Peer Evaluation

1. Play the game designed by the peer as assigned by your instructor.
2. Reflect on the peer's work, and evaluate the game for each of the five key areas of design identified in the rubric.
3. Rank each key area using a scale from 0 to 5. Record the value in the Score column.
4. Complete the Peer Evaluation rubric in the Commentary and Constructive Criticism section. Explain why you gave the score you did for each area of design.
5. Suggest improvements needed for the peer's game in the Peer Evaluation rubric in the Commentary and Constructive Criticism section.

Key Area	0	1	2	3	4	5	Score
Concept Is the idea well developed?	No main idea or theme.					Clear theme or main idea maintained on all levels.	
Aesthetics Does the look, color, contrast, and placement of objects fit the game?	Poor quality graphics, color, and contrast.					Awesome graphics and animations. Items contrasted well.	
Sound Effects Do the sounds play? Are the music and sounds appropriate?	No sound. Sound is too loud, too soft, or not related to the game.					Sounds enhance gameplay and play clearly.	
Functionality Does everything work as expected?	Unfinished. Could not play. Major errors.					Plays perfectly. No bugs, glitches, or errors.	
Replay How likely are you to play this game again?	Game solved. Too easy. Not interesting or impossible to win.					Cannot wait to play it again! Skill was challenging, but enjoyable.	
Add up the values in the Score column to get a total.						**Total Score**	

Commentary and Constructive Criticism

Explain why you assigned the score for each key item assessed. Provide details on what you liked in that area and what needed improvement. Cite specific examples from the game. Provide suggestions on how to improve the game.

Personal Evaluation

Key Area	Detailed Assessment
Concept	
Aesthetics	
Sound Effects	
Functionality	
Replay	
Suggested Improvements	

Peer Evaluation

Key Area	Detailed Assessment
Concept	
Aesthetics	
Sound Effects	
Functionality	
Replay	
Suggested Improvements	

Office Technology Integration

Creating a Blog Post

1. Launch Microsoft Word.
2. On the startup page, click in the search text box, enter blog post, and click the search button (magnifying glass).
3. In the list of search results, click the Blog post template. A preview is displayed, as shown.

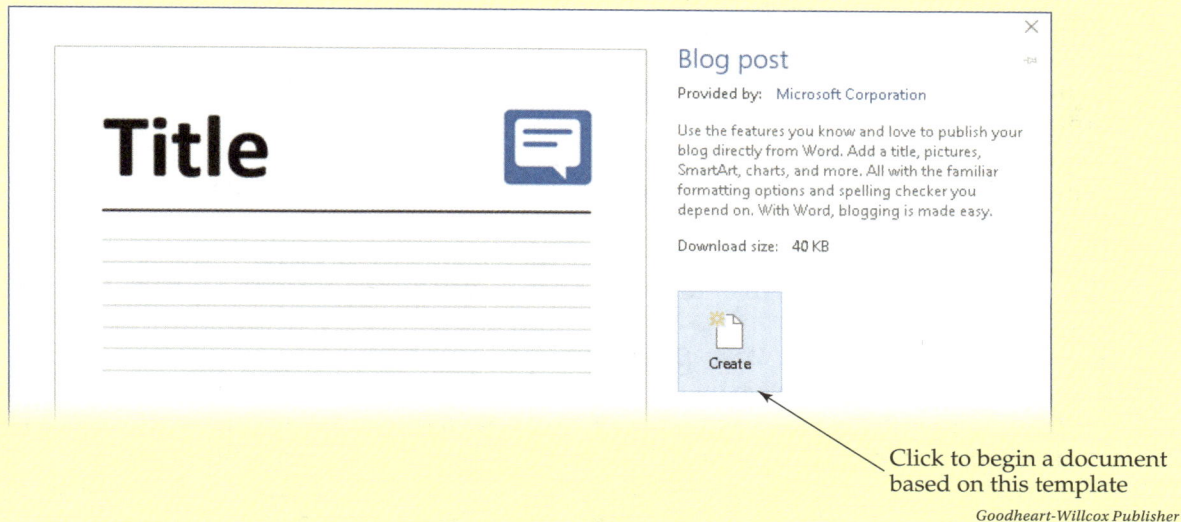

Title

Blog post

Provided by: Microsoft Corporation

Use the features you know and love to publish your blog directly from Word. Add a title, pictures, SmartArt, charts, and more. All with the familiar formatting options and spelling checker you depend on. With Word, blogging is made easy.

Download size: 40 KB

Create

Click to begin a document
based on this template

Goodheart-Willcox Publisher

4. Click the **Create** button in the preview to begin a new document for a blog post.
5. A message appears asking you to register a blog account, as shown. For this activity, click the **Register Later** button. Note: if you have a blog account already set up, you can click the **Register Now** button, but you can register later as well.

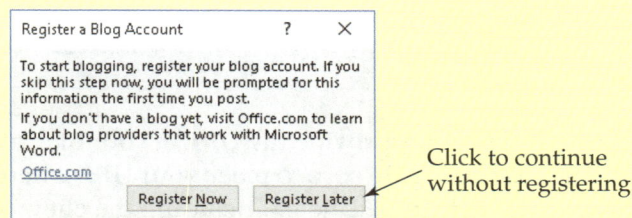

Register a Blog Account   ?   ✕

To start blogging, register your blog account. If you skip this step now, you will be prompted for this information the first time you post.

If you don't have a blog yet, visit Office.com to learn about blog providers that work with Microsoft Word.

Office.com

Register Now   Register Later

Click to continue
without registering

Goodheart-Willcox Publisher

6. Examine the template. There is placeholder text at the top of the page for the title. The rest of the template is blank. Also, notice the ribbon. Most of the tabs you are familiar with in Word do not appear. When creating a blog post, the ribbon is streamlined to show only the tools relevant to creating a post and blogging.
7. Click the placeholder text, and enter a title for your blog post. Remember, you are blogging a critique of a game you have reviewed in this lesson. The title should accurately reflect the content of the blog.

8. Click below the blog title. This is where the body of the blog should be written, as shown.

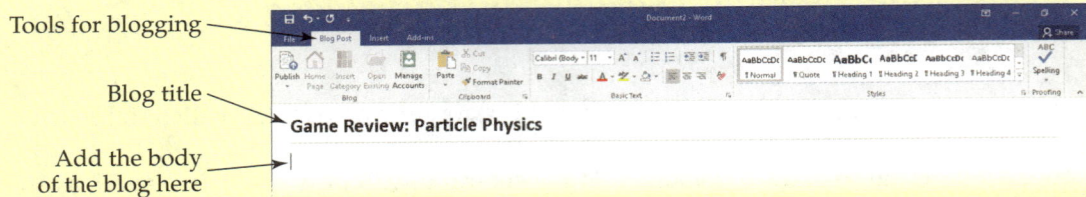

Tools for blogging ⟶

Blog title ⟶

Add the body of the blog here ⟶

Game Review: Particle Physics

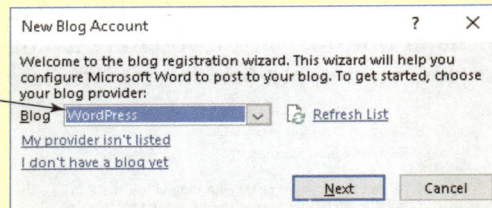

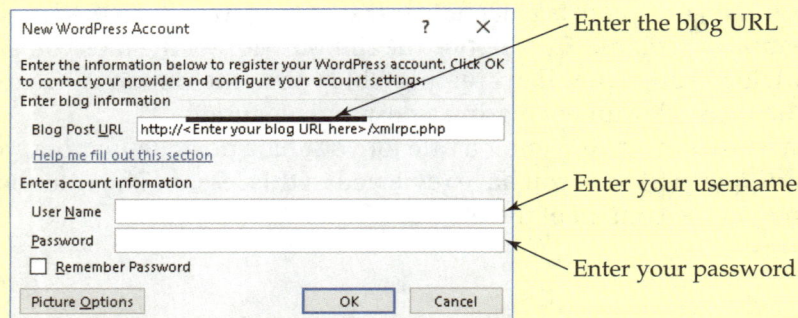

9. Write a paragraph introducing the blog post and what will be covered.
10. Add a heading for Personal Evaluation.
11. Below this heading, write one or two paragraphs describing your evaluation of your own game.
12. Add a heading for Peer Evaluation.
13. Below this heading, write one or two paragraphs describing your evaluation of your classmate's game.
14. Applying what you have learned, spell-check the document and display reading statistics.
15. If the reading level is too high or too low, edit what you have written to adjust the reading level.
16. Save the document as *LastName_*BlogPost in your working folder.
17. Click **Blog Post**>**Blog**>**Publish** on the ribbon. The remainder of this activity requires that you have a blog account and assumes you have not already registered the account with Word.

Publish

18. In the dialog box that is displayed, click the **Register an Account** button.
19. In the **New Account** dialog box, click the **Blog** drop-down arrow, and select your blog provider in the list, as shown. You can select Other if your provider is not listed.

Select your blog provider ⟶

New Blog Account

Welcome to the blog registration wizard. This wizard will help you configure Microsoft Word to post to your blog. To get started, choose your blog provider:

Blog [WordPress ▾] ⟳ Refresh List

My provider isn't listed

I don't have a blog yet

[Next] [Cancel]

20. Click the **Next** button. You must now provide the URL of your blog and enter your username and password, as shown. Be sure to place your URL where indicated. Your URL should replace <Enter your blog URL here> including the chevrons.

New WordPress Account

Enter the information below to register your WordPress account. Click OK to contact your provider and configure your account settings.

Enter blog information

Blog Post URL [http://<Enter your blog URL here>/xmlrpc.php] ⟶ Enter the blog URL

Help me fill out this section

Enter account information

User Name [   ] ⟶ Enter your username

Password [   ] ⟶ Enter your password

☐ Remember Password

[Picture Options]   [OK] [Cancel]

21. Once you have entered the URL, username, and password, click the **OK** button. Word will attempt to log in to your blog and upload the post. If the login is not successful, you may need to go through the steps of publishing and registering again.

Binary Number System

Learning Objectives

After completing this lesson, you will be able to:

- compare and contrast the binary and base-10 number systems.
- explain programming subroutines.
- construct an app to convert binary numbers into decimal numbers.
- identify the purpose of programming modes.

Situation

The Awesome Game Company is considering you for its smartphone app division. It would like you to prove your skills by creating a proof of concept for an app. The POC app will be a binary number converter, so you must first learn about binary and the binary number system.

Reading Materials

What happens when you enter a character, letter, or number on a computer? Regardless of the program you use to enter the information, the computer has to convert the keystrokes into information that it can process and store. To do this, the computer must first convert your input into binary digits to form binary code.

Binary simply means two. A **binary digit** is a number that uses only two digits (0 or 1). **Binary code** is a pattern of binary digits consisting of ones (1) and zeros (0) that the computer can interpret. A computer uses an on or off memory storage system called a bit. A **bit** of information is a single value of either on or off. The computer reads the information magnetically as either magnetic (on) or nonmagnetic (off). This can be represented in terms of a 1 (on) or 0 (off). A bit of data by itself has very little meaning. Only when that bit of data is arranged in a pattern with other

bits of data will the data represent something. Most modern computing systems arrange bits of data into bytes. One **byte** contains eight bits of data.

One Bit (off)	One Bit (on)	One Byte of Data (8 bits)	Two Bytes of Data (16 bits)
0	1	0110 0110	0110 0110 1010 1100

The pattern of the data in a byte is used to represent all letters, numbers, and symbols read and stored by a computer. You may have heard of a 32-bit processor or 64-bit processor on your computer. A 32-bit processor can read and assemble a 32-bit character pattern. A 64-bit processor can read and assemble a character pattern of up to eight bytes in length or a total of 64 bits of data.

Binary Numbers

The number system you learned in school is called base 10. In a **base-10 number system,** all of the number place values are based on the number 10. That means the numbers 0 through 9 can be held in a single placeholder position. For a number greater than 9, additional placeholders are assembled in a pattern for you to recognize. So, a number such as 249 has a 2 in the hundreds placeholder, 4 in the tens placeholder, and 9 in the ones placeholder. If you add 1 to the number 249 (1 + 249), the ones placeholder runs out of usable digits and the tens placeholder has to be increased. This creates the number 250.

Binary digits can be assembled to create binary numbers in much the same way. The placeholders of a binary number can only hold a 1 or a 0. This means it is a **base-2 number system.** Once the value exceeds 1, a new placeholder must be used. So, in binary number format, the value of zero is simply 0. The value of 1 is simply 1. After that, there are no further digits available to create the number 2, and a new placeholder needs to be used. The result is that the binary number for 2 has two placeholders and is represented as 10 (one-zero, not ten). The binary number placeholder values for one byte of data are:

128   64   32   16   8   4   2   1

To convert a binary number into a base-10 number, multiply the placeholder values by binary digit values. Then, add each of the products to get the total. Take the binary number 0001 0101 and try to figure out what base-10 number it represents.

Binary placeholder values	128	64	32	16	8	4	2	1	
Binary number	× 0	0	0	1	0	1	0	1	
Multiplied by placeholder	0	0	0	16	0	4	0	1	= 16 + 4 + 1 = 21

Binary numbers can be added or subtracted in the same way as Arabic (base-10) numbers when you understand the placeholder values. In this example, notice how the placeholder digit values are added to create the sum. The Arabic equivalent numbers are shown on the right, and the sums are equal.

$$
\begin{array}{rcl}
0100 &=& 4 \\
+\ 0001 &=& +1 \\
\hline
0101 &=& 5
\end{array}
$$

Notice in the next example that the 4 placeholder in both numbers contains a 1. Since a binary number can only be 1 or 0, adding 1 + 1 results in 0 and causes the next higher placeholder to increase by one. However, in this case, one of the binary numbers already has a 1 in the 8 placeholder, so adding another 1 causes another carryover into the 16 placeholder.

In this example, there is another carryover when the 64 placeholder digits are added, resulting in a 1 in the 128 placeholder.

$$
\begin{array}{rcr}
0110\ \ 1100 & = & 108 \\
+\ 0100\ \ 0101 & = & +\ 69 \\
\hline
1011\ \ 0001 & = & 177
\end{array}
$$

The principle of borrowing from a placeholder on the left to subtract applies in binary subtraction:

$$
\begin{array}{rcr}
0100 & = & 4 \\
-\ 0001 & = & -\ 1 \\
\hline
0011 & = & 3
\end{array}
$$

$$
\begin{array}{rcr}
0110\ \ 1100 & = & 108 \\
-\ 0100\ \ 0101 & = & -\ 69 \\
\hline
0001\ \ 0101 & = & 39
\end{array}
$$

To multiply or divide, the computer will actually add or subtract to perform the operation. A computer can add and subtract binary numbers very quickly. The computer has a speed advantage over humans. It can add and subtract numbers thousands of times per second, so the process seems instantaneous.

To complete multiplication, the computer actually performs addition. For example, look at what happens when the user instructs the computer to multiply 50 by 10. The computer performs nine additions:

$$50 + 50 + 50 + 50 + 50 + 50 + 50 + 50 + 50 + 50 = 500$$

The result is the same as if you were to manually calculate 50×10.

To divide, the computer performs subtraction and counts how many times it repeats the subtraction process. If the computer is told to divide 100 by 20, it repeatedly subtracts 20 from 100:

$$100 - 20 - 20 - 20 - 20 - 20 = 0$$

It counts the number of times the subtraction was performed and returns the result, which in this case is 5.

Unicode

Binary numbers are great, but what about all the other characters such as letters and symbols? All computer data are stored in binary form (1 or 0). There are no other options. So, then, how does a computer know the user wants to enter the letter A or the dollar sign symbol ($) using binary digits?

In most modern computers, characters such as letters, numbers, and symbols are stored in a pattern using up to four bytes of data called Unicode. **Unicode** is a system of using one- to four-byte patterns to represent all 1,112,064 characters a computer can read. Unicode uses a binary format to look up the value of the binary data set from a data table and display the correct character. UTF-8 is one of the encoding standards within the Unicode system. Most websites follow this standard.

Data Type

It is important for a computer programmer to write code that tells the computer what type of data the binary digits represent. If the programmer sets the data type to integer, which is a number type, then the computer can use the binary number format to read the integers. If the programmer sets the data type to string, which is a text type, then the computer will use

Unicode to look up the correct character as text. For this reason, computer languages include multiple data types to define the data that is present in a binary data set.

Game Build

The Awesome Game Company has assigned you the task of creating an app to convert numbers into binary format. This project requires you to build the app in HTML 5 format. If the company approves your app, another team will port it to various smartphone platforms.

How to Begin

1. Launch Clickteam Fusion 2.5, and begin a new application.
2. Applying what you have learned, set the frame size to 320 by 480, and name the frame Training Level.
3. Save the file as *LastName*_Binary_POC in your working folder.
4. Display the Training Level frame in the frame editor.
5. If the grid and snap are on, turn them off.
6. Create the game objects shown in **Figure 23-1.** Place them in the locations indicated. The frame should look like **Figure 23-2.**
7. Display the event editor for the Training Level frame.
8. On event line 1, program this pseudocode:
   IF at the start of the frame,
    THEN set the value of the Counter_Attempt object to 25
     AND disable the Button_Calc object.
9. Add a new event line, and program this pseudocode:
   IF the Button_Play object is clicked,
    THEN set the value of the Counter_1 object to 0
     AND set the value of the Counter_2 object to 0
     AND set the value of the Counter_4 object to 0
     AND set the value of the Counter_8 object to 0
     AND set the value of the Counter_16 object to 0
     AND set the value of the Counter_32 object to 0
     AND set the value of the Counter_Calc object to 0
     AND disable the Button_Play object
     AND enable the Button_Calc object.
10. In event line 2, right-click in the cell under the icon for the Counter_Binary object, and click **Set Counter** in the shortcut menu to display the expression editor.
11. In the expression editor, click the **Random range** button. An expression is created with placeholders for minimum and maximum values. Notice the expression is currently invalid. This is because you have not yet entered values in the placeholders.
12. Enter 1 as the minimum number and 31 as the maximum number so the expression reads RRandom(1,31). This will randomly generate numbers between 1 and 31. This will be the number that the player will have to convert to binary.
13. Close the expression editor.

Subroutines

To perform calculations, the game will operate in two different modes. There will be an input mode to allow the player to change the binary digits. The second mode is a calculate mode that computes the binary input and converts it to a number. Clickteam Fusion 2.5 has a function to create groups of events. A group of events can be activated or deactivated from the main game loop. As you learned in Lesson 16, in programming this is called a subroutine or sub. The two modes for this application will be created with groups of events.

Frame Editor

Show Grid

Snap to Grid

Event Editor

Name: _____

Object Type	Name	Starting Value	Location	Size	Format
String	Title	Binary Number Converter	(0, 0)	320 by 35	Center aligned, Arial, bold, 18 pt., red
String	Attempts	Remaining Attempts	(0, 40)	250 by 35	Right aligned, Arial, black oblique, 16 pt., black
String	Correct	Correct	(65, 85)	85 by 32	Left aligned, Arial, bold, 14 pt., black
String	Incorrect	Incorrect	(210, 85)	85 by 32	Left aligned, Arial, bold, 14 pt., black
String	Instruction	Create this number in binary.	(25, 130)	95 by 65	Left aligned, Arial, 14 pt., black
String	Directions	Input Binary Data Here	(0, 205)	320 by 32	Center aligned, Arial, bold, 20 pt., black
String	Digits	32 16 8 4 2 1	(65, 235)	200 by 32	Left aligned, Arial, 14 pt., black Three spaces between 32 and 16, four spaces between all other numbers.
String	Result	Binary Result	(72, 340)	200 by 32	Left aligned, Arial, bold, 20 pt., black
Button	Button_ Play	Play	(225, 145)	75 by 50	
Button	Button_ Reset	Reset Binary Data Input	(72, 300)	180 by 32	
Button	Button_ Calculate	Tap to Calculate Binary	(72, 380)	180 by 32	
Counter	Counter_ Attempt	0	(310, 75)	25 by 40	
Counter	Counter_ Correct	0	(60, 110)	20 by 32	Recolor all numbers green
Counter	Counter_ Incorrect	0	(200, 110)	20 by 32	Recolor all numbers red
Counter	Counter_ Binary	0	(220, 200)	45 by 65	
Counter	Counter_1	0	(252, 290)	18 by 28	
Counter	Counter_2	0	(220, 290)	18 by 28	
Counter	Counter_4	0	(190, 290)	18 by 28	
Counter	Counter_8	0	(160, 290)	18 by 28	
Counter	Counter_16	0	(125, 290)	18 by 28	
Counter	Counter_32	0	(85, 290)	18 by 28	
Counter	Counter_ Calc	0	(182, 480)	40 by 60	

Figure 23-1. These are the objects needed to build the binary app.

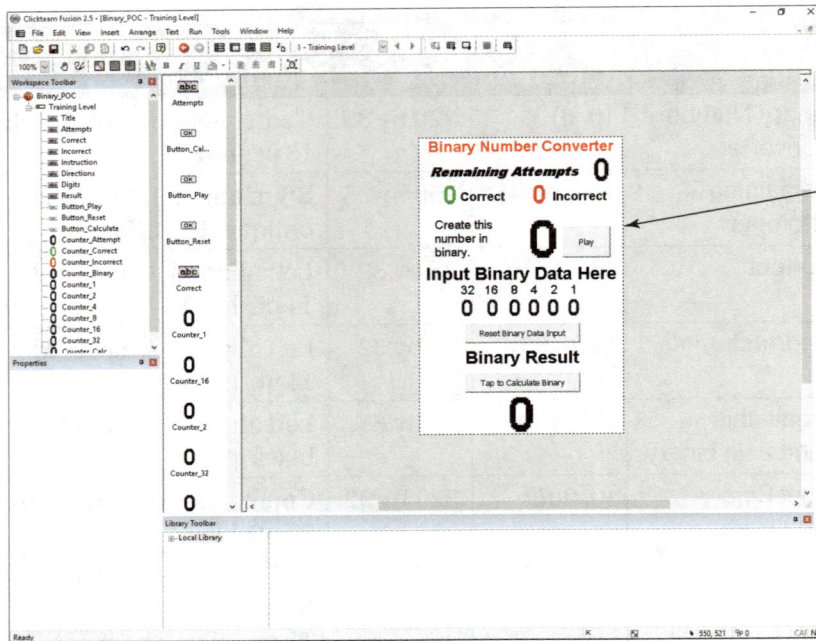

All objects are placed, sized, and formatted

Figure 23-2. The layout of the binary app.

14. Right-click on the number for event line 3, and click **Insert>A group of events** in the shortcut menu. The **Group Events** dialog box is displayed, as shown in **Figure 23-3.**

15. Click in the **Title of the group** text box, and enter Input Mode. This is the name of the sub.

16. Uncheck the **Active when frame starts** check box. In this application, subs will only be activated, or called, when the user enters a command.

17. Leave the **Password protection** and **Confirm password** text boxes empty, and click the **OK** button. The Input Mode group, or sub, begins on event line 3, and event line 4 is indented. All indented lines under a group name line are part of the sub. Also notice there are now two "new condition" lines, one inside the Input Mode sub and one below it that is not indented. The one that is not indented is used to add new events that are *not* part of the sub.

18. Applying what you have learned, create a new sub (group) on event line 5 called Calculate Mode that is inactive when the frame starts.

19. In event line 2, right-click in the cell under the **Special Conditions** icon, and click **Group of events>Activate** in the shortcut menu.

20. In the **Activate** dialog box, select the Input Mode sub, and click the **OK** button.

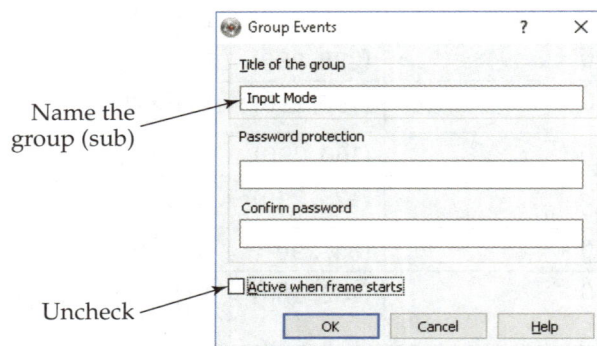

Name the group (sub)

Uncheck

Figure 23-3. In Clickteam Fusion 2.5, a subroutine is created by creating a group of events.

21. Right-click in the same cell, and click **Group of events>Deactivate** in the shortcut menu.
22. In the **Deactivate** dialog box, select the Calculate Mode sub, and click the **OK** button.

Input Mode

When the input mode is active, the user can enter numbers for the conversion. The input mode is controlled by the Input Mode subroutine. This sub needs to have programming added to be functional.

23. Add a new condition in event line 4 within the Input Mode sub. In the **New Condition** dialog box, click the **Special** icon, and click **Group of events>On group activation** in the shortcut menu. Since the event line is within the Input Mode sub, this condition refers to the Input Mode group of events (sub).
24. In event line 4, add an action to set the value of the Counter_Calc object to 0.
25. Add a new condition in event line 5 within the Input Mode sub, and program this pseudocode:
    IF the user left-clicks the Counter_1 object,
        THEN set the value of the Counter_1 object to 1.
26. Applying what you have learned, program the Counter_2 through Counter_32 objects to change to a value of 1 when left-clicked, as shown in **Figure 23-4.**
27. In event line 11 within the Input Mode sub, program this pseudocode:
    IF the Button_Calc object is clicked,
        THEN activate the Calculate Mode sub (group of events).
28. In event line 12 within the Input Mode sub, program this pseudocode:
    IF the Button_Reset object is clicked,
        THEN set the value of the Counter_1 through Counter_32 objects to 0.

Calculate Mode

Once the user taps the **Calculate** button, the application will go into calculate mode. This mode is controlled by the Calculate Mode subroutine. The sub contains the programming needed to add the value from each of the input counters (the Counter_1 through Counter_32 objects) and display the result. To evaluate the binary value input by the user, each counter value must be multiplied by the binary value equal to the position of the binary digit. Remember, the value of each counter will be a binary value of either 1 or 0.

29. In event line 15 within the Calculate Mode sub, program this pseudocode:
    IF on activation of the Calculate Mode sub (group of events),
        THEN disable the Button_Calc object.
30. In event line 15, right-click in the cell under the icon for the Counter_Calc icon, and click **Set Counter** in the shortcut menu to open the expression editor.

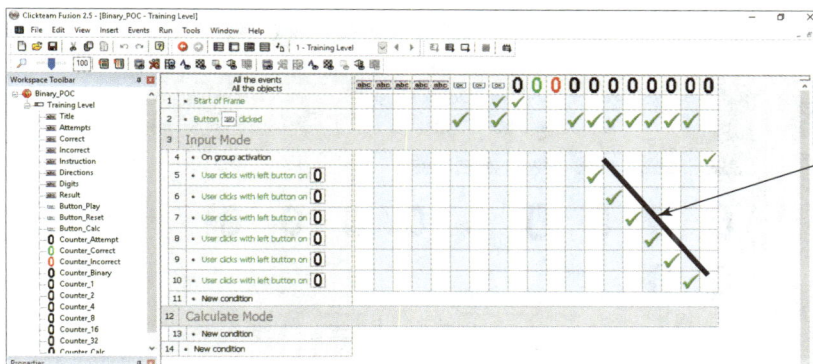

Programming to set counters to 1 when clicked

Goodheart-Willcox Publisher

Figure 23-4. The counters for binary position are programmed to allow the user input.

31. Applying what you have learned, create an expression that obtains the current value of the Counter_32 object. This is the value input by the user for binary position 32.

32. Add a left parenthesis at the beginning of the expression.

33. Add * 32) to the end of the expression so the expression reads (value ("Counter_32")* 32). This expression multiplies the value of the Counter_32 object by the binary position value (32).

34. Add an addition sign at the end of the expression.

35. Continue building the expression to add each counter value, as shown in **Figure 23-5.** Be sure to multiply each value by the correct binary position and to include an addition sign between parenthesis groups to add each binary digit to the others. When done constructing the expression, close the expression editor.

36. Run the frame. Test the functions that have been programmed to this point. Note any bugs. Close the game window when done testing.

Run Frame

Scoring

If the player enters a correct binary equivalent for the displayed number, the number of correct answers needs to be increased by one. If the player enters an incorrect equivalent, the number of incorrect answers needs to be increased by one. In both cases, the number of attempts remaining needs to be decreased by one.

37. In event line 16 within the Calculate Mode sub, program this pseudocode:
   IF the value of the Counter_Calc object is equal to the value of the Counter_Binary object,
      THEN add 1 to the value of the Counter_Correct object
      AND subtract 1 from the value of the Counter_Attempts object
      AND enable the Button_Play object
      AND disable the Button_Calculate object
      AND deactivate the Calculate Mode sub.

38. In event line 17 within the Calculate Mode sub, program this pseudocode:
   IF the value of the Counter_Calc object is not equal to the value of the Counter_Binary object,
      THEN add 1 to the value of the Counter_Incorrect object
      AND subtract 1 from the value of the Counter_Attempts object
      AND enable the Button_Play object
      AND disable the Button_Calculate object
      AND deactivate the Calculate Mode sub.

Build the expression →

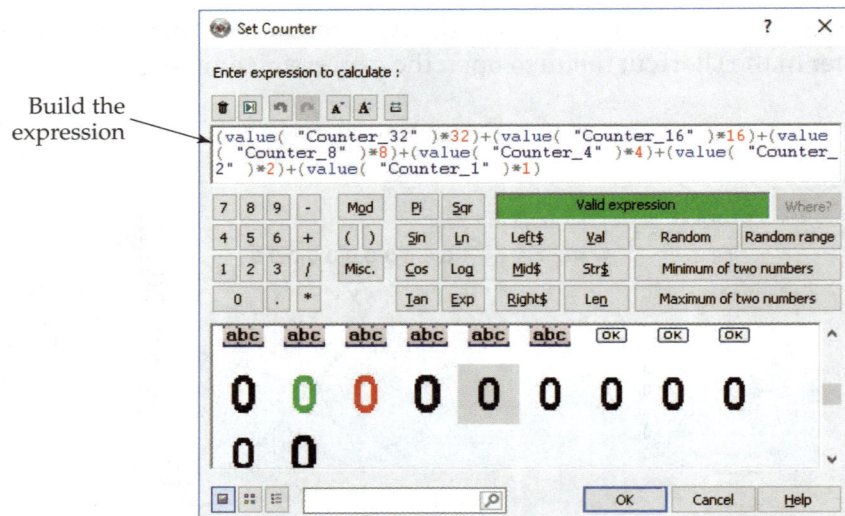

Figure 23-5. The expression obtains the value from each binary position counter, multiplies it by the correct number, and adds all products to find the final answer.

39. In event line 19, which is outside of either sub, program this pseudocode:
   IF the value of the Counter_Correct object is equal to 25,
      THEN go to the next frame.

40. In event line 20, which is outside of either sub, program this pseudocode:
   IF the value of the Counter_Attempt object is equal to 0,
      THEN restart the frame.

41. Move event lines 19 and 20 to before the Input Mode sub to make the programming more elegant.

42. Run the frame. Fully test the app. Note any bugs. Since you are running the frame, getting 25 correct answers or running out of attempts will both end the application. Close the game window when done testing.

Run Frame

Tuning

43. Applying what you have learned, duplicate the Training Level frame, and rename the copy as Level 1. Place the Level 1 frame after the Training Level frame.

44. Modify the Level 1 frame by deleting the Digits string object. This will make the level more difficult by not giving the player the value of each binary digit.

45. Modify the programming for the Level 1 frame by changing the random value generator for the Counter_Binary to select values from 1 to 63. This will bring binary position 32 into play, which is already accounted for in the programming.

46. Add a new frame as the first frame, and design it as a title frame.

47. Include buttons on the Title frame to allow the user to go to the training level or to the first level.

48. Include directions in the Title frame to tell the user how to use the app.

49. Modify the programming on the Level 1 frame to return to the Title frame when the user achieves 25 correct answers or to end the app when out of guesses.

50. Run the application. Fully test all elements of the app. Close the game window when done testing.

51. Debug as needed.

Porting

   If approved, this game will be ported to a smartphone app. Porting means making the program compatible with a particular computer platform. For the approval process, you will port the app to HTML 5 format.

52. Click the **Build and Run** button on the **Run Toolbar**. The **Save HTML5 Project** dialog box is displayed, as shown in **Figure 23-6**.

53. Click in the **Project name:** text box, and enter Binary App.

54. Click the **Browse** button next to the **Project path:** text box, navigate to your working folder, and select it. The HTML5 files will be added to a subfolder in this folder.

55. Click the **OK** button to compile the app. Note: the layout of your app screen may be altered during the compiling process. If this happens, do not worry about trying to correct it.

56. Save the file, and submit all work for grading.

Build and Run

Name the app

Save HTML5 Project	✕
Project name :	BinaryApp
Project path :	C:\Floor_Working	Browse
OK		Cancel

Click to locate a folder in which to save the files

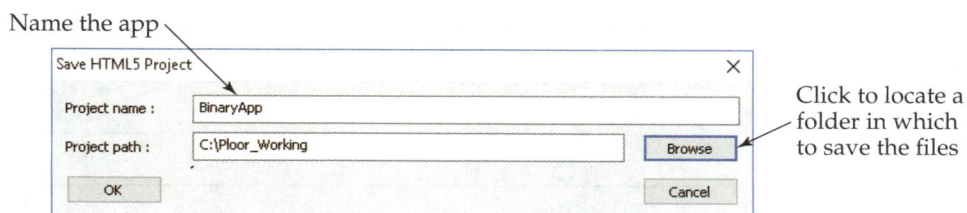

Goodheart-Willcox Publisher

Figure 23-6. Build the project as an HTML 5 app to submit it for approval.

Vocabulary

Write a definition for each of the key terms from this lesson. You will develop a personal glossary of key terms throughout this course.

binary

_____

_____

binary digit

_____

_____

binary code

_____

_____

bit

_____

_____

byte

_____

_____

base-10 number system

_____

_____

base-2 number system

_____

_____

Unicode

_____

_____

Review Questions

Language Arts

1. Describe the advantage a computer has over humans in performing mathematical calculations.

_____

_____

_____

_____

_____

Name: _____

2. Add the following binary numbers.

    0110 0010
    0000 1000
    0001 0010
    0000 0101

    _____
    _____
    _____
    _____
    _____

Mathematics

3. What is the expression in Clickteam Fusion 2.5 for generating a random number between 5 and 15?

    _____
    _____
    _____
    _____
    _____

Applied Technology

4. Write a brief description of how a subroutine is created in Clickteam Fusion 2.5.

    _____
    _____
    _____
    _____
    _____

Language Arts

5. Which data type would be used in programming to store: Programming is fun!

    _____
    _____
    _____
    _____
    _____

Applied Technology

Higher-Order Thinking Strategies

Applied Technology

6. A computer can be programmed to loop a process. A loop will repeat the process over and over for a programmed number of times. Consider the equation 5×35 in terms of how a computer will solve the equation. How will the computer solve this equation, and how many times will the computer have to run the loop to get the correct result?

_____
_____
_____
_____
_____

Social Science

7. Which Arabic number if translated into binary would best match the acronym for _laugh out loud_ used in social media posts and texting? Think of the 1s and 0s as letters to match the acronym.

_____
_____
_____
_____
_____

Applied Technology

8. Speculate why subroutines were used in the build created in this lesson.

_____
_____
_____
_____

Language Arts

9. In your opinion, what impact would there be if websites throughout the world used a different encoding standard than UTF-8?

_____
_____
_____
_____

Science

10. Unlike the solar system that includes Earth, some solar systems include a binary star. Infer from the reading what a binary star solar system would look like.

_____
_____
_____
_____

Office Technology Integration

Using Functions in a Spreadsheet

1. Launch Microsoft Excel or other spreadsheet software, and open the vocabulary spreadsheet you updated in previous lessons.
2. Applying what you have learned, add a new worksheet, and name it Lesson 23.
3. Add each of the vocabulary words and definitions from the Vocabulary section of this lesson.
4. Save the spreadsheet, and then close it.
5. Begin a blank new worksheet, and save the file as *LastName*_BinaryCalculator in your working folder.
6. In cell A1, enter the text Binary Calculator. You will create a utility to convert whole base-10 numbers into binary numbers.
7. Select the cell range A1:M1, and click **Home>Alignment>Merge and Center** on the ribbon.
8. In cell A4, enter the text Input a Whole Number Between 0 and 255.
9. Apply a thick outside border to cell A5 and cell A8.
10. In cell A7, enter the text Binary Number Result.
11. In cell A5, enter the number 254.
12. In cell M3, enter the number 1.
13. In cell L3, create a formula to multiply cell M3 by 2 (=M3*2).
14. Copy cell L3, select the cell range F3:K3, and paste. Cell F3 will have a value of 128 if done correctly.
15. In cell F4, create a formula to divide cell A5 by cell F3 (=A5/F3).
16. In cell G4, create a formula to divide cell F5 by cell G3(=F5/G3).
17. Copy cell G4, and paste into the cell range H4:M4.
18. Select cell F5, and click the **Formulas>Function Library>Insert Function** on the ribbon. The **Insert Function** dialog box is displayed.
19. Click in the **Search for a function:** text box, enter IF, and click the **Go** button. Functions related to "if" are displayed in the list at the bottom of the dialog box.
20. Select the **IF** function from the list, and click the **OK** button. The **Function Arguments** dialog box is displayed, as shown. There are three text boxes that will allow you to create **IF...THEN** events in Excel. The first text box is for the **IF** condition, which in Excel is the logical test. The second text box is for the **THEN** action when the condition is **TRUE**. The third text box is for the **ELSE** action, which occurs when the condition is **FALSE**.

Merge and Center

Thick Outside Borders

fx

Insert Function

IF   THEN   ELSE

Function Arguments		? ✕
IF		
Logical_test	F4>=1	= TRUE
Value_if_true	A5-F3	= 126
Value_if_false	A5	= 254
	= 126	

Checks whether a condition is met, and returns one value if TRUE, and another value if FALSE.

Value_if_false is the value that is returned if Logical_test is FALSE. If omitted, FALSE is returned.

Formula result = 127.984375

Help on this function   OK   Cancel

Goodheart-Willcox Publisher

21. Program this pseudocode in the **Function Arguments** dialog box, and then click the **OK** button:

    IF cell F4 is greater than or equal to 1,

        THEN subtract cell F3 from A5

            ELSE the value of cell A5.

22. Applying what you have learned, program this pseudocode in cell G5:

    IF cell G4 is greater than or equal to 1,

        THEN subtract G3 from F5

            ELSE the value of cell F5.

23. Copy and paste the formula from cell G5 to the cell range H5 to M5.

24. In cell F6, program this pseudocode:

    IF cell F4 is greater than or equal to 1,

        THEN 1

        ELSE 0.

25. Copy the formula in cell F6 to the cell range G6:M6.

26. Select in cell A8, and display the **Insert Function** dialog box.

27. Search for join text together.

28. Select the **CONCATENATE** function from the list of results, and click the **OK** button. To *concatenate* is to join together. This function takes the values or text from multiple cells and combines them into a single cell as a single text string.

29. In the **Function Arguments** dialog box, click in the **Text 1** text box, and enter F6 or simply click cell F6 in the spreadsheet.

30. Click in the **Text 2** text box. Notice that the **Text 3** text box appears. Enter G6 in the **Text 2** text box.

31. Continue entering cells H6 to M6 in each of the text boxes, and then click the **OK** button to create the formula. Make sure you enter the cells in alphabetical order.

32. Test the programming by entering values in cell A5 and check to see if the binary value is correct.

33. On Sheet 2, use your knowledge of programming and binary to create a utility that will accept binary input values and calculate the base-10 number.

34. Submit your work for grading.

Project Management

Learning Objectives

After completing this lesson, you will be able to:

- explain team integration through task organization.
- illustrate the stages in the three-stage production process.
- organize tasks using a Gantt chart.

Situation

The Awesome Game Company believes your cross-training on different skills has gone very well. The next step in the management-training program is to understand the workflow of how individual tasks are completed to make a game. This is the last section of training before you will be evaluated on your potential to lead a team. Continue doing great work.

Reading Materials

A video game build is a complex project that requires the balancing of time, tasks, and tender (money). The **project** is a temporary activity having defined beginning and ending points. By definition, the project has to be bound by time. There are many reasons why a game project must end on time.

To make sure all activities are completed by the deadline, each part of the project is broken down into individual tasks. A **task** is a single piece of work. The person or specialist who is best able to perform a task is given the task assignment. The **task assignment** is a small portion of the project defined by the outcome, or what that portion of the project is supposed to do.

Each project is also assigned a budget. A **budget** is a definition of how much money can be spent and on what it will be spent. The money in the budget must be allocated by task. Some tasks cost more money than others. Each task must be budgeted the correct amount of money for completion.

The **project manager** is in charge of making sure that all tasks are completed on time without going over budget. A lot of planning is needed to achieve this. The project manager needs to make sure everyone is always working on the proper part of the project. A common planning tool used in project management is the Gantt chart. A **Gantt chart** is a scheduling table displaying all tasks for the project, the time needed for each task, and which tasks are dependent on other tasks. Typically,

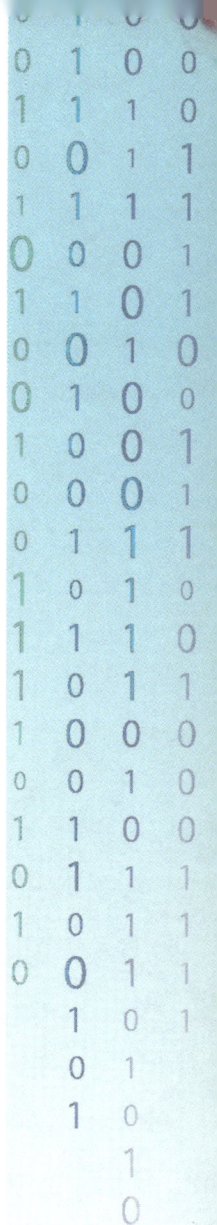

the tasks are displayed on the left, and the timeline for the project is displayed across the top, as shown in **Figure 24-1.**

The idea behind the Gantt chart is to visually see what needs to be done and to organize the workflow so tasks will be done when the next person needs the work. Imagine if you were designing a game and the artwork was not done. You cannot finish your job because the workflow for the artwork is behind schedule. You have nothing to do but wait for the assets to come from the art department. This also makes you behind, and it makes the next person down the line from you behind on delivery of the project. The Gantt chart helps break down the project into tasks so each task can be prioritized and assigned a deadline. By organizing tasks, each member of the team can see and understand the key function he or she plays on the team. This helps integrate each team member into a functioning team.

Look at the Gantt chart in **Figure 24-2.** This is a chart for a two-person game project. One person is the artist and the other the designer. On day 1, the artist works on the concept art, while the designer works on the title page. On day 2, the artist completes the model sheets, while the designer completes the score page. By day 3, the artist is making assets, while the designer is building the game level. Of course, at this point the final game assets are not completed, so the designer simply uses test objects that will be replaced with the correct sprites when the artist is finished. By day 5, the designer is getting final art from the artist and is able to put that into the game. Each person has a job to do and it gets done following the task timelines shown. By day 10, the final result is a game ready to show the customer in final form with artistic packaging.

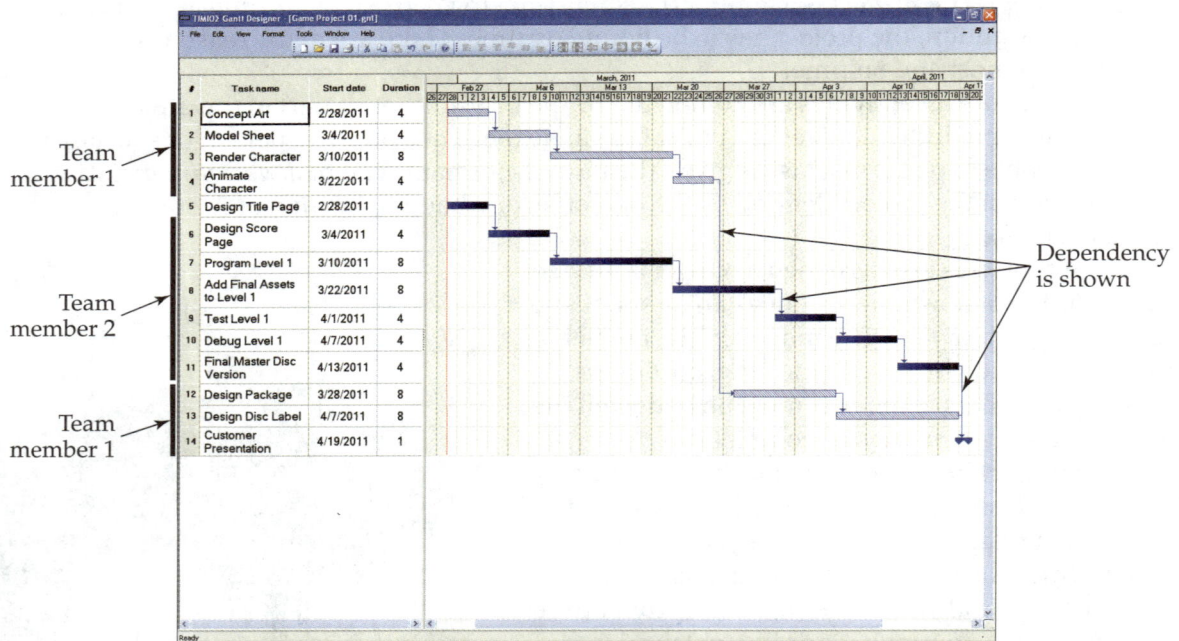

Goodheart-Willcox Publisher

Figure 24-1. This is a typical Gantt chart created in dedicated Gantt-chart software.

Task	Timeline									
	Day 1	Day 2	Day 3	Day 4	Day 5	Day 6	Day 7	Day 8	Day 9	Day 10
Concept Art	■									
Model Sheet		■								
Render Character			■	■						
Animate Character					■					
Design Title Page	■									
Design Score Page		■								
Program Level 1			■	■						
Add Final Assets to Level 1					■	■				
Test Level 1							■			
Debug Level 1								■		
Final Master Disc Version									■	
Design Package						■	■			
Design Disc Label								■	■	
Customer Presentation										■

Goodheart-Willcox Publisher

Figure 24-2. This Gantt chart shows the tasks for a two-person game project. Notice how many tasks must occur at the same time.

By organizing and managing tasks, the project can be completed on time and on budget. Proper project management will allow the project to move smoothly through the three-stage production process. The ***three-stage production process*** is concept, construction, and completion (tuning). Tasks are set up so ideas get worked out, the game is built, and the bugs are worked out. Each stage yields a new iteration, or version, of the game that is improved from previous iterations.

Plan Build

You have been assigned the task of creating a practice Gantt chart for use in a project. The company has assigned you a hypothetical project of managing a race pit crew. A pit crew must quickly complete its tasks as a team to get the driver back out in the race as quickly as possible.

1. Research the role of a NASCAR pit crew.
2. Create a list of tasks the pit crew needs to complete during a pit stop.
3. Use the table in **Figure 24-3** to plan the tasks and timeline.
4. Using spreadsheet software like Microsoft Excel or dedicated Gantt chart–creation software, create a Gantt chart for a 20-second pit stop.
5. Save your work, and submit it for grading.

Task	Timeline																			
	1	2	3	4	5	6	7	8	9	10	11	12	13	14	15	16	17	18	19	20

Goodheart-Willcox Publisher

Figure 24-3. Use this planning table to list the tasks to complete the project and how much time is required for each task.

Name:_____

Vocabulary

Write a definition for each of the key terms from this lesson. You will develop a personal glossary of key terms throughout this course.

project

_____

_____

task

_____

_____

task assignment

_____

_____

budget

_____

_____

project manager

_____

_____

Gantt chart

_____

_____

three-stage production process

_____

_____

Office Technology Integration

Creating a Spreadsheet Gantt Chart

1. Launch Microsoft Excel or other spreadsheet software, and open the vocabulary spreadsheet you updated in previous lessons.
2. Applying what you have learned, add a new worksheet, and name it Lesson 24.
3. Add each of the vocabulary words and definitions from the Vocabulary section of this lesson.
4. Save the spreadsheet, and then close it.
5. Launch Microsoft Excel.
6. On the startup screen, click in the search bar at the top, enter Gantt, and click the **Start searching** button (magnifying glass). Templates for creating a Gantt chart are displayed, as shown.

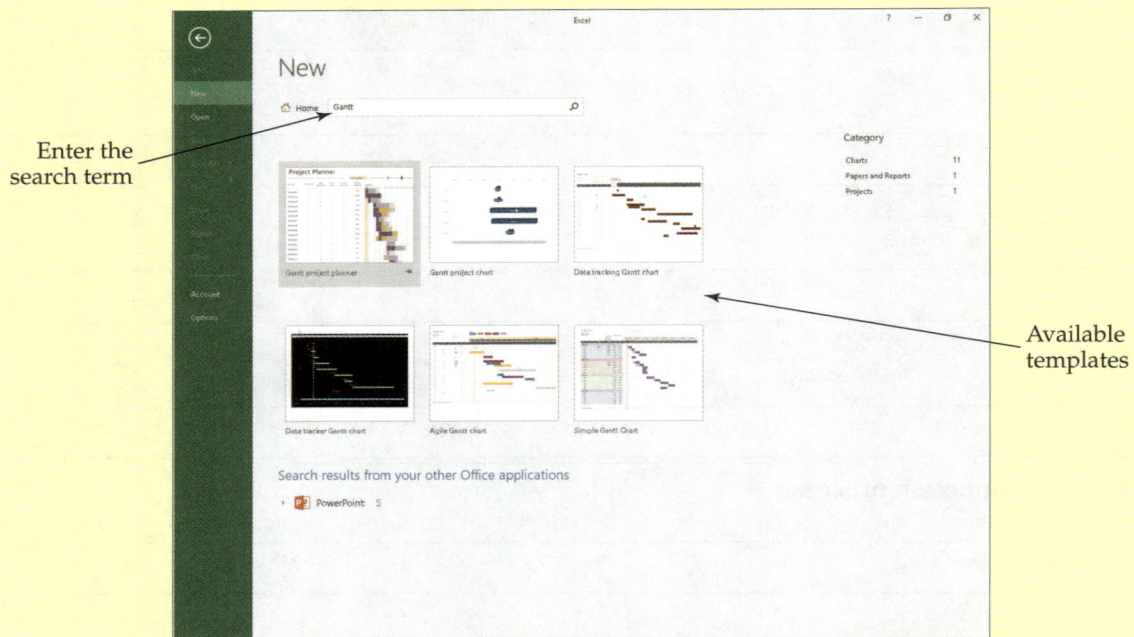

Enter the search term

Available templates

Goodheart-Willcox Publisher

7. Single-click on a template to see a larger preview and a description of the template. Investigate each template.
8. Select a Gantt chart template of your choice, and begin a new spreadsheet based on that template.
9. Save the file as *LastName_*Gantt in your working folder.
10. Using the information you gathered in this lesson, customize the Gantt chart template to match your data.
11. Save your work, and submit it for grading.

Concept Documents

Learning Objectives

After completing this lesson, you will be able to:

- explain project management of a game concept.
- create sprites using concept art.
- apply physics to a game project.
- program a drawing function that uses the mouse.

Situation

The Awesome Game Company conducted a contest on its website to generate new game ideas. In order to take the winning idea and make a game, you are responsible for creating the concept documents. Before creating these documents, you must learn what they are and how they are used.

Reading Materials

Design documents are used to record all decisions for the game development. The first stage of development is the concept stage. In this stage, all ideas about what the game will look like after it is built are recorded in the *concept documents,* or *pitch documents.*

If you have a great idea for a game, you need to be able to tell someone about it! The first document you create is the high-concept document. The *high-concept document* is the selling tool to get the company to agree to build your game. This is usually a letter that answers the five essential questions. The answers to the *five essential questions* form the foundation of the concept for the game:

- What is the game going to be about? (basic idea)
- Who is going to play this game? (audience, age, target market, desired ESRB rating)
- Who is the main character going to be in the game? (player role, character type)
- What will the player do in the game? (victory condition, obstacles, opponents)
- What will the world look like in the game? (settings, levels, backgrounds, perspective)

The high-concept document is supposed to help you get your game idea across to the decision-makers and make them want to hear more about your idea.

If the company likes the idea, it will have you come in and tell more about it. That is when you need a game-treatment document. This is part of your presentation. The *game-treatment document*

includes information on the concept, story outline or storyboard, and some drawings of the characters and game world. It is important to discuss in this document any unique selling point for your game.

A *unique selling point (USP)* is any feature that would make the game different from all other games. Think about a pitch for the game *Guitar Hero.* Before *Guitar Hero,* no other games used a guitar as the controller. Imagine walking into a meeting to pitch *Guitar Hero* with a guitar controller and showing everyone how different the gameplay would be. The guitar controller made the game unique, so the USP for *Guitar Hero* is the user interface.

After your game is approved, you still need to record all other decisions that will be made about the game. Even if you are making a small game by yourself, it is still a good practice to record your ideas and decisions so you do not forget what you are doing.

Game Build

The Awesome Game Company has received a new game idea from a contest it conducted on its website. The contest winner wants to see a game that allows the player to kick a ball and score a goal. But, this is not just any old soccer game. This game concept includes something unique. The game would be a platform-style game where the ball must be bounced around and off of obstacles to find the goal. Refer to the concept described in **Figure 25-1.** Since you have done such a great job and demonstrated you are able to lead a project, you have the

Online Contest Concept	
What is the game going to be about?	The game is about kicking a soccer ball through a maze of platforms. The player will have the ability to draw sloping lines between platforms to get the ball to fall properly. Once the player kicks the ball, it has to fall down to reach the goal by bouncing on platforms, lines, or moving objects inside the maze. This concept combines elements of soccer, basketball, billiards, and platform games.
Who is going to play this game?	Boys and girls age 5 to 15 would play this game. It would have to be rated E for Everyone, but could have some cool explosions or other effects if the audience was older.
Who is the main character going to be in the game?	The player avatar is a soccer player or might just be the ball. The player can choose which character will kick the ball on each level. Each character will have different skills or power to kick and the player must match the skills to the challenge.
What will the player do in the game?	The player must connect the platforms so the ball falls through the maze to reach the goal.
What will the world look like in the game?	The game is in 2D platform (side) view. The ball starts at the top and falls to the bottom. In each level, the maze design would change. Some platforms slant downward to speed up the ball and others slope upward to slow it down. Some springs or moving objects present obstacles or can be used by the player to bounce the ball.

Goodheart-Willcox Publisher

Figure 25-1. The five essential questions form the foundation for the concept of the game.

chance to lead this project to see if the game can work. Build the proof of concept to make sure the technology can be used for this type of gameplay.

How to Begin

1. Launch Clickteam Fusion 2.5, begin a new application, and save the file as *LastName_ Skill Shot Soccer POC* in your working folder.
2. Name the first frame Level 1.
3. Display the Level 1 frame in the frame editor.
4. Applying what you have learned, set up and display a grid that is 32 pixels by 32 pixels and activate snap.
5. Add the game objects described in the concept art document shown in **Figure 25-2**.
6. Insert a Physics Engine object anywhere outside the visible play area.
7. Select the Ground object, and use the **Properties** toolbar to set the Obstacle Type property to Platform.
8. Select the Ball object, and click the **Movement** tab in the **Properties** toolbar.
9. Change the Type property to Physics - Bouncing Ball Movement.
10. Set the Initial direction property to only direction 0 (right).

Frame Editor

Grid Setup

Movement

Concept Art						
Object Type	Object Name	Canvas Size	Description	Design	Position	Hotspot
Active	Pixel_ Dot	4 by 4	Fill entire canvas with red		(–64, 100)	Centered
Active	Ball	32 by 32	Black-filled circle with white patches		(47, 111)	Center of gravity
Active	Goal	64 by 32	Green-filled rectangle		(64, 448)	Centered
Backdrop	Ground	32 by 32	Blue-filled rectangle		(0, 128) and (0, 432)	Centered
Button	Button_ Reset	64 by 32	Add the display text Reset	 Reset	(192, 32)	
Button	Button_ Exit	64 by 32	Add the display text Exit	 Exit	(384, 32)	
Button	Button_ Start	64 by 32	Add the display text Start	 Start	(288, 32)	
Score	Score	24 by 32			(600, 64)	
Lives	Lives				(32, 32)	

Goodheart-Willcox Publisher

Figure 25-2. These are the game objects needed to build the game.

11. Set the Initial speed property to 0.

12. Set the Elasticity property to 50. Leave all other properties at the default settings.

13. Applying what you have learned, duplicate each of the Ground objects in one row and six columns, as shown in **Figure 25-3.**

Drawing Function

To make this game work, programming needs to be added so the player can draw lines to connect platforms (Ground objects) to reach the Goal object. The red dot (Pixel_Dot object) will be the pixel for creating the line. As the player drags the cursor, instances of the dot will be added, making a red line. This will be the path for the ball to follow. The physics engine will control how the ball moves.

14. Display the event editor for the Level 1 frame.

[Event Editor]

15. Add a new event, and in the **New Condition** dialog box, click **The mouse pointer and keyboard** icon, and click **The mouse>Repeat while mouse-key is pressed** in the shortcut menu. In the dialog box that is displayed, click the **Left button** radio button, and click the **OK** button to create the condition.

16. Applying what you have learned, add an action to create a new Pixel_Dot object at location (–100, –100). This will generate a new pixel outside of the visible play area, but additional actions are needed to correctly place the pixel at the location of the mouse.

17. Applying what you have learned, add a new action to set the X coordinate of the Pixel_Dot object to the X coordinate of the cursor, as shown in **Figure 25-4.**

18. Add a second action to set the Y coordinate of the Pixel_Dot object to the Y coordinate of the cursor.

[Run Frame]

19. Run the frame. Test if you can draw red lines on the frame. Notice the spacing of the pixels changes based on how quickly the mouse is moved. Close the game window when done testing.

Reducing Object Count

Currently, the computer has to track each active object on the screen. As you draw, you are placing hundreds of new objects for the computer to track. To reduce the load of

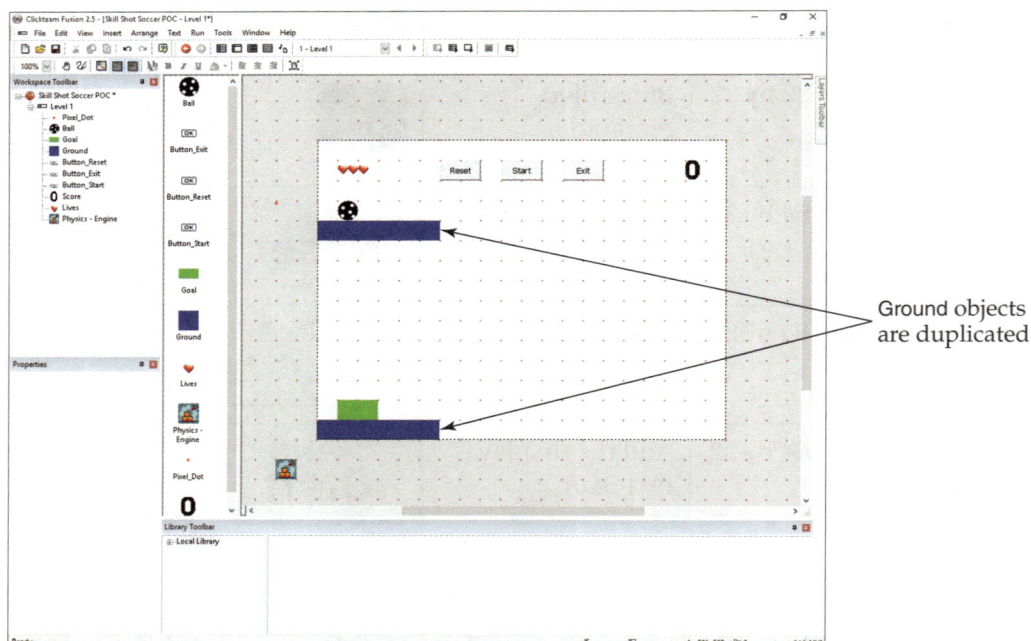

Ground objects are duplicated

Goodheart-Willcox Publisher

Figure 25-3. Create two platforms using the Ground objects.

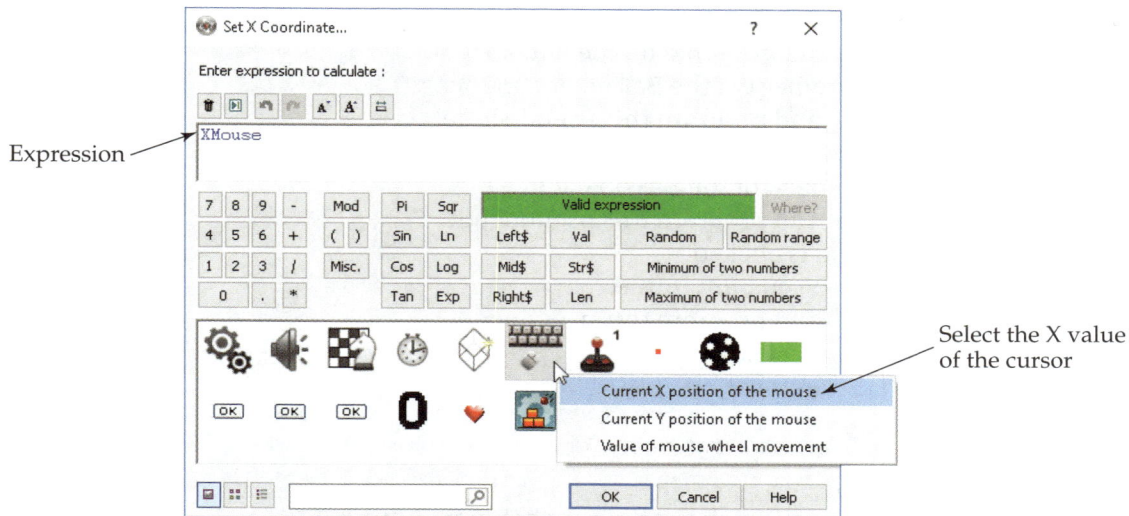

Expression

Select the X value
of the cursor

Goodheart-Willcox Publisher

Figure 25-4. An expression is used to set the X coordinate of the Pixel_Dot object to the X coordinate of the current cursor location.

the processor, any Pixel_Dot object can be pasted into the background. Once objects are pasted into the background image, the game engine will not need to track those objects. The converted objects can also serve as obstacles in the game. Because the Pixel_Dot objects do not move after being placed into the scene, pasting into the background is a great solution for this game.

20. In event line 1, right-click in the cell under the icon for the Pixel_Dot object, and click **Animation>Paste image into background** in the shortcut menu. The **Paste Image into Background** dialog box is displayed, as shown in **Figure 25-5.**
21. Click the **Obstacle** radio button.
22. Click the **OK** button. This makes the object part of the background and an obstacle that other objects can interact with later.

User Interface

The three buttons need to be programmed to make the game function. Also, you should have noticed in your testing that the ball drops off the screen. Programming needs to be added to tell the ball to stop when it hits the backdrop.

23. Add a new event line, and program this pseudocode:
      IF the Ball object collides with the backdrop,
          THEN stop the movement of the Ball object.

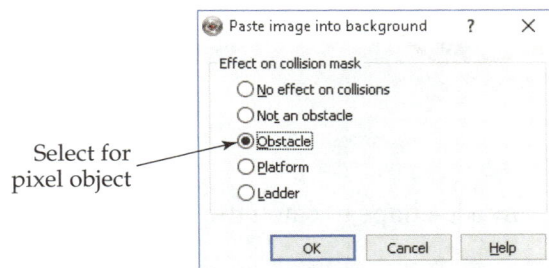

Select for
pixel object

Goodheart-Willcox Publisher

Figure 25-5. An object can be pasted into the background as an obstacle.

24. Add a new event line, and program this pseudocode:
      IF the Ball object exits the game on the left or right,
         THEN the movement of the Ball object bounces.
25. Add a new event line, and program this pseudocode:
      IF the **Start** button is clicked,
         THEN set the speed of the Ball object to 20.
26. Add a new event line, and program this pseudocode:
      IF the **Reset** button is clicked,
         THEN restart the current frame.
27. Add a new event line, and program this pseudocode:
      IF the **Exit** button is clicked,
         THEN end the application.

Testing

28. Run the frame.
29. Drawing a big U-shape to catch the ball, as shown in **Figure 25-6**.
30. Click the **Start** button to "kick" the ball. The ball should move forward, fall down, bounce around in the U, and eventually stop.
31. Click below the ball, and drag to draw another line. Notice that the drawing mechanism is still functioning and can be used to move the ball. This may present some interesting gameplay options!
32. Click the **Reset** button. The line should be removed and the ball placed back in the original position.
33. Close the game window, and debug any errors.

Run Frame

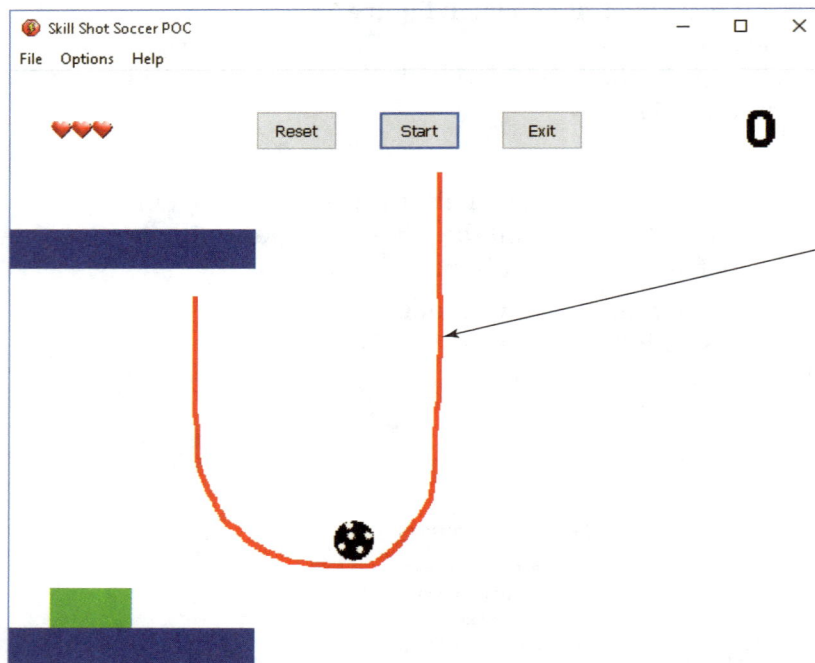

Goodheart-Willcox Publisher

Figure 25-6. For testing, draw a U-shape to catch the ball.

Victory Condition

Each time the player is able to complete the maze by hitting the goal with the ball, points need to be added to the player's score. However, if the player sends the ball off the top or bottom of the frame, a life should be removed. Also, the player needs to be moved to the next level when the goal is reached.

34. Add a new event line, and program this pseudocode:
    IF the Ball object collides with the Goal object,
       THEN add 1 to the player 1 score
          AND move to the next frame.
35. Add a new event line, and program this pseudocode:
    IF the Ball object leaves the play area on the top or bottom,
       THEN remove one life from player 1.
36. Add a new event line, and program this pseudocode:
    IF the number of lives for player 1 equals 0,
       THEN end the application.
37. Applying what you have learned, create programming modules as appropriate to make the programming elegant.

Completion of Concept

38. Display the Level 1 frame in the frame editor.
39. Create additional platforms with the Ground object to create a maze. An example is shown in **Figure 25-7.**
40. Copy the Level 1 frame, and name it Level 2.
41. Display the Level 2 frame in the frame editor, and change the location of the platforms and the goal.
42. Create a basic title page with instructions on how to play the game.

Frame Editor

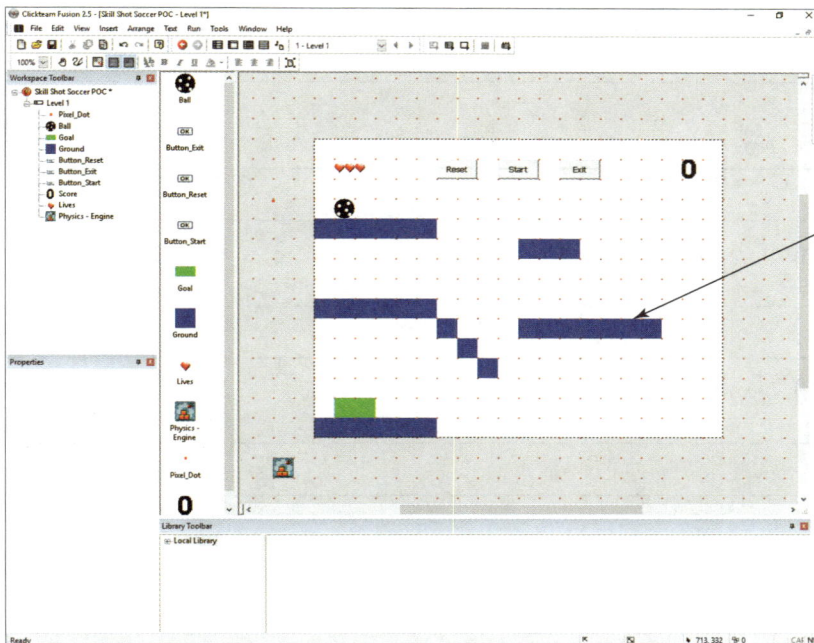

Create a maze with Ground objects

Goodheart-Willcox Publisher

Figure 25-7. The player must draw lines to guide the ball through the maze and to the goal.

Run Application

43. Run the application. Fully test the game. Close the game window when done testing.
44. Debug as needed.

Going Beyond

The Level 2 frame can be made more challenging. Try adding these elements to increase the difficulty and to add interest to the gameplay.

45. Create a system that will be able to kick the ball and apply different initial speed or direction to the ball. Refer to the physics-based game created in Lesson 21 for ideas.
46. Add additional objects that will change the physics properties of the ball when the ball contacts them.
47. Save your work, and submit it for grading.

Vocabulary

Write a definition for each of the key terms from this lesson. You will develop a personal glossary of key terms throughout this course.

concept document

_____

_____

pitch document

_____

_____

high-concept document

_____

_____

five essential questions

_____

_____

game-treatment document

_____

_____

unique selling point (USP)

_____

_____

Name: _____

Review Questions

1. Research games that require special controllers, such as Guitar Hero. Identify aspects of using the controller that may limit or prevent some users from playing the game.

_____

_____

_____

Social Science

2. The grid used in this game build is 32 by 32. If an object is 32 pixels high and 152 pixels wide, how many grid squares will the object occupy?

_____

_____

_____

Mathematics

3. Why is it beneficial for the active objects used to draw the line be replaced with as background images?

_____

_____

_____

Applied Technology

4. Select one of your favorite games, and write a brief description to answer the essential question: what will the player do in the game?

_____

_____

_____

Language Arts

5. How is real-world physics simulated in this game?

_____

_____

_____

Science

Higher-Order Thinking Strategies

6. Identify the unique selling point for one of your favorite games. Explain what technology (software, graphics, hardware, etc.) is used in the USP.

_____

_____

_____

Applied Technology

Mathematics

7. If the cursor is moved from the point (34,125) to (231,173), what is the linear distance moved? Hint: think of the coordinates as opposite corners of a rectangle, then split the rectangle into two right triangles and solve for the length of the hypotenuse.

_____

_____

_____

_____

Social Science

8. The age range for this game is 5 to 15. List several things that must be considered related to content for this wide range of ages.

_____

_____

_____

_____

Language Arts

9. In your own words, describe an application in one of your favorite games where pasting objects into the background would be an appropriate design technique to use.

_____

_____

_____

_____

Mathematics

10. The computer will place a Pixel_Dot object each time the main game loop repeats. Assume that it takes the computer .002 seconds to read the game loop programming. How many Pixel_Dot objects will the computer be able to place in one second? Show your work.

_____

_____

_____

_____

Office Technology Integration

Creating a Word Processor Letter

1. Launch Microsoft Excel or other spreadsheet software, and open the vocabulary spreadsheet you updated in previous lessons.
2. Applying what you have learned, add a new worksheet, and name it Lesson 25.
3. Add each of the vocabulary words and definitions from the Vocabulary section of this lesson.
4. Save the spreadsheet, and then close it.
5. Launch Microsoft Word.
6. On the startup screen, click in the search bar at the top, enter business letter, and click the **Start searching** button (magnifying glass). Templates for creating a business letter are displayed, as shown.

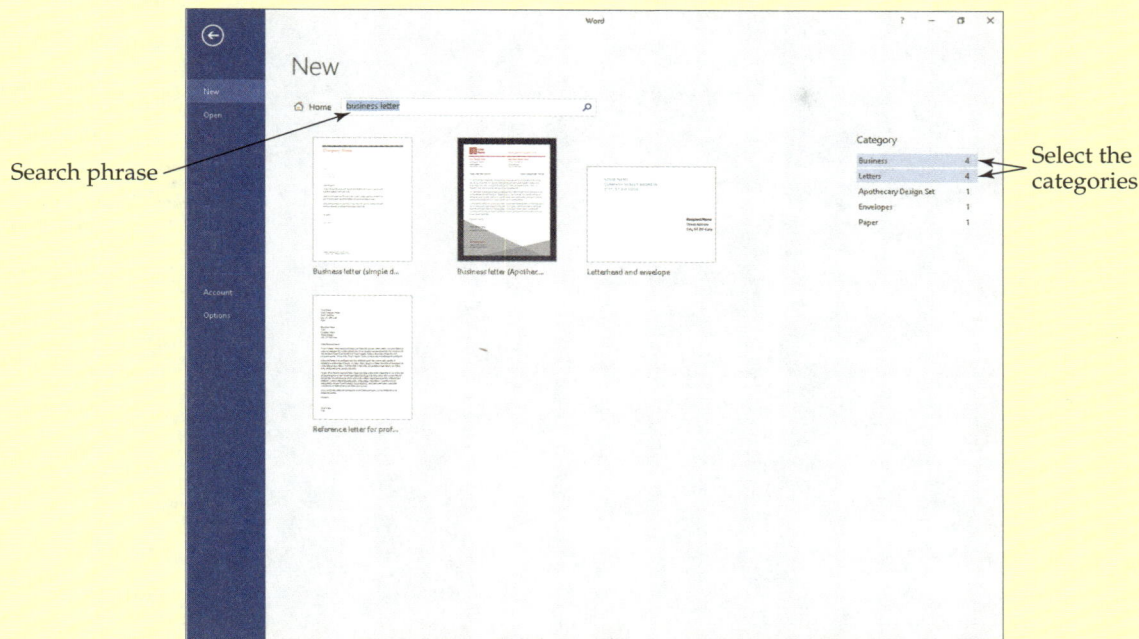

Search phrase

Select the categories

Goodheart-Willcox Publisher

7. Use the categories to filter the list.
8. Select a template you feel would be appropriate to create a business letter for a high-concept document, and begin a new document based on that template.
9. Address the letter to:
Awesome Game Company
1234 Five Street
Digital, Florida 35999
10. If the template includes phone numbers, use (555) 321-0987 as the phone number and (555) 321-7890 as the fax number for the Awesome Game Company.
11. Enter your name, and use Future Game Designer as your title.
12. Use your school address and phone number as your company address.
13. The recipient of the letter is the Creative Director, and use your instructor's name.
14. In the body of the letter, write an exciting letter to the Creative Director about the game concept created in this lesson to persuade the company to let you lead a team to develop the game into a sellable game.

15. Address each one of the five essential questions for the game in your write-up. Refer to **Figure 25-1,** but restate each answer in your own words.
16. Save the letter as *LastName*_High Concept Document in your working folder.
17. If a printer is available, print and sign your letter.
18. Submit your work for grading.

Construction Documents

Learning Objectives

After completing this lesson, you will be able to:

- complete world design document sketches.

- construct rules for a game concept.

- synthesize core mechanics programming to fit the rules.

- develop an original game concept according to the needs of a customer.

Situation

The Awesome Game Company management has reviewed the proof of concept game you built in Lesson 25 and thinks it will be perfect for a customer. The Hi-Flyer Rubber Ball Company (HFRBC) has been looking for a game to put on its website. When the Awesome Game Company sales staff pitched your proof of concept as an example, HFRBC loved it. Before you get started building the game, you must create a set of design documents for the creative director to review and approve. Once approved, this is your chance to wow everyone with your talents.

Reading Materials

To start the construction phase, draft the governing game design document. The *governing game design document* is a collection of the different documents used to display information needed for each designer, programmer, or artist working on the project. In most cases, these are referred to as the *design documents, d-docs,* or just "the documents." **Figure 26-1** shows design documents commonly used in the game industry.

The design documents contain the critical information needed for all aspects of the game build. They contain all decisions made related to the game. This information is recorded in the documents, and the documents are distributed to all team members.

With a game approved by management, it is time to get started getting the concept refined from the basic idea to exactly what the game will look like when it is finished. This is the beginning of

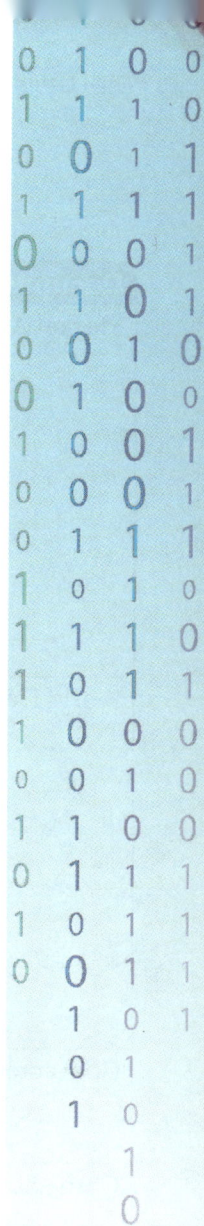

Document Name	Topics	Description
Market Analysis	Concept	Answers the five essential questions.
	Game Overview	Brief synopsis of the game action and how the protagonist will move from the beginning to the end of the story.
	Game Characteristics	A listing of the major element and features, such as worlds, levels, mood, etc.
	Target Market	Demographics on the age, income, maturity, etc., of the gamers. Additionally, a description of the competitors, USPs, and potential popularity of the game, genre, and theme are included.
	Gaming Platform	On what platform is the game built to play: Windows, Mac, Playstation, Xbox, Nintendo, iPhone, Android, or other platform?
World Design	Color Pallette	Colors used by all artists throughout the game to create the same mood and feel.
	Scene Drawings	Drawings of scenes from the game with mood, lighting, and contrast noted.
	Scene Notations	Background sounds needed/used and light direction, source, and intensity.
	Storyboard	Structure of the plot within the game showing as linear, mission based, nonlinear (sandbox), hub and spoke, etc.
	Game Controls	User interface, menu systems, in-game information, displays, health/skill database, and other game controls are listed.
Character Design	Concept Art	Basic sketches of characters, major objects.
	Model Sheets	Formal sketches of models, movements, facial expressions, and accessories.
Game Script	Decision Tree or Flowchart	Break down the storyline into the decisions and paths a player will take through the game. Levels, skills, and objectives for the player at each point in the story are shown.
	Game Mechanics	How the rules of the game will be applied.
	Game Physics	Gravity, speed, interactions, collision, etc., are defined and set for the game world.
	Animation Sets	Animations and player/nonplayer movements. For character movements, the user interface is indicated.
	Narrative Script	Narrations, voiceovers, and cut scenes.
Character Script	Player Movement	User interface controls that activate each character animation and movement. Nonplayer character (NPC) interactions are set. Active object list is created and interactions are set.
	Player Statistics	Database of attributes, skills, weapons, and health of player character. Checkpoints, storage, and restarting data for selected player are set.
Technical Design	Program Design	Game engine, physics engine, artificial intelligence (AI), etc.
	Poly Rendering	Game map controls and object draw and rendering controls.

Goodheart-Willcox Publisher

Figure 26-1. While there is not a standard set of documents included in the governing game design document, the documents described here are commonly included.

the construction or elaboration stage of production. All decisions are recorded in the design documents. Also, before making a decision, refer to the design documents to see what related information has already been recorded.

It is important to note that there is no standard set of documents required to build a game. Each project may have unique documents that best fit the decisions needed for that game build.

Game Build

The Hi-Flyer Rubber Ball Company wants to see a game with ten levels and lots of really cool obstacles, everything from springs to spinning hazards, vertical walls, and whatever else you can think of to keep the ball moving around to get to the goal. One key feature of the Hi-Flyer rubber ball is that it can bounce very high. Additionally, the ball is not a soccer ball. It is a yellow ball with green stripes and says Hi-Flyer on it, as shown in **Figure 26-2.** You need to modify the proof of concept game to better represent the product the customer manufactures.

How to Begin

1. Brainstorm ideas on how to modify the Skill Shot Soccer proof of concept game to meet the requirements of the customer.
2. Complete a set of four world design sketches to show levels 1, 4, 7, and 10. Use the templates provided on the next pages. Include sketches of the obstacles and objectives that each level will have. Each level should look different and require more skill to advance.
3. Complete a game script document to list rules and how they will be implemented by the core mechanics.
4. Turn in the world design and game script documents for approval before beginning the game build.

Game Design

5. Launch Clickteam Fusion 2.5, and open the *LastName*_Skill Shot Soccer POC file saved in Lesson 25.

Figure 26-2. The artwork created in the proof of concept game in Lesson 25 will need to be modified to match the Hi-Flyer ball manufactured by the customer.

6. Save the file as *LastName*_Hi-Flyer_Alpha in the folder specified by your instructor.
7. Save your work often as you construct the game. You may find it helpful to save several iterations, such as Hi-Flyer_Alpha1, Hi-Flyer_Alpha2, and so on. This will allow you to test programming on an iteration of the game and work out the problems without damaging any of the existing and functional programming.
8. Using your world design documents as a guide, create the game assets needed to construct all levels of the game.
9. Using your world design documents as a guide, create a series of three levels.
10. Using your game script documents as a guide, program the objects to react as set by the core mechanics of the game.
11. Save the final project as *LastName*_Hi-Flyer_Beta, and submit it for grading.

Office Technology Integration

Creating a Slideshow Sales Pitch

1. Launch Microsoft PowerPoint, and begin a new blank presentation.
2. Design and create an introduction slide to describe the game you are pitching.
3. Include two slides for each of the world design sketches you created in this lesson.
4. The first slide for a world design sketch should have the name or level as the title of the slide along with a bulleted list for the description of objects.
5. The second slide for a world design sketch should include a scan of the sketch or a recreation of the sketch using shapes, objects, and images available in PowerPoint.
6. Include a slide showing a design for a title frame for the game.
7. Include a slide showing a design for a winner frame for the game.
8. Include a transition for all slides (**Transitions>Transition to This Slide**).
9. Apply a theme to all slides (**Design>Themes**), as shown.

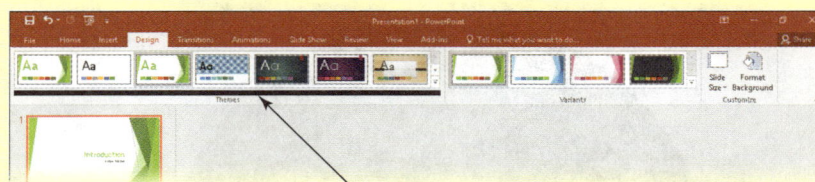

Select a theme to apply

10. Save the file as *LastName*_World Design in your working folder.
11. Export the presentation as a PowerPoint show that will play on its own in a continuous loop.
12. Prepare for delivering the presentation using the rehearse timings feature (**Slide Show>Set Up>Rehearse Timings**).
13. Submit your work for grading, and be prepared to deliver the presentation to the class.

Name: _____

World Design Document

Sketch	Name or level:
	Description of objects:

Sketch	Name or level:
	Description of objects:

Sketch	Name or level:
	Description of objects:

Sketch	Name or level:
	Description of objects:

Name: _____

Game Script Document

Rules

Example: The ball will bounce high.

1. _____
2. _____
3. _____
4. _____
5. _____
6. _____
7. _____
8. _____
9. _____
10. _____
11. _____
12. _____
13. _____
14. _____
15. _____
16. _____
17. _____
18. _____
19. _____
20. _____
21. _____
22. _____
23. _____
24. _____
25. _____
26. _____
27. _____
28. _____

Game Script Document

Core Mechanics

Example: The value for the Elasticity property for the Ball object will be 100.

1. _____

2. _____

3. _____

4. _____

5. _____

6. _____

7. _____

8. _____

9. _____

10. _____

11. _____

12. _____

13. _____

14. _____

15. _____

16. _____

17. _____

18. _____

19. _____

20. _____

21. _____

22. _____

23. _____

24. _____

25. _____

26. _____

27. _____

28. _____

Completion Documents

Learning Objectives

After completing this lesson, you will be able to:

- test a game for quality attributes.
- compare and contrast playability and functionality testing.
- properly program cheat codes.
- provide and receive constructive criticism.

Situation

You have made a remarkable amount of progress since you started in the management-training program. The Awesome Game Company has been very impressed with your ability to handle the task of bringing a successful game to the customer. It is now time to test the game.

Reading Materials

The completion or tuning stage is the final stage of the three-stage production process. During this stage, no additional game designing takes place. The team focuses on getting the game to work properly. The game must be tested and refined for both functionality and playability.

Functionality testing is the task of making sure all game controls and interactions work properly. Here is where the quality assurance (QA) team tests every button, function, and option trying to find any bugs and glitches in the game. It may take a long time to test every piece of the game.

To save time during testing, the programmers add cheat codes to the game. A *cheat code* is a command that can be used during game development to easily overcome a game challenge or defeat an enemy. These codes are used by the testers so they do not have to start over all the time or play the entire game. Imagine testing the obstacles of a game and having to restart a level or the entire game each time you lost your three lives. The cheat code for unlimited lives helps the tester check each part of the game that can take away a life. Cheat codes are supposed to be removed after testing, but sometimes they are left in and players discover them.

Playability testing seeks to find out if the story is completely told, the game holds true to the

Name: _____

Date: _____

Class: _____

concept, and the objectives are obtainable. First, the game needs to be tested to determine if the player can understand the story being told through the gameplay. When players enter the game world, they want to keep going until they reach the victory condition. Each risk players take must have an appropriate reward to make the gameplay meaningful. When side tasks and other trivial tasks in the game lead to no reward or do not move the game forward, consider removing them to keep the player focused on the main story.

Additionally, the game must be compared to the original concept to make sure it has achieved what was planned. The completion stage is actually a very poor time to figure out that the game has missed the original concept. For example, if the game is too violent for the age group or the game world does not fit the concept, it is hard to fix these errors at this late stage. Nonetheless, if the game needs to be corrected to match the original concept before it can be released, then this is the time to do so.

Lastly, playability testing must assure that the game objectives are attainable. Many players want to complete all objectives, even those not specifically required to win the game. It is really frustrating to play a game and not be able to complete objectives, whether primary or secondary. Even worse is if the game has failed to escalate the challenges.

Escalating the challenges means the objectives become harder to achieve as the game progresses. This is a way of teaching the players how to play the game and what they are supposed to do by making the first levels the easiest and the last levels the hardest. When the game is played by *newbs*—players who are new to the game—they need to have easy objectives to complete while learning how to use the controls and interface. Sometimes the design team forgets that they were all newbs once.

Any bugs or issues found are prioritized. Hopefully, there is enough time to fix all problems, but often this is not the case. The most serious problems must be fixed first. Minor problems are fixed if there is time to do so, but the game may be released with these problems in place. The quality assurance team sends out an error report, called a ***bug check,*** when it finds a problem. The bug check is prioritized by assigning a level, as shown in **Figure 27-1.** Level A bugs are the most serious and must be fixed. Level D bugs are minor and are fixed last as time permits.

Game Build

Now you are in the last phase of production on the Hi-Flyer project. It is time to get out all of the bugs that are meaningful to the gameplay. You only have a short period of time to tune this game, so use your time wisely.

How to Begin

1. Launch Clickteam Fusion 2.5, and open the *LastName_*Hi-Flyer_Beta file from the previous lesson.
2. Save the file as *LastName_*Hi-Flyer_Beta1 in your working folder.
3. Add a cheat code by programming this pseudocode on each frame:
   IF the player presses the [Q] key,
      THEN add one life.
4. Add a cheat code by programming this pseudocode on each frame:
   IF the player presses the [P] key,
      THEN go to the next level (frame).

Bug Type	Meaning	Examples
A	Major problem! The game cannot be released with this bug.	• Game is not fun to play. • Virus in game. • Game crashes. • Game features do not work properly. • Level is too difficult to complete. • Spelling errors. • Legal errors.
B	Big problem! The game can be released with this bug, but it will receive bad reviews for the error.	• Gameplay can typically be maintained. • Some features missing. • Graphic errors to backgrounds or other nonessential areas. • Incomplete menu or menu has options that are never available. • Levels are too easy to complete.
C	Common problem. This should be fixed if time permits, but release of the game will not be delayed by this bug. The easy fixes get done, while the difficult fixes are not done.	• Gameplay is uninterrupted by the error. • A minor problem that may be noted as a glitch by critics. • A problem that is not likely to be experienced by most players. • An error that is hard to duplicate.
D	Suggested feature. This bug will likely not be fixed prior to releasing the game unless there is remaining time.	• Gameplay is uninterrupted, but could be enhanced. • Adding a feature might make the gameplay better. • New technology could be applied. • Two buttons might be hard to press at the same time to activate a weapon.

Goodheart-Willcox Publisher

Figure 27-1. Bugs and other issues are categorized by level. The most critical bugs are level A, and fixing these are prioritized over all other issues.

QA Testing

5. Run the application, and play your game. Note any errors or bugs with the functionality and playability. Make a list of the bugs.
6. Have a classmate play your game and create a list of bugs while you do the same for his or her game.
7. Compile a comprehensive list of bugs for your game.
8. Prioritize the bugs from level A through level D.

Completion

9. Arrange the levels in your game to create escalating challenges to help players learn how to play your game.
10. Make sure the backgrounds and assets follow a logical progression of skill building.
11. Debug the game in the order of priority you identified earlier. Remember, you may not have enough time to fix all bugs.
12. Save the game as *LastName*_Hi-Flyer_Golden in your working folder.
13. Complete a personal evaluation and a peer evaluation in the Higher-Order Thinking Strategies.
14. Submit all work for grading.

Vocabulary

Write a definition for each of the key terms from this lesson. You will develop a personal glossary of key terms throughout this course.

functionality testing

_____

_____

cheat code

_____

_____

playability testing

_____

_____

escalating

_____

_____

newb

_____

_____

bug check

_____

_____

Review Questions

Applied Technology

1. How are cheat codes used in testing a game?

_____

_____

_____

_____

Language Arts

2. Describe the focus of the tuning stage.

_____

_____

_____

_____

Name: _____

3. How did you use escalating challenges to help players from different backgrounds learn how to play your game?

_____

_____

_____

_____

Social Science

4. Describe what defines the four levels of bugs, A through D.

_____

_____

_____

_____

Language Arts

5. Compare and contrast functionality testing and playability testing.

_____

_____

_____

_____

Language Arts

Higher-Order Thinking Strategies

6. You have been given 25 hours to fix bugs that were found during testing. There were three level A bugs, one level B bug, six level C bugs, and eleven level D bugs. Level A bugs will take 4.5 hours each to fix, level B bugs 2.75 hours each, level C bugs 3.25 hours each, and level D bugs .75 hours each. How many bugs will you be able to fix, and which levels are they?

_____

_____

_____

_____

Mathematics

7. How does escalating the challenges help make the game appealing to players with diverse backgrounds, both in game-playing experience and cultural experience?

_____

_____

_____

_____

Social Science

8. Explain what impact a game containing many bugs will have on a player if the bugs do *not* prevent the player from achieving the victory condition.

_____

_____

_____

_____

Language Arts

Applied Technology

9. Based on the testing you performed on your game, complete the following personal evaluation rubric. Be honest in your evaluation.

	0	1	2	3	4	5	Score
Concept Is the idea well developed?	No main idea.					Clear throughout.	
Aesthetics Do the look and colors fit the game?	Poor quality graphics and color.					Awesome graphics and theme-based colors.	
Sound Effects Do the sounds play well? Are the music and ambient sounds appropriate?	No sound; sounds too loud or not related to the game.					Good sound for each item at good levels.	
Functionality Does everything work?	Unfinished, could not play; major errors.					Plays perfectly; no bugs, glitches, or errors.	
Replay How likely are you to play this game again?	Game solved, too easy or uninteresting.					Cannot wait to play this again!	
						Total Score (higher is better)	

Applied Technology

10. Based on the testing you performed on your classmate's game, complete the following peer evaluation rubric. Be honest, but professional, in your evaluation. Provide this constructive criticism to your classmate.

	0	1	2	3	4	5	Score
Concept Is the idea well developed?	No main idea.					Clear throughout.	
Aesthetics Do the look and colors fit the game?	Poor quality graphics and color.					Awesome graphics and theme-based colors.	
Sound Effects Do the sounds play well? Are the music and ambient sounds appropriate?	No sound; sounds too loud or not related to the game.					Good sound for each item at good levels.	
Functionality Does everything work?	Unfinished, could not play; major errors.					Plays perfectly; no bugs, glitches, or errors.	
Replay How likely are you to play this game again?	Game solved, too easy or uninteresting.					Cannot wait to play this again!	
						Total Score (higher is better)	

Office Technology Integration

Spreadsheet Table

1. Launch Microsoft Excel or other spreadsheet software, and open the vocabulary spreadsheet you updated in previous lessons.
2. Applying what you have learned, add a new worksheet, and name it Lesson 27.
3. Add each of the vocabulary words and definitions from the Vocabulary section of this lesson.
4. Save the spreadsheet, and then close it.
5. Start a new blank workbook, and save it as *LastName*_BugCheck in your working folder.
6. Select the range A1:E10, and apply all borders formatting to the cells.
7. Enter the text Bug Level in cell A1.
8. Enter the text Levels Affected in cell B1.
9. Enter the text Description in cell C1.
10. Enter the text Solutions in cell D1.
11. Enter the text Progress in cell E1.
12. Select the range A1:E10.
13. Click **Insert>Tables>Table** on the ribbon. In the **Create Table** dialog box, check the **My table has headers** check box, then click the **OK** button to convert the range into a table format, as shown.

All Borders

Table

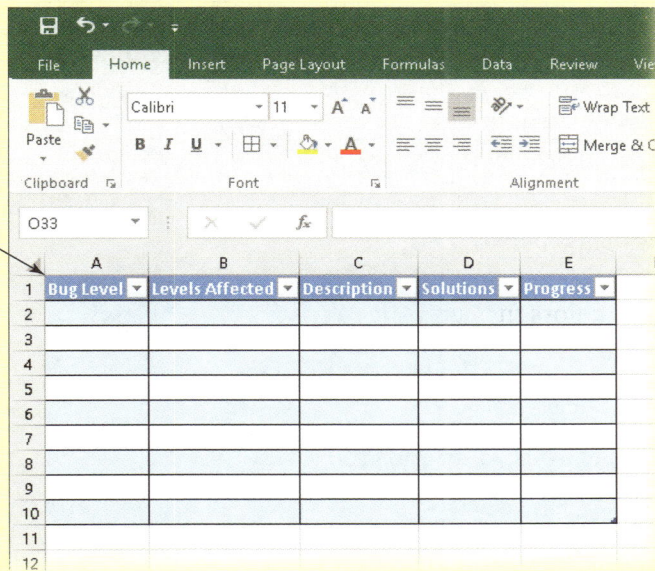

Goodheart-Willcox Publisher

14. Add data to first row of the table as follows.

Bug Level	Levels Affected	Description	Solutions	Progress
A	3, 6, and 9	Clickteam Fusion 2.5 free version will not allow movement between the affected levels.	Purchase full version.	Not yet done.

15. Using the bug list from your game analysis, complete the table to include the bugs found in your game while testing. Record the progress as either Not Done, Working, or Completed.

16. To add more rows, click the resizing handle at the bottom-right corner of the table, and drag downward.

17. Click the drop-down arrow next to the Bug Level header, and click **Sort A to Z** in the drop-down menu.

18. Click the drop-down arrow next to the Progress header, and click **Text Filters>Does Not Equal...** in the shortcut menu. In the dialog box that is displayed, enter Completed in the top text box, and click the **OK** button to filter out any bug fix that has been completed.

19. Save your work, and submit for grading.

Capstone—Exhibition of Mastery

Learning Objectives

After completing this lesson, you will be able to:

- demonstrate mastery in the design process from conception to production.

- develop design plans, character sketches, documentation, and storyboards for a proposed video game.

- construct an original video game.

- use a variety of software tools to design and construct a video game.

- provide and receive constructive criticism on a video game build.

Situation

The Awesome Game Company has asked your team to submit a proposal for a new video game design. A client named Jam Bee Yoose has contacted the company about having a game made for it. The client provided little details, but offered a huge bonus because the company is overflowing with cash. The Awesome Game Company needs to do well on this first game as this client could easily afford to buy more games in the future.

Game Build

Jam Bee Yoose shared some information about the company that could be used in a game context. Jam Bee Yoose produces and bottles a line of nutritious and healthy drinks from scratch every morning. It has a complex assembly line that peels fruit, removes seeds or pits, and carries the fruit to a machine that turns the fruit into pulp. Each fruit has its own assembly line. Once the fruit is turned into pulp, another machine creates the various flavors of drinks by mixing the fruit pulp in various proportions and bottles each flavor. The bottles are sent to the final station where they are boxed and prepared for shipment. The drinks are sold at the factory store, shipped to local grocery stores, and sold to local vending machine stockers.

Anything you would like to use from this information would make the customer smile. Use your imagination. There is only one restriction on

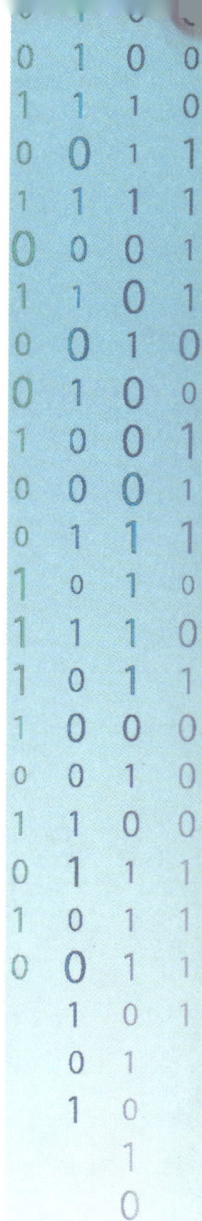

Name: _____

Date: _____

Class: _____

the game concept. The client asked that you please not try to create an exact model of their factory. If creating a factory, it should be a very fun factory with unusual means of getting the same task accomplished. That might include baby elephants to smash the fruit into pulp or animated hoses to fill each bottle. The company likes wacky stuff.

- Audience: boys and girls, ages 6 to 14
- Rating: E for Everyone
- Complexity: at least two levels
- Reward: a coupon on the winner page for a free case of the nutritious drinks; winner page appears when the player reaches a certain amount of points

How to Begin

1. Assemble your team according to the directions given by your instructor. Your team should include three to four members with different skill strengths to create a balanced team. The team needs people good in management, design, programming, and art.
2. Brainstorm ideas that support the customer requirements.
3. Use Microsoft Word or other word processing program to create a high-concept document in the format of a business letter. Address the letter to your instructor (Director of New Products for the Awesome Game Company) with your school address.
4. Turn in the high-concept document to your instructor for review. Only written concepts will be reviewed and approved. This allows your team to keep its concept confidential from other teams, so your cool ideas are not used by other teams. Remember, the video game industry is highly competitive.
5. When the director of new products (your instructor) approves the concept, your team can begin preparing the design documents.

Design Documents

Using the ideas from the team's high-concept document, expand the ideas, and record these decisions as design documents.

6. Create a storyboard to tell why the character is motivated to go through the game activities. A storyboard is a set of sketches and captions that lay out the action in the game.
7. Create a world-design document to display no less than two sketches and details for the game environment.
8. Create a character document to sketch the main character and the action poses needed for the game.
9. Create a game-script document to record the rules and how to program the core mechanics of the objects.

10. Create a Gantt chart for the main tasks and expected beginning and completion times. Your instructor will provide the deadlines.
11. Review all documents with the director of new products (your instructor) before proceeding with creating game assets and designs.

Construction

Your design documents should help your team get the project completed quickly. Time is limited, so work quickly and efficiently.

12. Use Clickteam Fusion 2.5 to build your game.
13. Use other programs such as Paint and Audacity (a freeware sound editor) as needed. The Internet can be used to help research and create the assets for your game.
14. Use equipment as needed, such as a digital camera or microphone. Equipment must be signed out according to the schedule and procedures of the class. Do not wait until the last day to use equipment shared by the class or it may not be available and your schedule will not be met.
15. Work together as a team to complete the tasks and problem solve to overcome design obstacles.
16. Save often to avoid errors or crashes that could ruin your project.
17. Save copies as iterations so it is easy to return to a previous point if needed.
18. Create two game levels and a winner page.
19. Program any cheat codes needed to complete thorough testing.
20. Test the game.
21. Create a bug report for each game error.

Completion

Your team is allotted only one day for tuning and completion. What you do not complete by the end of the day simply does not get finished.

22. Prioritize the bugs to get the most important bugs fixed first.
23. As a team, come up with the best way to repair the game.
24. Fix the bugs you can in the allotted time.
25. Save the game as *TeamName*_GameName_Gold Master in the folder specified by your instructor.

Evaluation

26. As a team, complete a personal review of your game.
27. As a team, complete a peer review of another team's game.
28. Assemble your design documents, personal review, and peer review from another team into an artistically designed packet.
29. Submit all materials for grading.

Personal Review

	0	1	2	3	4	5	Score
Concept Is the idea well developed?	No main idea.					Clear throughout.	
Aesthetics Do the look and colors fit the game?	Poor quality graphics and color.					Awesome graphics and theme-based colors.	
Sound Effects Do the sounds play well? Are the music and ambient sounds appropriate?	No sound; sounds too loud or not related to the game.					Good sound for each item at good levels.	
Functionality Does everything work?	Unfinished, could not play; major errors.					Plays perfectly; no bugs, glitches, or errors.	
Replay How likely are you to play this game again?	Game solved, too easy or uninteresting.					Cannot wait to play this again!	
						Total Score (higher is better)	

Bugs

List the bugs found on each level.

_____

_____

_____

_____

_____

_____

_____

_____

_____

_____

_____

_____

_____

_____

Name: _____

Improvements and Suggestions

_____

_____

_____

_____

_____

_____

_____

_____

_____

_____

_____

_____

_____

_____

_____

_____

Peer Review

	0	1	2	3	4	5	Score
Concept Is the idea well developed?	No main idea.					Clear throughout.	
Aesthetics Do the look and colors fit the game?	Poor quality graphics and color.					Awesome graphics and theme-based colors.	
Sound Effects Do the sounds play well? Are the music and ambient sounds appropriate?	No sound; sounds too loud or not related to the game.					Good sound for each item at good levels.	
Functionality Does everything work?	Unfinished, could not play; major errors.					Plays perfectly; no bugs, glitches, or errors.	
Replay How likely are you to play this game again?	Game solved, too easy or uninteresting.					Cannot wait to play this again!	
						Total Score (higher is better)	

Bugs

List the bugs found on each level.

_____
_____
_____
_____
_____
_____
_____
_____
_____
_____
_____
_____
_____

Improvements and Suggestions

_____
_____
_____
_____
_____
_____
_____
_____
_____
_____
_____
_____